# ARCO

# Guide to Teacher

# Certification

# Testing

ARCO

Guide to Teacher

Certification

Testing

# ARCO
# GUIDE TO TEACHER CERTIFICATION TESTING

**6th Edition**

THOMSON
PETERSON'S

Australia • Canada • Mexico • Singapore • Spain • United Kingdom • United States

**THOMSON**

**PETERSON'S**

An ARCO Book

ARCO is a registered trademark of Thomson Learning, Inc., and is used herein under license by Thomson Peterson's.

**About Thomson Peterson's**

Thomson Peterson's (www.petersons.com) is a leading provider of education information and advice, with books and online resources focusing on education search, test preparation, and financial aid. Its Web site offers searchable databases and interactive tools for contacting educational institutions, online practice tests and instruction, and planning tools for securing financial aid. Thomson Peterson's serves 110 million education consumers annually.

For more information, contact Thomson Peterson's, 2000 Lenox Drive, Lawrenceville, NJ 08648; 800-338-3282; or find us on the World Wide Web at www.petersons.com/about.

Additional information provided by Practical Strategies, Inc.

Editor: Wallie Walker Hammond; Production Editor: Teresina Jonkoski; Manufacturing Manager: Ivona Skibicki; Composition Manager: Gary Rozmierski

ISBN-13: 978-0-7689-2311-7
ISBN-10: 0-7689-2311-5

Printed in the United States of America

10  9  8  7  6  5  4  3  2        08  07  06

Sixth Edition

## OTHER RECOMMENDED TITLES

*ARCO Master the Praxis I: PPST Exam*
*ARCO Master the Praxis II Exam*

# CONTENTS

## Contents

## Introduction

# HOW TO GET THE MOST FROM THIS BOOK

Teaching is considered a portable profession, which is very convenient in our increasingly mobile society. It used to be relatively easy to get a teaching position in elementary or secondary schools when moving from one state to another. Now, however, each state has its own set of teacher preparation requirements, and many states have their own certification tests. Nearly all these state tests are different, making it difficult for a teacher in one state to be credentialed to teach in another state. Teachers moving from one state to another may find that they have additional requirements to satisfy in order to be licensed.

Then there is the issue of career changers. States have separate requirements for people who want to move into teaching from another career. These alternate routers may find the bureaucracy of state education departments difficult to navigate in order to find out how they can become teachers.

This book is here to help! Whether you are coming from a traditional teacher preparation course, moving from one state to another, or interested in teaching as a second career, *ARCO Guide to Teacher Certification Testing* provides the basic information for becoming licensed to teach in all 50 states and the District of Columbia. In addition, you will find contact information for each department of education and for various agencies within each department. This contact information includes Web addresses for specific agencies as well as teacher recruitment and employment sites. The final section offers four practice tests and complete explanations for all questions.

## GETTING STARTED
The information in the State Profiles is divided into traditional and alternate routes followed by information on special credentials. Each State Profile also discusses the testing requirements for each state.

### Traditional Teacher Preparation Route
If you are presently enrolled in a traditional teacher preparation course and know the state in which you wish to teach and the grade level (elementary, middle, secondary),

- find your state in the State Profiles.
- locate information about general requirements including testing for the traditional route.

If you are specializing in a field such as speech therapy,

- note if there are any special requirements including testing.

### College Degree but No Teacher Preparation
If you are graduating from college but have not had a teacher preparation course, which usually means you have not done student teaching, many states require that you have special on-the-job training. If you fit this category,

- find your state in the State Profiles.
- see if the state requires any additional coursework, mentoring, or testing.

### Moving from One State to Another to Teach
If you will be moving from one state to another to teach,

- find the new state in the State Profiles.
- locate information about credentialed teachers moving into the state from another.
- also read about state reciprocity for teachers moving within certain state consortia, pages 6–7.
- note if there are any additional requirements for specialties such as music teachers.
- note which, if any, additional tests you may need to take.

### Alternate Route
If you are interested in going into teaching from another career,

- find your state in the State Profiles.
- locate information about academic requirements, on-the-job coursework and/or mentoring once you begin teaching, and testing.

Once you have the basic information, contact the appropriate agency within the state's department of education. Each State Profile has the telephone number, street address, and Web site for the department and appropriate agencies. Sign up for the appropriate tests and then test your knowledge by completing the appropriate practice tests beginning on page 129.

## GIVE US YOUR FEEDBACK

We welcome any comments or suggestions you may have about this publication and invite you to complete our survey at www.petersons.com/booksurvey or complete the survey at the back of this book, tear it out, and mail it to us at:

Publishing Department
Thomson Peterson's
2000 Lenox Drive
Lawrenceville, NJ 08648

Your feedback will help us to provide personalized solutions for your educational advancement.

# Part I

# BECOMING A TEACHER

# Chapter 1

# WHY BECOME A TEACHER?

How did you get to where you are today? Who were the teachers who guided you, inspired you, answered your questions, made you laugh, and helped you learn to enjoy the process of learning?

We have all had the good fortune to encounter teachers who are among the best. These were people who could have prospered in any field but chose to teach, and we have benefited greatly from their decision. However, teachers also benefit from teaching. Take a moment to consider just a few of the benefits, material and otherwise, to be gained in this anything-but-thankless profession.

## MAKING THE WORLD (OR AT LEAST SOME SMALL PARTS OF IT) A BETTER PLACE

Looking at your own life, or inquiring about the lives of family members, friends and neighbors, you will surely find countless stories of the overwhelmingly positive influence of teachers. This influence can take many forms.

Most obviously, teachers pass on knowledge. In doing so, they stimulate the interest of students so that students gain enthusiasm for learning more about a subject on their own. Fortunately, students are not alone in their explorations. Teachers continue to help them in their quest for more knowledge, and who knows where students' inquiring minds may lead them?

Doctors recount stories of the high school biology teacher who first encouraged their interest in the inner workings of living things. Lawyers and politicians tell of the English and social studies teachers who encouraged them to take part in classroom debate, allowing them to hone the skills that would later prove useful in the courtroom and in the halls of government. Engineers describe the math teachers who showed them the many ways that numbers can be fun and interesting, patiently answering their questions when number theory became increasingly complex. How many artists have taken up painting as a career because of the guidance of an art teacher? For that matter, how many of us would read, write, or think critically if we had not had a patient professional helping us gain these skills?

Still, this passing on of skills and information is only part of what teachers do. They make it possible for students to stage school musicals and plays. They moderate after-school clubs and help students learn how to edit and produce school newspapers, magazines, and yearbooks—whether in print or on DVD's and videos. They coordinate science fairs and school trips.

But teachers do more than their job descriptions list. How many of us had teachers who listened to our personal problems and helped ease the pain of growing up? How many of us would have gone on to higher education if we hadn't had teachers who not only gave us information but showed us that learning could be fun? With intelligence, good humor, and compassion they led us to discover information, helped us develop and sharpen skills, spurred creativity, answered our questions, and listened sympathetically to our problems. They guided us to become the people we are today. Some even became our friends.

Can good teachers single-handedly change everything that is bad in the world? No, but they can make a small, but significant difference in the lives of many of their students, just by "being there for them," listening and encouraging them.

## YOU MIGHT NOT GET RICH, BUT . . .

You won't be poor, either. While it is true, as any aspiring teacher will likely be told, that one is unlikely to attain vast wealth and a life of untold luxury in the teaching profession, the field is not without financial rewards. Teachers' salaries are, in fact, competitive with many other fields. While salaries vary dramatically from one state to the next and from district to district within a state, the average salary for teachers with some experience can be as high as $55,000 a year in California. Average starting pay in Alaska is $37,000 a year. A first-grade teacher with 25 years' experience, a master's degree, and additional credits can make $80,000 in a Pennsylvania. Teaching salaries generally keep up with the rate of inflation.

In most states, teachers also enjoy good benefit packages, as well as pension plans that allow for retirement after 25 years of service or age 60, depending on the district. Of course, retirement packages vary significantly in different parts of the country. In most states, however, packages include guaranteed retirement income as well as survivor and disability protections. Increasingly, options also exist for 401k plans and other investment-based packages.

Some states and districts may offer signing bonuses and even relocation help in order to attract teachers in high-needs subjects such as math and science. Some areas offer similar aid to teachers willing to teach in high-needs schools.

## JOB SECURITY

Significantly, during this era of corporate downsizing and career paths that change direction without warning, teachers are far more likely to *reach* retirement age while still employed than most other professionals. At a time when the very concept of job security seems to be steadily receding into the past for workers in many jobs, teaching is looking better and better as a career. Certainly, districts lay off employees in tight budgets and schools close as populations shift. However, teaching tends to be far more stable than most occupations, and districts tend to hold onto their employees, particularly teachers.

Thanks to strong teachers' unions, teachers at any stage of their careers are rarely laid-off and cannot be casually dismissed without reason. Current shortages of qualified teachers throughout much of the United States, of course, increase this security. At this time, shortages are especially acute in math and science. In some states, teachers are being recruited from other countries to make up for these shortages. Most importantly, teachers who have taught for anywhere from two to five years can be awarded tenure. The number of years needed for tenure varies from state to state, as do other tenure requirements, which may include testing and/or acquiring an advanced degree. A large majority of teachers, however, are successful in attaining tenure.

Once tenured, a teacher's job is secure to a significant degree. This is not to say that teachers can stagnate. Rather, states are increasingly requiring continued professional development and the gaining of advanced degrees. In most districts, the salary scale increases commensurate with master's or doctoral degrees. Ultimately, this means that teachers are expected not only to pass on what they've learned to students, but to *continue learning* themselves. Teaching is a profession in which continued growth is not only desirable, but expected.

## TIME OFF

Of course, it must be mentioned that one great advantage of working in the teaching field is the time when one is *not* working. Perhaps the best known "perk" of teaching involves time off. Most entry-level workers feel fortunate to have two weeks' paid vacation, along with a few holidays off such as Thanksgiving, Christmas, New Years' Day, and the Fourth of July. They look back with nostalgia on those days of youth when they had a winter break, a spring break, and summer vacations as well as all of those holidays and even snow days off. Teachers, of course, get almost all the time off that they had as students. For this reason, teaching is an ideal career for working parents.

This is not, of course, to say that a teacher's work is limited to the hours of the school day. Like their students, teachers have homework. There are papers and tests to grade, lesson plans to create or revise, as well as parent-teacher conferences, school nights and other school-related activities. Teachers also have to get all those professional development hours and classes for their own advanced degrees. What this means is that teachers are not necessarily free whenever their children are. However, teachers' schedules are closer to those of school-age children than those of people in almost any other job.

Twelve weeks of vacation a year, on average, are unique in the working world and allow teachers more time with family, for travel, for hobbies, or for supplementing income by working at second careers. It is, therefore, no coincidence that so many writers, artists, and other creative people use teaching as their "day job." Teaching is a career that allows for and even encourages these other pursuits.

## EXPLORING YOUR INTERESTS

Of course, free time is hardly the only appeal of teaching to a writer, artist, musician, or athlete. Teaching allows the teacher to explore and share his or her interests with others. There are few "job wanted" ads for painters, creative writers, or basketball players. Teaching, however, allows those dedicated to these pursuits not only to exercise their talents, but to share them.

It is interesting to note that, in the Hebrew language, the word *lamad* stands for both "teaching" and "learning." A teacher is always learning—about teaching itself, about the subject matter being taught, about students, and about him- or herself.

## BENEFITS OF WORKING WITH YOUNG PEOPLE

As a teacher, a person stays in contact with young people for the length of his or her career. Every year a new group of students enters the classroom. At any age, a teacher is witness to a steady stream of fresh ideas, newfound talents, and limitless youthful energy.

While maturity certainly has its advantages, in many ways the company of children and adolescents can be preferable to a constant diet of fellow adults. Students tend to be willing to explore new ideas, are open to new experiences, and are certainly ready to laugh and have fun. A teacher has the pleasure and joy of seeing the eyes of students light up as they discover something new—an interesting new fact, a new idea, or even an entirely new and different way of looking at life.

Of course, it is not only the eyes of students that can light up from learning the new and different. Every student has unique experiences and perspectives. A teacher is in the unusual position of learning about these experiences and perspectives, while helping students to express what they want to say and be. This can be particularly rewarding when one is teaching students from different backgrounds. While some teachers prefer to teach in familiar environments, others have the opportunity to serve populations that are far different from themselves. These can range from the most privileged to the least privileged. Teachers are needed everywhere that children live, from upscale suburban environments to Native American reservations, from the urban school to the regional rural school.

## IF YOU ARE THINKING ABOUT TEACHING

There are, of course, advantages to every career choice. There are simply very few careers that carry as many different advantages as teaching.

As a teacher, you can spend your life immersed in subjects that interest you while passing on that interest to others. You can do so with a secure paycheck, ever in touch with youth, and with time to spend with your family or to pursue your interests. While others wonder if what they do matters, you will always know, whenever a child under your guidance moves a small step toward becoming an adult, that you are making a difference.

# Chapter 2

# PATHS TO TEACHER PREPARATION

In its report *Profile of Teachers in the U.S. 2005,* the National Center for Education Information (NCEI) reports that 70 percent of current public school teachers obtained their certification through traditional undergraduate teacher preparation programs, and 24 percent came through graduate teacher preparation programs. Six percent were certified by completing alternative programs. States are approving more alternative certification routes to meet the growing demand for teachers, and the ratio of preparation methods is changing.

## TRADITIONAL ROUTE

The traditional route to certification is much the same in every state. Potential teachers must earn a bachelor's degree in arts or science and complete a teacher preparation program for the area in which they want to teach. Elementary teachers usually have a liberal arts education, whereas secondary teachers are required to have the equivalent of a major in their subject area. Some states have a minimum GPA requirement, usually 2.5 or higher on a 4.0 scale. Teacher preparation programs include a supervised teaching experience such as student teaching, which is a requirement in all states.

Generally, colleges and universities offer programs that lead to both the bachelor's degree and certification. There are also some post-baccalaureate programs leading to certification or to a master's degree and certification. In every state, the preparation program must be a state-approved program and accredited either through one of the regional accrediting organizations or by the National Council for Accreditation of Teacher Education (NCATE). According to NCATE, one-third of states now require their public institutions to have NCATE accreditation. The Council for Higher Education Accreditation (CHEA) Web site provides links to the regional accrediting organizations, which maintain lists of accredited institutions on their Web sites. In addition, each state certification Web site has a list of approved programs.

In addition to educational requirement, all states except Iowa and Montana require prospective teachers to pass standardized exams. Most states require a basic skills assessment such as the Praxis I: Pre-Professional Skills Test in reading, writing, and mathematics. This is often a requirement for admission to the teacher preparation program. Most states also require subject area tests, which may be specific for elementary education, middle school specialization, or secondary subject areas. The Praxis II:

Subject Assessments are commonly used. Some states also require a pedagogy test, such as the Praxis II: Principles of Learning and Teaching, which are specific to the grade level. Although many states use the ETS Praxis series of tests, a number of states have their own basic skills, subject, and pedagogy exams based on their state standards. The subject area exams and pedagogy exams are usually taken near the end of the teacher preparation program.

Although many states use the Praxis series, not all Praxis assessments are approved in every state. Candidates should confirm that the test they plan to take is the one required in the state where they are being certified. Also, each state sets its own passing score for each assessment based on performance of a pilot group of teachers in that state. Therefore, a passing score in one state may not be a passing score in another state.

Finally, many states have special requirements and these vary widely among the states. They include passing exams on the principles of the U.S. and state Constitutions; courses in child abuse and violence prevention; courses for teaching reading; human relations and cultural relations courses; competency in the use of technology; and U.S. citizenship. Some states have a recency requirement, which means that the teacher preparation program, additional coursework, or teaching experience must have been completed within the preceding specified number of years.

## ALTERNATE ROUTES

In response to teacher shortages in particular subject areas, notably math and science, and geographic areas, particularly urban and rural districts, all states except Alaska, Michigan, and North Dakota have approved alternative routes to teacher certification. These routes allow persons who have not completed a traditional teacher preparation program to become teachers. Many programs are limited to prospective secondary teachers and even to specific subject areas, but some also include prospective elementary teachers. Some programs are specifically for special education teachers. Most programs limit the number of candidates that are accepted each year. Each state maintains a list of approved programs on its certification Web site. The National Center for Alternative Certification (NCAC) is also a good source for information about alternate programs.

The National Center for Education Information (NCEI) published a report in 2005 entitled "Profile of Alternate Route Teachers" using data collected by the NCAC. This report contains a list of characteristics common to many alternate route programs. In general, the programs are designed to attract persons who have careers outside of education and who hold a bachelor's degree. The screening process is rigorous and only about half of the candidates who apply are accepted. These are on-the-job programs that include professional education coursework or the equivalent, and candidates receive mentoring and support. High standards of performance are required for completion of the programs and only about two thirds of those who enter programs complete them and receive certification. About half of the programs are administered by colleges and universities and about a fifth are administered by school districts. The rest are administered by regional centers, state departments of education, and consortiums.

Alternative route programs almost always require a person to have a bachelor's degree in the subject area they will teach. Many programs have a minimum GPA requirement, and many also require a basic skills assessment and/or subject assessment for admission to the program. Some have a requisite number of years of work experience in the subject area.

The candidate often begins the process by securing an offer of employment with a school district, which will have a major responsibility in supporting the candidate by mentoring and evaluations. All states with alternate routes have some provision for issuing an alternate route or provisional certificate that allows a candidate to be the teacher of record while completing the requirements of the program. These certificates generally are issued for one year and must be renewed one or two times. The professional education component may include courses at a college or university or seminars and workshops offered regionally. Most alternate route programs require summer sessions and evening and/or weekend courses in addition to full-time teaching in a mentoring situation. About half the programs can be completed in two years, about a third in one year, and the rest take three years, according to the NCEI report. In most states, these programs lead to the entry-level certificate. Candidates must then meet the same testing and other requirements as candidates in traditional programs, with the exception of the student teaching component.

The NCEI "Profile of Alternate Route Teachers" reports that about 35,000 persons were certified through alternate route programs in 2004. The percent of males, minorities, and older people certified through alternative routes is higher than for those certified in traditional routes.

### Licensure via Portfolio

Some states including Minnesota and Vermont use this alterative process for licensing. Candidates prepare a portfolio demonstrating how they meet state standards. The portfolio is reviewed by a committee and an interview usually follows. If successful, the candidate is eligible for a license or certificate.

### Teach for America

This program recruits outstanding new college graduates in all majors who commit to teach for two years. They are placed in about 1,000 schools in twenty-two high-needs urban and rural districts across the country. Graduates are selected particularly for their leadership qualities and potential to inspire others to succeed. They complete an intensive summer institute and are supported in the process of becoming certified in the states where they receive teaching assignments.

## RECIPROCITY

Reciprocity is the process by which a teacher who is trained or holds a certificate in one state becomes certified to teach in another state. Each state determines its own policy. Many states participate in interstate agreements that facilitate certification of teachers coming from other states. These agreements are not a guarantee of certification. Applicants usually have some requirements to meet. Also, applicants from states who do not participate in the agreements may become certified in other states if they have completed an accredited preparation program, particularly one accredited by NCATE. Each state has a process for reviewing credentials and usually issues some type of provisional certificate to allow persons to teach for a limited time while meeting requirements.

### National Association of State Directors of Teacher Education and Certification (NASDTEC) Interstate Agreement

NASDTEC is the most widely accepted interstate certification agreement. It was formerly called the Interstate Certification Compact (ICC), and this name is still widely used. Many states, the District of Columbia, U.S. territories, and the Department of Defense Education agency typically sign the agreement. States and jurisdictions determine if they will participate and for which categories—teachers, administrators, support personnel, or vocational educators. Although the agreement is valid for a five-year period (i.e., 2005–2010), states may change their status at any time. The list of participating states is updated twice each year. To find out if your state belongs to the agreement, check the state's Web site.

States that choose to participate agree to grant certification to applicants who have completed approved teacher preparation programs in other member states. The program must be in an area comparable to an approved area in the receiving state. Member states also agree to grant comparable certificates to applicants who have completed an approved program, hold a current full certificate, and have at least three years of satisfactory half-time experience during the past seven years. In all cases, applicants must meet all ancillary requirements of the state in which they seek certification. These may include graduate study, testing, citizenship, recency, and special coursework. Some states waive testing requirements for applicants with three years' experience.

Member states are not required to grant certification based on alternate route certificates from other states. However, states may agree to certify applicants who have completed an alternate route program and hold at least an entry-level certificate. States may also agree to grant certificates to applicants who hold certificates above the entry-level certificate and have at least three years of satisfactory half-time experience. States may also grant advanced certification to applicants who hold NBPTS certification in a comparable area. In this case, testing requirements are usually waived. A few states also accept the American Board for Certification of Teacher Excellence (ABCTE) Passport to Teaching.

### Northeast Regional Credential (NRC) Program

The NRC is an agreement that promotes mobility of educators among the seven member states and increases the pool of applicants for education positions. States that issue and accept the NRC are Connecticut, Maine, Massachusetts, New Hampshire, New York, Rhode Island, and Vermont. Persons who hold a full certificate or license in one of the participating states may apply for the NRC and be employed for one year in Maine or Connecticut, or for two years in the other participating states. After that time, educators must meet state certification requirements to continue teaching in the state. Credentials are not available in all disciplines, particularly general science and history, and each state determines the subject areas for which it accepts the credential. Connecticut also has additional requirements. Persons interested in the NRC should see the Web site for more information.

### Mid-Atlantic Regional Teacher Project (MARTP)

Delaware, Maryland, New Jersey, Pennsylvania, Virginia, and the District of Columbia collaborate in this project to enhance reciprocity and teacher mobility. The American Association of Colleges of Teacher Education (AACTE) facilitates the program. The program offers limited reciprocity, but it may be of particular value to outstanding new graduates who may apply to become a Meritorious New Teacher Candidate (MNTC) and receive reciprocity in several states.

### Central States Teacher Exchange

Formerly the Midwest Regional Exchange, this agreement among nine states grants a provisional license to persons who completed a teacher education program and hold a standard license in one of the other states. They have two years to meet all requirements in the receiving state. Participating states are Illinois, Iowa, Kansas, Michigan, Missouri, Nebraska, Oklahoma, South Dakota, and Wisconsin.

## SPECIAL CIRCUMSTANCES

### Special Service and Support Personnel

This category includes school counselors, school psychologists, school psychometrists, library-media specialists, reading specialists, speech-language pathologists, occupational and physical therapists, and school nurses. In most states, counselors, psychologists, psychometrists, library-media specialists, and speech-language pathologists are required to have master's degrees. Some states also require that they hold a teaching certificate. In most states also, counselors, psychologists, and speech-language pathologists are required to hold professional licenses or national certification. School nurses are required to be registered

nurses in most states, and some states require that they also hold teaching certificates. Occupational and physical therapists are not required to be certified in most states, but usually must hold professional licenses. Approved programs or certification programs are required in most states.

### Career Technical Education or Vocational Education

Completion of an approved program may be required in states that require candidates for these certificates hold bachelor's degrees. However, many states grant at least provisional certification to persons with a high school diploma and significant work training and experience. Nearly all states require some work experience, but usually, the higher the education level acquired, the fewer years of work experience needed. Many states require trade licenses or national certification.

### Foreign Applicants

In all but a few states, applicants who were trained in other countries must have their credentials evaluated by a credential evaluation service to be considered for certification. Applicants must submit the evaluation with their application for certification. These are generally compared to state requirements and standards to determine if the applicant qualifies for certification.

Credential evaluation services translate foreign certifications and transcripts and determine their equivalents in the United States. Most states post a list of evaluation services on their certification Web site, which may be found in the "Useful Web sites" section of the state summaries in Chapter 3. The National Association of Credential Evaluation Services (NACES®) and the Association of International Credential Evaluators, Inc. (AICE®) are associations of foreign credential evaluation services. Both provide lists of their members on their Web sites. The Web site of NAFSA: Association of International Educators (formerly the National Association of Foreign Student Advisers) provides guidelines for selecting an evaluation service. The Teachers4America Web site describes the process and prospects for foreign applicants seeking certification and employment in the United States.

### Paraprofessionals

As a result of No Child Left Behind (NCLB) legislation, paraprofessionals who work in Title I programs are required to demonstrate competency either through postsecondary study or through formal state or local assessment. State policies vary in how state or local assessments are implemented. These are described in the state summaries in Chapter 3. Useful information for paraprofessionals may also be found on the National Resource Center for Paraprofessionals Web site and on the Colorado Department of Education Web site.

### RESOURCES FOR ADDITIONAL INFORMATION

AllEducationSchools.com: www.alleducationschools.com
  Links to accredited teacher preparation programs, including online programs. Resources regarding careers in education including requirements and salary information. Description of support services, including requirements.

Association for Career and Technical Education (ACTE): www.acteonline.org
Information for career and technical educators, including career resources and a limited job bank.

Association of International Credential Evaluators, Inc. (AICE®): www.aice-eval.org
Links to foreign credential evaluation services.

Bureau of Labor Statistics, U.S. Department of Labor, *Occupational Outlook Handbook, 2006–07 Edition,* on the Internet at www.bls.gov/oco/home.htm (visited April 17, 2006).
Descriptions of programs and requirements for teachers at all levels, teaching assistants, and some support services.

Colorado Department of Education: www.cde.state.co.us/cdepara/ResourcesPage.htm
Resources for paraprofessionals.

Council for Higher Education Accreditation (CHEA): www.chea.org/Directories/regional.asp
Links to regional accreditation organizations.

Mid-Atlantic Regional Teacher Project (MARTP): www.aacte.org/programs/martp/aboutmartp.cfm
Reciprocity project including five states and District of Columbia.

NAFSA: Association of International Educators (National Association of Foreign Student Advisers): www.nafsa.org
Search "credential evaluation")
*A Guide to Selecting Foreign Credentials Evaluation*

National Association of Credential Evaluation Services (NACES): www.naces.org
Links to foreign credential evaluation services.

National Association of State Directors of Teacher Education and Certification (NASDTEC) Interstate Agreement: www.nasdtec.org/agreement.tpl
Reciprocity agreement among many states and U.S. territories.
REFNational Center for Alternative Certification: www.teach-now.org
Maintains links to alternate route state contacts and programs in all 50 States. Conference information. Publications include *Profile of Alternate Route Teachers* and *Alternate Teacher Certification: A State-by-State Analysis 2006.*

National Center for Education Information: www.ncei.com

National Council for Accreditation of Teacher Education (NCATE): www.ncate.org
Accreditation for teacher education programs. Provides lists of accredited institutions by state.

Northeast Regional Credential Program: www.wested.org/cs/li/view/pj/185
Nine-state reciprocity agreement.

National Resource Center for Paraprofessionals: www.nrcpara.org
Resources for paraprofessionals.

Teach For America: www.teachforamerica.org
Nationwide alternate program placing teachers in high-needs districts.

Teachers4America: www.teachers4america.net
Information for foreign applicants.

The College Board: www.collegeboard.com/csearch/majors_careers/profiles/majors/13.0101.html
Advice on finding a teacher preparation program. Career profiles.

# Part II

# LICENSURE AND CERTIFICATION/ PROFILES OF STATE PROGRAMS

# Chapter 3

# TEACHER LICENSURE AND CERTIFICATION REQUIREMENTS: STATE PROFILES AND THE DISTRICT OF COLUMBIA

The information in the State Profiles is divided into traditional and alternate routes followed by information on special credentials. Each State Profile also discusses the testing requirements for each state.

Once you have the basic information, contact the appropriate agency within the state's department of education. Each State Profile has the telephone number, street address, and Web site for the state's department of education and other appropriate agencies.

Every state and the District of Columbia requires teachers and school staff to be certified. Each state determines its own certification requirements and the types and levels of certificates or licenses it offers. This chapter summarizes the certification requirements for each of the 50 states and the District of Columbia. Most states grant certificates for classroom teachers, special service personnel, and administrators. The state summaries focus on the requirements for classroom teachers and point out special requirements for special service personnel. The chapter does not address certification of administrators.

Most states grant an entry-level certificate and a standard certificate. Some states also have an advanced level for the most experienced educators or those with graduate degrees. The emphasis in this chapter is on the requirements for entry-level certification at the bachelor's degree level, so the more advanced levels and professional growth requirements are not treated extensively. Those certificate designations that are mainly used for salary purposes are not mentioned, such as the "Master's plus 30 hours" that is offered in some states.

## TRADITIONAL ROUTE

This section in each profile outlines the basic, minimum requirements for initial certification. For example, if a bachelor's degree is required, it should be understood to be a bachelor's degree or higher. It may be either a Bachelor of Arts or a Bachelor of Science. Similarly, if a GPA is specified or if semester hours are given, it is the minimum that fulfills the requirements. The GPA is always relative to a 4.0 scale. Similarly, "completion of a teacher preparation program" always means a state-approved accredited program at a four-year degree-granting institution of higher education. Generally, these programs lead to both the bachelor's degree and certification, although there are some traditional post-baccalaureate education programs. In addition, every state requires the recommendation of the Certification Officer of the institution to verify that the candidate has successfully completed the program and to specify what the candidate is qualified to teach.

## ALTERNATE ROUTE

Requirements for alternate route certification are on the state-level. Programs available through universities or area education agencies are also described. In some states, this process is called licensure via portfolio.

## ENDORSEMENTS

In most states, endorsements, also called authorizations, licensure areas, certification fields, and specializations, specify the grade level and/or subject area that a person is authorized to teach. The profile for each state reflects the terminology used in that state.

## SPECIALTY CERTIFICATES

This section describes special requirements such as advanced degrees for special service personnel, also called pupil personnel in some states. The section also lists special requirements for career technology teachers, school nurses, coaches, and school librarians.

## TESTING AND SPECIAL REQUIREMENTS

The standardized tests that are required in each state are listed. In addition, requirements that vary from state to state are also given, such as recency, citizenship, training in abuse prevention, human relations and cultural studies, teaching reading, and constitution requirements. Every state requires a background check and fingerprint check for all educators.

## SPECIAL SITUATIONS AND NOTES

This section generally contains information about reciprocity, foreign applicants, paraprofessionals, substitute teachers, and incentive programs.

## USEFUL WEB SITES

Web addresses for each state certification/licensure division are given as well as Web addresses for testing information, contacts, recruitment, jobs searching, school directories, state-approved teacher preparation programs, alternate routes, and application materials (forms). In addition, many states have Web addresses for online applications, foreign applicant information, paraprofessionals, substitute teachers, NBPTS certification incentive programs, and Troop-to-Teachers (TTT) programs. Of particular interest in many states are the "Teach" Web sites such as "Teach in Florida," "Teach Oregon," and "Teaching in Hawaii." These sites often contain recruitment information, information on alternate route programs, online vacancy posting and job applications, and information about living in the state, among other useful information. See also Chapter 4 about jobs.

## ABBREVIATIONS

Various abbreviations are used in the state and District of Columbia profiles. Consult the following list as you read the profiles of interest to you.

| | |
|---|---|
| ABCTE | American Board for Certification of Teacher Excellence www.abcte.org |
| ACT | ACT Assessment www.act.org |
| ACTFL | American Council on the Teaching of Foreign Languages Proficiency Assessments: www.actfl.org/i4a/pages/index.cfm?pageid=3642 |
| ASHA | American Speech-Language-Hearing Association www.asha.org |
| ASLTA | American Sign Language Teachers Association www.aslta.org |
| CEU | Continuing Education Unit |
| EIPA | Educational Interpreter Performance Assessment: clwilliams@ucc.edu or jlcohen@comdenucc.edu |
| ABCTE | American Board for Certification of Teacher Excellence www.abcte.org |
| ESOL | English for Speakers of Other Languages |
| ESL | English as a Second Language |
| GED | General Educational Development High School Equivalency Diploma |
| GMAT | Graduate Management Admission Test www.gmac.com/gmac/thegmat |
| GRE | Graduate Record Examinations www.ets.org/gre |
| HELP | Higher Education Learning Profile www.eriworld.com/help.htm |
| ICC | Interstate Certification Compact (now NASDTEC Interstate Agreement) |
| NASDTEC | National Association of State Directors of Teacher Education and Certification www.nasdtec.org |
| NBPTS | National Board for Professional Teaching Standards www.nbpts.org |
| NCATE | National Council for Accreditation of Teacher Education www.ncate.org |
| NCLB | No Child Left Behind www.ed.gov/nclb/landing.jhtml |
| NTE | New Teacher Exam (no longer offered) |
| PPST | Praxis I: Pre-professional Skills Test www.ets.org/praxis |
| SAT | Scholastic Aptitude Test www.collegeboard.com/splash |
| SCPI | Sign Language Communication Proficiency Interview www.lexnyc.com/vocational_services.html |
| TOEFL | Test of English as a Foreign Language www.ets.org/toefl |
| TTT | Troops to Teachers www.proudtoserveagain.com |

# ALABAMA

## OVERVIEW

*Teachers at the elementary, middle, and secondary levels in Alabama are required to hold a Professional Educator Certificate. This is granted upon completing a program for the certificate and satisfying testing requirements. A candidate may obtain an alternative or preliminary certificate to teach in the meantime, but these are valid for only three years.*

## TRADITIONAL ROUTE

The **Professional Educator Certificate: Class B** (Baccalaureate Level) requires a bachelor's degree from a teacher preparation program, or a bachelor's degree and a fifth year of study in a teacher preparation program. Applicants must meet the requirements of the Alabama Prospective Teacher Testing Program (APTTP) as described below. The certificate is valid for five years. Varying combinations of teaching experience and/or professional development satisfy the renewal requirements.

## ALTERNATE ROUTE

The **Alternative Baccalaureate-Level Certificate** is available to applicants who hold at least a bachelor's degree with 32 semester hours, or a major in the subject area for which they will be certified. The superintendent of the employing district must request the initial certificate and also assign a mentor to the prospective teacher. The certificate is valid for one year and may be renewed twice. To obtain the Professional Educator Certificate, an applicant must complete the Alternate Baccalaureate Level program coursework, have three years of continuous full-time experience, and meet the APTTP requirements.

The **Special Alternative Certificate** allows applicants who hold at least a bachelor's degree to complete the requirements for the Professional Educator Certificate: Class A (Master's Level) by completing a fifth-year program. The certificate is valid for one year and may be renewed twice. The applicant must complete the Alternate Class A program coursework and meet the APTTP requirements to obtain the Professional certificate.

## SPECIALTY CERTIFICATES

Alabama awards the following specialty certificates:

Preliminary Certificate for Counselor, Library-Media Specialist, and Speech-Language Specialist; Reading Specialist; Library-Media Specialist; Counselor; Speech-Language Pathology; Career/Technical Alternative Baccalaureate Level Certificate; Career/Technical Certificates Endorsed in Health Sciences; Career/Technical Certificates Endorsed in Technical Education

Applicants for these certificates must meet the requirements of the APTTP (except those applying for Career/Technical Certificates Endorsed in Health Sciences or Technical Education). The Preliminary Certificate for Counselors requires a counselor license. Valid Professional Educator Certificates are required for Reading Specialist, Library-Media Specialist, and Counselor.

## TESTING

- The Alabama Prospective Teacher Testing Program (APTTP) consists of the ACT WorkKeys basic skills assessments in Mathematics, Reading for Information, and Writing, and the Praxis II: Subject Assessments. Out-of-state applicants may substitute the Praxis I: Pre-Professional Skills Test (PPST) for the basic skill assessments.

- Applicants for the Professional Educator Certificate must pass both portions of the APTTP.

- For the initial Alternative or Preliminary Certificate, applicants must be registered for both parts of the APTTP, and for the renewal, they must pass both parts.

- Testing is not required for Career/Technical Certificates.

## SPECIAL SITUATIONS AND NOTES

- Out-of-state applicants who have a bachelor's degree and/or certification may obtain the Professional Educator Certificate by completing an out-of-state teacher preparation program at an NCATE-accredited institution or by meeting the requirements of the NASDTEC Interstate Agreement. Recognition may be extended to programs in states that do not participate in the NASDTEC agreement. Applicants must meet the APTTP test requirements

- Applicants who completed their education in a foreign country must have their credentials evaluated by an evaluation service. See the Web site below.

- The Substitute Certificate requires a high school diploma or equivalent. The substitute's certificate is valid for five years.

## USEFUL WEB SITES

- **AL Certification, approved programs, testing, renewal, endorsements, foreign applicants, contacts, NBPTS, TTT:** www.alsde.edu/html/sections/section_detail.asp?section=66&footer=sections

- **Recruiting (AL Teacher Quality Enhancement Project):** www.alsde.edu/html/sections/section_detail.asp?section=75&footer=sections

- **Alabama Prospective Teacher Testing Program (APTTP):**
ACT WorkKeys System Basic Skills Assessment (Applied Mathematics, Reading for Information, and Writing): www.act.org/alabamapttp
Praxis II: Subject Assessments: www.ets.org/praxis (select state requirements)

- **Jobs and school directory:** www.alsde.edu/html/JobVacancies.asp

# ALASKA

## OVERVIEW

*Becoming certified in Alaska to teach at the elementary, middle, or secondary level is a two-step process: Initial Teacher Certificate and then Professional Teacher Certificate.*

### TRADITIONAL ROUTE

- The **Initial Teacher Certificate** allows a candidate to begin teaching while completing all requirements for the Professional certificate. The Initial certificate is valid for three years and is nonrenewable. Requirements for the Professional certificate must be met during this three-year period. The applicant for an Initial Certificate must hold a bachelor's degree and meet state testing requirements. For the elementary level (K–8), candidates must complete a teacher preparation program. For the secondary level (7–12), candidates may be enrolled in a teacher preparation program, but need not have completed it to begin teaching.

- The **Professional Teacher Certificate** requires an Initial certificate, completion of a teacher preparation program, Alaska Studies coursework, Multicultural/Cross-Cultural Communications coursework, 6 semester hours of credit within the past five years, and two satisfactory performance reviews. The Professional certificate is granted when all requirements have been met. It is valid for five years and requires 6 semester hours of additional coursework and current employment in an Alaska public school (or submission of fingerprints, if not employed) for renewal.

### ALTERNATE ROUTE

No alternate route is available.

### SPECIAL CERTIFICATES

Certificates are designated by type as follows:

- The basic requirements for the **Type C Special Services Certificate** are the same as those for a Professional certificate; however, Type C also requires completion of a special services area program. Endorsements include audiology, occupational therapy, physical therapy, recreation, school nursing, school psychology, school psychometry, social work, speech pathology, school counselor, and library science-media. School psychologists and speech pathologists must hold a master's degree and complete an approved program in their respective areas.

- **Type E Early Childhood Certificate** allows the holder to be an instructional aide at the primary level or to help in preschool. It requires completing a program in early childhood education and 400 hours of supervised practice.

- **Limited Type I Instructional Aide Certificate** enables an experienced aide to complete requirements for a Professional Teacher Certificate. The person must have three years' experience as an instructional aide and expertise in Alaska Native culture, be enrolled in a bachelor's degree program, complete a teacher preparation program, and pass Praxis I. The certificate is valid for one school year and may be renewed three times.

- Type M Limited Certificates are available in Alaska Native language or culture, military science, and vocational or technical education. Applicants must show subject expertise and teaching competency, but are not required to have a bachelor's degree.

### ENDORSEMENTS

Endorsements may be added to a Professional certificate. To add a grade level endorsement, a teacher must complete a grade-level endorsement program. To add a subject area, candidates must either have a degree with a major or minor in the subject area or pass the appropriate Praxis II exam (English, Math, General Science, French, and German are the only subjects available by exam).

- For a Special Education endorsement, applicants must have an Initial or Professional certificate and complete a teacher preparation program in special education.

- For a Preschool Handicapped endorsement, a person must complete 6 hours in early childhood special education.

- For a Gifted Education endorsement, a candidate must have an Initial or Professional certificate and complete 6 hours in gifted education.

- For vocational education, a person must have an endorsement in vocational education or a Type M Limited Certificate to teach.

### TESTING AND SPECIAL REQUIREMENTS

- Candidates must pass one of the following for certification: Praxis I Pre-Professional Skills Test (PPST), Praxis I Computer-Based Test (CBT), California Basic Educational Skills Test (CBEST), or Washington Educator Skills Test—Basic (WEST-B).

- All candidates for the Professional certificate must complete approved Alaska Studies and Multicultural Education/Cross-Cultural Communication courses. See the certification Web site for a list of approved courses.

- Paraprofessionals may demonstrate competency by passing the HELP assessment.

## SPECIAL SITUATIONS AND NOTES

- Out-of-state applicants who hold a valid certificate in another state are required to meet the testing requirements. A one-year certificate is available to allow applicants to complete test requirements.

- Foreign applicants must have a Social Security Number and have their credentials evaluated by an evaluation service. See the Web site for more information.

- Paraprofessionals must have a high school diploma (or equivalent) and have an associate's degree or two years of college study (48 semester hours) or demonstrate competency through the state HELP assessment.

## USEFUL WEB SITES

- **Certification, approved programs, foreign applicants contacts:** www.educ.state.ak.us/TeacherCertification

- **Teaching in AK (recruitment, placement, jobs):** alaskateacher.org

- **School directory:** www.eed.state.ak.us/Alaskan_Schools/Public

- **Certification inquiry:** www.educ.state.ak.us/TeacherCertification/CertSearchForm.cfm

- **Forms:** www.educ.state.ak.us/TeacherCertification/app02.html

- **Fees:** www.educ.state.ak.us/TeacherCertification/fees.html

- **Testing:** www.educ.state.ak.us/TeacherCertification/praxis.html
www.ets.org (select state requirements)
www.CBEST.nesinc.com
www.WEST.nesinc.com

- **HELP assessment:** www.eriworld.com/help.htm

- **NBPTS:** www.educ.state.ak.us/TeacherCertification/NationalBoard/NationalBoardGrant.html

- **Approved programs:** www.educ.state.ak.us/TeacherCertification

- **AK TTT:** www.eed.state.ak.us/TTT/Home.cfm

# ARIZONA

## OVERVIEW

*Becoming a fully certified teacher in Arizona is the same whether a candidate comes through the traditional or alternate route and wants to teach at the elementary or secondary level. A person must first obtain the Provisional Teaching Certificate and then the Standard Teaching Certificate.*

### TRADITIONAL ROUTE

- The **Provisional Teaching Certificate** allows the holder to accept initial employment, is valid for two years, and is nonrenewable, although it may be extended once for two years. The Provisional certificate requires a bachelor's degree and one of the following: (1) completion of the appropriate grade-level teacher preparation program; (2) education coursework (45 semester hours for the elementary certificate, 30 hours for secondary, and 37 hours for the early childhood—birth to age eight) including 8 semester hours of practicum or two years of full-time teaching experience for the elementary or secondary levels; or (3) a valid certificate from another state. Candidates must also meet the Arizona Educator Proficiency Assessment (AEPA) test and constitution test requirements.

- The final step is the **Standard Teaching Certificate.** The candidate must hold the Provisional certificate for two years and complete two years of full-time teaching. In addition for the elementary certificate, teachers must take 45 clock hours (3 semester hours) of coursework in phonics. The Standard certificate is valid for six years and requires 180 clock hours of professional development, or 12 semester hours of coursework for renewal.

### ALTERNATE ROUTE

The **Alternative Secondary Path to Certification (ASPC)** allows candidates who hold a bachelor's degree with 3.0 GPA, meet the AEPA test requirements, and have an "intent to hire" to begin teaching while completing training. The program is only available at the secondary level (9–12) and in the core subjects: math, science, English, reading language arts, foreign languages, civics and government, economics, fine arts, history, and geography. Candidates must complete an initial intensive summer training program. They then receive the Teaching Intern Certificate. While teaching, candidates must complete a two-year teacher induction program including coursework and mentoring. Upon completion of the two-year program and satisfaction of all test requirements, they receive a Provisional certificate. Requirements for obtaining the Standard certificate are the same as those in the traditional program.

### ENDORSEMENTS

The following endorsements may be added to teaching certificates: Art, Bilingual Education, Computer Science, Cooperative Education, Dance, Dramatic Arts, Drivers Education, Early Childhood, Elementary Foreign Language (K–8), English as a Second Language (ESL), Gifted, Library Media Specialist, Mathematics Specialist (K–8), Middle Grade (5–9), Music, Physical Education, Reading Specialist, and Structured English Immersion (SEI).

### SPECIALTY CERTIFICATES

- Special Education Certificates are offered in the following areas: Cross-Categorical, Early Childhood (birth to age five), Hearing Impaired, Severely and Profound Disabled, Speech and Language Impaired, and Visually Impaired. All certificates are for Grades K–12 except as noted. The process for obtaining these certificates is essentially the same as the traditional route in elementary education.

- Career and Technical Education Certificates are offered in the following areas for K–12: Agriculture, Business and Marketing, Family and Consumer Science, Health Careers, and Industrial Technology.

- The Athletic Coaching Certificate 7–12 is offered for coaches who do not hold a teaching certificate. See the certification Web site for requirements.

- Professional Non-Teaching Certificates are offered for Guidance Counselors (PreK–12) and School Psychologist.

### TESTING AND SPECIAL REQUIREMENTS

- Arizona Educator Proficiency Assessment (AEPA) includes the following: Professional Knowledge Tests, Subject Knowledge Tests, and Constitutions of the United States and Arizona Test.

- All applicants for a teaching certificate must pass the AEPA Professional Knowledge Tests at the appropriate grade level. Tests are offered for elementary (K–8), secondary (7–12), special education, and career and technical education.

- All applicants must pass the AEPA Subject Knowledge Tests in the area in which they seek certification. If a test is not offered in a particular subject area, they may take approved courses. To add an additional subject area to a certificate, the candidate must take the appropriate Subject Knowledge Test. If a test is not offered in that subject area, the candidate must complete 24 hours of approved coursework.

- Candidates in the ASPC program must pass the Subject Knowledge exam before beginning the first year of the program and must pass the Professional Knowledge exam before beginning the second year.

- Applicants must complete a college course covering the Arizona Constitution or pass the AEPA constitution exam. Similarly, applicants must complete a college course covering the U.S. Constitution or pass the AEPA exam.

- Endorsement in Spanish requires passing the Arizona Classroom Spanish Proficiency Examination. Endorsements in other foreign languages require verification of proficiency by a college or university language department. Endorsements in Native American languages require proficiency verification by an official of the tribe. English as a Second Language requires proficiency in either Spanish or Native American languages.

## SPECIAL SITUATIONS AND NOTES

- Out-of-state applicants who hold valid certificates in elementary, secondary, or special education may obtain a comparable Reciprocal Provisional Teaching Certificate valid for one year. During that year, applicants must complete the AEPA and constitution requirements to qualify for a Professional Certificate. Applicants with three years' experience are exempt from the Professional Knowledge Assessment. Applicants with a master's degree are exempt from the Subject Knowledge Assessment. Applicants who otherwise qualify for the Professional Certificate have three years to fulfill the constitution requirement unless they teach a social studies course and then they have only one year. Arizona has fingerprint reciprocity with 19 states (AL, AR, CA, CO, FL, GA, ID, MN, NE, NV, NM, ND, OR, SC, UT, VT, WA, WI, WY).

- Foreign applicants must have their credentials evaluated by an evaluation service. See the Web site for more information.

- Paraprofessionals in Title I programs must have a high school diploma or equivalent and an associate degree or the equivalent of two years of full-time study at an institution of higher education or pass one of the following exams: ETS ParaPro Assessment, MASTER Teacher's ParaEducator Learning Network, or ACT WorkKeys Proficiency Certificate.

- The Substitute Certificate allows a person to substitute up to 120 days in the same school. It requites a bachelor's degree, is valid for six years, and may be renewed. Substitutes are exempt from the AEPA test requirements.

- The Teaching Intern Certificate allows a person who is enrolled in a teacher prep program to perform paraprofessional or intern services at any grade level.

## USEFUL WEB SITES

- **Certification, approved programs (see general information):** www.ade.state.az.us/certification

- **Jobs:** www.arizonaeducationjobs.com
www.ade.az.gov/empl_opp.asp

- **School directory:** www.ade.az.gov/schools/schools/districts.asp

- **Contacts:** www.ade.state.az.us/certification/contact.asp

- **Alternate routes:** www.ade.az.gov/asd/altpath

- **Forms:** www.ade.state.az.us/certification/certforms.asp

- **Testing:** www.aepa.nesinc.com
Paraprofessionals: www.ets.org/parapro
www.paraeducator.net
www.act.org/workkeys/overview/profcert/index.html

- **Foreign applicants:** www.ade.state.az.us/certification/faqs.asp

- **Fees:** www.ade.state.az.us/certification/newfees.asp

- **AZ TTT:** www.ade.az.gov/troops2teachers

# ARKANSAS

## OVERVIEW

Becoming certified in Arkansas is a two-step process for candidates in the traditional route and a three-step process for candidates in the nontraditional route. Each process is the same whether a person wants to teach at the Early Childhood level (P–4), Middle Childhood/Early Adolescence level (4–8), or Adolescent/Young Adulthood level (7–12).

## TRADITIONAL ROUTE

- Step 1: **Initial Teaching License** is granted to novice teachers. Candidates must have a bachelor's degree, complete a teacher education program, and meet the test requirements. The license is valid for up to three years while the novice teacher completes an on-site induction program.

- Step 2: **Standard Teaching License** is granted when a candidate has completed the induction program and the performance assessments. The license is valid for five years and requires 60 clock hours of professional development activities each year. Applicants for renewal must also have two years of experience during the past five years (only one year if it is the past year) or 6 hours of coursework.

## ALTERNATE ROUTE

**The Non-Traditional Licensure Program (NTLP)** is offered in the following teaching areas Early Childhood (P–4), Middle Childhood (4–8), Secondary (7–12) for subject areas (Math, English, Social Studies, Physical Science, Earth Science, Life Science); for all levels (P–12) for subject areas (Physical Education, Drama/Speech, Art, Music, Spanish, French); and for grade levels 4–12 for subject areas (Family and Consumer Science, Agriculture, Industrial Technology, Business Education, Marketing Technology).

- Step 1: **Provisional Teaching License** is granted to candidates entering the NTLP to enable them to begin teaching while completing the requirements for the Initial or Standard license. Candidates must hold a bachelor's degree, have met the test requirements, and must have an employment offer or declare willingness to accept employment in a high-needs district. During the two-year program, candidates participate in teacher preparation modules, meet additional test requirements, and receive mentoring.

- Step 2: **Initial Teaching License** is granted to candidates who have completed the NTLP and have met test requirements but have not passed the performance assessment. Candidates may skip this step if they have successfully completed the performance assessment.

- Step 3: **Standard Teaching License** is granted to candidates who have met all requirements. The terms and renewal requirements are the same as those for traditionally prepared teachers.

## AREAS OF LICENSURE AND ENDORSEMENTS

Additional areas of licensure may be added to initial and standard licenses only if teachers are assigned in the new area rather than in areas for which they are already licensed. Additional areas may be added in one of two ways. (1) If an assessment is offered and the new area is not an Exception Area (such as Special Education and Non-Instructional Student Services), the teacher may successfully complete the required assessment. (2) If the new area has no assessment, is an Exception Area, or is at a different level than the teaching license, the teacher must complete a program and pass the Praxis II assessment (if available). Teachers have three years to meet the requirements while teaching out-of-area.

Endorsements are offered in Library Media Science, Reading, Guidance and Counseling, Gifted and Talented, English as a Second Language, Educational Examiner, Coaching, and Journalism. There is also a teaching endorsement for grades 5 and 6 only.

## TESTING AND SPECIAL REQUIREMENTS

- All candidates must pass the Praxis I: Pre-Professional Skills Test (PPST) in Reading, Writing, and Mathematics. Candidates entering the traditional or nontraditional program must pass this test for admission to the programs. Candidates with advanced degrees may substitute graduate assessments such as the GRE for PPST.

- All candidates must pass the appropriate Praxis II: Subject Assessments. Candidates in traditional programs must meet this requirement to qualify for the initial license. Candidates in the nontraditional program must meet this requirement for admission to the program.

- To add a licensure area, the appropriate Praxis II: Subject Assessment is required.

- All candidates must pass Praxis II: Principles of Learning and Teaching for the appropriate grade level. Candidates in traditional programs must meet this requirement to qualify for the initial license. Candidates in the nontraditional program must meet this requirement during the second year of the program.

- Candidates for the Standard license must successfully complete the Praxis III: Classroom Performance Assessments. Teachers with traditional preparation complete this during their first year of teaching under the Initial license. Those with nontraditional preparation complete it during their second year in the program.

- An Arkansas History course is required for licensure in Early Childhood, Elementary, and Middle School, and for Secondary Social Studies. This is included in traditional programs. Candidates in the NTLP must complete this requirement before beginning the second year of the program.

- For Early Childhood licensure, candidates in the NTLP must complete coursework for teaching reading before beginning the second year of the program.

## SPECIAL SITUATIONS AND NOTES

- Arkansas offers reciprocity for teaching certificates from all states as well as U.S. territories and countries included in the NASDTEC Interstate Agreement. For the Five-Year Standard license, applicants must pass the Praxis II: Subject Assessments and Principles of Learning and Teaching (or corresponding exams from other states) or have three years' experience. Applicants must also meet the Arkansas History requirement. Applicants are eligible for a One-Year Provisional nonrenewable license to complete the testing, experience, or Arkansas History requirements.

- Foreign applicants must enter through the Non-Traditional Licensure Program. They must also have their credentials evaluated by an evaluation service. See the Web site for more information.

- The ETS ParaPro Assessment is the only formal assessment approved for paraprofessionals.

## USEFUL WEB SITES

- **Licensure, contacts:** arkedu.state.ar.us/teachers/teachers. html

- **Teach AR (recruitment):** www.teacharkansas.org

- **Teachers-Teachers (recruitment):** www.teachers-teachers.com/Arkansas.cfm

- **School directory:** arkedu.state.ar.us/schools/schools_public.html

- **Jobs:** www.as-is.org/classifieds

- **Licensure inquiry:** arkedu.state.ar.us/teachers/accessing_licensure_info.html

- **Approved programs:** arkedu.state.ar.us/teachers/approved_programs.html

- **Forms:** arkedu.state.ar.us/teachers/teachers_application. html

- **Testing:** arkedu.state.ar.us/teachers/praxis.html
www.ets.org (select state requirements)
www.ets.org/parapro

- **Alternate routes:** www.teacharkansas.org/non-trad-lic-program.html
arkedu.state.ar.us/teachers/licensure_mentoring.html#Traditiona

- **Scholarships:** www.starark.com

- **AR TTT:** www.teacharkansas.org/troops-teachers.html

- **Foreign applicants:** arkedu.state.ar.us/teachers/reciprocity.html

- **NBPTS:** arkedu.state.ar.us/teachers/certification_program. html

# CALIFORNIA

## OVERVIEW

*Becoming certified in California is the same whether a candidate comes through the traditional or alternate route and wants to teach at the elementary, middle, or secondary level. A candidate first obtains a Preliminary MS or SS Teaching Credential and then the Professional Clear Teaching Credential.*

*Credentials are designated as Multiple Subject (MS) or Single Subject (SS). A Multiple Subject credential allows a person to teach any grade level in a self-contained classroom such as in elementary school. A Single Subject credential allows a person to teach a specified subject in departmentalized classes such as in middle or secondary school, but the holder may teach that subject at any grade level.*

## TRADITIONAL ROUTE

The **Preliminary MS or SS Teaching Credential** allows a person to teach while completing requirements for the Professional Clear Credential. The Preliminary credential is valid for five years and is nonrenewable. It requires a bachelor's degree, completion of a MS or SS teacher preparation program including student teaching, and meeting the testing requirements described below.

The **Professional Clear MS or SS Teaching Credential** requires the Preliminary Teaching Credential (MS or SS) and either completion of an approved Professional Teacher Induction Program, or NBPTS certification in Early Childhood, Middle Childhood, Early Adolescence, or a subject area. Professional Clear Teaching Credential is awarded when all requirements are met. It is valid for five years and requires professional development for renewal.

## ALTERNATE ROUTES

**Teachers Certified in Other States:** For the Preliminary Teaching Credential, individuals who hold or are eligible for a comparable certificate in another state must have a bachelor's degree and have completed a professional preparation program in elementary education for the MS credential or in secondary education with a subject major for the SS credential. Additional requirements depend on the person's number of years of experience and whether California has determined that the other state has standards equivalent to its own.

The Professional Clear Teaching Credential (MS or SS) requires the Preliminary Certificate and various experience, coursework and/or test requirements, depending on the person's years of experience and whether the other state's standards are considered equivalent to California's. Persons holding the NBPTS certification receive the Professional Clear MS or SS Credential depending on the NPBTS certification.

**Teachers with Private School Experience:** The Preliminary Teaching Credential has the same requirements as for the Traditional Route. In addition, applicants must either have three to five years of full-time experience and complete a professional preparation program in elementary or secondary education excluding student teaching, or have a minimum of six years full-time experience. The Professional Clear Teaching Credential requires completion of an approved Professional Teacher Induction Program or a fifth year in a MS or SS teacher preparation program.

## AUTHORIZATIONS

Authorizations allow individuals who hold teaching credentials to obtain additional credentials without completing a professional preparation program for those credentials. Authorizations allow teachers holding a MS credential to add a SS credential, or those holding a SS credential to add a MS or another SS credential. There are coursework and/or testing requirements for each situation.

Supplementary Authorizations allow a person holding a MS credential to teach specific subjects in grade 9 and below, or for a person holding a SS credential to teach specific subjects at any grade level.

Introductory Subject Matter and Specific Subject Matter Authorizations determine what grade levels and subject areas the holder may teach. Both require a prerequisite teaching credential and coursework.

## SPECIALTY CREDENTIALS

Specialty Credentials are offered in the following areas: Designated Subject Vocational Ed; Child Development; Clinical or Rehabilitative Services; Cross Cultural, Language, and Academic Development (CLAD) and Bilingual CLAD (BCLAD); Serving English Learners (EL); Library-Media Specialist; Pupil-Personnel Services; Reading Certificate; School Nurse Services; Education Specialist Instruction (Special Ed); Specialist Instruction; and Specialist in Reading and Language Arts. The requirements for each are available on the credential requirements Web site.

## TESTING AND SPECIAL REQUIREMENTS

■ Applicants for any credential, certificate, or permit must pass the California Basic Educational Skills Test (CBEST). Teachers certified in other states may obtain the Preliminary Teaching Credential without CBEST, but they must pass it within one year to obtain the Professional Clear Credential unless they hold the NBPTS certification.

- Applicants for any Preliminary Teaching Credential or Authorizations must pass the California Subject Examinations for Teachers (CSET) or complete required coursework. Teachers certified in other states with equivalent standards are exempt from CSET under some options. See Web sites below for more information.

- Applicants for the Preliminary MS Teaching Credential must pass the Reading Instruction Competence Assessment (RICA) unless they completed a California teacher preparation program with student teaching. Teachers certified in other states may be exempt in some cases. Applicants adding a MS authorization and teachers certified in some other states must also pass RICA or complete the Developing English Language Skills for Beginning Readers course.

- A foundational computer technology course is required for the Preliminary Credential. Applicants with private school experience may pass the Preliminary Educational Technology Test (PET) instead.

- A U.S. Constitution course is required of all applicants or applicants may pass an exam given by the college or university instead.

- CPR training is required of applicants prepared in some alternate routes.

## SPECIAL SITUATIONS AND NOTES

- For reciprocity, lists of states having agreements with California and states with equivalent teacher preparation programs are located on the credential requirements Web site under "Individuals Prepared Outside California."

- Applicants who completed their education in a foreign country must have their credentials evaluated by an evaluation service. See the Web site below.

- The Paraprofessional Teacher Training Program is a career ladder program ultimately leading to a teaching credential.

- Substitute and Emergency Substitute credentials are available. Requirements vary depending on whether the individual is a prospective teacher or a career substitute. See the credential requirements Web site for details.

## USEFUL WEB SITES

- **Teach CA:** www.teachcalifornia.org
- **CA Commission on Teacher Credentialing:** www.ctc.ca.gov/default.html
- **Credential requirements:** www.ctc.ca.gov/credentials/requirements.html
- **Approved programs:** www.ctc.ca.gov/educator-prep/approved-programs.html
- **Forms:** www.ctc.ca.gov/credentials/materials.html
- **Teacher credential look-up and renewal:** teachercred.ctc.ca.gov/teachers/index.jsp
- **Contacts:** www.ctc.ca.gov/contact.html
- **Fees:** www.ctc.ca.gov/credentials/fee-and-fingerprint.html
- **Foreign applicants:** www.ctc.ca.gov/credentials/leaflets/c1635.html
- **Test requirements:** www.ctc.ca.gov/credentials/CAW-exams.html
  CA Basic Educational Skills Test:(CBEST): www.cbest.nesinc.com
  CA Subject Examinations for Teachers (CSET): www.cset.nesinc.com
  Reading Instruction Competence Assessment (RICA): www.rica.nesinc.com
  Preliminary Educational Technology Test (PET): www.cset.nesinc.com
- **School directories:** www.slocoe.org/resource/calpage1.htm
  www.kern.org/fcmat/resources/state/all.html
- **Jobs:** www.edjoin.org
- **NBPTS:** www.cde.ca.gov/pd/ps/te/nbpts.asp
- **CA TTT:** www.scoe.net/troops

# COLORADO

## OVERVIEW

*Becoming licensed to teach in Colorado through the traditional route is a two-step process. The process is the same whether a person wants to teach at the elementary, middle, or secondary level. Becoming licensed through an alternate route is a three-step process and requirements vary by level.*

## TRADITIONAL ROUTE

■ Step 1: **Initial License** is the entry-level license. It is valid for three years and may be renewed if the candidate has not completed an induction program.

■ Step 2: **Professional License** is granted to candidates who hold the Initial license and have completed an approved induction program. The Professional license is valid for five years. Renewal requires 6 semester hours of credit or 90 clock hours of professional development. Applicants for the Initial license must complete an education preparation program and meet test requirements. Applicants in special service areas must have a valid professional license, certificate, or registration. After completing an induction program, candidates receive the Professional License.

## ALTERNATE ROUTE

■ Step 1: Either the **Alternate Teacher's License in the Alternate Program** or **Teacher in Residence Authorization in the Teacher in Residence Program** allows a candidate to teach while completing requirements for the Initial license.

■ Step 2: **Initial License** has the same term and renewal requirements as those for the traditional route.

■ Step 3: **Professional License** has the same term and renewal requirements as those for the traditional route.

The two programs, Alternate Teacher's License in the Alternate Program and Teacher in Residence Authorization in the Teacher in Residence Program, are offered only in specific endorsement areas. The most important difference between the two programs is location. Some school districts offer only one program. The process and requirements are the same for admission to either program. Candidates must have a bachelor's degree with a minimum of 30 semester hours of courses in the endorsement area, and must pass the content exam in order to obtain a Statement of Eligibility that allows a candidate to seek employment. The Statement of Eligibility is valid for three years while candidates look for a job and may be renewed once.

Upon accepting employment, candidates in the Alternate Program receive the Alternative Teacher's License, which is valid for one year. During this time, candidates must take 225 clock hours, or equivalent semester hours, of instruction and activities including performance evalua-

tions. Upon completing the one-year program, candidates are eligible for the three-year Initial license. To move to the Professional license, candidates must complete an induction program.

Upon accepting employment in the Teacher in Residence Program (TIR), candidates receive the Teacher in Residence Authorization, which is valid for two years. During this time, candidates take teacher preparation courses and receive 100 hours of supervision and observation. Upon completing the two-year program, candidates are eligible for the three-year Initial license. If candidates also complete an induction program during the two years, they are eligible for the five-year Professional license.

## ENDORSEMENTS

Additional endorsements may be added to Initial and Professional licenses by completing an endorsement program or with a combination of credits and experience. Only specific endorsements are available through the credit-and-experience route. In either case, candidates must pass the appropriate content area exam.

## SPECIALTY CERTIFICATES

Following are the license areas for special service providers: Audiologist, Occupational Therapist, Orientation/Mobility, Physical Therapist, School Counselor, School Nurse, School Psychologist, School Social Worker, and Speech Pathologist. Some of these areas require master's degrees, Colorado professional licenses, or special exams. See the licensing Web site for details.

## TESTING AND SPECIAL REQUIREMENTS

■ All candidates for initial licenses through traditional or alternate routes, or those adding an endorsement area must pass the appropriate content area exam. This may be the PLACE (Program for Licensing Assessments for Colorado Educators) assessment or certain Praxis II: Subject Assessments.

■ The following Praxis II: Subject Assessments are accepted for licensing in Colorado: Audiology; Elementary Education; English Language, Literature, and Composition; Mathematics; School Psychologist; General Science; Social Studies; and Speech-Language Pathology.

- Audiologists and speech pathologists must pass the ASHA assessment.

- School psychologists must pass the National School Psychology exam.

- School social workers may take the Association of Social Work Boards assessment or the PLACE exam or hold a professional license.

## SPECIAL SITUATIONS AND NOTES

- Out-of-state applicants who hold valid licenses and have three years of consecutive full-time experience may be exempt from the PLACE requirement. An Interim Authorization is available for applicants who do not have three years of full-time experience and have not met the PLACE requirement. The authorization is valid for one year and may be renewed once. Upon completing the PLACE requirement, applicants receive the Initial license and must then meet the same requirements for the Professional license as candidates prepared in state. Applicants who hold NBPTS certification are exempt from completing an induction program.

- Foreign applicants must have their credentials evaluated by an evaluation service, except for Canadian transcripts in English. See the Web site for more information.

- Paraprofessionals in Title I schools must have an associate degree or two years of study at an institution of higher education, or demonstrate competency through the ETS ParaPro Assessment, the ACT WorkKeys Proficiency Certificate assessment, or local assessment.

- Colorado offers three Substitute Authorizations, none of which carry any grade level or subject area endorsements. The five-year Substitute Authorization requires an expired Colorado license or a valid out-of-state license. The three-year authorization requires a bachelor's degree. The one-year authorization requires a high school diploma or equivalent and experience working with children.

## USEFUL WEB SITES

- **Licensing, contacts:** www.cde.state.co.us/index_license.htm

- **Teach in CO (job search, school directory):** www.teachincolorado.org

- **School directory:** www.cde.state.co.us/edulibdir/directory.htm

- **Paraprofessionals:** www.cde.state.co.us/cdepara

- **Substitutes:** www.cde.state.co.us/cdeprof/wizard_substitute.asp

- **Testing:** www.cde.state.co.us/cdeprof/liassm.htm www.cde.state.co.us/cdeprof/wizard_PRAXIS.asp www.ets.org (Select state requirements) Paraprofessionals: www.ets.org/parapro www.act.org/workkeys/overview/profcert/index.html

- **Alternate routes:** www.cde.state.co.us/cdeprof/wizard3.asp

- **Fees:** www.cde.state.co.us/cdeprof/lifees.htm

- **Foreign applicants:** www.cde.state.co.us/cdeprof/wizard_outstate.asp

- **TTT:** www.mwttt.com

# CONNECTICUT

## OVERVIEW

Connecticut has a "three-tier continuum" for teacher certification for elementary, middle, and secondary school. The process is the same for traditional and alternate routes, except that candidates in alternate route programs must teach under a Temporary 90-Day Certificate before they are eligible for the Initial Educator Certificate.

- Step 1: **Initial Educator Certificate** is valid for three years and may be renewed five times.

- Step 2: **Provisional Educator Certificate** is valid for eight years.

- Step 3: **Professional Educator Certificate** is valid for five years and requires 9 continuing education units (CEU's) or graduate coursework (1 semester hour is equivalent to 1.5 CEU's) for renewal.

## TRADITIONAL ROUTE

The **Initial Educator Certificate** requires a bachelor's degree, completion of the test requirements, and one of the following: (1) completion of a teacher preparation program for the grade level and field for which the candidate will be endorsed, or (2) teaching for 20 months in the same public school or an approved nonpublic school, and completing required coursework.

The **Provisional Certificate** requires completion of all requirements, including tests, for the Initial Educator Certificate at the grade level and field for which the candidate will be endorsed, and one of the following: (1) completing 10 months of experience and the Beginning Educator Support and Training (BEST) program, or (2) completing 30 months of experience in 10 years in a public school or approved nonpublic school in Connecticut or another state.

The **Professional Educator Certificate** requires completing 30 months of experience in a Connecticut public or approved nonpublic school, and completing any additional course requirements.

## ALTERNATE ROUTE

Connecticut offers two **Alternate Routes to Certification (ARC) Programs.** A bachelor's degree and subject major are required for both programs.

**ARC I Program** consists of nine weeks of full-time summer school instruction and is available in the following subject areas: Middle Grades (4–8) endorsed in English, earth science, general science, or mathematics; Secondary (7–12) English, Mathematics, Science (general science, biology, physics, chemistry, or earth science), or History/Social Studies; for all grade levels (PreK–12) World Languages (Spanish, French, or Latin).

**ARC II Program** consists of 24 weeks of part-time instruction (Friday evenings and all day Saturday from October to May). It is available in the following subject areas: Mathematics (7–12); Science (7–12) (general science, biology, physics, chemistry, or earth science; Middle Grades (4–8) History/Social Studies; for all grade levels (PreK–12) Art, World Languages (all languages), Music, Family and Consumer Science, or Technology Education.

Upon completing either program and meeting the Praxis II and ACTFL (for world languages) test requirements, candidates receive a **Temporary 90-Day Certificate** in the endorsement area of the program. After 90 days of full-time teaching (or 180 days part-time, with renewal of the certificate) candidates apply for the Initial Educator Certificate. Under the Initial certificate, candidates must teach for 20 months, complete 30 hours of continuing education, and complete the BEST program. At this point the candidate is eligible for the Provisional Educator Certificate, the requirements for which are the same as those for the traditional route.

## ENDORSEMENTS

There are teaching, special services, and vocational endorsements and all certificates have endorsements. Grade-level endorsements include Elementary Education (Grades 1–6); Middle Grades (4–8), which are for specific subjects; and Secondary (7–12) subjects, which may be taught down to grade 5 (grade 4 for World Languages) in a departmentalized setting. Special services endorsements may not be cross-endorsed to each other or to teaching endorsements.

## SPECIALTY CERTIFICATES

- Coaches must hold either the Five-Year Renewable Coaching Permit or the Temporary Emergency Coaching Permit.

- The Library Media Specialist Certificate may be obtained through an Advanced Alternate Program offered by Area Cooperative Educational Services (ACES). See the ACES Web site for more information.

## TESTING AND SPECIAL REQUIREMENTS

- The Praxis I: Pre-Professional Skills Test (PPST) in reading, writing, and mathematics is required for the Initial Educator Certificate or for admission to a teacher education program. This test may be waived with acceptable official scores on the SAT, ACT, or PAA (Prueba de Aptitud Academica—Puerto Rico) exam.

■ All candidates must pass the Praxis II: Subject Assessments appropriate to their endorsement area (grade level and field). Teachers adding endorsements must also pass the appropriate Praxis II exams.

■ Candidates seeking endorsement in world languages or bilingual education must pass the ACTFL oral and written proficiency tests.

■ The Beginning Educator Support and Training (BEST) Program is a one- to three-year program depending on the field. Core academic fields generally require the three-year program, whereas special education and vocational field generally require only one year. The program includes of mentoring and assessment.

## SPECIAL SITUATIONS AND NOTES

■ Connecticut does not have reciprocity with any other state, but does participate in the NASDTEC Interstate Agreement. Out-of-state applicants who have completed a teacher preparation program or have 27 months of experience in another member state under a Level II certificate do not need additional coursework. Other out-of-state applicants who meet the requirements for the Initial Educator Certificate under the traditional route may also be eligible. Applicants must still meet all test requirements. A nonrenewable, one-year Interim certificate with deferral of testing is available. All test requirements must be met before it expires.

■ Connecticut participates in the Northeast Regional Credential (NRC) program, which allows teachers certified in the following states to teach temporarily in the other states: Connecticut, Maine, Massachusetts, New Hampshire, New York, Rhode Island, and Vermont. However, Connecticut still requires a Connecticut certificate.

■ Foreign applicants must have their credentials evaluated by an evaluation service. See the Web site for more information.

■ Paraprofessionals in Title I schools must have a high school diploma or GED and an associate degree or two years of study at an institution of higher education or pass the ETS ParaPro Assessment.

■ Long-term substitutes must complete the BEST program.

■ Connecticut offers a minority teacher incentive grant. See the CT Teacher Recruitment and Retention Web site for more information on financial aid.

## USEFUL WEB SITES

■ **Certification, contacts:** www.state.ct.us/sde/dtl/cert/index. htm

■ **CT Teacher Recruitment & Retention (job search):** www.csde.state.ct.us/public/der/teacherrecruitment/index. htm
ACES: www.aces.k12.ct.us/pdsi/index.aspx

■ **School directory:** www.csde.state.ct.us/public/csde/ publicmenu.asp

■ **Jobs:** www.ctreap.net

■ **Approved programs:** www.state.ct.us/sde/dtl/cert/links. htm

■ **NBPTS:** www.state.ct.us/sde/deps/NBS/index.htm

■ **Testing:** www.state.ct.us/sde/dtl/cert/tocassess.htm
Paraprofessionals: www.ets.org/parapro/index.html

■ **Alternate routes:** www.ctdhe.org/ARC/default.htm

■ **ACES:** www.aces.k12.ct.us/programs/pdsi/lmsp/index. asp

■ **Northeast Regional Credential:** www.wested.org/cs/we/ view/pj/185

■ **Forms, fees:** www.state.ct.us/sde/dtl/cert/toccert.htm

■ **Foreign applicants:** www.state.ct.us/sde/dtl/cert/facts01/ fact112.htm

■ **CT TTT:** www.state.ct.us/sde/dtl/cert/howto4.htm

# DELAWARE

## OVERVIEW

*Educators in Delaware must hold both a license and a certificate. The license allows the person to teach. The certificate specifies the grade level, subject area, or special service. Delaware has a three-tiered licensure system that is the same whether a person comes through the traditional or alternate route and wants to teach at the elementary, middle, or secondary level.*

- *Step 1: **Initial License** is granted to individuals who meet all requirements and becomes active when a person is hired. It is valid for three years from the date of hire and is nonrenewable.*

- *Step 2: **Continuing License** is issued to candidates who have met all requirements under the Initial license. It is valid for five years and requires 90 clock hours of professional development for renewal.*

- *Step 3: **Advanced License** is granted to educators who receive NBPTS certification. It is valid for 10 years and may be renewed if the NBPTS certification is renewed. If NBPTS certification is not renewed, the educator moves to a continuing license.*

*Delaware offers two classes of certification.*

- ***Standard Certificate** is issued to candidates who complete an approved program and approved coursework, pass the appropriate tests, hold a valid full certificate in another state, or who hold NBPTS certification. Certificates do not expire for educators who hold valid Delaware licenses.*

- ***Emergency Certificate** is issued to an educator who holds a license but who has not met the requirements for certification in the specific area. The emergency certificate is valid for three years, during which the holder must complete the requirements for the standard certificate.*

## TRADITIONAL ROUTE

The requirements for an Initial license include a bachelor's degree, completion of a student teaching program through an educator preparation program or minimum of 91 days of long-term teaching at one assignment. During the term of the license, holders must participate in a three-year mentoring program that incorporates elements from the ETS PATHWISE Framework Induction Program. When all requirements have been met under the Initial license, a Continuing license will be issued.

## ALTERNATE ROUTE

**Alternative Routes to Certification (ARTC) Program** is a licensure program for noneducation majors. It allows candidates who hold bachelor's degrees with a major (at least 30 semester hours) in a critical needs subject to begin teaching while completing education training at the University of Delaware. Candidates must meet the test requirements and secure a job offer in a district with a critical need in their subject area. Candidates receive an Initial license and Emergency certificate upon enrollment in the program. They must complete all coursework and student teaching required for the program as well as all requirements for a certificate in the appropriate area. When all requirements have been met under the Initial license, they receive their Continuing license.

Critical needs areas include all the sciences, technology education, business education, English, mathematics, and world languages (major languages only, not bilingual or ESOL).

## PROFESSIONAL LICENSES

- School nurses must hold Delaware educator licenses, Delaware professional licenses, and CPR certification.

- School psychologists must hold Delaware educator licenses and professional licenses from Delaware or the National School Psychology Certification Board or another state.

- School counselors and school social workers must hold educator licenses.

- Occupational therapists, physical therapists, audiologists, and speech-language pathologists do not hold educator licenses, but they must hold Delaware professional licenses.

- All professionals may be eligible for salary increases if they hold national certification in their respective areas.

- Individuals seeking Trade and Industry Licensure/ Certification should contact the school districts directly. These licenses/certificates generally require two years of college or technical training and six years of experience. See the Web site for more information.

## TESTING AND SPECIAL REQUIREMENTS

- All candidates for initial licensure (traditional or alternate route) are required to pass the Praxis I: Pre-Professional Skills Test (PPST) in reading, writing, and math. Acceptable scores on the following exams qualify as exemptions to this requirement: SAT, GRE,

NTE Communications (for writing portion only), or California Basic Educational Skills Test (CBEST). An applicant who is employed will be issued a license without passing Praxis I, but must pass the test by the end of the next fiscal year.

- Candidates in the ARTC program must pass the appropriate Praxis II exam, if one is approved in their subject area. Not all Praxis II exams have been approved.

- Praxis II: Subject Assessments may be used to add an area of certification.

## SPECIAL SITUATIONS AND NOTES

- Out-of-state applicants who hold valid full certification in other states, the District of Columbia, Guam, and Puerto Rico receive comparable Delaware licenses. These applicants are exempt from the Praxis I requirement. Applicants with less than three years' experience receive an Initial license and must participate in an alternate mentoring program. Applicants with three years experience receive a Continuing license. Applicants who hold NBPTS certification receive an Advanced license.

- Foreign applicants must have their credentials evaluated by an evaluation service and meet all Delaware requirements including the Praxis I test. See the Web site for more information.

- Paraprofessionals in Title I schools must hold a Paraeducator Permit. The permit requires a high school diploma (or equivalent) and a passing score on the ETS ParaPro assessment, an associate degree, or 2 years of study at an institution of higher education. The permit is valid for five years and requires 15 clock hours of professional development for renewal.

## USEFUL WEB SITES

- **Certification:** deeds.doe.k12.de.us

- **Teach DE (job search):** www.teachdelaware.com

- **School directory:** www.doe.k12.de.us/info/schools/sites.shtml

- **Contacts:** deeds.doe.k12.de.us/deeds_contactus.aspx

- **DE TTT contact:** wbarton@doe.K12.de.us

- **Approved programs:** deeds.doe.k12.de.us/certificate/deeds_caep.aspx

- **Certification inquiry, online application and status:** deeds.doe.k12.de.us/public/deeds_pc_findeducator.aspx

- **Forms:** deeds.doe.k12.de.us/certificate/deeds_forms.aspx

- **Paraprofessionals:** deeds.doe.k12.de.us/deeds_home_para.aspx

- **Testing:** deeds.doe.k12.de.us/certificate/deeds_testing.aspx
www.ets.org/praxis (select state requirements)
www.ets.org/parapro

- **Alternate routes:** deeds.doe.k12.de.us/certificate/deeds_artc.aspx

- **Trade and industry:** deeds.doe.k12.de.us/certificate/deeds_trade.aspx

- **Foreign applicants:** deeds.doe.k12.de.us/certificate/deeds_nonuscred.aspx

- **NBPTS:** deeds.doe.k12.de.us/certificate/deeds_nbct.aspx

- **Substitutes:** deeds.doe.k12.de.us/certificate/deeds_substitute.aspx

# DISTRICT OF COLUMBIA

## OVERVIEW

All teachers must hold a valid District of Columbia license to teach in public, private, or charter schools at the elementary, middle, or secondary level. Licensure is a two-step process for candidates in the traditional route and a three-step process for alternate route candidates.

## TRADITIONAL ROUTE

- Step 1: **Standard License** is granted to novice teachers and is valid for five years. For renewal, it requires 6 semester hours of professional development.

- Step 2: **Professional License** is granted to teachers who have met all the requirements for a Standard license and have received tenure. It is valid for five years and requires 6 semester hours or 90 clock hours of professional development for renewal.
  For the Standard license, candidates must have a bachelor's degree, complete a teacher education program with a major in a subject area, and meet all test requirements. Upon receiving tenure, teachers are granted the Professional license.

## ALTERNATE ROUTE

- Step 1: **Provisional Alternate Route License** is granted to novice teachers in the alternate route programs and is valid for three years. It is nonrenewable.

- Step 2: **Standard License** is granted to teachers who have completed all requirements under the Provisional license. It is valid for five years and requires 6 semester hours of professional development for renewal.

- Step 3: **Professional License** has the same term and requirements as those in the traditional route.
  Candidates for the Provisional License must complete all test requirements, enroll in a teacher education program for the subject area they will teach, and be hired or contracted to teach in a public, private, or charter school.

## SPECIAL LICENSES

- The Restricted License is a Provisional license that may be granted to applicants who have 33 semester hours or a bachelor's degree in a major not defined as a core content area according to NCLB, have met the Praxis I requirement, and have been hired or contracted to teach in a public, private, or charter school. It is valid for three years and is nonrenewable.

- The following special service licenses require master's degrees: Audiologist, Psychometrist, School Counselor, School Librarian/Media Specialist, School Psychologist, Speech Language Pathologist, and School Social Worker. See the Web site for specific requirements.

## TESTING AND SPECIAL REQUIREMENTS

- All candidates for a Provisional and Standard licenses must pass all portions of the Praxis I: Pre-Professional Skills Test (PPST) and the appropriate Praxis II: Subject Assessments. The exception is the Restricted Provisional license, which requires passing Praxis I only.

## SPECIAL SITUATIONS AND NOTES

- Out-of-state applicants who have completed a teacher education program, hold a valid Standard or Professional license with a subject endorsement, and have three years' experience receive a Standard license. They are exempt from testing requirements. Out-of-state applicants who have completed a teacher education program and hold a valid Standard or Professional license with a subject endorsement but have less than three years' experience receive a Provisional Out-of-State license. It is valid for three years and is nonrenewable. Applicants have to meet all test requirements during the term of the Provisional license. Applicants holding NBPTS certification receive the Professional license in the same subject area as their NBPTS certification.

- Paraprofessionals must have a high school diploma or equivalent and two years (60 credits) of study at an institution of higher education, or an associate degree, or demonstrate competence by passing the ETS ParaPro assessment.

- Two substitute licenses are offered. The Full Substitute License requires a bachelor's degree and allows the holder to substitute throughout the school year. The Limited-Term Substitute License requires at least 60 credit hours at an institution of higher education and allows the holder to substitute a maximum of 90 days per school year. Both licenses are valid for two years and may be renewed.

- Critical needs areas include Elementary, Special Education, and Reading.

## USEFUL WEB SITES

- **Certification:** www.k12.dc.us/dcsea/certification

- **Teach DC (recruitment):** www.teachdc.org/index.asp

- **School directory:** www.k12.dc.us/dcps/schools/schoolsmain.html

- **Online job application:** www.teachertrack.org/dcsd

- **Alternate routes:** www.k12.dc.us/dcsea/certification/licensing/initialteacher.html

- **Contacts:** www.k12.dc.us/dcsea/certification/home/staff2.html

- **Fees:** www.k12.dc.us/dcsea/certification/licensing/faq_3.html

- **NBPTS:** www.k12.dc.us/dcps/ProfDev/nbpts/nbcapp.htm

- **Testing:** www.k12.dc.us/dcsea/certification/licensing/faq_5.html
  www.ets.org/praxs (select state requirements)
  www.ets.org/parapro

- **Forms:** www.k12.dc.us/dcps/schools/schoolsmain.html

- **Paraprofessionals:** www.k12.dc.us/DCPS/OWPD/professionaldevt/pdparaprotitle1.htm

- **Approved programs:** www.k12.dc.us/dcsea/certification/licensing/faq.html

- **Substitutes:** www.k12.dc.us/dcsea/certification/licensing/substitute.html

- **TTT (See VA TTT):** www.odu.edu/educ/education/ttt/index.htm

# FLORIDA

## OVERVIEW

*Teachers in Florida elementary and secondary schools must hold either a Professional Certificate or a Temporary Certificate with appropriate subject specialization. The Temporary Certificate allows candidates to complete requirements for the Provisional Certificate while teaching. The Temporary Certificate is valid for three years and is nonrenewable. The Professional Certificate is valid for five years and requires a minimum of 6 semester hours or the equivalent for renewal.*

### TRADITIONAL ROUTE

To qualify for a Temporary Certificate, a candidate must have a bachelor's degree from a teacher preparation program. Degrees from teacher prep programs in other states or U.S. territories are accepted if they lead to certification in those jurisdictions. Candidates may have a bachelor's degree with an education major or minor without having completed a program. These candidates must then complete a professional education competence demonstration system. Candidates for the Temporary Certificate must pass the appropriate Florida Teacher Certification Examinations (FTCE) Subject Area Exams. To qualify for a Professional Certificate, candidates must meet the remaining FTCE requirements.

### ALTERNATE ROUTE

The process for alternate certification is essentially the same as for traditional certification. The only difference is that candidates in the alternate route program have not completed a teacher preparation program. Candidates must be eligible for a Temporary Certificate (i.e., hold a bachelor's degree and meet FTCE requirements) and be hired by a school district where they will participate in an on-the-job alternative preparation program. Upon completing the program and meeting the remaining FTCE requirements, candidates are eligible for the Professional Certificate.

### SUBJECT SPECIALIZATION AND ENDORSEMENTS

All applicants for Professional and Temporary Certificates must meet the requirements for at least one subject specialization, which could be grade level, academic subject, or special service. Candidates must meet degree or course requirements or pass the appropriate FTCE Subject Area Exam. Valid out-of-state certificates, or NBPTS or ABCTE certificates in the same subject area also qualify. The requirements are the same for adding additional subject specializations.

An endorsement is a rider that denotes a particular area of specialization within a subject area on an existing certificate. Therefore, applicants must already hold a certificate in the subject area before they can obtain an endorsement. Applicants apply for a Statement of Status of Eligibility to determine the exact requirements they must meet before beginning work on an endorsement.

### TESTING AND SPECIAL REQUIREMENTS

- Florida Teacher Certification Examinations (FTCE) consist of three tests: Professional Education, General Knowledge, and Subject Area Exams.

- Candidates for the Professional Certificate must pass the Professional Education exam. Exemptions include the following: candidates who complete a Florida alternative certification program; candidates who hold a valid Standard certificate from another state or U.S. territory or NBPTS certification; candidates who hold valid ABCTE certification if they have also completed a professional education competence demonstration system; candidates who have two semesters of full-time college teaching experience. Candidates holding a Temporary Certificate must complete this requirement within the first year of teaching.

- Candidates for the Professional Certificate must pass the General Knowledge exam. Exemptions include candidates who hold a valid Standard certificate from another state or U.S. territory or NBPTS or ABCTE certification and candidates who have two semesters of full-time college teaching experience.

- Candidates for the Professional Certificate or who are adding a subject specialization to an existing certificate must pass the appropriate Subject Area Exams. Candidates who hold a valid Standard certificate in the same subject area at the same degree level from another state or U.S. territory or NBPTS or ABCTE certification are exempt.

### SPECIAL SITUATIONS AND NOTES

- Out-of-state applicants may qualify for a Florida Professional Certificate if they hold a valid Standard certificate from another state or U.S. territory and the subject areas are comparable to Florida's, or if they hold valid NBPTS certification.

- Foreign applicants must have a Social Security Number and have their credentials evaluated by an evaluation service. See the Web site for more information.

- Paraprofessional and substitute training is offered through Educator Preparation Institutes. See the Web site for more information.

## USEFUL WEB SITES

- **Certification:** www.fldoe.org/edcert

- **Teach in FL (job search):** www.teachinflorida.com

- **School directory:** www.fldoe.org/schoolmap/flash/schoolmap_text.asp

- **Approved programs:** www.firn.edu/doe/profdev/teachprep/teachprep.htm

- **Contacts:** www.fldoe.org/edcert/contact.asp

- **Certification inquiry:** www.fldoe.org/edcert/public.asp

- **Application status:** nwrdc.fsu.edu/kmtcstat

- **Testing:** www.firn.edu/doe/sas/ftcehome.htm

- **Time to Teach (recruitment):** www.timetoteach.org

- **Educator preparation institutes:** www.teachinflorida.com/PreCollegiate/EPI.asp

- **Alternate routes:** www.altcertflorida.org

- **Foreign applicants:** www.fldoe.org/edcert/foreign.asp

- **NBPTS:** www.firn.edu/doe/etp/nbpts.html

- **FL TTT:** www.firn.edu/doe/profdev/troopste.htm

- **Online application:** www.fldoe.org/edcert/mat_req.asp

# GEORGIA

## OVERVIEW

*Teachers in Georgia must be certified in the fields they teach. Grade level fields are Early Childhood (P–5), Middle Childhood (4–8), Secondary (7–12), and P–12 for Special Education and noncore subjects. The Clear Renewable Certificate is the full professional certification and may be obtained via traditional and alternate routes. It is valid for five years and requires continuing education or coursework for renewal.*

## TRADITIONAL ROUTE

In the traditional route, candidates may choose a preparation program that leads to a degree and a certificate, or if they already have a bachelor's degree, they may choose a preparation program for the certificate only. In either case, candidates must meet testing and special requirements as noted below. Candidates who have met all requirements except student teaching may take a one-year supervised practicum. Upon completing all requirements, the candidate receives the **Clear Renewable Certificate.**

## ALTERNATE ROUTE

In the **Georgia Teacher Alternative Preparation Program (TAPP),** applicants must have a bachelor's degree and a 2.5 GPA, meet test requirements, and be employed in a district with a TAPP. The two-year program includes coursework and mentoring. Upon completing the program, candidates receive the Clear Renewable Certificate.

The **Test-Based Option,** candidates must have a bachelor's degree in the field or a closely related field, meet the test requirements, and complete a one-year supervised practicum. At the end of the practicum, successful candidates receive the Clear Renewable Certificate.

The **Non-Renewable Test-Based Option** is available to candidates who have an approved bachelor's degree and a job offer but have not yet completed all requirements. Candidates who have passed Praxis I and Praxis II subject assessments must affiliate with a program to complete remaining requirements. Candidates who have passed Praxis I, Praxis II subject assessments, and Principles of Learning and Teaching may complete a one-year supervised practicum. Candidates in Special Education who have passed Praxis I and have an offer of employment in special education may obtain the nonrenewable certificate. In all cases, remaining testing and special requirements must be met within the term of the certificate in order to receive the Clear Renewable Certificate.

Candidates with an expired Georgia certificate may obtain the **Non-Renewable Certificate-Based Option** in the same field(s) and one additional field. Candidates with a Clear Renewable Certificate may obtain a Non-Renewable certificate in another field. In both cases, outstanding requirements for the Clear Renewable Certificate must be met within the term of the certificate.

## ENDORSEMENTS

Endorsements are supplementary fields. Each requires a prerequisite certificate and completion of an endorsement program. Endorsements are offered in the following teaching fields: Career Exploration, Coordinator of Cooperative Education, Diversified Cooperative Training, English to Speakers of Other Languages, Gifted In-Field, Preschool Handicapped, Related Vocational Instruction, and Safety and Drive Education. The only service endorsement field is Teacher Support Specialist. See the Web site for details.

## SPECIALTY CERTIFICATES

- Vocational certificates allow persons with full-time occupational experience to become teachers with the minimum education required for the field.

- Permits allow eligible retired teachers, performing artists, Junior ROTC personnel, and native foreign language speakers to teach. See the Web site for details.

## SPECIAL GEORGIA REQUIREMENTS

All applicants for certification in Georgia must satisfy requirements in the following five areas. Candidates completing in-state teacher preparation programs meet all requirements except testing. Teachers new to Georgia have five years to complete the requirements.

- Content Knowledge Assessments: Applicants must pass the content knowledge assessments described below or have a valid exemption (out-of-state teachers meeting specific experience requirements, NBPTS certification except Middle Grades Generalist, or a content area for which no test has been approved).

- Standards of Conduct: This is an FBI background check and fingerprints.

- Recency of Study/Experience: Applicants must have completed 6 semester hours, or 10 professional learning units, or 10 continuing education units within the past five years. One year of full-time college teaching, NBPTS certification, or a valid professional license for special services meets this requirement.

- Special Education: All persons certified to teach or provide special services must have 3 hours of coursework or 5 professional learning units in special education. NBPTS certification qualifies.

- Computer Skill Competency: Competency may be demonstrated by test or coursework and is required for all renewals. NBPTS certification and NCATE qualify. In addition, certification in early childhood, elementary, middle grades, and special education requires coursework in the teaching of reading.

## TESTING

- The Praxis I Pre-Professional Skills Test (PPST) is required for admission to alternate TAPP programs and for Provisional certificates in all areas except Trade and Industry and Healthcare Science Technology Education. Appropriate scores on ACT, SAT, or GRE will be accepted in place of Praxis I.

- All in-state applicants for certification must pass the appropriate Praxis II subject area assessment. Out-of-state applicants may be exempt if they hold a certificate in another state and passed the required content knowledge exams in that state. If such exams were not required, they must take the appropriate Praxis II exam. Candidates in the TAPP program must complete Praxis II tests within the first year (except Early Childhood and Special Education candidates, who have two years to pass).

- Candidates in the Test-Based Alternate Option must pass Praxis II Principles of Learning and Teaching for the appropriate grade level.

## SPECIAL SITUATIONS AND NOTES

- Out-of-state candidates who have completed an educator training program or hold a valid certificate with three years' experience may be eligible for the Clear Renewable Certificate if they have met all Georgia requirements. If they have not met all requirements, they may obtain employment and a Non-Renewable certificate to allow them to complete all requirements. Georgia participates in the NASDTEC Interstate Agreement and has reciprocity with all participating states for all certificate types.

- Non-U.S. citizens who have teaching credentials and experience may teach in Georgia for three years under the International Exchange Certificate. Applicants must have the equivalent of a U.S. bachelor's degree, have a

job offer, and be proficient in English. Evaluation of credentials by an evaluation service is required. See the Web site for details.

- Paraprofessionals must demonstrate competency through two years of study at an institution of higher education, an associate degree, or by passing the ParaPro assessment. See the Web site for more information.

- Georgia's Reach to Teach program is an initiative to recruit and prepare teachers to teach in critical districts in math, science, and special education. See the Web site for details.

- Various conditional certificates are available to allow applicants to teach temporarily without completing all requirements. See the Web site for details.

## USEFUL WEB SITES

- **Certification:** www.gapsc.com/TeacherCertification.asp
- **Teach GA (job search and recruitment):** www.teachgeorgia.org/
- **School directory:** public.doe.k12.ga.us/findaschool.aspx?contacts=ALL
- **Certification inquiry:** www.teachgeorgia.org/
- **Approved programs:** www.gapsc.com/Approved Programs/EducationProgram.asp
- **Forms:** www.gapsc.com/TeacherCertification/Certification FormsandApplications.asp
- **Paraprofessionals:** www.gapsc.com/ParaPro/home.asp
- **Testing:** www.gapsc.com/TeacherTesting.asp www.ets.org (select state requirements) Computer competency: www.gapsc.com/Teacher Certification/TestReminders.asp
- **Alternate routes:** www.gapsc.com/GATAPP/home.asp
- **Endorsements:** www.gapsc.com/TeacherCertification/Endorsements.asp
- **GA Reach to Teach:** www.reachtoteachingeorgia.com
- **NBPTS:** www.gapsc.com/AboutNBPTS/National_board.asp
- **GA TTT:** www.tttga.net

# HAWAII

## OVERVIEW

*All teachers and education specialists in Hawaii must hold a valid teaching license obtained via traditional or alternate routes, or reciprocity. The license is valid for five years and requires 60 points of professional development (1 semester hours equals 5 points) for renewal. After 4 semesters of satisfactory teaching, teachers are eligible for tenure.*

### TRADITIONAL ROUTE

Candidates must hold a bachelor's degree earned through a teacher education program for the grade level/subject they wish to teach and meet all test requirements.

### ALTERNATE ROUTE

**Post-Baccalaureate Certificate in Secondary Education (PBCSE)** is for candidates who have a bachelor's degree in an area other than education. Candidates must have a 2.75 cumulative GPA and a 2.75 GPA in their major and meet all test requirements for admission to the program. In addition, they must have 40 hours of paid or volunteer group leadership with youth and demonstrate communication skills in a personal admissions interview. The program consists of 33 hours of coursework leading to the Initial Teaching Certificate.

**Transition to Teaching** is a PBCSE alternate route program leading to an Initial Teaching Certificate in secondary mathematics or science. Requirements are the same as for other PBCSE programs.

**Alternative Route to Licensure in Special Education (ARLISE)** allows candidates to be hired into a special education position while completing requirements. The program consists of seminars, coursework, mentoring, and field experience. Upon completing the program and meeting all test requirements, candidates are licensed. There are two strands with different prerequisites. Candidates in the **Respecialization in Special Education (RISE) 1-Year Strand** must have completed a teacher education program in an area other than special education. Candidates in the **Alternative Basic Certification in Special Education (ABCSE) 2-Year Strand** have a bachelor's degree, but have not completed a teacher education program.

**Bachelor of Arts in Special Education (BASE)** is a two-year Bachelor of Arts in Education program that includes coursework, video conferencing, seminars, and student teaching. Prospective candidates must be employed in a Hawaii school and have 60 semester hours of college courses with a 2.0 GPA in English composition, college math, humanities, social sciences including developmental psychology, and natural science including a lab. Candidates must make a commitment to complete the program with a 2.5 GPA, meet all financial obligations, and teach for at least three years in a Hawaii special education classroom.

**Online Degree Programs** are also considered alternative programs. A program must be a state-approved program in the state where the sponsoring institution is located, the institution must be regionally accredited, and the applicant must meet the reciprocity requirements. The applicant must hold a license in the state where the sponsoring institution is located and must have at least three years experience, or complete a teacher education program with supervised student teaching in Hawaii.

### TEACHING FIELDS CERTIFICATES

Teaching Fields Certificates may be added to existing licenses through one of three options. In Option A, candidates must complete a teacher education program for the new grade level or field. This is the only option for adding the school librarian field. In Option B, candidates complete 18 hours of coursework in the new grade level or field and have two years' experience teaching in the new field or hold an out-of-state license in the new field. In Option C, candidates have two years' teaching experience in the new field and pass the appropriate Praxis II: Subject Assessments.

### SPECIALTY CERTIFICATES

Industrial Arts/Trades and Industry certificates may be based on experience rather than on a degree. One or two years of experience are required depending on the area.

### TESTING AND SPECIAL REQUIREMENTS

- All candidates must pass the Praxis I: Pre-Professional Skills Tests (PPST) in reading, writing, and mathematics.

- All candidates must pass the Praxis II: Principles of Learning and Teaching for the grade level of their teacher education program. Those in middle-level programs are required to take the complete 5–9 version. Those in early childhood programs are required to take the PK–3 test.

- Candidates in early childhood (PK–3) and elementary (K–6) teacher education programs must take the Praxis II: Subject Assessments in those areas. Candidates in middle-level programs must take exams in the area related to their student teaching. Those in secondary or specialist programs must take the exams in their major area.

- Candidates for the PBCSE programs must pass Praxis I: PPST and the appropriate Praxis II: Subject Assessments for admission to the program. Praxis II is an exit requirement for candidates in Art, Business, Home Economics, ESL, and Industrial Arts/Trades and Industry.

## SPECIAL SITUATIONS AND NOTES

■ Out-of-state applicants must have completed a teacher education program approved in the state where they are licensed. Otherwise applicants must hold a valid license and have three years of at least half-time experience. Applicants must meet all test requirements, but applicants holding NBPTS certification are exempt from the test requirements.

■ Foreign applicants must have their credentials evaluated by an evaluation service. They must also have authorization to work in the U.S. See the Web site for more information.

■ Paraprofessionals in Title I schools must meet requirements in one of the following options: (1) 48 credits from an institution of higher education; (2) an associate degree; (3) completion of a two-year Educational Assistant Training Program including practicum; (4) completion of Educational Assistant Foundation Courses (12 hours) including practicum; (5) passing score in the ETS ParaPro Assessment. In addition, Options 3 and 4 require professional courses in reading, writing, and math, or three credits each in math and English, or passing the ParaPro Assessment.

■ Class III substitutes must be licensed in Hawaii and have completed a teacher education program. They have first priority for jobs. Class II substitutes must hold a bachelor's degree. All applicants must complete a 30-hour substitute teacher course. Upon completion, they receive the Substitute Teacher Course Certificate valid for five years.

## USEFUL WEB SITES

■ **Licensing, approved programs:** www.htsb.org

■ **Teaching in HI (recruitment and jobs):** doe.k12.hi.us/personnel/teachinginhawaii.htm

■ **Jobs:** www.rrsc.k12.hi.us

■ **School directory:** 165.248.6.166/data/schoollist.asp

■ **Online application:** fms-web2.k12.hi.us/OnlineApp/OnlineApp.asp

■ **Forms:** www.htsb.org/forms

■ **Contacts:** www.htsb.org/contact.html

■ **NBPTS:** www.htsb.org/nbpts/index.html

■ **HI TTT:** www.rrsc.k12.hi.us/ttt.html

■ **Paraprofessionals:** rrsc.k12.hi.us/ea/index.htm
www.rrsc.k12.hi.us/ea/nclbpamphlet.htm

■ **Foreign applicants:** doe.k12.hi.us/personnel/teachernonuscitizens.htm

■ **Testing:** www.htsb.org
www.ets.org/praxis (select state requirements)
www.ets.org/parapro

■ **Alternate routes:**
ARLISE: www.rrsc.k12.hi.us/tc/index.html
BASE: www.rrsc.k12.hi.us/base
Transition to Teaching: www.hawaii.edu/coe/departments/ttt/index.html
PBCSE: www.hawaii.edu/coe/departments/ite/prog_pbcse.html
Online programs: www.htsb.org/licensing/onlinedegree.html

■ **Substitutes:** doe.k12.hi.us/personnel/teachersubstitute.htm

# IDAHO

## OVERVIEW

*All Idaho educators must hold an educator credential, which may be the Standard Teaching Certificate or one of several temporary certificates for candidates in alternate programs or for out-of-state applicants. The Standard Teaching Certificate is valid for five years and for renewal requires 6 semester credits or the equivalent of professional development. In addition, educators who are employed at the time of renewal must meet the technology and literacy requirements.*

### TRADITIONAL ROUTE

To qualify for Standard certification, candidates must complete a bachelor's degree in a teacher training program and meet all technology, literacy, and test requirements.

### ALTERNATE ROUTE

**Alternative Certification** allows individuals who hold a bachelor's degree to become certified secondary teachers. To be eligible, candidates must have a 2.0 GPA, have earned their degree at least five years earlier, hold a major or minor in the subject area they will teach, meet all other nonacademic requirements, and have an offer of full-time employment in an Idaho school. The Alternative Certification is valid for three years. During that time, candidates must complete required courses with a 2.5 overall GPA and teach for two years under a Teacher Trainee Letter of Permission. During the two-year training period, they are mentored and evaluated. Upon successfully completing courses, training, and the technology and test requirements, they are eligible for the Standard Secondary Teaching Certificate.

Idaho has three **Alternative Authorization Programs** that allow persons lacking the necessary certification or endorsement to teach while completing requirements. The requirements for the programs are similar to the Alternative Certification program described above except that applicants receive a Letter of Authorization to teach.

- In the **Teacher to New Certification** program, persons who hold a valid teaching certificate but lack the necessary certificate or endorsement may complete an alternate teacher preparation program in the new area. The authorization is valid for three years.

- The **Content Specialist** program expedites the certification process for a person who has unique qualifications in the subject area. The authorization is valid for three years.

- The **Para-Educator to Teacher** program allows para-educators to become certified teachers. The program must be completed in five years.

- Candidates who hold a bachelor's degree may use the **Computer-Based Alternate Route to Teacher Certification** program for initial certification, additional certification, or for adding endorsements. Candidates must complete the program and meet the Praxis II test requirements in order to receive an Interim Certificate, which is valid for three years and is nonrenewable. With the Interim Certificate, they must teach for two years under a mentoring program to be eligible for the Standard certificate.

- **American Board for Certification of Teacher Excellence (ABCTE)** is approved as an alternate route to certification in the following areas: Biology, Elementary Education, English, General Science, and Math. It may be used for the initial certificate, additional certificates, or adding endorsements. Candidates who complete the ABCTE test program and receive the ABCTE Passport to Teaching certificate are eligible for the Interim Certificate, which enables them to teach. The certificate is valid for three years. During this time, candidates must complete a two-year mentoring program, which may be either a program offered by the employing district or be the ABCTE program. Candidates must also meet the technology requirement, and candidates for Elementary Education (K–8) must meet the literacy requirement. After completing all requirements, candidates are eligible for the Standard certificate.

### CERTIFICATES AND ENDORSEMENTS

Educator credentials are defined by certificates and endorsements. Certificates generally designate the grade level the holder is authorized to teach. Each certificate carries endorsements that generally designate the subject area the holder is authorized to teach. There are Praxis II test requirements for certificates and endorsements. Endorsements also require 20 semester hours of coursework in the subject area.

Certificates include Early Childhood/Early Childhood Special Education Blended Certificate (Birth–Grade 3), Standard Elementary Certificate (K–8), Standard Secondary Certificate (6–12), Native American Language Teacher, Standard Exceptional Child Certificate (K–12), Pupil Personnel Services Certificate (PreK–12), Limited Approvals (Alternate Routes), Pupil Personnel Services, and Professional-Technical (6–12). Endorsements for Audiologist, Counselor, School Psychologist, Speech-Language Pathologist or Social Worker require a master's degree. Candidates for school nurse must be registered nurses with a bachelor's degree in nursing.

## SPECIALTY CERTIFICATES

- The Standard Secondary Certificate for Professional-Technical Education with endorsement in an occupational area requires completion of a bachelor's degree teacher preparation program.

- The Occupational Specialist Certificate requires work experience and/or a bachelor's degree in the occupational area.

## TESTING AND SPECIAL REQUIREMENTS

- All candidates must pass the appropriate Praxis II: Subject Assessments. Elementary (K–8) certification requires Elementary Education: Content Knowledge plus Principles of Learning and Teaching K–6 or 5–9.

- All persons adding a certification or endorsement must pass the appropriate Praxis II: Subject Assessment.

- All candidates must hold the Basic Educational Technology Competency Certificate. To obtain this certificate, candidates must pass the Idaho Educator Technology Assessment, the Idaho Technology Portfolio Assessment, or the Idaho Technology Performance Assessment. This is also a requirement for certification renewal. Employed educators applying for renewal may request one five-year waiver for this requirement. Those not employed in Idaho at the time of renewal automatically receive a waiver.

- Candidates for Elementary Education (K–8) certification must complete the Idaho Comprehensive Literacy Course or pass the Idaho Comprehensive Literacy Assessment (ICLA). This is also a requirement for renewal, but is waived for those not employed at the time of renewal.

## SPECIAL SITUATIONS AND NOTES

- Out-of-state applicants who hold a valid license with three years' experience in any state covered by the NASDTEC Interstate Agreement is issued a three-year nonrenewable Interim Certificate to allow time to meet Idaho requirements. During this period, they must meet the technology and literacy requirements. Upon completion, they receive a Standard certificate.

- Foreign applicants must have their credentials evaluated by an evaluation service. They must also meet the Praxis II requirements. See the Web site.

- Positions that are difficult to fill are Special Education, Math, Music, ESL, Foreign Language, Early Childhood Special Education, Counselor, English, Speech Pathologist, and Speech/Drama.

## USEFUL WEB SITES

- **Certification:** www.sde.state.id.us/certification

- **Jobs:** www.idahoeducationjobs.com/index.html

- **School directory:** www.sde.state.id.us/admin/eddirectory

- **Contacts:** www.sde.state.id.us/certification/staff.asp

- **Approved programs:** www.sde.state.id.us/certification/resourceed.asp

- **Alternate routes:** www.sde.state.id.us/certification/altroutes.asp

- **ABCTE:** www.sde.state.id.us/certification/abcte.asp

- **Forms:** www.sde.state.id.us/certification/certforms.asp

- **Fees:** www.sde.state.id.us/certification/certfees.asp

- **Paraprofessionals:** www.sde.state.id.us/sasa/law.asp

- **Testing:** www.sde.state.id.us/certification/praxisinfo.asp www.ets.org/praxis

- **Technology assessment:** www.sde.state.id.us/bots/testing.asp

- **ICLA:** www.sde.state.id.us/instruct/curriculum/ComList.asp

- **Foreign applicants:** www.sde.state.id.us/certification

- **Professional-Technical Education:** www.pte.idaho.gov/certif/certic.htm

- **NBPTS:** www.sde.state.id.us/certification/nationalboard.asp

- **Northern Plains TTT:** www.montana.edu/ttt

# ILLINOIS

## OVERVIEW

There are three levels of Professional Teaching Certificates that may be obtained through traditional preparation, alternate routes, or reciprocity.

- **Initial Certificate** is issued to new teachers. It is valid for four years, during which they must complete one professional development activity required for moving to the Standard Certificate.

- **Standard Certificate** requires four years of teaching under the Initial Certificate and one professional development activity. It is valid for five years and requires professional development for renewal.

- **Master Certificate** is granted to persons who achieve NBPTS certification and is valid for ten years.

## TRADITIONAL ROUTE

Candidates for the Initial Certificate must complete an approved Illinois teacher education program for the certificate and subject area in which they will teach. The Initial Certificate is considered an "entitlement certificate." Candidates must pass the Basic Skills Test before entering the program and must meet the Illinois Certification Testing System (ICTS) requirements.

## ALTERNATE ROUTE

The **Alternative Teacher Certification** program is limited to 260 new candidates per year. Candidates must have a bachelor's degree and five years' experience in their field (except when applying for provisional teaching in Chicago) and must meet all test requirements. After completing the first phase of the program, candidates receive a one-year nonrenewable Provisional Alternative Teaching Certificate. After completing required courses, candidates must teach full-time for one year with mentoring and complete performance assessments to receive a nonrenewable Initial Alternative Teaching Certificate valid for four years. After four years of teaching, candidates are eligible for the Standard Teaching Certificate.

For **Resident Teacher Certification,** candidates must have a bachelor's degree, enroll in an approved preparation program, and meet all test requirements. Upon admission to the program, they receive a nonrenewable Resident Teacher Certificate valid for four years. After teaching for four years under direct supervision and mentoring, meeting all test requirements, and completing a Master of Education degree, they are eligible for the Standard Teaching Certificate.

**Illinois Teacher Corps** is a Resident Teacher Certification program for persons who have a bachelor's degree with a 3.0 GPA, five years' experience in their field, and are enrolled in a Master of Education degree program. The degree program can take no longer than two academic years and three summers. Upon completion, candidates are eligible for the Initial Teaching Certificate.

## ENDORSEMENTS

Endorsements on certificates indicate the grade level or subject the holder is authorized to teach. At the secondary level, endorsements require a major (32 semester hours), or 24 semester hours plus a passing grade on the Content Test. Endorsements for middle grades (5–8 on elementary certificate or 6–8 on the secondary certificate) require 18 semester hours of content courses and 6 semester hours of education courses specific to the middle grades.

## SPECIALTY CERTIFICATES

Provisional Vocational and Temporary Provisional Vocational Certificates may be issued to persons with appropriate work experience and/or coursework.

## TESTING AND SPECIAL REQUIREMENTS

- The Illinois Certification Testing System (ICTS) consists of a Basic Skills Test, a Content Test, and the Assessment of Professional Teaching (APT). The APT is given for four grade levels: Birth to grade 3, K–9, 6–12, K–12/P–21 for special subjects.

- Candidates for Initial or Standard certification in Early Childhood, Elementary, Secondary, or Special Education are required to pass the Basic Skills Test before entering a teacher education program. They must pass the Content Test and the appropriate level APT before receiving the certificate.

- Persons holding Provisional Teaching Certificates must pass all ICTS tests within nine months unless waived (see out-of-state information below).

- Candidates for School Service Personnel Certificates must pass the Basic Skills Test and Content Test before receiving the certificate. Persons holding Provisional School Service Personnel Certificates must pass both tests within nine months.

- Candidates for admission to alternate route programs must pass the Basic Skills Test and Content Test.

- Candidates who already hold a certificate but wish to gain another certificate must attend an approved program for the other certificate (at a different grade level) and must take the appropriate APT.

- Endorsements require passing the appropriate Content Test unless the candidate has a major (32 semester hours) in the subject.

- Candidates for the Transitional Bilingual Certificate must pass the appropriate Language Proficiency Test before receiving the certificate.

## SPECIAL SITUATIONS AND NOTES

- Illinois participates in the Central States Teacher Exchange Agreement and the NASDTEC Interstate Agreement. Out-of-state applicants who hold a valid certificate and have completed a teacher preparation program including student teaching or have three years of experience (four years for Standard Certificate) will receive a comparable certificate.

- Foreign applicants must have their credentials evaluated by an evaluation service. See the Web site for more information.

- Paraprofessionals in Title I programs must have an associate degree, or 60 semester hours credit or a passing score on the ETS ParaPro Assessment or ACT WorkKeys test, or 30 semester hours credit and 300 professional training points, or complete an approved paraprofessional training program and 300 professional training points.

- Applicants for Substitute Certificates must hold a regular certificate or have a bachelor's degree or two years teaching experience with appropriate coursework. The certificate is valid for 4 years. A substitute may not teach more than 90 days in any district in a single year.

## USEFUL WEB SITES

- **Certification:** www.isbe.net/certification/default.htm

- **Recruit IL (recruitment and job search):** www.recruitillinois.net

- **Jobs:** www.iasaedu.org/Jobbank/default.htm

- **School directory:** www.isbe.net/research/htmls/directories.htm

- **Contacts:** www.isbe.net/certification/html/chicago_office.htm

- **Online application and certification inquiry:** www.isbe.net/otis/default.htm

- **Approved programs:** www.isbe.net/profprep/PDFs/Directory.pdf

- **Substitutes:** www.isbe.net/certification/requirements/do_not_require.htm

- **Testing:** www.isbe.net/certification/html/testing.htm
  www.icts.nesinc.com
  Paraprofessionals: www.ets.org/parapro
  www.act.org/workkeys

- **Alternate routes:** www.isbe.net/profprep/alternative.htm

- **Foreign applicants:** www.isbe.net/certification/html/foreign_credential.htm

- **Paraprofessionals:** www.isbe.net/certification/html/paraprofessional.htm

- **Forms:** www.isbe.net/certification/html/forms.htm

- **IL TTT:** www.isbe.net/troops/default.htm

- **NBPTS:** www.isbe.net/certification/html/national_board_experienced.htm

# INDIANA

## OVERVIEW

All teachers and special service providers in Indiana must hold a Professional Educator License, which may be an Instructional or School Services Personnel Professional license. Each has three levels, whether a person comes through the traditional or alternate route and wants to teach in an elementary, middle/junior high, or high school setting.

- **Initial Practitioner** is the license issued to new teachers. They are required to participate in the Indiana Mentoring and Assessment Program (IMAP) for two years. Assessment is in the form of a portfolio. The license is valid for two years and may be renewed once for one year if IMAP is not completed, or twice if the holder is not employed.

- **Proficient Practitioner License** is the next step and is valid for five years. It requires a Professional Growth Plan for renewal.

- The next step is **Accomplished Practitioner License** issued to those who complete an advanced degree or achieve NBPTS certification.

## TRADITIONAL ROUTE

Candidates for the Initial Practitioner License must have a bachelor's degree in education or have completed a teacher education program and have met all test requirements.

## ALTERNATE ROUTE

**Transition to Teaching** is open to candidates with a bachelor's degree. They must complete an approved program consisting of 18 hours of education courses for secondary or 24 hours for elementary. They must also meet all test requirements for the Initial Practitioner License. After completing the Beginning Teacher Assessment Program under the Initial license, they are eligible for the Proficient Practitioner License. They then follow the requirements for Accomplished Practitioner.

## CONTENT AREAS AND SCHOOL SETTINGS

Licenses list the Content Areas and School Settings (grade level) for each Content Area that the holder is authorized to teach. School Settings are Preschool (PreK), Elementary/Primary (K–3), Elementary/Intermediate (4–6), Junior High/Middle School, and High School. Completing an approved program is required for adding an area to a license.

## SPECIALTY CERTIFICATES

- School Service Personnel licenses require a master's degree except school nurse, which requires a bachelor's degree and registered nurse license.

- Occupational Specialist licenses are for grades P–12. Workplace Specialist licenses are for secondary level only. These require a high school diploma or GED and occupational experience.

- The license for Communication Disorders requires a master's degree in Speech Language Pathology. The license for Reading Specialist requires a master's degree.

## TESTING AND SPECIAL REQUIREMENTS

- All candidates for the Initial Practitioner License must pass the Praxis I: Pre-Professional Skills Test (PPST). In addition, Praxis II: Specialty Area Tests are required for most content areas.

- There are no test requirements for school service personnel.

- Candidates for the Initial elementary (primary or intermediate) license must pass the Praxis II: Reading Specialist test.

## SPECIAL SITUATIONS AND NOTES

- Indiana participates in the NASDTEC Interstate Agreement. Applicants who completed an NCATE-accredited program or an approved program in a NASDTEC state may not have additional course requirements, but must complete IMAP if they have less than two years' experience. Out-of-state applicants are issued a Reciprocal Permit valid for one year if they have completed an approved program, hold a valid license, and have met all prerequisites. Applicants who hold a license and have three years' experience are exempt from the test requirements.

- Foreign applicants must have their credentials evaluated by an evaluation service.

- Paraprofessionals in Title I schools must have an associate degree, or two years of study at an institution of higher education, or pass the ETS ParaPro Assessment.

- Substitute Permits, not licenses, are issued by the employing school district. Each district sets its own requirements. Permits are valid for three years. Persons holding an Indiana license may substitute without obtaining a permit.

## USEFUL WEB SITES

- **Certification:** www.doe.state.in.us/dps/welcome.html

- **Jobs:** iseasjob.indstate.edu

- **School directory:** www.doe.state.in.us/htmls/k12.html

- **Approved programs:** www.doe.state.in.us/dps/licensing/approvedprograms.html

- **Contacts:** www.doe.state.in.us/dps/visitors/contact.html

- **Certification inquiry:** mustang.doe.state.in.us/TEACH/teach_inq.cfm

- **Fees:** www.doe.state.in.us/dps/licensing/fees.html

- **Paraprofessionals:** www.doe.state.in.us/dps/parapro/welcome.html

- **Testing:** www.doe.state.in.us/dps/teacherprep/testing/welcome.html
www.ets.org/praxis (select state requirements)
www.et.s.org/parapro

- **Forms:** www.doe.state.in.us/dps/quicklinks.html

- **Alternate routes:** www.doe.state.in.us/dps/specialtopics bulletin.html

- **TTT (See Michigan TTT):** RatajikD@Michigan.gov

- **Substitutes:** www.doe.state.in.us/dps/licensing/substitute/welcome.html

# IOWA

## OVERVIEW

*Becoming licensed to teach in Iowa at the elementary, middle, or secondary level by the traditional route is a two-step process. The alternate route is available only to people wishing to teach on the secondary level.*

### TRADITIONAL ROUTE

- Step 1: The **Initial License** is valid for two years and may be renewed twice, but only if the holder does not have two years of teaching experience.

- Step 2: The **Standard License** requires two years of teaching experience, is valid for five years, and requires six credits of professional development for renewal.
  The Initial License requires a bachelor's degree; completion of an approved teacher preparation program, an approved human relations component, and requirements for one teaching endorsement; and meeting the Recency Requirement described below. The Initial License may be converted to the Standard License after two years of teaching experience with evidence of competence in the Iowa teaching standards.

### ALTERNATE ROUTE

The **Teacher Intern License** allows a person who holds a bachelor's degree to become a secondary teacher. The applicant must meet the subject matter requirements for one of the secondary teaching endorsements, have a 2.5 GPA, have worked for at least three years beyond the bachelor's degree, and complete an approved introductory teacher intern program. The license is valid for one year, during which the person must participate in an approved mentoring and induction program, complete a teacher intern seminar, and complete a concluding intern teacher program.

### ENDORSEMENTS

Endorsements are required for all licenses and designate the grade level and subject area that may be taught. Endorsements are also required for special services and special education. To add an endorsement, the applicant must complete the endorsement requirements in a teacher prep or education program. These include specific subject courses and may also include core education courses.

The Middle School Endorsement (Grades 5–8) authorizes the holder to teach all subjects at this grade level except reading, art, music, industrial arts, physical education, and special education. It requires specific coursework and an Iowa teaching license with either the elementary (K–6) classroom endorsement or the secondary (7–12) classroom endorsement.

### TESTING AND SPECIAL REQUIREMENTS

- Iowa has no testing requirements.

- All applicants for new licenses and renewals must have completed an approved "Mandatory Child and Depen-dent Adult Abuse Reporter Training" program within the past five years. See the Web site for a list of approved programs.

- The Recency Requirement stipulates that the applicant meets all requirements for a valid license but has less than 160 days (two years) of experience during the past five years.

### SPECIAL SITUATIONS AND NOTES

- Out-of-state applicants must have three years' experience to qualify for the Standard License. Those who completed alternate programs without student teaching must also have three years' experience. Applicants must meet minimum requirements for each endorsement.

- Applicants who completed their education in a foreign country must have their credentials evaluated by an evaluation service. See the Web site below.

- Applicants for the Paraeducator Certificate must have at least a high school diploma or equivalent, complete an approved paraeducator training program, and satisfy the child abuse prevention requirement. The certificate is valid for five years and requires 3 hours college credit for renewal. Areas of concentration may be added by meeting additional requirements.

- A substitute teaching license requires completion of a teacher education program and authorizes the holder to substitute in any grade level or subject for no more than 90 days per assignment. The license is valid for five years and may be renewed with either 30 days of substitute experience or approved coursework.

- A substitute authorization requires a bachelor's degree or paraprofessional certificate and completion of a substitute training program. It authorizes the holder to substitute in middle, junior, or high school for no more than five days per assignment. It is valid for one year and requires 15 clock hours for renewal.

### USEFUL WEB SITES

- **IA Board of Educational Examiners:** www.state.ia.us/boee/#a

- **Teach IA (job search):** www.iowaeducationjobs.com/

- **School directory:** www.state.ia.us/educate/directory.html

- **Teacher Intern License:** www.state.ia.us/boee/tilal. html

- **Contacts:** www.state.ia.us/boee/boeedir.html

- **Forms:** www.state.ia.us/boee/getapp.html

- **Approved programs:** www.state.ia.us/boee/Coldir.html

- **Out-of-state and foreign applicants:** www.state.ia.us/ boee/getapp.html

- **Paraeducators:** www.state.ia.us/boee/para.html

- **Substitutes:** www.state.ia.us/boee/sub.html

- **NBPTS:** www.state.ia.us/educate/ecese/nbc/list.html

- **Child Abuse Prevention Programs:** www.state.ia.us/ boee/abuse.html

- **TTT (contact national office):** www.ProudToServe Again.com

# KANSAS

## OVERVIEW

*Teachers in Kansas must hold a Standard Teaching License to teach at the elementary, middle, or secondary level. There are three levels of licensure for those who complete traditional programs, Conditional License, Professional License, and Accomplished License. Candidates who come through the alternate route have an additional level, the Restricted Teaching License, which precedes the Conditional License.*

## TRADITIONAL ROUTE

The **Conditional License** is the initial teaching license, is valid for two years, and may be renewed once. Candidates for the Conditional Teaching License must have a bachelor's degree with a 2.5 GPA, complete a teacher preparation program, and meet the recency and test requirements.

The **Professional License** is granted to persons who hold the Conditional License and complete the Kansas Performance Assessment (KPA). This second-level license is valid for five years. Renewal requires 160 points of professional development including 80 points of college credit.

The **Accomplished License** is granted to persons who hold a Professional License and achieve NBPTS certification. It is valid for 10 years.

## ALTERNATE ROUTE

The alternate route program allows candidates to teach for three years in a middle/secondary position under the **Restricted Teaching License.** Candidates for the Restricted license must hold a bachelor's degree or have coursework in the content area in which they wish to teach. The coursework must be equivalent to what is offered in a traditional program. Candidates must also have a 2.5 GPA and a job offer in their content area from a school district. During the first year of the program, candidates must pass the appropriate Praxis II: Subject Assessment. During the three years, they must make adequate progress in their coursework, maintain a 2.5 GPA, and submit annual progress reports. When candidates complete the program and the testing requirements, they receive a Conditional License. To move to the Professional License, they must complete the KPA.

## ENDORSEMENTS

To add endorsements for new subjects, candidates must complete an endorsement program and meet test requirements. Persons who already hold a teaching or school specialist license and have been hired to teach in a new area are issued a Provisional license until they complete the endorsement program. However, to qualify for the Provisional license, they must complete 50 percent of the endorsement program. Special education is an endorsement.

## SPECIALTY LICENSES

- Candidates for the School Specialist Conditional License, which is valid for five years, must hold a master's degree, complete a graduate level program with a 3.25 GPA, hold a valid Professional Teaching license (for counselor, library media, or reading specialist), and meet the recency and test requirements. In addition, for the Professional License, they must complete a performance assessment, which consists of a supervised internship.

- Technical Certificates are issued to persons who have occupational work experience, complete a training program consisting of 18 semester hours, pass a trade exam or hold an occupational license, and have been hired by a school district. A Restricted Certificate allows persons to teach while completing requirements.

- A Special Needs Certificate requires an additional 9 semester hour credits.

## TESTING AND SPECIAL REQUIREMENTS

- Candidates for the Conditional License must pass the appropriate Praxis II: Subject Assessments and the appropriate level Praxis II: Principles of Learning and Teaching (PLT).

- Candidates for School Specialist Conditional License must pass the appropriate Praxis II: Specialty Assessment.

- Educators adding an endorsement area must pass the appropriate Praxis II: Subject Assessments.

- The Kansas Performance Assessment (KPA) is required to upgrade to the Professional License. It consists of a written teaching unit including goals, objectives, and plans for instruction and assessment.

- Foreign applicants whose primary language is not English must pass the ETS Test of English as a Foreign Language (TOEFL).

- To meet the recency requirement, candidates must have 8 credit hours or one year of teaching experience within the past six years.

## SPECIAL SITUATIONS AND NOTES

- Out-of-state applicants must meet the same degree, GPA, program, recency, and test requirements as those in prepared in-state for the Conditional License. For a

Professional License, they must also hold an out-of-state professional level license and have a successful performance assessment or three years' experience. If applicants only need to meet the test requirements, they may apply for a two-year Exchange License, a one-year Nonrenewable License if hired, or a substitute license. To upgrade to the Conditional License, applicants must remove any deficiencies, meet the test and recency requirements, and have a 2.5 GPA. Those who have completed comparable exams or who hold NBPTS certification are exempt from the test requirement.

- The Exchange License is based on an agreement among Illinois, Iowa, Kansas, Michigan, Missouri, Nebraska, Oklahoma, South Dakota, and Wisconsin. It is valid for two years and allows persons who completed a teacher education program and hold a standard license in these states to teach while removing any deficiencies. Applicants who have been trained through alternate routes do not qualify.

- Foreign applicants must have their credentials evaluated by an evaluation service. They must meet the same requirements for the Conditional License as candidates trained in-state and also pass an English proficiency exam. See the Web site for more information.

- Paraprofessionals paid by Title I funds or in Title I schools must have a high school diploma or GED and 48 hours of study at an institution of higher education, or an associate degree, or pass the ETS ParaPro Assessment, the ACT WorkKeys assessments, or the ParaEducator Learning Network assessments.

- The Standard Substitute License requires a bachelor's degree and completion of a teacher preparation program. It is valid for 5 years and requires 100 professional development points for renewal. The Emergency Substitute License requires 60 semester hours. The type of license determines the number of days a substitute may serve.

- Teacher Service Scholarships encourage students to enter the teaching profession by granting funding in exchange for one or two years of teaching. Some scholarships are specifically for math and science teachers. See the financial aid Web site for more information.

## USEFUL WEB SITES

- **Licensure:** www.ksde.org/cert/licensure_info.htm

- **Job search:** www.kansasteachingjobs.com

- **School directory:** www.ksde.org/eddir/eddir.html

- **Contacts:** www.ksde.org/cert/cert.html

- **Licensure inquiry:** online.ksde.org/teal/cert_search.aspx

- **Approved programs:** www.ksde.org/cert/approvedprogs.html

- **Foreign applicants:** www.ksde.org/cert/outofcountry.htm

- **Paraprofessionals:** www.ksde.org/sfp/nclb/paraprofessionals/para_info_11-04.doc

- **Testing:** www.ksde.org/cert/testing.htm
www.act.org/workkeys
Paraprofessionals: www.ets.org/parapro
www.adt.org/workkeys
www.paraeducator.net
English proficiency: www.ets.org/toefl

- **Alternate routes:** www.ksde.org/cert/resteaching.htm

- **Forms**: www.ksde.org/cert/1ask4app.html#1Download

- **Financial Aid:** www.kansasregents.org/financial_aid/awards.html

- **NBPTS:** www.ksbe.state.ks.us/cert/nbpts.html

- **KS TTT:** www.mwttt.com

- **Substitutes:** www.ksde.org/cert/substitute.htm

# KENTUCKY

## OVERVIEW

*Professional Certificates are required for teaching elementary, middle, and secondary school in Kentucky. The certificates are valid for five years and require graduate study or continuing education for renewal. Provisional Certificates are available to candidates in some alternate route programs to allow completion of all requirements while teaching.*

### TRADITIONAL ROUTE

Applicants for the **Professional Certificate** must complete a college or university teacher preparation program including student teaching and meet the test requirements described below.

### ALTERNATE ROUTE

Kentucky offers seven alternate routes to certification for teaching primary to grade 12.

- **Option 1: Exceptional Work Experience Certification:** The applicant must have a bachelor's degree, a major in the subject area (or passing score on the Praxis II: Subject Area exam), at least 10 years of "exceptional work experience" beyond the bachelor's degree, and an employment offer from a local school district.

- **Option 2: Local District Training Program Certification:** The applicant must have a bachelor's degree, 30 hours of subject coursework or five years of field experience, and an employment offer from a school district with an approved training program. Upon completion of the one-year training program, the applicant receives a one-year Provisional Certificate and must participate in a Kentucky Teacher Internship Program (KTIP). Upon completion of the KTIP program, the applicant receives the Professional Certificate.

- **Option 3: College Faculty Certification:** The applicant must have a master's degree in the subject area and five years of teaching experience or equivalent (90 semester credit hours) at an institution of higher education. The applicant who meets these requirements receives a Statement of Eligibility. The applicant must then obtain employment and the one-year Provisional Certificate. Upon completion of a one-year KTIP program, the applicant receives the Professional Certificate.

- **Option 4: Adjunct Instructor Certificate:** The applicant must have a bachelor's degree for all levels and a major or minor in the subject area for middle and secondary levels. For vocational education, the applicant must have a high school diploma and four years of occupational experience. In either case, applicants must have an employment offer from a school district. The applicant may be employed part-time or on a contract basis, but this route does not lead to Professional Certification.

- **Option 5: Troops to Teachers Program:** See the Web site below for details.

- **Option 6: University-Based Alternative Route to Certification:** Applicants complete a preparation program while teaching. Candidates must have a bachelor's or master's degree and meet admission requirements. They receive a Temporary Provisional Certificate and must participate in a KTIP. All requirements and tests must be completed within three years.

- **Option 7: University Institute Alternative Route to Certification:** The applicant must have a bachelor's, professional, or graduate degree and meet minimum score requirements on the Graduate Record Exam (GRE). No universities currently offer this program.

### CERTIFICATION AREAS

- Teaching certificates are offered in three areas: Base Teaching Certificates (specific grade levels), Restricted Base Certificates (non-core academic areas), and Other Instructional Services (special and administrative services).

- Endorsements are available in the following licensure areas: Computer Science, Instructional Computer Technology, Reading and Writing, Gifted Education, Driver Education, Environmental Education, School Safety, School Nutrition, ESL, Learning and Behavior Disorders, and Special Education. The last three require passing the appropriate Praxis II Specialty Area exam.

- Guidance Counselor Certification requires completion of a master's level guidance counselor program for the Provisional certificate. The Standard certificate has additional requirements.

### TESTING AND SPECIAL REQUIREMENTS

- All applicants must pass the Praxis II Principles of Teaching and Learning for the appropriate grade level and the Praxis II Specialty Area test for each certification area.

## SPECIAL SITUATIONS AND NOTES

- Out-of-state applicants must complete a teacher preparation program (traditional or alternate) and meet minimum GPA, testing, and internship requirements. Applicants who hold a valid certificate and have two years' experience are exempt from the testing and internship requirements. Kentucky participates in the NASDTEC Interstate Agreement.

- Foreign applicants must have completed a bachelor's degree teacher prep program with student teaching in a subject recognized by Kentucky. In addition, they must meet minimum GPA requirements and have their credentials evaluated by an evaluation service. See the Web site below.

- Kentucky has a Minority Educator Recruitment and Retention Program that provides financial assistance. See the alternate routes Web site for details.

- The Substitute Teacher Certification, which is valid for five years, requires a statement of eligibility for a Kentucky teaching certificate or a previous Kentucky certificate based on a bachelor's degree and four-year teacher preparation program.

- Emergency Substitute Teacher Certificates are available from individual school districts. A bachelor's degree is required.

- Paraprofessionals must have at least a high school diploma or GED. Therapeutic and nursing assistants must meet additional qualifications.

## USEFUL WEB SITES

- **KY certification:** www.kyepsb.net/certification/certstandardroutes.asp

- **KY Educators (teacher recruitment):** www.kyeducators.org

- **Jobs:** www.education.ky.gov/KDE/HomePageRepository/jobs/default.htm

- **School directory:** www.education.ky.gov/KDE/About+Schools+and+Districts/Kentuckys+Schools+and+Districts/default.htm

- **Applications:** www.kyepsb.net/certification/certquicklinks.asp

- **NBPTS:** www.kyepsb.net/certification/nationalboard.asp

- **TTT:** www.kyepsb.net/certification/troopstoteachers.asp

- **Testing:** www.kyepsb.net/assessment/teachertests.asp www.ets.org (select state requirements) www.ets.org/praxis

- **Alternative routes:** www.kyepsb.net/certification/certaltroutes.asp

- **Approved programs:** www.kyepsb.net/teacherprep/index.asp

- **Foreign applicants:** www.kyepsb.net/certification/certstandardroutes.asp

- **Certification inquiry:** www.kyepsb.net/certification

- **Substitutes:** www.kyepsb.net/certification/substitutecert.asp

# LOUISIANA

## OVERVIEW

*Louisiana offers certification for early childhood (grades Pre-K–3), elementary (grades 1–5), middle school (grades 4–8), and secondary (grades 6–12). All-level certification (K–12) is available for art, dance, foreign languages, health and physical education, and music. The licensure structure has three levels of Professional Certificates.*

■ *Level 1: This is the entry-level Professional Certificate and may be obtained through traditional or alternate routes and is valid for three years.*

■ *Level 2: Teachers with a Level 1 Professional Certificate must teach for three years and satisfy the requirements of the Louisiana Teacher Assistance and Assessment Program (LaTAAP) to obtain the Level 2 certificate, which is valid for five years. Renewal requires 150 clock hours of professional development.*

■ *Level 3: Teachers with a Level 1 or Level 2 Professional Certificate may obtain the Level 3 certificate by completing a master's degree, teaching for three years, and meeting the requirements of the LaTAAP. Level 3 certificates are valid for five years and require 150 clock hours of professional development for renewal.*

## TRADITIONAL ROUTE

For the Level 1 Professional Certificate, applicants must graduate from a teacher preparation program and meet the testing requirements described below.

## ALTERNATE ROUTE

Louisiana offers three alternate routes leading to the Level 1 Professional Certificate. Applicants for all programs must have a bachelor's degree with a 2.5 GPA and meet the testing requirements for admission to and completion of any of the programs.

**Practitioner Teacher Alternate Certification Program** combines coursework and full-time teaching. Candidates receive the Practitioner License upon entering the program, which is valid for three years and may not be renewed.

**Master's Degree Alternate Program** leads to certification and a master's degree. A candidate who is employed receives the Practitioner License.

**Non-Master's/Certification-Only Alternate Certification Program** leads to certification for candidates who are not eligible for the Master's or Practitioner alternate programs. The program requires a 2.2 GPA, whereas the other two require 2.5. A candidate who is employed receives the Practitioner License while pursuing completion of the program.

## SPECIALTY CERTIFICATES

■ Ancillary Certificates are offered for special services such as school nurse, social worker, speech therapist, and school psychologist. Requirements vary. See the Web site for more information.

■ Career and Technical Trade and Industrial Education (CTTIE) Certificates are available for the secondary level. A degree is not required. However, with a degree, fewer hours of coursework are required to convert a temporary certificate to a permanent certificate and to maintain that certificate.

## TESTING AND SPECIAL REQUIREMENTS

■ All applicants for admission to teacher preparation programs (traditional or alternate) must pass the Praxis I Pre-Professional Skills Test (PPST). Applicants with advanced degrees may be exempt.

■ Applicants for the Level 1 Professional Certificate in traditional programs must pass the appropriate Praxis II content exam for the grade level or subject area. Elementary Education: Content Knowledge is required for Pre-K–3 and grades 1–5. The appropriate middle school content area exams are required for grades 4–8, and the appropriate subject area exams are required for grades 6–12 and All-Level K–12. Candidates for the Special Education Certificate must pass the appropriate content exams for the specific grade level.

■ Applicants for the Level 1 Professional Certificate in traditional programs must pass the Praxis II pedagogy exams: Early Childhood Education for Grades Pre-K–3 and the appropriate Principles of Learning and Teaching exam for all other grade levels. Candidates for the Special Education certificate must also pass the appropriate Praxis II Special Education exams.

■ For admission to the Practitioner Teacher, Master's Degree, and Non-Master's alternate programs, applicants must pass the same Praxis II content exams as candidates in traditional programs.

■ To complete all alternate programs, candidates must pass the same Praxis II pedagogy exams as candidates in traditional programs. They must also demonstrate reading competency through coursework or assessment.

- The Louisiana Teacher Assistance and Assessment Program (LaTAAP) is a mentoring and evaluation professional development program for new teachers. Teachers with Level 1 certificates must meet the requirements within four semesters.

## SPECIAL SITUATIONS AND NOTES

- The Out-of-State Certificate is given to a teacher who is certified in another state but has not met the Praxis testing requirements. It is valid for three years and is nonrenewable. The teacher must pass the appropriate Praxis exams or have four years of teaching in another state and one year in Louisiana. Teachers must also meet the requirements of the LaTAAP or have two years of teaching experience.

- Foreign applicants must have their credentials evaluated by the Education Department of an accredited college or university or by the American Association of Collegiate Registrars and Admissions Officers (AACRAO). See the Web site below.

- Paraprofessionals must have a high school diploma and one of the following: pass the ParaPro Assessment, complete two years (48 semester hours) of full-time study, earn an associate degree, or pass the ACT WorkKeys skills assessment with on-the-job observation. See the Web site for more information.

- The STAR (Students Teaching and Reaching) program is aimed at high school juniors and seniors who want to learn about teaching as a career.

## USEFUL WEB SITES

- **Certification Requirements:** www.doe.state.la.us/lde/tsac/603.html

- **Teach LA (online certification and recruitment center, job vacancies):** www.teachlouisiana.net

- **School directory:** www.doe.state.la.us/lde/directory/home.html

- **Jobs:** www.doe.state.la.us/lde/hr/1317.html

- **Certification inquiry:** www.teachlouisiana.net/Certification/FindCTSRecord.asp

- **Forms, foreign applicants, ancillary certificates:** www.doe.state.la.us/lde/tsac/610.html

- **Testing:** www.doe.state.la.us/lde/tsac/613.html www.ets.org (select state requirements)

- **Approved programs:** www.doe.state.la.us/lde/tsac/605.html

- **Alternate route:** www.doe.state.la.us/lde/tsac/614.html

- **NBPTS:** www.doe.state.la.us/lde/pd/626.html

- **Paraprofessionals:** www.doe.state.la.us/lde/tsac/621.html www.doe.state.la.us/lde/tsac/1790.html

- **TTT (contact national office):** www.proudtoserveagain.com/pages/808014/index.htm

# MAINE

## OVERVIEW

Persons employed as teachers or educational specialists in Maine must hold a valid certificate to teach at the elementary, middle, or secondary level. There are three levels of certification.

- **Initial Certification** differs for traditional and alternate route candidates. The **Provisional Certificate** is the Initial Certification for teachers and educational specialists in the traditional route. It is valid for two years and is nonrenewable except under special circumstances. For candidates in alternate route programs, the Initial Certification may be the **Conditional Certificate,** the **Targeted Need Certificate,** or the **Transitional Endorsement.** Each is issued for one year and may be renewed twice.

- The **Professional Certificate** is granted to persons who have been employed for two years under the Provisional Certificate or a Conditional Certificate. It is valid for five years and requires 6 credits of approved study for renewal.

- **Master Certificate** is granted to persons who hold the Provisional Certificate and achieve NBPTS certification or demonstrate other exemplary skills. It is valid for five years and may be renewed for as long as the requirements for receiving the certificate continue.

## TRADITIONAL ROUTE

Candidates for the Provisional Certificate must hold a bachelor's degree, complete a teacher preparation program, and meet testing requirements, the requirement for teaching exceptional students, and the physiology and hygiene requirement.

## ALTERNATE ROUTE

Maine offers three certificates that are considered alternate routes to certification, and candidates may be employed under them. Each one is valid for one year and may be renewed twice. The first renewal is contingent upon passing the Pre-Professional Skills Test and completing 6 semester hours. The second renewal is contingent upon passing the Praxis II: Subject Assessment and Principles of Learning and Teaching exams and completing 6 additional semester hours or completing an alternate program. By the end of the third certification period, all coursework and test requirements must be completed.

- **Conditional Certificate** is issued to persons who hold a bachelor's degree, but have not met all the requirements for a Provisional or Professional Certificate.

- **Targeted Need Certificate** is intended to fill positions where a shortage of fully certified applicants exists. It is issued to a person who holds a bachelor's degree with at least 6 semester hours in the area of the certification or endorsement, but who is not eligible for any other certificate.

- **Transitional Endorsement** is issued to persons who hold a Provisional or Professional certificate and have completed at least 6 semester hours relevant to the additional endorsement, but lack some requirements for the endorsement.

## ENDORSEMENTS

Teaching certificates carry one or more endorsements that specify the grade level and subject area a teacher is authorized to teach. Educational specialist certificates do not carry endorsements, but they are issued for a specific grade level and subject area.

## SPECIALTY CERTIFICATES

- Candidates for the Professional School Nurse Certificate must hold a Registered Professional Nurse license. Candidates for School Psychologist Certificates must have a master's degree, a National School Psychology Certificate, or a valid Maine professional psychologist license.

- School Counselor Certificate and Speech and Language Clinician require master's degrees.

- Career and Technical Education certificates may be based on work experience rather than a degree, or a combination of work experience and coursework.

- Native Language teachers may receive certification without a bachelor's degree if they meet certain criteria.

## TESTING AND SPECIAL REQUIREMENTS

- All applicants for the Provisional Teaching Certificate must pass the reading, writing, and mathematics portions of the Praxis I: Pre-Professional Skills Test (PPST) or the Computer Based Test (CBT), the appropriate Praxis II: Subject Assessments, and the appropriate grade level Praxis II: Principles of Learning and Teaching (PLT).

- Candidates for the Conditional or Targeted Needs Certificates must pass PPST during year 1 of the program and Praxis II: Subject Assessments and PLT during year 2.

- Candidates for the Transitional Endorsement are not required to take PPST or PLT.

- Candidates for Career and Technical Education Certificates are required to take all portions of the PPST, the Praxis II: Subject Assessments, and PLT.

- Applicants for the Native Language endorsement are not required to take the PPST or PLT. The Praxis II: Subject Assessment is not available.

- Applicants for endorsement in foreign languages must complete 24 semester hours or obtain an advanced level score on the ACTFL Oral Proficiency Interview in the appropriate language.

- All candidates for certification must complete an approved course for "Teaching Exceptional Students in the Regular Classroom."

- All candidates for Initial Certification must demonstrate knowledge of hygiene and physiology and the effects of alcohol and drugs in particular.

## SPECIAL SITUATIONS AND NOTES

- Maine participates in the Northeast Regional Credential Program (NRC) along with Connecticut, Massachusetts, New Hampshire, New York, Rhode Island, and Vermont. The credential is accepted as a certificate in Maine for one year. After that, the applicant must obtain Maine teaching or educational specialist certification.

- Maine participates in the NASDTEC Interstate Agreement. Applicants from a NASDTEC state who have completed an approved preparation program or have three years' experience (five years for the Professional Certificate) under a certificate comparable to a Maine certificate may receive the Conditional license in order to complete the testing and teaching exceptional students requirements.

- Foreign applicants must have their credentials evaluated by an evaluation service. See the Web site for more information.

- There are three levels of paraprofessionals: (1) Educational Technician I Authorization requires a high school diploma or GED; (2) Educational Technician II Authorization requires 60 credits; (3) Educational Technician III Authorization requires 90 credits. All are valid for five years and require 3 credits of approved study for renewal.

- Substitutes do not need certification or authorization. The length of time a person may substitute depends upon his or her qualifications.

## USEFUL WEB SITES

- **Certification, contacts:** www.maine.gov/education/cert/index.html

- **Job search:** www.maine.gov/education/jobs.htm

- **School directory:** www.maine.gov/education/schoolinfolist.htm

- **Certification inquiry, application status:** www.medms.maine.gov/medms%5Fpublic/ReportPortal/Portal.aspx?CurrentLocation=/Public%20Reports

- **Fees:** www.maine.gov/education/forms/fingerprint/letter_1.htm

- **Approved programs:** www.maine.gov/education/highered/Teacher%20Education/TeacherEduc.htm

- **Testing:** www.ets.org/praxis (select state requirements) Paraprofessionals: www.ets.org/parapro

- **Forms:** www.maine.gov/education/forms/cert.htm

- **Alternate routes, substitutes (Ch 115, Pt I):** www.maine.gov/sos/cec/rules/05/chaps05.htm

- **NBPTS:** www.maine.gov/education/pressreleases/Press%20Release%20-%20Subsidy%20Notice%207-03.htm

- **Foreign applicants:** www.maine.gov/education/cert/faq.htm#18

- **Paraprofessionals:** www.maine.gov/education/edletrs/2004/ilet/04ilet21.htm

- **ME TTT:** www.nnettt.org

# MARYLAND

## OVERVIEW

*All teachers in Maryland must hold a valid certificate to teach at the elementary (grades 1–6 and middle school) or secondary (7–12) levels. There are three levels of professional certificates for teachers coming through the traditional route. For teachers prepared through the alternate route, the Resident Teacher Certificate is the initial certificate. Maryland also offers a **Conditional Certificate**, which is valid for two years, for persons who are employed but do not meet all requirements for certification.*

## TRADITIONAL ROUTE

Candidates for initial certification must have graduated from a Maryland Approved Program (MAP) and meet all test requirements and the reading content requirement.

- **Standard Professional Certificate I (SPC I)** is issued to candidates who meet all requirements and who are employed in public or accredited nonpublic schools. It is valid for five years and may be renewed only once if service is interrupted.

- **Standard Professional Certificate II (SPC II)** is issued to educators who complete SPC I, have three years' experience and 6 semester hours credit, and have a professional development plan for the Advanced Professional Certificate. SPC II is valid for five years and is nonrenewable.

- **Advanced Professional Certificate (APC)** is issued to educators who have three years of full-time experience and 6 semester hours credit, and have earned a master's degree or 36 hours of post-baccalaureate courses including 21 semester hours of graduate level courses. It is also issued to educators who achieve NBPTS certification and have 12 semester hours of graduate courses. The certificate is valid for five years and may be renewed with 6 credits of professional development including reading, if the reading content requirement has not been met.

## ALTERNATE ROUTE

**Resident Teacher Certificate (RTC)** is the initial certificate in the alternate route program. It allows candidates to begin teaching while completing requirements for full certification. Candidates must have a bachelor's degree with a B average in content area courses, pass the basic skills and content exams, and complete 135 clock hours of study prior to employment. During the course of the program, they must complete an additional 45 clock hours of study for the secondary level or an additional 135 clock hours for the elementary level, be mentored each year, and pass the Praxis II: Principles of Learning and Teaching exam. The certificate is valid for one year and may be renewed once at the secondary level and twice at the elementary level.

## ENDORSEMENTS

Educators who hold a valid certificate may add an endorsement for another grade level or subject by completing necessary coursework or a graduate degree, and meeting the testing requirements.

## SPECIALTY CERTIFICATES

- The following special service areas require a master's degree: Guidance Counselor, Library Media Specialist (or 36 hours of graduate work), Pupil Personnel Worker, Reading Specialist, Psychometrist, and School Psychologist.

- Trades and Industry Certificates may be obtained without a bachelor's degree. A combination of training and work experience is required.

## TESTING AND SPECIAL REQUIREMENTS

- Candidates for initial certification must pass the Praxis I: Pre-Professional Skills Tests and the appropriate Praxis II: Subject Assessments and Principles of Learning and Teaching (PLT).

- Educators applying to add an endorsement must pass the appropriate Praxis II: Subject Assessments and PLT. Those who have previously passed the appropriate level PLT do not need to retake it.

- All teachers must complete the Reading Content Requirement. For those in a MAP or endorsement program, this must be completed by the end of the program. Those renewing Early Childhood, Elementary, or Special Education (birth–grade 3 or grades 1–8) must complete a total of 12 semester hours (6 hours in the first renewal period and 6 hours in the second). Those renewing Secondary, Secondary Special Education, or Specialty (PreK–12) certificates must complete 6 semester hours during the first renewal period. Resident Teachers at the same grade levels must complete their requirements by the time they complete the Resident Teacher program.

## SPECIAL SITUATIONS AND NOTES

- Out-of-state applicants must submit all documentation to the Certification Branch for evaluation. Applicants must either have a bachelor's degree, have completed an educator preparation program, and meet all Maryland test requirements; or they must have a bachelor's degree, hold a valid certificate, and have met their state's test requirements. Out-of-state applicants who have a bachelor's degree, hold a professional certificate, and have two years of full-time experience will be exempt from the testing requirements.

■ Foreign applicants must have their credentials evaluated by an evaluation service. See the Web site for more information.

■ Paraprofessionals in Title I programs must have a high school diploma or GED. In addition, they must have two years of study at an institution of higher education (48 credit hours), hold an associate degree, or pass the ETS ParaPro Assessment.

## USEFUL WEB SITES

■ **Certification, contacts:** www.marylandpublicschools.org/ MSDE/divisions/certification/certification_branch

■ **Teach MD (recruitment):** www.marylandpublicschools. org/MSDE/divisions/certification/certification_branch/ teach_md

■ **School directory:** www.marylandpublicschools.org/ MSDE/schoolsystems

■ **Application status:** educator.marylandpublicschools.org

■ **Approved programs:** www.marylandpublicschools.org/ MSDE/divisions/certification/certification_branch/teacher_ preparation/md_approved_programs

■ **NBPTS:** www.marylandpublicschools.org/MSDE/ divisions/certification/certification_branch/national_board_ certification/nbpts_overview

■ **Paraprofessionals:** www.marylandpublicschools.org/ msde/programs/esea/teacher_quality_reg.htm

■ **Testing:** www.marylandpublicschools.org/MSDE/ divisions/certification/certification_branch/testing_ information/testing_info_general
www.ets.org/praxis (select state requirements)
Paraprofessionals: www.ets.org/parapro

■ **Jobs:** www.marylandpublicschools.org/MSDE/divisions/ certification/certification_branch/teach_md/teacher_ positions

■ **Alternate routes:** www.marylandpublicschools.org/ MSDE/divisions/certification/certification_branch/certifi-cation_inf/apply/docs/obtain11.htm

■ **Foreign applicants:** www.marylandpublicschools.org/ msde/divisions/certification/certification_branch/certifica-tion_inf/apply/docs/approved_foreign_evaluation

■ **MD TTT:** www.marylandpublicschools.org/msde/ programs/troops_teachers

# MASSACHUSETTS

## OVERVIEW

*Teachers, specialists, and support personnel in Massachusetts must hold a license to serve at the elementary, middle, or secondary levels. There are three levels of licensure and four routes to obtain certification. Candidates in Apprenticeship and Performance Review Programs begin with the Preliminary License. Those in traditional or post-baccalaureate teacher preparation programs usually begin with the Initial License.*

- **Preliminary License** *is valid for five years and is granted to candidates who have completed some but not all requirements for the Initial License.*

- **Initial License** *is granted to candidates who have completed a traditional or post-baccalaureate teacher preparation program including a practicum. Those who hold the Preliminary License must complete an approved district-based training program to gain this license. All candidates must also meet the Massachusetts Tests for Educator Licensure (MTEL) requirements. The license is valid for five years and may be extended for an additional five years.*

- **Professional License** *is issued to persons who have worked for three years under an Initial License, completed a one-year mentor induction program plus an additional 50 hours with mentoring, and completed either a Performance Assessment Program, a master's degree, or a district-based program. Persons who have achieved NBPTS certification also qualify. The license is valid for five years. For renewal, educators must have an Individual Professional Development Plan that includes 150 Professional Development Points for renewal of the primary area plus 30 points for each additional area.*

## TRADITIONAL ROUTE

The traditional route is known as **Route One** and begins with the Initial License. This route may not be used to prepare for a library teacher license.

## ALTERNATE ROUTE

For **Route Two,** candidates for the Preliminary License must have a bachelor's degree, complete specific courses depending on the subject area, and complete the Massachusetts Tests for Educator Licensure (MTEL) test requirements. Candidates for the Initial License who hold a bachelor's degree outside of education complete a post-baccalaureate education program and meet the MTEL requirements. There are three types of post-baccalaureate programs. (1) Programs in colleges or universities usually lead to a master's degree and Initial License. (2) Apprentice programs allow candidates to obtain the Initial License while working as an apprentice or intern for half an academic year. (3) District-based programs allow candidates to complete most requirements for the Initial License while teaching full-time.

In **Route Three,** candidates who hold the Preliminary License and are employed or in a supervised apprenticeship must complete an approved program for the Initial License.

**Route Four** is the Performance Review Program for teachers who hold a Preliminary License and are employed in a district that does not have an approved program leading to the Initial License. Candidates must have three years of employment under the Preliminary License, complete required seminars and courses, and pass a competency review for fields where no subject matter test is available.

This route is not available for licensure in early childhood, elementary, special education, academically advanced, library, or speech/language/hearing disorders.

## LICENSES ISSUED

Licenses are issued for the grade level and subject area. These are early childhood (PreK–2), elementary (1–6), middle subjects (5–8), secondary subjects (8–12), special education (PreK–8 or 5–12), and all-level subjects.

## SPECIALTY CERTIFICATES

- Specialist Teacher Licenses are offered in Academically Advanced (PreK–8); Reading (all levels); and Speech, Language, and Hearing Disorders (all levels). The Academically Advanced and Reading Initial Licenses require an Initial License and one year of experience under that license. The Speech, Language, and Hearing Disorders License requires a master's degree and a passing score on the MTEL Communication and Literacy Skills test.

- Professional Support Personnel Licenses are offered for School Guidance Counselor, School Nurse, School Psychologist, and School Social Worker. The Initial License requires a master's degree, except for School Nurse, which requires a bachelor's degree and Registered Nurse License.

- Candidates for the Preliminary Vocational Technical Teacher License must have a high school diploma or GED, have the required experience, meet test requirements, and for some areas, have an occupational license.

To be eligible for the professional license, candidates must work for three years under the Preliminary License and complete a one-year induction program and required courses.

## TESTING AND SPECIAL REQUIREMENTS

■ Candidates for the Initial or Preliminary License must pass the Massachusetts Tests for Educator Licensure (MTEL). MTEL consists of a Communication and Literacy Skills Test and PreK-12 Subject Matter Tests. If a candidate holds a Preliminary License and passed the required tests for that license, he or she do not have to retake them for the Initial License.

■ For Special Education and fields where no Subject Matter Test is available, candidates must complete a competency review.

■ The Foreign Language Tests include a written and an oral assignment. The English Language Learner Test also includes an oral assignment.

■ Candidates for the Preliminary Vocational Technical License must pass the MTEL Vocational Technical Literacy Skills Test and written and performance subject matter tests.

## SPECIAL SITUATIONS AND NOTES

■ Out-of-state applicants who have a bachelor's degree and completed an NCATE-accredited program or a program in a NASDTEC state and pass the MTEL exams for initial licensure qualify for the Initial License. These are the only out-of-state programs recognized in Massachusetts. Those who hold a license in a NASDTEC state and have three years' experience must pass the MTEL exams. They may obtain a one-year Temporary License while completing the MTEL test requirements. The Temporary License is not be granted to individuals who have failed any part of the MTEL. All out-of-state applicants must pass meet the MTEL requirements for an Initial License.

■ The Northeast Regional Credential (NRC) is accepted in Massachusetts for up to two years. After that, the applicant must obtain a Massachusetts license.

■ Paraprofessionals in Title I schools must have a high school diploma or GED and two years (48 credit hours) of study at an institution of higher education, or an associate degree, or pass the ETS ParaPro Assessment or the ACT WorkKeys Proficiency Certificate for Teacher Assistants.

■ Substitutes apply directly to school districts.

## USEFUL WEB SITES

■ **Licensure:** www.doe.mass.edu/educators

■ **Job search:** www4.doemass.org/elar/mecccommon/MeccAnchorPageControl.ser

■ **GEM (recruitment):** www.doe.mass.edu/gem

■ **School directory:** www.doe.mass.edu/infoservices

■ **Contacts:** www.doe.mass.edu/contact

■ **Approved programs:** www.doe.mass.edu/edprep

■ **Alternate routes:** www.doe.mass.edu/lawsregs/603cmr7.html?section=05

■ **Testing:** www.doe.mass.edu/mtel
www.mtel.nesinc.com

■ **Paraprofessionals:** www.ets.org/parapro
www.act.org/workkeys

■ **Online application and status (ELAR):** www4.doemass.org/auth/Login

■ **NBPTS:** www.doe.mass.edu/eq/mt

■ **MA TTT:** www.nnettt.org

■ **Paraprofessionals:** www.doe.mass.edu/nclb

# MICHIGAN

## OVERVIEW

*Teachers and special service providers in Michigan must have a certificate to teach at the elementary, middle, or secondary levels. There are two levels of certification for traditional route applicants. Michigan does not have an alternate route, but provides for special circumstances.*

## TRADITIONAL ROUTE

- **Provisional Certificate** is the initial certificate issued to candidates who have graduated from a teacher preparation program and passed the appropriate Michigan Test for Teacher Certification (MTTC). It is valid for six years and may be renewed for three years with 10 semester hours in a planned program or a master's degree. It may be renewed for an additional three years with a total of 18 semester hours in a planned program or master's degree. A third renewal is possible only if the candidate has met all requirements except three years' teaching experience and has a job offer.

- **Professional Education Certificate** is the advanced certificate issued to persons who have three years' experience under the Provisional Certificate, have completed 18 semester hours in a planned program under the Provisional Certificate or have a master's degree, and complete the reading requirement. It is valid for five years and requires 6 semester hours credit or 18 Continuing Education Units for renewal.

## ALTERNATE ROUTE

Michigan does not have an alternate route program. All teaching candidates must complete a teacher preparation program. However, the following authorization that allows a person to teach while completing a program is available in certain circumstances. Authorization may be granted to a district to employ a person who is not certified or endorsed to teach in certain subjects in grades 9–12 only when a fully certified teacher is not available. The subject areas include biology, chemistry, computer science, engineering, foreign languages, mathematics, physics, and robotics. The person must have a bachelor's degree with a major in the subject area and must have two years of work experience in the field during the past five years. These requirements may be waived if the person is continually enrolled and in the process of completing a teacher preparation program leading to certification or endorsement, and the person has a plan leading to certification on file with the school district. If the employment continues more than one year, the person must meet the MTTC test requirements for the Provisional Certificate.

## ENDORSEMENTS

Endorsements on a certificate specify the grade level and subject area the holder is authorized to teach. The elementary certificate is for all subjects in grades K–5, or for all subjects in grades K–8 in a self-contained classroom. An elementary certificate with a subject area endorsement allows the holder to teach that subject in grades 6–8 in a middle school setting. The secondary certificate is for specific subject areas in grades 7–12. Adding an endorsement to a teaching certificate requires completing an endorsement program and passing the appropriate MTTC Subject Area test.

## SPECIALTY CERTIFICATES

- **School Guidance Counselors** must hold a master's degree, complete a guidance counselor program, and meet the MTTC test requirements. A three-year nonrenewable temporary authorization is available to those who have 34 semester hours in a program and meet the MTTC requirements.

- Candidates for a **Temporary Vocational Authorization** must have a bachelor's degree with a major or minor in the occupation and two years of relevant work experience. After teaching three years and completing 10 semester hours, they are eligible for the full Occupational Education Certificate. It is valid for five years and requires 6 semester hours or the equivalent of Continuing Education Units for renewal.

## TESTING AND SPECIAL REQUIREMENTS

- The Michigan Test for Teacher Certification (MTTC) consists of the Basic Skills test (reading, mathematics, and writing), the Elementary Education test, and Subject Area tests.

- Candidates for the Provisional Certificate are required to pass the Basic Skills test.

- Candidates for the elementary certificate must pass the Elementary Education test.

- Candidates for the secondary certificate or the elementary certificate with subject endorsements are required to take the appropriate Subject Area test.

- Teachers adding an endorsement area to an existing certificate must pass the appropriate MTTC Subject Area test.

- To advance from the Provisional Certificate to the Professional Education Certificate, elementary teachers must complete 6 semester hours of reading methods coursework. Secondary teachers must complete 3 semester hours.

- All candidates for the Provisional Certificate must complete CPR and First Aid training from either the American Red Cross or the American Heart Association.

## SPECIAL SITUATIONS AND NOTES

- A Temporary Teacher Employment Authorization is granted to out-of-state applicants who hold a valid teaching certificate and meet all requirements for the Provisional Certificate except the MTTC test requirements. The nonrenewable authorization allows one year to complete the MTTC requirements. A Professional Education Certificate is issued to out-of-state applicants who hold a valid teaching certificate and a master's degree or 18 semester credits in a program following their initial certificate. In this case the MTTC requirement is waived.

- Foreign applicants must have their credentials evaluated by an evaluation service except those who completed a teacher preparation program in Canada and hold a valid teaching certificate from Newfoundland, Ontario, Quebec, or Saskatchewan. See the Web site for more information.

- Paraprofessionals in Title I schools must have an associate degree, two years (60 semester hours) of study at an institution of higher education, or pass one of the following: ACT WorkKeys (Reading for Information, Writing, and Applied Mathematics), MTTC Basic Skills, ETS ParaPro Assessment, or complete the Michigan Paraprofessional Portfolio Assessment.

- Substitute Permits require 90 semester hours of credit. Substitutes apply directly to the school district for a permit. The permit allows the holder to teach 150 days per school year but not in an extended assignment.

## USEFUL WEB SITES

- **Certification:** www.michigan.gov/mde/0,1607,7-140-5234_5683_14795—-,00.html

- **Job search:** mtn.merit.edu/joblistings.html
metb.merit.edu
www.mireap.net

- **School directory:** www.cepi.state.mi.us/scm

- **Certification inquiry:** mdoe.state.mi.us/teachercert

- **Contacts:** www.michigan.gov/mde/0,1607,7-140-5234_5683_14795-22288—,00.html

- **Foreign applicants:** www.michigan.gov/mde/0,1607,7-140-6530_5683_5708-32537—,00.html

- **Paraprofessionals:** www.michigan.gov/mde/0,1607,7-140-28815—-,00.html

- **MI TTT:** www.michigan.gov/mde/0,1607,7-140—36797—,00.html

- **Testing:** www.act.org/workkeys

- **Paraprofessionals:** www.michigan.gov/documents/Guidelines_for_Michigan_Paraprofessional_Portfolio_84950_7.pdf
www.ets.org/parapro
www.act.org/Workkeys

- **Forms:** www.michigan.gov/mde/0,1607,7-140-6530_5683_5708—-,00.html

- **Fees:** www.michigan.gov/mde/0,1607,7-140-5234_5683_14795-32154—,00.html

- **NBPTS:** www.michigan.gov/documents/ANNOUNCE-MENT_76650_7_106390_7.doc

- **Approved programs:** mdoe.state.mi.us/proprep

# MINNESOTA

## OVERVIEW

*All teachers, related service providers, and substitutes in Minnesota public elementary or secondary schools must hold valid teaching licenses. Licenses are valid for five years and require 125 clock hours of professional development for renewal.*

## TRADITIONAL ROUTE

To obtain the **First-Time Full Professional Education License,** applicants must complete an approved teacher preparation program in the appropriate licensure field and meet the test requirements and human relations requirement outlined below.

## ALTERNATE ROUTE

**Licensure via Portfolio** is a pathway to state licensure for individuals who have not completed a state teacher prep program. Applicants must provide evidence in the following areas: (1) academic preparation; (2) professional development, training, and workshops; (3) teaching and related experiences. Upon approval, candidates are eligible to submit a Minnesota Teaching License Application. Applicants must have a bachelor's degree, meet minimum GPA requirements in the major field of study, and also meet the test requirements described below.

## LICENSURE FIELDS

Licensure fields specify the grade level or subject area for which the teacher is qualified. Licensure fields also include related and special services. Applicants must meet the test requirements described below. Applicants adding a field to a license must also complete college or university work for the licensure field.

## TESTING AND SPECIAL REQUIREMENTS

- All first-time applicants (traditional or alternate) are required to pass Praxis I: Pre-professional Skills Test (PPST), Praxis II: Principles of Learning and Teaching (PLT), and Praxis II: Subject Assessments or Specialty Area tests.

- Applicants adding a licensure field must pass the appropriate Praxis II: Subject Assessments or Specialty Area tests.

- All applicants must satisfy the Human Relations Requirement. This may be accomplished through a Minnesota teacher prep program; an approved Minnesota Human Relations Program; a teacher prep program in Iowa, Ohio, Nebraska, or South Dakota; or Peace Corps, Americorps, Vista, or Teacher Corps programs.

- School administrators, counselors, social workers, nurses, psychologist, and speech-language pathologists are exempt from these testing and human relations requirements.

## SPECIAL SITUATIONS AND NOTES

- Minnesota does not have reciprocity with any other state. Teacher prep programs completed at colleges and universities in other states must have equivalent content to those in Minnesota. In addition, applicants must complete the Human Relations Requirement and pass the appropriate Praxis I and Praxis II exams as described above. To complete these requirements, teachers who meet all other requirements can be granted a one-year, nonrenewable license.

- Applicants who completed their education in a foreign country must have their credentials evaluated by an evaluation service. See the Web site below.

- Limited Full-Time Licenses are available to persons with a bachelor's degree and at least a minor in the subject area but who have not completed a teacher prep program, and to persons who have completed a program but have not passed the required exams. The employing district must request the license, which is valid for one school year and may be renewed twice.

- A Short Call Substitute License requires completion of a teacher prep program (in-state or out-of-state) leading to full licensure. It is valid for five years.

- A Limited Intern License is available to persons who have completed at least three years of a teacher prep program.

- Teacher shortage areas include science (all fields), special education (all areas), technology, mathematics, agriculture, world languages, English as a second language, and bilingual education.

- Paraprofessionals must have an associate degree (or equivalent) or demonstrate competency via the ParaPro Assessment, local assessment, or portfolio.

## USEFUL WEB SITES

- **MN EducatorLicensing, requirements, contacts:** www.education.state.mn.us/mde/Teacher_Support/Educator_Licensing/index.html

- **MN Teacher Recruitment Center (job bank, school districts, TTT):** www.education.state.mn.us/mde/Teacher_Support/Minnesota_Teacher_Recruitment_Center/index.html

- **License Look-up:** www.education.state.mn.us/mde/ Teacher_Support/Educator_Licensing/View_an_Individual_Educators_License/index.html

- **Licensure via Portfolio:** www.education.state.mn.us/ mde/Teacher_Support/Educator_Licensing/Licensure_Via_Portfolio/index.html

- **Paraprofessionals:** education.state.mn.us/mde/Learning_Support/Special_Education/Paraprofessional_Resources/index.html

- **Testing:** www.education.state.mn.us/mde/Teacher_Support/Educator_Licensing/Teacher_Testing_Requirements/index.html

Praxis assessments: www.ets.org/praxis (select state requirements)
ParaPro Assessment: www.ets.org/parapro

- **Approved programs, foreign applicants, licensure fields:** www.education.state.mn.us/mde/Teacher_Support/Educator_Licensing/Resources/index.html

- **Human Relations Programs:** www.education.state.mn.us/mde/Teacher_Support/Educator_Licensing/Types_of_Licenses/First_Time_Licensure_Adding_to_Existing/000480.html

- **Forms:** www.education.state.mn.us/mde/Teacher_Support/Educator_Licensing/Licensure_Forms/index.html

# MISSISSIPPI

## OVERVIEW

*The Five-Year Educator License is the standard license for teaching in Mississippi and may be obtained through traditional or alternate routes. Licenses are valid for five years and require continuing education, coursework, or NBPTS certification for renewal.*

### TRADITIONAL ROUTE

Candidates for the **Five-Year Educator License Class A** (bachelor's level) in the traditional route must earn a bachelor's degree from an approved program or NCATE program and meet the test requirements.

### ALTERNATE ROUTE

Mississippi offers three alternate route programs. Each program is only available in specific subject areas. See the alternate route Web site for a list.

**Mississippi Alternate Path to Quality Educators (MAPQE) (One-Year Alternate Route License Class A, bachelor's level):** For admission to the program, candidates must hold a bachelor's degree and meet test requirements. To obtain the One-Year Alternate Route License, candidates must complete 90 hours of training in the program, and secure a job. To convert this license to a five-year license, candidates must complete the New Teacher Practicums program, participate in mentoring and evaluation in the local district during the first year of teaching, and complete test requirements.

**Teach Mississippi Institute (One-Year Alternate Route License):** For admission to the program, candidates must hold a bachelor's degree and meet test requirements. To obtain the One-Year Alternate Route License, candidates must complete an eight-week training session or ten-week online program and secure a job. To convert this license to a five-year license, candidates must complete a one-year internship with a mentoring and induction program in the local district.

**Masters of Arts in Teaching (MAT) (Three-Year Alternate Route License):** For admission, candidates must hold a bachelor's degree and meet test requirements. To obtain the Three-Year Alternate Route License, candidates must complete 6 hours of preteaching courses in a MAT program. To convert this license to a five-year license, candidates must secure a job and complete an additional 6 hours of coursework including a supervised internship.

### SPECIALTY CERTIFICATES

- Five-Year Educator Licenses are offered in the following areas: Audiologist, Child Development (PreK–K), Emotional Disability, Guidance and Counseling, Library/Media, Performing Arts, Psychometrist, School Psychologist, Speech/Language Clinician, and Special Education (all levels). These require specific degrees and test requirements. See the certification Web site for details.

- Three- and Five-Year Vocational Educator Licenses are available for nondegreed applicants. A Three-Year License may be converted to a Five-Year Class A License. See the certification Web site for requirements.

- Expert Citizen Educator Licenses and Three-Year Educator License-JROTC Instructor are also available to qualified individuals. See the certification Web site.

### SUPPLEMENTAL ENDORSEMENTS

Supplemental Endorsements may be added to a three- or five-year license. Applicants must hold a bachelor's degree and the three- or five-year license, complete an approved content area program, pass the Praxis II Specialty Area exam, complete approved coursework at Mississippi State University, complete an approved Middle Level Professional Development Institute, or obtain NBPTS certification in each subject area. Renewal is at the same time as the Educator License and requires continuing education or coursework.

### TESTING AND SPECIAL REQUIREMENTS

- Praxis II Principles of Learning and Teaching (PLT) and Praxis II Specialty Area tests are required for candidates in the traditional route.

- Candidates for admission to any alternate route program must pass Praxis I Pre-Professionals Skills Test (PPST) and Praxis II Specialty Area tests. Candidates in the MAPQE program may submit an Instructional Portfolio in place of Praxis II when applying for the Five-Year Educator License.

- Candidates for Five-Year Educator Licenses in special services must pass Praxis I PPST and Praxis II Specialty Area tests. Some licenses also require PLT.

### SPECIAL SITUATIONS AND NOTES

- Out-of-state applicants who hold a valid credential with less than two years' experience or a license that is less than standard may obtain a Two-Year Educator License-Reciprocity. Applicants must meet all requirements for the Five-Year Educator License through an approved route. Those with a standard out-of-state credential in areas that Mississippi recognizes and at least two years of experience may qualify for the Five-Year Educator License-Reciprocity. This carries the same renewal requirements as Mississippi's Five-Year Educator License.

- Foreign applicants must have their credentials evaluated by an evaluation agency and must have a social security number. See the Web site for information.

- Paraprofessionals must have a high school diploma and demonstrate competency through two years of study at an institution of higher education, by obtaining an associate degree, or through formal state or local assessment.

- Mississippi offers scholarship incentives for new teachers in science, math, special education, and foreign languages. See the alternate routes Web site for more information.

## USEFUL WEB SITES

- **Certification:** www.mde.k12.ms.us/ed_licensure/index.html

- **MS Teacher Center (job placement):** www.mde.k12.ms.us/mtc

- **School directory:** www.mde.k12.ms.us/districts/msmap2.htm

- **Contacts:** www.mde.k12.ms.us/ed_licensure/staff.html

- **Online application and certification inquiry:** www.mde.k12.ms.us/OVTE/License/TN3270.htm

- **Approved programs:** www.mde.k12.ms.us/ed_licensure/teacher_education.html

- **Testing:** www.mde.k12.ms.us/ed_licensure/praxis_test.html
www.ets.org (select state requirements)

- **Forms:** www.mde.k12.ms.us/ed_licensure/licensure_application.htm

- **Vocational forms:** www.mde.k12.ms.us/ed_licensure/post_secondary.html

- **Foreign applicants:** www.mde.k12.ms.us/ed_licensure/foreign.html

- **Alternate routes:** www.mde.k12.ms.us/ed_licensure/alternate_path.html

- **NBPTS:** www.mde.k12.ms.us/mtc/National_Board_Certification.htm

- **MS TTT:** www.mde.k12.ms.us/mtc/ttt.htm

# MISSOURI

## OVERVIEW

*Teachers and those providing student services in Missouri must have a certificate to teach at the elementary, middle, or secondary levels. There are two levels of professional certification for candidates in the traditional route. Candidates in alternate route programs have an initial additional level with two options.*

## TRADITIONAL ROUTE

- **Initial Professional Certificate** is the first certificate issued to graduates of teacher education programs. They must have had student teaching and a 2.5 GPA overall and in the subject area, and meet the Praxis II test requirements. The Initial certificate is valid for four years during which teachers must have one year of beginning teacher assistance, two years of mentoring, and annual evaluations. Teachers with this certificate must also complete 30 contact hours in their professional development plan.

- **Career Continuous Professional Certificate** is issued to teachers who meet all the requirements for the Initial Certificate and have four years of experience. The Career certificate is valid for ninety-nine years but requires 15 contact hours of professional development annually. A "high quality" career certificate is granted to individuals who have two of the following: ten years of experience, a master's degree, or NBPTS certification. These individuals are exempt from the professional development requirement.

## ALTERNATE ROUTE

Candidates coming through the alternate route must first qualify for one of the following certificates as part of their alternate route program:

- **Provisional Certificate** allows a person with a bachelor's degree to teach while completing the requirements for the Initial Certificate through a college program. It is valid for two years.

- **Temporary Authorization** allows a person with a bachelor's degree to teach for three years while completing requirements for the Initial Certificate through a district program. It is valid for one year and maybe renewed twice.

- **Transition to Teaching** is an alternate route program leading to Initial certification for career-changers. It includes a two-week summer institute, the coursework required for certification, workshops during the school year, and coaching. Applicants must qualify for Temporary Authorization (i.e., a bachelor's degree with a subject major and a 2.5 GPA overall and in their major). Each institute (possibly several at different locations each year) is limited to 40 participants per year

who have been hired to teach in high-demand subject areas or schools with low-income populations.

- Candidates for **Alternative or Innovative Route** must have a bachelor's degree with a subject major and a 2.5 GPA. They receive a Provisional Certificate that allows them to teach while completing a two-year college education program consisting of 30 to 35 credits. Upon completing the program and meeting the Praxis II test requirements, candidates receive the Initial Certificate.

- Candidates for the **Temporary Authorization Route** must have a bachelor's degree with a subject major and a 2.5 GPA overall and in their major. They take 24 college credits of "self-directed courses" to meet various competencies while teaching for three years under a one-year Temporary certificate that requires nine credits each year for renewal. During the three years, candidates must continue employment with successful performance evaluations and participate in a two-year mentoring program. They must also meet the Praxis II test requirements. Upon completing all requirements, candidates receive the Initial Certificate. This route does not include early childhood, elementary, and some special education areas.

- In the **Doctoral Route,** candidates with a doctoral degree in a subject area may qualify for the Initial Certificate by passing the appropriate Praxis II: Principles of Learning and Teaching exam. This route is limited to teachers for middle and secondary subjects.

## CERTIFICATION AREAS

Certification areas designate the grade level and subjects that the holder is authorized to teach. Grade levels include early childhood (birth–grade 3), elementary (1–6), middle (5–9), and secondary subjects (9–12). The Provisional Certificate and Temporary Authorization may be used to complete coursework to add certification areas to an existing certificate. Certain additional areas may be added by passing the appropriate Praxis II exams.

## SPECIALTY CERTIFICATES

- Student Service Certificates include School Counselor, School Psychologist, School Psychological Examiner, Speech-Language Pathologist, Career Education Counselor, and Career Services Counselor. These require a master's degree except School Psychologist, which requires a specialist degree plus 60 credits of graduate study, and Career Services Counselor, which requires a bachelor's degree. Speech-Language Pathologists may obtain certification by a teacher preparation program or a professional license.

- Career Education Certificates do not require a bachelor's degree, but do require work experience.

## TESTING AND SPECIAL REQUIREMENTS

- Candidates for admission to teacher education programs must pass the College Basic Academic Subjects Examination (CBASE), which assesses reasoning skills in language arts, mathematics, science, and social studies.

- For certification, all school professionals must pass the appropriate Praxis II: Subject Assessments/Specialty Area exams and the appropriate level Praxis II: Principles of Learning and Teaching (PLT).

## SPECIAL SITUATIONS AND NOTES

- Missouri does not have reciprocity with other states. Out-of-state applicants who hold a valid license/ certificate may obtain a comparable Missouri certificate, which may be an Initial or Career Continuous Certificate depending on years of teaching experience. They are also exempt from the Praxis II requirements. Approved teacher education programs in other states are accepted for Initial certification if candidates meet all other requirements for the traditional route.

- Foreign applicants must have their credentials evaluated by an evaluation service. See the Web site for more information.

- Paraprofessionals in Title I programs must have a high school diploma or GED and two years of study at an institution of higher education, or an associate degree, or pass the ETS ParaPro Assessment.

- The Substitute Certificate requires 60 hours of college credit and is valid for one year. Substitutes apply directly to the school district.

- A number of scholarships are available for prospective teachers, in particular minority teachers. See the scholarships Web site for more information.

## USEFUL WEB SITES

- **Certification:** www.dese.mo.gov/divteachqual/teachcert/ index.html

- **Job search:** www.moteachingjobs.com

- **School directory:** www.dese.mo.gov/directory

- **Contacts:** www.dese.mo.gov/divteachqual/teachcert/ certstaff.html

- **Application status:** k12apps.dese.mo.gov/webapps/logon. asp

- **Certification inquiry:** k12apps.dese.mo.gov/webapps/ tcertsearch/tc_search1.asp

- **Approved programs:** www.dese.mo.gov/divteachqual/ teached/directory/index.html

- **Substitutes:** www.dese.mo.gov/divteachqual/teachcert/ subcerts.html

- **MO TTT:** chad.schatz@dese.mo.gov

- **Paraprofessionals:** www.dese.mo.gov/divimprove/ fedprog/instrucimprov/qualpara.html

- **Testing:** www.dese.mo.gov/divteachqual/teached/ assessment.htm

- **CBASE:** www.arc.missouri.edu www.ets.org/praxis (select state requirements)

- **Paraprofessionals:** www.ets.org/parapro

- **Forms:** www.dese.mo.gov/divteachqual/teachcert/forms. html

- **Scholarships:** www.dese.mo.gov/divteachqual/scholar- ships/index.html

- **Alternate routes:** www.dese.mo.gov/divteachqual/ teachcert/certclass.html

- **Transition to Teaching:** www.dese.mo.gov/divteachqual/ teachrecruit/TTP.html

- **Foreign applicants:** www.dese.mo.gov/divteachqual/ teachcert/forms.html

- **NBPTS:** www.dese.mo.gov/divteachqual/teachcert/ national_board.html

# MONTANA

## OVERVIEW

*All teachers in Montana must have a license to teach at the elementary (K–8) or secondary (7–12) level. There are two levels of licensure for teachers prepared by the traditional route. Teachers prepared through alternate route programs have an additional initial license.*

### TRADITIONAL ROUTE

**Class 2 Standard Teacher's License** is the license issued to beginning teachers who have completed a professional educator preparation program with student teaching and a performance-based assessment. This assumes that candidates have a bachelor's degree and have maintained a 2.5 GPA overall and in their major and minor. The license is valid for five years and requires three semester credits plus 15 renewal units (or four semester credits) for renewal.

**Class 1 Professional Teacher's License** is granted to teachers who hold the Class 2 Standard Teacher's License (or meet the qualifications for it), have a master's degree or one year (30 graduate credits) of study beyond the bachelor's degree, and have three years' experience. The license is valid for five years and requires 60 renewal units for renewal.

### ALTERNATE ROUTE

The first step is the **Class 5 Alternate Teaching License,** which allows persons who hold a bachelor's degree to teach while completing requirements for a Standard License.

**Class 5 Alternative Teaching License or Specialist License:** Candidates for any Class 5 Alternative License must have a bachelor's degree plus requirements listed below for specific endorsements. Candidates must file a Plan of Professional Intent to obtain a Class 1, 2, or 6 license within three years of receiving the alternative license. Any endorsements available for Class 1, 2, or 6 licenses are available for a Class 5 license. The alternative license is valid for three years, is nonrenewable, and may not be reinstated. To upgrade from a Class 5 license, candidates must complete all requirements on their Plan of Professional Intent.

- Candidates seeking an elementary endorsement must also have 60 semester credits in liberal arts subjects plus 6 semester credits in human development, reading or language arts, social studies, and arithmetic.

- Candidates seeking a secondary subject endorsement must also have 30 semester credits in the subject area and 6 semester credits of professional educator preparation.

- Candidates seeking endorsement for School Psychologist must also have a master's degree and required coursework, specifically including coursework in individual intelligence testing.

- Candidates seeking endorsement for School Counselor must have a master's degree, required coursework, and 600 hours of supervised internship.

### ENDORSEMENTS

Endorsements to a license specify the grade level and subject area that the holder is authorized to teach. Endorsements may be added to an existing Class 1 or 2 teacher's license by completing an endorsement internship program. Applicants must have a contract to teach in the new endorsement area and be enrolled in 6 semester hours in the program. The program must be completed in three years.

### SPECIAL LICENSES

Class 4 Career and Vocational/Technical License requires work experience.

Class 6 Specialist License is offered only with endorsements for School Psychologist and School Counselor. It is valid for five years and requires 60 renewal units (or 4 semester graduate credits) for renewal. It may be obtained directly by qualified candidates or as an upgrade from the Class 5 Alternative License. School psychologist candidates must have current credentials from the National Association of School Psychologists (NASP) or a master's degree with specific courses. School counselor candidates must have a master's degree and 600 hours of supervised internship.

Candidates for the Class 7 American Indian Language and Culture Specialist License must receive approval from the tribe verifying their competence and they must meet all nonacademic requirements for licensure. The license is valid for five years and for renewal requires 60 renewal units that are authorized by the tribe.

### TESTING AND SPECIAL REQUIREMENTS

Montana currently has no test requirements. Candidates for admission to teacher education programs may write an essay or take the Praxis I: Pre-Professional Skills Test (PPST). All applicants must submit a notarized Oath of Allegiance.

### SPECIAL SITUATIONS AND NOTES

- Montana participates in the NASDTEC Interstate Agreement. Out-of-state applicants who hold a valid professional license (not provisional or alternative) and have completed a teacher preparation program that is

NCATE-accredited and included student teaching (or one year of supervised teaching) receive a comparable Montana license.

- Foreign applicants must have their credentials evaluated by an evaluation service. See the Web site for more information.

- Paraprofessionals in Title I programs must have a high school diploma or GED and two years of study at an institution of higher education, or an associate degree, or demonstrate competency through formal assessment.

- Substitutes apply directly to school districts. There is no substitute license.

- The Northern Plains Transition to Teaching is a distance-learning alternate program at Montana State University that leads to licensure in Montana. It is designed for teachers in rural or high-needs schools. See the Web site for more information.

## USEFUL WEB SITES

- **Licensure, Jobs for Teachers:** www.opi.state.mt.us
- **School directory:** www.opi.mt.gov/Directory/Index.html

- **Contacts:** www.opi.state.mt.us (select educator licensure)

- **Forms:** www.opi.state.mt.us (select educator licensure)

- **Certification inquiry:** www.opi.state.mt.us (select educator licensure, other licensure tools)

- **Approved programs:** www.opi.state.mt.us (select educator licensure, other licensure tools)

- **Alternate routes:** www.opi.state.mt.us (select educator license, alternative licenses) www.teachforachange.com

- **Transition to Teaching:** www.montana.edu/nptt

- **Foreign applicants:** www.opi.state.mt.us (select educator licensure, alternative licenses)

- **Paraprofessionals:** www.opi.mt.gov/pdf/SpecED/guides/ParaGuide.pdf

- **MT TTT:** www.montana.edu/ttt

# NEBRASKA

## OVERVIEW

*Teachers and special service providers in Nebraska must hold one of three levels of certification to teach at the elementary, middle, or secondary levels. The state has no alternate route to certification, but an option is available in certain circumstances.*

## TRADITIONAL ROUTE

**Initial Teaching Certificate** is the certificate issued to beginning teachers. It is valid for five years and requires 6 semester hours for renewal. To qualify, candidates must have a bachelor's degree, complete a teacher preparation program, and also meet the basic skills, special education, human relations, and recency requirements.

**Standard Teaching Certificate** is issued to persons who hold the Initial Teaching Certificate and have two consecutive years of at least half-time experience under that certificate. The Standard certificate is valid for seven years and for renewal requires 6 semester hours credit or two years of at least half-time experience during the past five years.

**Professional Teaching Certificate** is granted to persons who hold or qualify for the Standard Teaching Certificate and complete a master's degree in the same area as the current endorsement or hold NBPTS certification. The Professional certificate is valid for 10 years and for renewal requires 6 semester hours credit or two years of at least half-time experience during the past five years.

## ALTERNATE ROUTE

Nebraska does not have an alternate route program. Candidates must complete a teacher preparation program. However, the **Transitional Teaching Certificate,** which allows a person to teach while completing a program, is available in certain circumstances. A district may hire a person to teach under this certificate if a fully qualified teacher is not available. The candidate must have a bachelor's degree that includes three quarters of the course requirements in the endorsement area, must have developed a plan and signed an agreement with an institution for completing an Initial certification program, and must complete a pre-teaching seminar. The hiring district must have a plan for mentoring and supervision. The certificate is valid for one school year and may be renewed for a maximum of five years provided the candidate completes at least 6 semester hours per year toward completion of the program.

## ENDORSEMENTS

Endorsements to a certificate are areas of specialization. Adding an endorsement requires completing a program.

## SPECIALTY CERTIFICATES

Candidates for Special Services Certificates must complete a program for the specific endorsement. The following certificates are offered: Special Services Counseling Certificate; School Nurse Special Services Counseling Certificate available only to candidates who hold a valid Registered Nurse license; School Psychology Special Services Counseling Certificate; Coaching Special Services Certificate available to candidates who complete portions of the American Sport Education Program training; Speech Technology; and Provisional Trades Certificate, which allows persons to be endorsed in vocational trades and ROTC without college credit.

## TESTING AND SPECIAL REQUIREMENTS

- All candidates for their first regular teaching certificates (not special services) must demonstrate basic skills competency by passing the Praxis I: Pre-Professional Skills Test (PPST).

- All candidates for their first teaching certificate must meet the special education requirement in one of the following ways: (1) completing a teacher education program for special education; (2) completing a special education course at a teacher education institution; (3) having employment experience that provides competence in the five skills required to teach the exceptional child in the regular classroom.

- All candidates for regular teaching certificates (not substitute) must meet the recency requirement. This requirement may be met by completing one of the following in the past 5 years: (1) a teacher education program; (2) teaching half-time for two consecutive years in the same school system under a valid regular teaching license; (3) 6 semester hours (for out-of-state applicants with a valid regular license who have not taught); or (4) completing 15 semester hours if the teacher education program was completed more than five years ago.

- Applicants who have an employment offer and meet all requirements except basic skills, special education, or recency may qualify for a one-year Provisional or Substitute Certificate.

- All candidates for new teaching or special services certificates must meet the human relations requirement. Anyone renewing a teaching or special services certificate must meet this requirement if they have not already done so. This requirement may be met by one of the following: (1) taking a pre-approved course at a

Nebraska college or university or in another state; (2) taking a course at a teacher education institution; (3) having employment experience that provides competence in the six required human relations skills. Applicants who have an employment offer and meet all requirements except the human relations requirement may qualify for a two-year nonrenewable Temporary Certificate. The requirement must be met within two years.

## SPECIAL SITUATIONS AND NOTES

- Out-of-state applicants must meet the basic skills, special education, recency, and human relations requirements. The basic skills requirement is waived for applicants who have three consecutive years of teaching under a certificate based on completion of a teacher education program or who hold NBPTS certification.

- Nebraska participates in a Regional Exchange Agreement with the following states: Arkansas, Illinois, Iowa, Kansas, Michigan, Missouri, Oklahoma, South Dakota, and Wisconsin. Applicants who hold a regular certificate in these states are eligible for a two-year Provisional Certificate to meet the basic skills, special education, or human relations requirements. Deficiencies must be removed in two years.

- Paraprofessionals in Title I programs must have a high school diploma or GED and two years (48 hours) of study at an institution of higher education, or an associate degree, or pass one of the following: ETS ParaPro Assessment, ACT WorkKeys, or ParaEducator Learning Network Assessment.

- The State Substitute Teaching Certificate is issued to persons who have previously held a regular teaching certificate. It allows the substitute to teach an unlimited number of days per year but no more than 90 in the same assignment and is valid for five years. It requires 50 days of teaching or 3 semester hours credit for renewal.

- The Local Substitute Teaching Certificate requires 60 hours of credit and completion of the human relations requirement. This certificate allows the substitute to teach 40 days per year, is valid for three years, and may be renewed.

## USEFUL WEB SITES

- **Certification:** www.nde.state.ne.us/TCERT

- **Teach in NE (job search):** www.nebraskaeducationjobs. com

- **Contacts:** www.nde.state.ne.us/TCERT/Ptchcert.html

- **School directory:** ess.nde.state.ne.us/DataCenter/ EducationDirectory/Default.htm

- **Online systems (application, status, inquiry):** www. nde.state.ne.us/TCERT

- **Paraprofessionals:** www.nde.state.ne.us/title1/03. 03paramemo.pdf

- **Testing:** www.nde.state.ne.us/TCERT/ApWithInst.html (select First Time Applicant Manual)

- **Paraprofessionals:** www.ets.org/parapro www.act.org/workkeys www.paraeducator.net

- **Approved programs:** www.nde.state.ne.us/TCERT/index. html www.nebraskateachereducation.org

- **Forms:** www.nde.state.ne.us/TCERT/ApWithInst.html www.nde.state.ne.us/TCERT/TCpdfs.html

- **Substitutes:** www.nde.state.ne.us/TCERT/Etchcert.html

- **NE TTT:** www.mwttt.com

# NEVADA

## OVERVIEW

*Teachers and specialists in Nevada are required to hold a license to teach at the elementary, middle, or secondary levels. Alternate route programs are limited.*

## TRADITIONAL ROUTE

**Elementary or Secondary License** is granted to candidates who complete a teacher education program including student teaching for the grade level they will teach and meet all other requirements. Candidates for the Elementary License must have 9 semester hours of literacy language arts and 9 semester hours of elementary methods. Candidates for the Secondary License must have a major and 22 semester hours of professional secondary or occupational education. The license is valid for five years.

**Elementary or Secondary Professional License** is issued to persons who meet all requirements for an Elementary or Secondary License, have a master's degree, and have three years' experience. It is valid for six years and requires courses or other professional development for renewal.

**Special License** covers grades K–12 with specific endorsements and is valid for eight years. Special Licenses require a degree with specific coursework. Candidates for school counseling must complete a practicum, and candidates for school psychologist must complete an internship or hold national certification.

## ALTERNATE ROUTE

Some Nevada colleges and universities offer nontraditional teacher preparation programs. Candidates should contact the institutions for requirements.

## LICENSES AND ENDORSEMENTS

Completing an endorsement program is required for adding an endorsement.

- The Elementary License covers grades K–8. The state does not require endorsements, but some districts do. Endorsements available on this license include Art, Computers, English, Health, Mathematics, Literacy, Science, Social Studies, Physical Education, Bilingual Education, and Music. Endorsements require 12 semester hours credit except English, which also requires 3 semester hours of advanced coursework, and Bilingual Education, which also requires an exam.

- The Secondary License with specific middle school endorsements covers middle school grades 7–9. Middle school endorsements include Art, English/Language Arts, Foreign Language, Mathematics, Music, Science, and Social Science. Endorsements generally require a major, minor, or area of concentration.

- The Secondary License covers grades 7–12. Endorsements to specify the field of concentration are required on this license. There are numerous academic endorsements available that generally require a major or minor in the field and also a variety of occupational endorsements that generally require two years of work experience and an occupational license if latter is available in the state.

- Some endorsements are available for grades K–12, for special education areas for ages 3–21, and for early childhood (birth–K or birth–grade 2).

- The Special License (K–12) requires a base license at the appropriate grade level and an endorsement in the special area. Endorsements are available for Counselor, Library, Nurse, Psychologist, Social Worker, Reading Specialist, and Special Education.

- The Teacher of English as a Second Language (TESL) requires a base license at the appropriate grade level with a TESL or bilingual endorsement.

- The Teacher of Computer Education license requires a base license at the appropriate grade level with a computer endorsement and allows the holder to teach computer education as a single subject.

## TESTING AND SPECIAL REQUIREMENTS

- Candidates for the initial license are required to take the Praxis I: Pre-Professional Skills Test (PPST). Candidates who have a master's degree, have a minimum score on the GRE exam and a 3.0 GPA, or have passed the California Basic Education Skills Test (CBEST) are exempt from the PPST requirement.

- Candidates for the initial license are required to take the appropriate level Praxis II: Principle of Learning and Teaching (PLT). Candidates for the elementary endorsement who are required to take the Praxis II: Curriculum Instruction and Assessment and the Content Area Exercises tests are exempt. Candidates for a subject endorsement may take either PLT or the pedagogy test for their subject area. Candidates for a Special License (K–12) may take either level (K–6 or 7–12). Candidates for the Physical Education endorsement may substitute both physical education specialty area exams for PLT.

- Candidates for the initial license are required to take the appropriate Praxis II: Subject Area/Specialty Area Test.

Only one test is required, so candidates may take either the test in their major or minor area.

- Candidates for the Speech and Language Handicapped endorsement are exempt from the specialty area exam if they have passed the Speech-Pathology test given by the American Speech-Language-Hearing Association (ASHA) or have a Certificate of Clinical Competence from ASHA.

- Candidates for the Home Economics endorsement are exempt from the subject area test if they have passed the National Family and Consumer Sciences Examination given by the Council for Certification of the American Association of Family and Consumer Sciences.

- Candidates for the initial license must complete coursework or pass exams covering Nevada School Law, the Nevada Constitution, and the U.S. Constitution.

- After July 1, 2008, candidates must meet all test requirements when applying for the initial license.

- Candidates must be U.S. citizens or file an intent to become a citizen. An Oath of Allegiance is required.

## SPECIAL SITUATIONS AND NOTES

- Nevada participates in the NASDTEC Interstate Agreement for teachers. Out-of-state applicants who hold full licenses and have three years' experience during the past five years are eligible for a comparable Nevada license upon completing all ancillary requirements and are exempt from the PPST and PLT requirements. Applicants who have one year of experience and a provisional or restricted license for which they passed exams may be exempt from one or more of the test requirements. Nevada accepts exams required by many states on a state-by-state basis. The testing Web site provides a list of accepted exams. Nevada also accepts competency exams for graduates of teacher education programs from any state if the exams were required by the program. Nevada does not have reciprocity with any state for school services, but does have reciprocity with all states for special education.

- Foreign applicants must have their credentials evaluated by an evaluation service. See the Web site for more information.

- Paraprofessionals in Title I schools must have a high school diploma or equivalent and an associate degree. Persons who have a language proficiency that is needed for children with limited English in Title I programs are exempt.

- The Substitute License (K–12) requires 62 semester credits with 6 semester credits in professional education, or a bachelor's degree. Licenses are valid for five years.

## USEFUL WEB SITES

- **Licensing, contacts, NBPTS:** www.doe.nv.gov/licensing.html

- **Teach for NV:** www.teachfornevada.com

- **Job search:** www.teachers-teachers.com/nevada.cfm www.doe.nv.gov/employ.html www.doe.nv.gov/employ/districtjobs.html

- **School directory:** www.doe.nv.gov/schools.html

- **Approved programs:** www.teachfornevada.com/education.htm

- **Paraprofessionals:** www.ed.gov/legislation/ESEA/Title_I/profdev.html

- **Testing:** www.doe.nv.gov/licensing/appforms.html www.ets.org/praxis (select state requirements)

- **NV TTT:** www.mwttt.com

- **Alternate routes (Nevada State College):** www.nsc.nevada.edu/academics/programs/teaching/career.lqm

- **Forms, Foreign Applicants:** www.doe.nv.gov/licensing/appforms.html

- **Substitutes:** www.doe.nv.gov/licensing/endorsements.html

# NEW HAMPSHIRE

## OVERVIEW

Educators and specialists in New Hampshire must hold a certificate to teach at the elementary, middle, or secondary levels. There are three levels of certification for educators prepared in traditional programs and two routes. Candidates in the three alternate route programs receive an Intern License prior to initial certification. The process is then the same as the traditional route.

## TRADITIONAL ROUTES

In **Alternative 1: New Hampshire Preparation Program,** candidates must have graduated from a teacher education program including a student teacher practicum. This route is for in-state preparation.

The second route is **Alternative 2: Out-of-State Candidates.** New Hampshire participates in the NASDTEC Interstate Agreement. However, New Hampshire accepts applicants from all states and U.S. territories who have completed a traditional teacher education program comparable to those in New Hampshire or a comparable alternate program, as well as applicants who hold a valid license and have three years of experience during the past seven years. Depending on experience, applicants qualify for the Beginning or Experienced Educator credential. All candidates must meet the Praxis I and Praxis II test requirements unless they have a master's degree and seven years' experience. Some alternate tests are also accepted. New Hampshire may deny certification in specialist areas that require advanced degrees if the sending state does not have the same requirements.

- **Beginning Educator Certificate** is issued to educators with less than three years experience and is valid for three years.

- **Experienced Educator Certificate** is issued to persons who hold the Beginning Educator Certificate and complete three years of full-time experience under that certificate. The certificate is valid for three years and requires 75 continuing education units for renewal. Each additional endorsement requires an additional 30 units.

- **Master Teacher** is issued to persons who hold the Experienced Educator Certificate and have seven years of full-time experience during the past ten years. NBPTS certification qualifies. The certificate is valid for three years.

## ALTERNATE ROUTE

Candidates for **Alternative 3: Demonstrated Competencies and Equivalent Experience** must hold a bachelor's degree and have three consecutive months of educational employment in the endorsement area they are seeking. Experience may be acquired in a private school. After establishing eligibility for the program, candidates must submit a written portfolio describing how they have demonstrated competence in each required standard. When the portfolio is approved, candidates must then pass an oral exam. Candidates must also meet testing requirements. Candidates may also demonstrate competence through national or regional certification.

**Alternative 4: Critical Shortage Areas and Career and Technical Education** allows candidates to begin teaching in critical shortage areas while completing a program leading to initial certification or to a new endorsement. The list of critical shortage areas is published each year (see the certification Web site). To be hired, candidates must obtain a Statement of Eligibility, which requires meeting the basic skills requirement and developing an Individualized Professional Development Plan for completing a bachelor's degree and certification. For academic subject areas, candidates must have passed two courses in the subject area. Candidates in General Special Education must enroll in a certification program for this area and have experience with special education students. Candidates in specialist areas must demonstrate academic preparation and, in some cases, work experience. Candidates in career and technical specialties must have an associate degree and two years' work experience or four years' work experience, and a trade license if applicable. Candidates receive an Intern License valid for three years. During that time they teach under a mentor and must meet subject area test requirements and complete the individualized plan to qualify for the either a Beginning or Experienced License.

**Alternative 5: Site-Based Certification Plan** allows candidates who have a bachelor's degree with a 2.5 GPA to begin teaching while completing a program leading to initial certification for the elementary or secondary level. Vocational and special education are excluded. For eligibility, candidates for elementary education must also have coursework in mathematics, English, social studies, and science. Candidates for secondary education must also have a major (30 credits) in the subject area. Candidates must be hired by a school district and develop a site-based plan. They receive an Intern License valid for two years, during which they must complete the plan. For the Beginning License, candidates must meet all test requirements and teach for one year under a mentor.

## ENDORSEMENTS

Endorsements on a certificate specify the grade level and subject area the holder is authorized to teach. Elementary covers grades K–8 and Secondary covers grades 7–12. Some endorsements are specifically for middle school subjects, grades 5–8 or 5–9.

## SPECIALTY CERTIFICATES

- Advanced degrees are required for School Psychologist, Associate School Psychologist, Guidance Counselor, Speech and Language Pathologist, and some areas of special education.

- Career and Technical Education Specialty Certificate requires a bachelor's degree, training, and work experience.

## TESTING AND SPECIAL REQUIREMENTS

- Candidates for initial certification must satisfy the basic skills requirement by taking the Praxis I: Pre-Professional Skills Test (PPST).

- Candidates for initial certification must take the appropriate Praxis II: Subject Assessments. Subject areas for which tests are approved are Biology, Chemistry, Earth/Space Science, English, General Science, Mathematics, Middle/Junior High School Mathematics, Physical Science, and Social Studies. Other subject area tests may be approved in the future. Some equivalent tests may be accepted for the basic skills and subject area tests. These alternatives include the GRE and GMAT exams and NBPTS certification. The testing Web site lists additional tests that are accepted.

- Candidates who are adding an endorsement area must pass the Praxis II: Subject Assessments in the subjects listed above.

- Persons who hold a master's degree are exempt from the test requirements.

- Educational Interpreters must have an associate degree and pass the New Hampshire Educational Interpreter Knowledge Assessment.

## SPECIAL SITUATIONS AND NOTES

- For out-of-state applicants, see above.

- Paraeducators in Title I programs must have a high school diploma or equivalent and two years (48 semester hours with a 2.0 GPA) of study at an institution of higher education or an associate degree or complete a New Hampshire training and assessment program. The Paraeducator Certificate is valid for three years and requires 50 continuing education units for renewal.

- Substitutes are not required to hold a credential to teach up to 20 consecutive days in the same position.

## USEFUL WEB SITES

- **Certification, traditional and alternate routes:** www.ed.state.nh.us/education/beEd.htm www.ed.state.nh.us/education/doe/organization/programsupport/boc.htm

- **Job search:** www.ed.state.nh.us/education/doe/employ.htm

- **School directory:** www.measuredprogress.org/nhprofile

- **Contacts:** www.ed.state.nh.us/education/doe/organization/programsupport/boc.htm

- **Approved programs:** www.ed.state.nh.us/education/doe/organization/programsupport/Certification/Approved%20Collegiate%20Programs%20List.htm

- **Paraprofessionals:** www.ed.state.nh.us/education/doe/organization/instruction/boip/ParaeducatorStandards.htm

- **Testing:** www.ed.state.nh.us/education/doe/organization/programsupport/Certification/PraxisInfo.htm www.ed.state.nh.us/education/doe/organization/programsupport/Certification/AltCredInfo.htm www.ets.org/praxis (select state requirements)

- **Equivalent tests:** www.ed.state.nh.us/education/doe/organization/programsupport/Certification/COMP%20PRAXIS%20II%20TESTS.htm

- **Forms:** www.ed.state.nh.us/education/doe/organization/programsupport/Certification/CredForms.htm

- **NH TTT:** www.nnettt.org

- **Fees:** www.ed.state.nh.us/education/doe/organization/programsupport/Certification/feeschedule.htm

# NEW JERSEY

## OVERVIEW

Becoming certified in New Jersey is a three-step process. The process is the same whether a person comes through the traditional or alternate routes and wants to teach at the elementary, middle, or secondary levels.

- **Step 1: Certificate of Eligibility with Advanced Standing (CEAS)** in the traditional route and **Certificate of Eligibility (CE)** in the alternate route: Both certificates are valid for life and allow the holder to accept initial employment.

- **Step 2: Provisional Certificate:** The applicant must be employed and be part of a state-approved district training program if the person holds a CEAS or a mentoring program, called a residency, for holders of a CE. The certificate is valid for two years.

- **Step 3: Standard Certificate:** This permanent certificate is granted to applicants who have met all requirements and have at least one year of satisfactory full-time teaching experience under a Provisional Certificate. Although the certificate is permanent, active teachers must complete 100 hours of professional development every five years.

## TRADITIONAL ROUTE

The CEAS requires a bachelor's degree with a 2.75 GPA and completion of a teacher preparation program that includes student teaching. This teacher prep program is the only difference from the CE. For the elementary level (K–5), applicants must have at least 60 credits of liberal arts and must pass the Praxis II Elementary Education: Content Knowledge exam. To teach at the middle-school level (5–8), applicants must also pass the appropriate Praxis II middle-school subject area exam. For the secondary level, applicants must have a major in a subject area and must pass the appropriate Praxis II subject area exam. The next step is the Provisional Certificate and the final step is the Standard Certificate.

## ALTERNATE ROUTE

A person coming into teaching from a different career must fulfill the same degree, GPA, and test requirements as prospective teachers coming from traditional teacher preparation programs in colleges and universities. For the CE at the elementary level, applicants must have at least 60 credits of liberal arts or the sciences. For the secondary level, applicants must have at least 30 credits in a subject area. The second and third steps are the same as the traditional route, except that the training program under the Provisional Certificate requires formal instruction (200 hours or 13 to 17 credits) and additional mentoring.

## ENDORSEMENTS AND TESTING

Endorsements are required for all Standard Certificates. Regardless of level, all teachers must have endorsements for the grade level or subject area they teach, or for the special service they provide. Requirements vary according to the endorsement.

- Grade level and subject area endorsements have coursework requirements and applicants must pass the appropriate Praxis II: Subject Area exam.

- Endorsements in ESL, Bilingual/Bicultural, and Special Education require an instructional CE, CEAS, or Standard Certificate plus endorsement in the subject or grade level. Special Education also requires 6 semester hours in special education. Applicants for ESL or Bilingual/Bicultural education must pass the ACTFL oral and written proficiency exams in English.

- Special Services Endorsements are available for Speech-Language Specialist, World Languages, Educational Interpreter, and Sign Language for Hearing-Impaired. In addition to the subject area requirements, World Languages also requires the ACTFL oral proficiency exam for each language. Applicants for Speech-Language Specialist must pass Praxis II Speech-Language Pathology Specialty Area exam. Applicants for Educational Interpreter must pass the EIPA and applicants for Sign Language must pass the SCPI.

- Vocational/technical endorsements require four years' experience for the CE or a major in the occupational area for the CEAS. No testing is required.

## SPECIAL SITUATIONS AND NOTES

- Out-of-state applicants who qualify under the ICC reciprocity agreement must pass the same exams as teachers prepared in state.

- Applicants must pass a physiology and hygiene exam, including the effects of alcohol and narcotics, administered by the county offices of education. Military training or college study in biology, health, or nutrition may take the place of the exam.

- Applicants who completed their education in a foreign country must have their credentials evaluated by an evaluation service. See the Web site below.

- Paraprofessionals must have an associate degree or equivalent (two years at an institution of higher education or formal assessment) and must demonstrate proficiency through a written or performance-based assessment.

- Short-term substitutes apply directly to the county offices of education.

- Applicants must be U.S. citizens or sign an affidavit of intention to become a citizen within five years. In addition, an Oath of Allegiance is required.

## USEFUL WEB SITES

- **Careers and job opportunities:** www.state.nj.us/njded/educators/career.htm

- **Jobs:** www.njhire.com

- **School directory:** www.state.nj.us/njded/directory/index.shtml

- **NJ TTT:** www.nj.gov/njded/tttnj/contact/

- **NJ Educators:** www.state.nj.us/njded/educators

- **NJ DOE licensing, forms, fees, contacts:** www.state.nj.us/njded/educators/license

- **Test requirements:** www.ets.org (select state requirements)

- **Online application and certification status:** www6.state.nj.us/DOE_TCIS_ONLINEED/login.jsp

- **Approved programs:** www.state.nj.us/njded/aps/heqi/licensure.htm

- **Foreign applicants:** www.state.nj.us/njded/educators/license/1145.htm

- **NBPTS:** www.state.nj.us/njded/profdev/nbct/

- **Voc/Tech:** www.state.nj.us/njded/voc/sle/hazards.htm

# NEW MEXICO

## OVERVIEW

*Teachers and instructional support providers in New Mexico must have a license to teach at the elementary, middle, or secondary levels. New Mexico has a three-tiered licensure system. Candidates in alternate route programs have an initial beginning level. Teachers at all levels must develop a professional development plan each year and have annual performance evaluations. To advance from one level to the next, educators must submit a Professional Development Dossier.*

### TRADITIONAL ROUTE

**Level I Provisional Teacher** is issued to beginning teachers who have a bachelor's degree with 24 to 36 semester hours in a content area and meet the New Mexico Teacher Assessments (NMTA) requirements and the reading requirement. They also must have completed a teacher preparation program with 14 weeks of student teaching. The license is valid for three years and is nonrenewable. However, it may be extended for two years. While teaching, candidates must complete a beginning teacher mentoring program lasting from one to three years. After three to five years, teachers must move to Level II to continue teaching.

**Level II Professional Teacher** is issued to teachers who have three years experience under the Level I license, have completed the mentoring program, and whose Professional Development Dossier demonstrates the required competencies. The license is valid for nine years and may be renewed as long as the teacher continues to demonstrate the required competencies.

**Level III-A Instructional Leader** is optional. It requires a master's degree or NBPTS certification. Teachers must complete at least three years under a Level II license and demonstrate required competencies through the Professional Development Dossier. The license is valid for nine years and may be renewed as long as the teacher continues to demonstrate the required competencies.

### ALTERNATE ROUTE

The alternative programs allow persons to begin teaching under an **Intern License** while completing requirements for the **Level I Alternative License.** The Intern License is valid for one year and may be renewed. Candidates have one to three years to complete all requirements. Candidates for all alternative programs must have a bachelor's degree with 30 semester hours in the major content area and 24 semester hours in another content area. All candidates must meet the NMTA test requirements and the reading requirement. Upon completing all requirements, candidates receive the Level I Alternative License. They then must complete a mentoring program lasting one to three years in the local district. Alternative licensure is only available for classroom teachers, not support services.

**Alternative Licensure Program Pathway** for elementary and special education teachers requires 12 to 21 semester hours. Secondary education candidates require 12 to 18 semester hours. Student teaching is required for both grade levels. Financial aid is available through New Mexico Teacher Loan for Service. The Transition to Teaching program supports candidates teaching in high-needs districts.

Candidates in the **Alternative Licensure Portfolio Pathway** must demonstrate by a portfolio that they meet the competencies for the Level I license. To be eligible, candidates must be registered for the NMTA and enrolled in courses to meet the reading requirement. They may complete their portfolio while teaching under an Intern License, a Substitute License, or an Educational Assistant License. The Transition to Teaching program is available in certain locations.

Candidates in the **District Alternative Licensure Pathway** must demonstrate competencies over a two-year period while participating in a district-based or statewide teacher preparation program. The Transition to Teaching program is available.

**Master's + Licensure Program** enables candidates to earn a master's degree while completing requirements for a teaching license. This program requires student teaching. The Transition to Teaching program and New Mexico Teacher Loan for Service are available to candidates.

### ENDORSEMENTS

Licenses are offered for teaching at the following grade levels: Early Childhood (birth–grade 3), Elementary (K–8), Middle subject areas (5–9), Secondary subject areas (7–12), all level subject areas (K–12), and Special Education (K–12). Endorsements specify subjects and require either 24 to 36 semester hours of coursework or for certain areas, NMTA Content Knowledge tests.

### SPECIALTY CERTIFICATES

- Candidates for Vocational Technical Education must have a bachelor's degree and/or work experience. The NMTA are not required.

- Candidates for School Nurse must have a Registered Nurse License or be a Licensed Practical Nurse.

- Candidates for Level II School Psychologist must hold a professional license.

- Candidates for the Certificate in Native Language and Culture are not required to have a bachelor's degree, but they must be approved by the tribe or pueblo. The NMTA are not required.

## TESTING AND SPECIAL REQUIREMENTS

- The New Mexico Teacher Assessments (NMTA) consist of the New Mexico Assessment of Teacher Basic Skills, the New Mexico Assessment of Teacher Competency (Elementary, Secondary, or Early Childhood), and the New Mexico Content Knowledge tests in Elementary Education, Reading, Language Arts, Social Studies, Math, Science, Modern and Classical Languages, Visual Arts, and Music.

- The secondary Content Knowledge tests are required for licensure for grades 7–12. Teachers holding an elementary license (K–8) have the option of taking one of the middle level Content Knowledge tests to demonstrate that they are "highly qualified" in a subject.

- All candidates for initial licensure must pass the NMTA exams. Candidates with a one-year license must meet the NMTA requirements before the license expires.

- Applicants who are adding certain endorsements may take the appropriate Content Knowledge test in lieu of coursework.

- Candidates for School Psychologist who have a one-year license must pass the Praxis II: School Psychologist exam before the license expires.

- Candidates for elementary or special education must have 6 semester hours in teaching reading. Candidates for secondary or K–12 must have 3 hours.

## SPECIAL SITUATIONS AND NOTES

- Out-of-state applicants who hold a bachelor's degree, have completed a teacher preparation program, passed a competency exam, hold a valid license, and have experience teaching are eligible for the Level I License. Out-of-state applicants who obtain licensure through reciprocity must teach for two years in New Mexico before applying for the Level II or Level III license.

- Foreign applicants must have their credentials evaluated by an evaluation service. See the Web site for more information.

- Paraprofessionals in Title I programs must hold a Level III Educational Assistant License. A high school diploma or equivalent is required along with two years (48 semester hours) of study at an institution of higher education, or an associate degree, or demonstrated competency on a local formal assessment.

- The Substitute Teaching License covers grades K–12. Applicants must have a high school diploma or equivalent and some training or experience.

## USEFUL WEB SITES

- **Licensing, forms, foreign applicants:** sde.state.nm.us/div/ais/lic/index.html

- **Teach NM (Recruitment, job search, approved programs):** www.teachnm.org

- **School directory:** www.ped.state.nm.us/districts/alphadistricts.html

- **Jobs:** www.nmreap.net

- **Contacts:** sde.state.nm.us/contact/index.html

- **NM TTT:** www.mwttt.com

- **Testing:** www.ped.state.nm.us/div/ais/lic/requirements.html
www.nmta.nesinc.com
www.ets.org/praxis (select state requirements)

- **Transition to Teaching:** teachnm.org/transition_to_teaching/t2t.htm

- **Alternate routes:** teachnm.org/becoming_a_teacher/alternative_licensure.htm

- **Paraprofessionals:** www.ped.state.nm.us/fedpro/programs/titleI/downloads.html

- **NBPTS:** teachnm.org/prof_dev_opportunities/national_board.htm

# NEW YORK

## OVERVIEW

*Classroom teachers in New York are required to be certified to teach at the elementary, middle, or secondary level. There are two levels of certification.*

- *Initial Certificate is issued to beginning teachers in the traditional route. The certificate is for specific grade levels and subjects, is valid for five years, and is nonrenewable although it may be reissued with additional professional development.*

- *Professional Certificate is the advanced certificate, is for specific grade levels and subjects, and is continuously valid but requires 175 hours of professional development every five years. Candidates must have a master's degree, three years' experience, and one year of mentoring.*

- *Pupil personnel professionals also have two levels of certification.*

- *Provisional Certificate is the entry-level certificate and is for specific grade levels and specialties. It is valid for five years.*

- *Permanent Certificate is the advanced certificate for pupil personnel professionals. Candidates must have two years experience and some areas require a master's degree. The certificate is valid for life.*

## TRADITIONAL ROUTE

Candidates must complete a bachelor's degree with a 2.5 GPA through a teacher preparation program and meet the New York State Teacher Certification Examination (NYSTCE) requirements. They must also meet the child abuse and violence prevention requirements.

## ALTERNATE ROUTE

**Alternative Teacher Preparation Program (ATP)** allows persons who hold a bachelor's degree with a subject major to begin teaching while completing requirements for certification. Candidates must complete 200 clock hours of introductory work and meet the NYSTCE test requirements. Upon completion, they receive the **Transitional B** teaching certificate and may be employed. The certificate is valid for three years. During this time, candidates complete coursework in an alternative teacher certification program and receive mentoring. Upon completing the program, candidates are eligible for the Initial Certificate.

**Individual Evaluation** enables candidates who hold a bachelor's degree with a 2.5 GPA to may submit their credentials for evaluation. They must meet specific course requirements in liberal arts and sciences, content core, and pedagogy; pass the NYSTCE test requirements; and complete student teaching.

Applicants to the **Graduate Teacher Preparation Program** must hold a bachelor's degree to enter the program. They earn an advanced degree while completing requirements for the Initial Certificate. This program usually includes an internship, and candidates must meet the NYSTCE test requirements.

**New York State Professional License** is given to speech language pathologists who are licensed in New York and who complete the child abuse and violence prevention requirements.

## CERTIFICATE TITLES AND EXTENSIONS

The certificate title determines the grade level and subject that the holder is authorized to teach. Grade levels include Early Childhood (birth–grade 2), Childhood Education (1–6), Middle Childhood Education (5–9), Secondary subjects (7–12), and Special Subject (all grades). Extensions to a certificate allow the holder to teach additional grade levels, subjects, or student populations. Teachers may add an additional certificate title by completing 30 semester hours of required courses and taking the appropriate content test. Adding another subject area requires 12 semester hours and passing the content test.

## SPECIALTY CERTIFICATES

- Candidates for School Nurse must be licensed Registered Nurses.

- Career and Technical Education certificates do not require a bachelor's degree.

## TESTING AND SPECIAL REQUIREMENTS

- The New York State Teacher Certification Examination (NYSTCE) program consists of the Liberal Arts and Sciences Test (LAST), the Assessment of Teaching Skills-Written (ATS-W), the Content Specialty Test (CST), the Bilingual Education Proficiency Assessment (BEA), and the Assessment of Teaching Skills-Performance (ATS-P).

- All candidates for initial teaching certificates are required to take the LAST, the ATS-W, and the appropriate CST.

- Candidates in the alternate program must take the LAST and appropriate CST to receive the Transitional B certificate.

- There is an elementary version and a secondary version of the ATS-W. Candidates for certificates covering all levels may take either.

- The CST in foreign languages includes written, listening, and speaking sections.

- Candidates for the bilingual extension are required to take the BEA in English and the language of instruction. The test includes listening, speaking, and a written section.

- Candidates for a second classroom teaching certificate need take only the CST for the new area.

- Candidates for the Professional Certificate in certain subjects must take the ATS-P, which requires a videotape.

- Candidates for permanent nondegree and associate degree Career and Technical Education certificates must take the LAST and ATS-W.

- Candidates for the Initial or Provisional Certificate must complete a Child Abuse Identification Workshop and the School Violence Prevention and Intervention Workshop.

- Candidates for the Professional or Permanent Certificate must be U.S. citizens or have INS Permanent Residence status.

## SPECIAL SITUATIONS AND NOTES

- New York participates in the NASDTEC Interstate Agreement. Applicants who complete a teacher preparation program in a participating state may apply for certification under reciprocity. They must meet the NYSTCE test requirements. Applicants who hold certificates from NASDTEC states and have three years' experience may apply for a Conditional Initial Certificate, which is valid for two years and allows time to complete the NYSTCE test requirements and qualify for the Initial Certificate.

- Candidates from states that do not participate in the NASDTEC Interstate Agreement must have a bachelor's degree with a 2.5 GPA, satisfy specific course requirements, and meet the NYSTCE test requirements.

- New York participates in the Northeast Regional Credential program. Candidates who hold this credential may teach in New York for two years while completing the NYSTCE test requirements.

- Out-of-state applicants who hold NBPTS certification qualify for a comparable New York certificate and are exempt from the NYSTCE test requirements, although they are required to take the CST in certain subjects.

- Foreign applicants must submit original credentials and transcripts with notarized English translations. Reports from evaluation agencies are not accepted. A social security number is required. See the Web site for more information.

- There are four levels of certification for teaching assistants: Level I, Level II, Level III, and Pre-Professional Teaching Assistant. Candidates for initial certification must have a high school diploma or GED, are required to take the NYSTCE Assessment of Teaching Assistant Skills Test (ATAS), and must meet the child abuse and violence prevention requirements. Paraprofessionals in Title I programs must also have two years of study at an institution of higher education or an associate degree or pass a formal assessment. The formal assessment may be the ATAS, ETS ParaPro Assessment, the ACT WorkKeys Proficiency Certificate for Teacher Assistants, or other local assessment.

- There are no substitute certificates. Any person who holds a valid New York certificate or who is in a preparation program may substitute any number of days. Persons who do not hold certificates or who are not in a certification program may substitute 40 days a year.

- Teachers of Tomorrow and Teacher Opportunity Corps are two incentive programs. See the Web site for more information.

## USEFUL WEB SITES

- **Certification:** usny.nysed.gov/licensing/teachercertlic.html

- **Teaching in NY (recruitment, job bank):** www.highered.nysed.gov/tcert/career/index.html

- **School directory:** www.nysed.gov/admin/bedsdata.html

- **Contacts:** www.highered.nysed.gov/tcert/certificate/regionalcenters.htm

- **Application status:** www.highered.nysed.gov/tcert/certificate/core.htm

- **NBPTS:** www.highered.nysed.gov/tcert/resteachers/albertshanker.htm

- **Approved programs:** www.highered.nysed.gov/tcert/certificate/teachrecommend.htm

- **Teaching Assistants:** www.highered.nysed.gov/tcert/faqta.htm Substitutes:

- **Teachers of Tomorrow, Teacher Opportunity Corps:** www.highered.nysed.gov/kiap/TEACHING/Teacherdevprogramunit.htm

- **Testing:** www.highered.nysed.gov/tcert/certificate/certexam.htm
www.nystce.nesinc.com

- **Paraprofessionals:** www.ets.org/parapro
www.act.org/workkeys/overview/profcert/index.html

- **Forms:** www.highered.nysed.gov/tcert/certificate/chartuserightform.htm

- **Alternate routes:** www.highered.nysed.gov/tcert/certificate/teachalt.htm

- **NY TTT:** www.highered.nysed.gov/tcert/career/troopsteachers.htm

- **Foreign applicants:** www.highered.nysed.gov/tcert/certificate/evalforeigncred.htm
www.highered.nysed.gov/tcert/substituteteaching.htm

- **Fees:** www.highered.nysed.gov/tcert/certificate/fees.htm

# NORTH CAROLINA

## OVERVIEW

*All teachers and special service personnel in North Carolina must hold a license to teach at the elementary, middle, or secondary levels. There are two levels of licensure for traditionally prepared candidates, and candidates in alternate route programs have an additional initial level.*

### TRADITIONAL ROUTE

**Initial License** is issued to beginning teachers who have graduated from a teacher education program with student teaching and meet test requirements. The license is valid for three years. During this time, teachers participate in the North Carolina Initial Licensure Program.

**Continuing License** is issued to persons who hold the Initial License, complete the North Carolina Initial Licensure Program, and have three years' experience. The license is valid for five years and requires 10 semester hours or 15 renewal units for renewal.

### ALTERNATE ROUTE

**Lateral Entry License** is valid for two years and may be extended for an additional year. Lateral Entry allows persons who hold a bachelor's degree in the subject area to teach while completing requirements for the Initial License. Candidates must have a 2.5 GPA and be employed in a school. Prior to beginning teaching, they complete a two-week training program. While teaching, they complete an education program at a college or a Regional Alternative Licensing Center (RALC) and receive mentoring. During the first two years of the Lateral Entry License, candidates must meet the test requirements. The license is valid for two years and may be extended for an additional year with 6 semester hours of coursework.

There are a number of lateral entry programs including NC TEACH, NC Model Teacher Education Consortium, and NC RISE. See the alternate route Web sites for details.

### LICENSURE AREAS

Teaching areas are Birth-K, Elementary (K–6), Middle Grades (6–9), Secondary (9–12), Special Subjects (K–12), and Exceptional Children (K–12). Additional areas of licensure may be added to an existing license by completing a program and meeting the test requirements.

### SPECIAL SERVICE PERSONNEL

- Licenses in the following areas require a master's degree: Curriculum Instructional Specialist, Instructional Technology Specialist-Computers, Media Supervisor, Media Coordinator, Counselor, Audiologist, and Speech-Language Pathologist.

- The School Psychologist License requires education at the sixth-year level.

### TESTING AND SPECIAL REQUIREMENTS

- All candidates for Initial Certification must pass the appropriate Praxis II: Subject Area/Specialty Area exams. One or two exams may be required depending on the area.

- Applicants adding an area of licensure must pass the appropriate Praxis II exams.

- In teacher education programs, students may be required to take the Praxis I: Pre-Professional Skills Test (PPST). Each program has its own requirements.

### SPECIAL SITUATIONS AND NOTES

- North Carolina participates in the NASDTEC Interstate Agreement. Applicants who complete a teacher preparation program in a NASDTEC state or an NCATE-accredited program are eligible for an Initial or Continuing License, depending on experience. Applicants must meet the test requirements and a temporary license may be issued to allow applicants to complete test requirements.

- Foreign applicants must have their credentials evaluated by an evaluation service and must have a social security number.

- Title I Teacher Assistants must have a high school diploma or equivalent and must have two years (48 semester hours) of study at an institution of higher education or an associate degree or complete an assessment.

- Substitutes are evaluated and approved by local superintendents.

- Areas of highest need include math, science, and special education.

### USEFUL WEB SITES

- **Licensure, Employment:** www.dpi.state.nc.us/employment

- **Teach 4 NC (recruitment, jobs):** www.teach4nc.org

- **School directory:** www.dpi.state.nc.us/school_personnel_support/lealist.htm

- **Contacts:** www.ncpublicschools.org/licensure/contact.html

- **Approved programs:** www.teach4nc.org/certification

- **Scholarships:** www.ncpublicschools.org/scholarships

- **Testing:** www.dpi.state.nc.us/licensure/forms.html
www.ets.org/praxis (select state requirements)

- **Jobs:** schooljobs.dpi.state.nc.us

- **Alternate routes:** www.teach4nc.org/alternate_routes
www.teach4nc.org/certification

- **Forms:** www.dpi.state.nc.us/licensure/forms.html

- **Paraprofessionals:** www.ncpublicschools.org/fbs/InstructGuide.htm

- **NBPTS:** www.ncpublicschools.org/nbpts

- **NC TTT:** www.dpi.state.nc.us/troops

# NORTH DAKOTA

## OVERVIEW

All persons must hold the Educator's Professional License to teach in North Dakota at the elementary, middle, or secondary levels. There are three levels of this licensure. There is no alternate route program for general education.

## TRADITIONAL ROUTE

**Initial License Level I** is issued to beginning teachers, is valid for two years, and may be renewed for two years if the applicant has less than 18 months' experience. Candidates for the Initial License must hold a bachelor's degree with a 2.5 GPA from a teacher education program including 10 weeks of full-time student teaching. Candidates for secondary or K–12 content-specific areas must have a major with 32 semester hours of coursework beyond the introductory level.

**Regular License Level II** is issued to persons who hold the Initial License and have 18 months' experience. This license is valid for five years. For renewal, applicants must have been under contract at least 30 days and completed 4 semester hours of study.

**Level III** is issued to persons who have earned an advanced degree or NBPTS certification.

## ALTERNATE ROUTE

**Transition to Teaching** is for Career and Technical Education only. It is a three-year program that allows a person who holds a bachelor's degree to teach while completing requirements for full licensure. Candidates must be under contract with a school district and obtain either an Interim (Emergency) License or a Provisional Trade and Industry Credential.

## ENDORSEMENTS

Endorsements on a license extend the grade levels or subject areas that the holder is authorized to teach. General Endorsements include Kindergarten, Elementary (1–6), Middle School (5–8), Secondary (7–12), and English as a Second Language (ESL)/Bilingual. These endorsements require 8 to 22 semester hours in a teacher education program, depending on the grade level, and may also require field experience. Major Equivalency Endorsements and Minor Equivalency Endorsements add subject areas to an existing license.

## SPECIAL CREDENTIALS

- Applicants for Professional Credentials must hold valid Professional Educator's Licenses. Credentials include Reading, Reading and Mathematics, Gifted and Talented Teacher, Drivers Education, and several areas of special education. School Counselor, Library Media, and School Psychology require a master's degree to be eligible for the Professional Credential.

- Applicants for Career and Technical Education Licenses must hold valid Professional Educator's Licenses for secondary and post-secondary teaching. A bachelor's degree with major in the subject area is required for teaching at the secondary level.

## TESTING AND SPECIAL REQUIREMENTS

- All candidates for the Initial license must take the Praxis I: Pre-Professional Skills Test (PPST) and Praxis II: Subject Area exams in those subjects where exams have been approved. Candidates for Elementary Education must also take elementary level Praxis II: Principles of Learning and Teaching (PLT).

- All candidates must take a course in Native American and Multicultural Studies, which must be completed by the time the Initial License expires.

- An Oath of Allegiance is required.

## SPECIAL SITUATIONS AND NOTES

- North Dakota has limited reciprocity. Out-of-state applicants submit their transcripts for review. Those who meet North Dakota requirements receive the Initial License. Those who meet minimum requirements, have graduated from a teacher education program or hold a valid license, and have a plan for completing the remaining requirements receive a two-year Interim Reciprocal License, which may be renewed once provided adequate progress is made toward removing deficiencies. Applicants must take Native American and Multicultural Studies.

- Foreign applicants must provide acceptable translations of their transcripts.

- Paraprofessionals in Title I programs must hold a Certificate of Completion, which requires 20 contact hours of in-service training. They must also have an associate degree or two years (48 semester hours) of postsecondary study or pass one of the following: Higher Education Learning Profile (HELP), Praxis I: Pre-Professional Skills Test (PPST), or ETS ParaPro Assessment.

- Substitutes must hold an Educator's Professional License.

## USEFUL WEB SITES

- **Licensure:** www.nd.gov/espb

- **Career and Technical:** www.nd.gov/cte

- **Credentials:** www.dpi.state.nd.us/cred/index.shtm

- **Jobs:** www.jobsnd.com

- **Contacts:** www.nd.gov/espb/misc/contact.html

- **School directory:** www.dpi.state.nd.us/resource/directry/index.shtm

- **Approved programs:** www.nd.gov/espb/progapproval/general.html

- **Paraprofessionals:** www.dpi.state.nd.us/cred/index.shtm

- **Substitutes:** www.nd.gov/espb/profdev/6710.html

- **Testing:** www.nd.gov/espb/licensure/testing.html www.ets.org/praxis (select state requirements)

- **Paraprofessionals:** www.ets.org/parapro www.eriworld.net/help.asp

- **Forms:** www.nd.gov/espb/licensure/forms.html www.dpi.state.nd.us/approve/credentials.shtm

- **Transition to Teaching:** www.nd.gov/cte/statewide-inits/trans-to-teach.html

- **NBPTS:** www.nd.gov/espb/profdev/national.html

- **ND TTT:** www.montana.edu/ttt

# OHIO

## OVERVIEW

*All teachers in Ohio must hold a license to teach at the elementary, middle, or secondary levels. For persons in a traditional preparation program, there are two levels of licensure. For persons in the alternate route program, there are one or two additional initial levels depending upon their educational background.*

### TRADITIONAL ROUTE

**Two-Year Provisional License** is issued to beginning teachers, is valid for two years, and is nonrenewable. During this time, teachers participate in the Entry Year mentoring program and complete the performance-based assessment. Candidates for the Initial License must have a bachelor's degree from a teacher education program and meet the test requirements.

**Five-Year Professional License** is issued to persons who hold the Provisional License and have completed the mentoring program and the performance-based assessment. The license is valid for five years. Renewal requires 6 semester hours of coursework or 18 Continuing Education Units (CEUs) according to an Individual Professional Development Plan. The second renewal requires a master's degree or 30 semester hours of graduate courses with at least 6 semester hours or 18 CEUs during the that cycle.

### ALTERNATE ROUTE

The alternate route is limited to specific secondary (7–12) subjects, except for the Intervention Specialist license, which is for K–12. Candidates entering an alternate route program must have a bachelor's degree with 30 hours of coursework in the subject area with a 2.5 GPA. Extensive work experience during the past five years in the subject area may qualify in place of the major.

**One-Year Conditional Teaching Permit** allows a person with a bachelor's degree to begin teaching while completing requirements for the Two-Year Alternate Educator License. The One-Year license is nonrenewable. To qualify for the Two-Year license, candidates must complete 6 semester hours of education coursework, including a supervised field experience, with a 2.5 GPA, and pass the Praxis II content area exam. The employing district must provide mentoring.

**Two-Year Alternative Educator License** is valid for two years and is nonrenewable. By the end of two years under the Alternate license, candidates must have passed the Praxis II pedagogy test and completed 12 hours of additional coursework. At this point, they are eligible for the Two-Year Provisional Teaching License. Under the Provisional License, they must complete the Entry Year mentoring program and the performance-based assessment to qualify for the Five-Year Professional License.

Candidates may apply for the **One-Year Conditional Teaching Permit** to allow them to begin teaching while completing requirements for the Two-Year Alternate Educator License. The permit requires 15 semester hours in the subject area plus 6 semester hours with a 2.5 GPA within the past five years. Candidates must also pass the Praxis I basic skills assessment. To qualify for the alternate license, they must complete an additional three semester hours in the subject area. The employing district must provide mentoring. Candidates must agree to apply for the Alternate Educator License at the end of the year.

### AREAS OF LICENSURE AND ENDORSEMENTS

Areas of licensure include Early Childhood (PreK–3), Middle Childhood (4–9), Adolescent to Young Adult (7–12), and Multi-Age (PreK–12). Endorsements include Adapted Physical Education, Bilingual Education, Career Based Intervention, Computer/Technology, Driver Education, Early Education of Handicapped Children, Literacy Specialist, PreKindergarten, Middle Childhood Generalist, Reading (PreK–12), Teaching English to Speakers of Other Languages, Transition to Work, and Career Technical.

### SPECIALTY CERTIFICATES

- The following Pupil Service Licenses require Ohio State Board licenses: Audiologist, Social Worker, School Speech-Language Pathologist, Nurse, Occupational Therapist, Physical Therapist, Occupational Therapy Assistant, and Physical Therapy Assistant.

- Pupil Service Licenses are available for School Counselor and School Psychologist.

- The Provisional Career-Technical License requires either a bachelor's degree and two years of work experience, or a high school diploma and five years of work experience.

### TESTING AND SPECIAL REQUIREMENTS

- Candidates for initial licensure must take the appropriate exams in Praxis II: Subject Area/Specialty Area and Praxis II: Principles of Learning and Teaching (PLT).

- Candidates moving from the Two-Year Provisional License to the Five-Year Professional License must complete the performance-based assessment, which is the Praxis III: Classroom Performance Assessments for Beginning Teachers.

- Candidates for the One-Year Conditional Teaching Permit must pass Praxis I: Pre-Professional Skills Assessment (PPST).

- Candidates for the Two-Year Alternate Educator License must pass the appropriate Praxis II: Subject Area exam.

- Candidates for the Two-Year Provisional License in the alternate route program must pass the Praxis II: Principles of Learning and Teaching.

- Candidates adding an endorsement must pass the appropriate Praxis II: Subject Area exam.

- Candidates for Professional Pupil Services Licenses must pass the appropriate Praxis II: Specialty Area exam.

- Persons who are advancing from the Two-Year Provisional License to the Five-Year Professional License in Early Childhood, Middle Childhood, and Intervention Specialist must complete 12 semester hours of courses in teaching reading.

## SPECIAL SITUATIONS AND NOTES

- Ohio participates in the NASDTEC Interstate Agreement. Out-of-state applicants with less than three years' experience are eligible for the Two-Year Provisional Teaching License. Applicants with three years' experience under a standard license are eligible for the Five-Year Professional License. They meet Praxis II test requirements.

- Foreign applicants must have their credentials evaluated by an evaluation agency.

- Paraprofessionals must hold an Educational Aide Permit, which requires a high school diploma or equivalent. In addition, those in Title I programs must have two years (48 semester hours) of study at an institution of higher education or an associate degree or a passing score on the ETS ParaPro Assessment.

- The Substitute Teaching License requires a bachelor's degree. A Short-Term Substitute License allows a person to teach up to five days in the same classroom. A Long-Term Substitute License allows a person to teach longer than five days, but candidates must be employed and complete additional coursework specific to the grade level they wish to teach. Licenses must be requested by the school district.

## USEFUL WEB SITES

- **Certification, contacts, fees:** www.ode.state.oh.us/teaching-profession/teacher/certification_licensure

- **Job search:** www.ode.state.oh.us/jobs

- **Certification inquiry:** webapp2.ode.state.oh.us/core/Educator_Information/default.asp

- **Application status:** www.ode.state.oh.us/Teaching-Profession/Teacher/Certification_Licensure/www-cert-status.asp

- **Approved programs:** www.ode.state.oh.us/Teaching-Profession/Teacher/Educator_Preparation/inst_prog.asp

- **Substitutes:** www.ode.state.oh.us/Teaching-Profession/Teacher/Certification_Licensure/rule_temp.asp

- **Testing:** www.ets.org/praxis (select state requirements)

- **Paraprofessionals:** www.ets.org/parapro

- **School directory:** www.ode.state.oh.us/data/OEDdistbuild.asp

- **Alternate routes:** www.ode.state.oh.us/Teaching-Profession/Teacher/Recruitment_Retention/alt_cond/default.asp?pfv=True

- **Forms:** www.ode.state.oh.us/teaching-profession/teacher/certification_licensure/application.asp

- **NBPTS:** www.ode.state.oh.us/teaching-profession/teacher/national_board_cert

- **OH TTT:** www.ode.state.oh.us/teaching-profession/teacher/Certification_Licensure/ohiot3.asp?pfv=True

# OKLAHOMA

## OVERVIEW

Teachers and specialists in Oklahoma must have a license or certificate to teach at the elementary, middle, or secondary levels. There are two levels for both the traditional and alternate routes.

- A **License** is issued to beginning traditionally prepared teachers or to teachers in the Alternative Placement Program. For traditionally prepared teachers, the License is valid for one year, during which the teacher must participate in a Residency Program that includes mentoring. Candidates in the Alternative Placement Program may hold a License for three years.

- **Standard Certificate** is issued to teachers with at least one year of experience who have completed the Residency Program and all test requirements. It is valid for five years and requires three years' experience for renewal. Applicants with less than three years' experience may renew with a combination of experience, professional development points, and college courses.

## TRADITIONAL ROUTE

Candidates for a License must complete a bachelor's degree through a teacher education program and meet the Certification Examinations for Oklahoma Educators (CEOE) general education and subject area requirements. To advance to a Standard Certificate, candidates must have one year of experience, complete the Residency Program, and pass the CEOE professional education exam.

## ALTERNATE ROUTE

**Alternative Placement Program** allows individuals who hold a bachelor's degree with a subject major to teach while completing requirements for a Standard Certificate. The program is limited to specific secondary and all grade level (PreK–12) subjects, and Career Technology Education. Candidates must also have two years of work experience in the subject area or graduate coursework. Once eligibility for the program is established, candidates must pass the general education and subject area test, and apply to the Teacher Competency Review Panel to receive a License. Only upon receiving a License may candidates take employment in a district. Candidates must agree to earn a Standard Certificate within three years. Requirements include completing the professional education component, the Resident Teacher Program, and the CEOE professional education exam.

## CERTIFICATION AREAS AND ENDORSEMENTS

Certificate areas include Early Childhood (PreK–3), Elementary (1–8), Middle/Junior High subjects (6–8), High School subjects (9–12), all level subjects (PreK–12), and Special Education (PreK–12). Endorsements are for specific middle or secondary subjects. Candidates may add an endorsement by completing a Professional Development Institute or by passing the appropriate CEOE subject area test. Additional subject areas may be added by passing the appropriate CEOE subject area test.

## SPECIALIST AND CAREER TECHNOLOGY CERTIFICATES

- Specialist Certificates are offered in the following areas: Library-Media Specialist, School Counselor, School Psychometrist, School Psychologist, Speech-Language Pathologist, and Reading Specialist. All require completing a graduate program and passing the appropriate CEOE subject area test. The following national certifications fulfill all testing and program requirements in their respective areas: Nationally Certified School Counselor (NCSC), Nationally Certified School Psychologist (NCSP), and Certificate of Clinical Competence (CCC) from the American Speech-Language-Hearing Association (ASHA).

- The Provisional Level I Certificate in Career Technology Education requires a high school diploma or GED and three years' work experience, completion of a Career and Technology Education Orientation Training Program, and an approved plan of study to complete requirements for the Level II and Standard Certificates.

## TESTING AND SPECIAL REQUIREMENTS

- The Certification Examinations for Oklahoma Educators (CEOE) consist of the Oklahoma General Education Test (OGET), the Oklahoma Professional Teaching Examination (OPTE), and the Oklahoma Subject Area Tests (OSAT). All candidates for an initial License are required to take the OGET and the appropriate OSAT. All candidates for a Standard Certificate are required to take the appropriate OPTE.

- Adding a certification area or subject requires passing the appropriate OSAT. Persons who hold NBPTS certification in the same area are exempt.

## SPECIAL SITUATIONS AND NOTES

- Out-of state applicants who hold a valid full teaching credential in any state are eligible for a comparable Oklahoma certificate after one year of employment in

Oklahoma. Oklahoma participates in the NASDTEC Interstate Agreement. Persons who have completed a teacher education program in any member state are eligible for certification in the same subject area. Applicants who have no experience receive a License and are required to participate in a Resident Teacher Program. All applicants must also meet the CEOE test requirements. Evaluation of comparable tests from other states is available. Contact the Oklahoma Commission for Teacher Preparation or see the testing Web sites below for more information. A two-year certificate is available for candidates who need to fulfill test requirements. Those holding NBPTS certification are immediately eligible for a Standard Certificate in the same area and are exempt from test requirements.

■ The Paraprofessional Title I Credential requires two years of study at an institution of higher education, an associate degree, or passing either the OGET or a local assessment. The credential is not required, but it is one way paraprofessionals may demonstrate they are highly qualified.

■ Substitutes who are employed on a monthly or annual basis must hold a teaching certificate. Any substitute who is employed in the same assignment for more than 20 days must hold a valid certificate for the subject and grade level. Any person who holds an expired Standard Certificate may substitute any number of days a year. Persons who hold a bachelor's degree but no certificate may teach only 70 days a year.

## USEFUL WEB SITES

■ **Licensing, Certification, contacts, school directory, job search, approved programs, forms:** sde.state.ok.us/home/defaultns.html
www.octp.org

■ **Approved programs:** www.okhighered.org

■ **School directory:** www.sde.state.ok.us/link/oklaeduc.html

■ **NBPTS:** www.octp.org

■ **Testing:** www.octp.org
www.ceoe.nesinc.com

■ **OK Teachers-Teachers (job search):** www.sde.state.ok.us/home/defaultns.html

■ **Jobs:** www.oklahomateachingjobs.org

■ **Forms:** www.sde.state.ok.us/pro/tcert/profstd.html

■ **OK TTT:** sde.state.ok.us/pro/trps.html

# OREGON

## OVERVIEW

*Teachers, school counselors, and school psychologists in Oregon must hold a license to teach at the elementary, middle, or high school levels. Oregon has a four-tiered system.*

- *Candidates in **Pre-Service Preparation** in traditional and alternative programs work toward meeting program and test requirements including a supervised teaching experience.*

- ***Initial License** allows candidates to enter the profession from a variety of backgrounds. While holding this license, beginning teachers receive mentoring. The license is valid for three years and may be renewed once.*

- ***Continuing License** is issued to teachers who hold the Initial License and have three years' experience. Candidates must complete a master's degree and an approved Continuing License Program or achieve NBPTS certification. The license is valid for five years.*

- ***Career Educator** is granted upon the first renewal of the Continuing License. It is valid for five years and requires completing a Continuing Professional Development Plan or NBPTS certification for renewal.*

## TRADITIONAL ROUTE

Candidates for the Initial License must hold a bachelor's degree, complete a teacher education program, and must meet all test, civil rights, and recency requirements.

## ALTERNATE ROUTE

**Restricted Transitional License** is intended for persons who are making a career change. A district may hire someone with a Restricted Transitional License when a fully licensed teacher is not available. Candidates for this license must have a bachelor's degree and be employed in a school district. The license is valid for three years during which candidates must participate in a district mentoring program, complete a teacher education program, and meet all test requirements. Upon completing all requirements, candidates receive the Initial License.

**Approved No Child Left Behind Alternative Route Teaching License** is granted to candidates who hold a bachelor's degree and are employed in a district. They must demonstrate subject mastery by having a major in a core academic subject, or passing a subject area exam (for secondary) or the Multiple Subject Examination (for elementary). The license is valid for three years during which candidates must participate in a mentoring or supervised support program, and complete all requirements for the Initial License.

Alternate route licenses are not available for school counselors and school psychologists.

## AUTHORIZATION LEVELS AND ENDORSEMENTS

Authorization levels on a license specify the grade level. Authorization levels include Early Childhood (age 3–grade 4), Elementary (3–8), Middle Level (5–10), and High School (7–12). The Elementary authorization allows a person to teach grades 5 and 6 in self-contained classes in a middle school. The Middle Level authorization allows a person to teach departmentalized classes in a middle school. Adding an authorization level requires 4 semester hours and a practicum if the level is contiguous to the level already held, or completing an approved program including practicum if the level is not contiguous.

Endorsements may be added to initial or advanced licenses. To qualify, candidates must pass the required test or complete a program of coursework as well as a practical experience, which may be a practicum, one year of teaching under a Conditional Assignment Permit, or five years of teaching in a private school. Completion of a program is always required for Special Education, Communication Disorders, Hearing Impairment, Visual Impairment, Reading, Drama, Japanese, Latin, Russian, and Adaptive Physical Education. Some endorsements require multiple grade level authorizations.

## SPECIALTY LICENSES

- Limited License is for persons who teach a highly specialized subject for which no endorsement exists. Candidates must have an associate degree or equivalent and be employed in a district, which provides mentoring. The license is valid for three years and may be renewed by passing a basic skills assessment and meeting the civil rights requirement. The license is only valid in the employing school district.

- Professional Technical License requires that candidates be employed in a school, have recent work experience, and pass an exam given by an Instructor Appraisal Committee. The license is valid for three years and is nonrenewable. Candidates who meet specified requirements during the three years receive the Five-Year Professional Technical License.

- American Indian Languages Teaching License requires that applicants be certified by the tribe whose language they will teach.

## TESTING AND SPECIAL REQUIREMENTS

- The Oregon Educator Licensure Assessments (ORELA) are the Multiple Subject Examinations (MSE) for candidates for Early Childhood, Elementary, and Middle Level. The MSE consists of three subtests. Subtest I includes Language Arts, Social Science, and the Arts; Subtest II includes Mathematics, Science, Health, and Physical Education; and Subtest III includes Language Arts, Social Science, the Arts, and Reading Instruction. Graduates of teacher education programs in Oregon must take Subtests I and II. Graduates of out-of-state programs must take Subtests II and III.

- Candidates for the initial license must pass a basic skills assessment, which consists of the reading, writing, and mathematics portions of the California Basic Educational Skills Test (CBEST) or the written Praxis I: Pre-Professional Skills Test (PPST). A mixture of CBEST and PPST passing scores is acceptable.

- Candidates for Middle Level authorization must pass the ORELA MSE. Candidates for High School authorization must pass the appropriate Praxis II: Subject Area/Specialty Area exam.

- Candidates for the Initial License must have recent experience during the preceding three years. This may be completing a teacher education program, teaching, or completing 9 quarter hours in an approved program.

- All candidates must complete a course and pass an exam on U.S. and Oregon civil rights laws.

## SPECIAL SITUATIONS AND NOTES

- Out-of-state applicants who completed a teacher education program or hold a full-time teaching license are eligible for the Transitional License, which is valid for three years and is nonrenewable. It allows applicants to teach while completing requirements for the Initial License. Applicants must take a basic skills assessment, but the subject matter exam may be waived if they have five years' experience teaching the subject under a valid license. Applicants must meet the civil rights requirement.

- Foreign applicants must have their credentials evaluated by an evaluation service. See the Web site for more information.

- Paraprofessionals in Title I programs must have two years of study at an institution of higher education or an associate degree or demonstrate competency through a formal local assessment.

- Applicants for the Substitute Teaching License must have completed a teacher education program in any state, hold a bachelor's degree related to teaching, or hold a full teaching license from any state. Applicants must meet the civil rights requirement. The license is valid for substituting at any level, but the substitute may not replace the same teacher for more than three months. The license is valid for three years and requires passing the basic skills test for renewal.

## USEFUL WEB SITES

- **Licensure:** www.tspc.state.or.us

- **Teach OR (job search, recruitment):** www.teachoregon.com

- **Jobs:** www.edzapp.com

- **Contacts:** www.tspc.state.or.us/contact.asp

- **School directory:** www.ode.state.or.us/search/results/?id=227

- **Application status:** www.tspc.state.or.us/lookup_query.asp

- **License inquiry:** www.tspc.state.or.us/lookup_query.asp

- **Approved programs:** www.ous.edu/teachedguide.htm

- **Paraprofessionals:** www.ode.state.or.us/news/announcements/announcement.aspx?=1000

- **Testing:** www.tspc.state.or.us/GenInfo_Item.asp?id=7
www.orela.nesinc.com
www.cbest.nesinc.com
www.ets.org/praxis (select state requirements)

- **Forms:** www.tspc.state.or.us/forms.asp?op=5&id=0

- **Alternate routes:** www.tspc.state.or.us/pub.asp?op=0&id=3

- **Fees:** www.tspc.state.or.us/faqs.asp?op=3&id=0#answer12

- **OR TTT:** www.ode.state.or.us/search/results/?id=104

- **Foreign applicants:** www.tspc.state.or.us/GenInfo_Item.asp?id=8

- **NBPTS:** www.ode.state.or.us/groups/teachers/awards/nbct

# PENNSYLVANIA

## OVERVIEW

*All professional employees of public schools in Pennsylvania must have Professional Educator Certification to teach at the elementary, middle, or secondary levels. There are two levels of instructional and specialist certification for traditionally prepared educators. Candidates coming through an alternate route have an additional initial certification level. All persons holding Level I or II certificates must complete 6 college credits, 6 in-service credits, 180 continuing education hours, or a combination of these every five calendar years to maintain active certificates.*

*There is an additional initial certification level for those in alternate route programs.*

■ ***Intern Certificate.*** *This certificate allows a person who holds a bachelor's degree and is enrolled in a Teacher Intern Program to begin teaching while completing requirements for the instructional Level I certificate.*

## TRADITIONAL ROUTE

**Level I Certificate** is the initial certificate issued to beginning educators. Candidates must have a bachelor's degree with a 3.0 GPA from a teacher education program and meet all test requirements. During the first year of teaching, candidates participate in an induction program. The certificate is valid for six years of service and is nonrenewable. After six years of service, educators must meet requirements for the Level II Certificate.

**Level II Certificate** is the permanent certificate issued to educators who hold the Level I Certificate, and complete an induction program, three years of teaching, and a master's degree or 24 post-baccalaureate credits.

## ALTERNATE ROUTE

**Teacher Intern Certification Program** allows individuals to hold a full-time teaching position while completing requirements for certification. It is not available to educational specialists. Candidates for a Teacher Intern Program must hold a bachelor's degree in the area in which they intend to be certified, have a 3.0 GPA, meet the test requirements, and meet the mathematics and English requirements for admission to the program. The Intern Certificate is issued when the candidate obtains employment. The certificate is valid for three years and is nonrenewable. Candidates must be enrolled continuously in the program, maintain a 3.0 GPA, and complete the program before the certificate expires. When candidates complete all requirements of the program including passing a Student Teacher Assessment, they are eligible for the Instructional Level I Certificate. Their coursework, but not their experience, counts toward the requirements for the Level II certificate.

## CERTIFICATES AND SUBJECT AREAS

Certificates include Early Childhood (nursery–grade 3), Elementary Education (K–6), Middle Level subjects (7–9), Secondary subjects (7–12), all level subjects (K–12), and Special Education (nursery–12).

Additional subject areas may be added to an existing certificate. Candidates must complete a preparation program and meet the test requirements.

## SPECIALIST CERTIFICATES

■ Specialist Certificates include Dental Hygienist, Elementary Counselor (K–6), Secondary Counselor (7–12), Home and School Visitor, Instructional Technology, School Nurse, School Psychologist, and Social Restoration. All are for grades K–12, except Counselor. Candidates who hold a valid Pennsylvania professional license as a registered nurse, dental hygienist, psychologist, counselor, or social worker are exempt from the specialty area test requirement. However, they must still take the basic skills assessment.

■ Vocational Instructional Certificates are available for grades 7–12. Candidates for the Level I certificate must have two years' work experience, pass an occupational competency exam, complete 18 credit hours in an approved vocational teacher education program, and pass appropriate tests.

■ The Program Specialist-ESL Certificate is available for candidates who have a Level I or II Certificate and have completed an approved ESL (English as a Second Language) training program.

## TESTING AND SPECIAL REQUIREMENTS

■ Candidates for the Level I Certificate must take the reading, writing, and mathematics portions of the Praxis I: Pre-Professional Skills Test (PPST) and the appropriate Praxis II: Subject Assessment/Specialty Assessment. Candidates for K–6 or K–12 certificates must also take Praxis II: Fundamental Subjects: Content Knowledge.

■ Candidates for Teacher Intern Programs must pass PPST, the Fundamental Subjects: Content Knowledge (for K–6 or K–12 certification), and the Subject Assessment for admission to the program.

- Candidates who are adding a subject area must take the appropriate Praxis II: Subject Assessment.

- Candidates for the Vocational Instructional I Certificate must take the reading and writing portions of the PPST. Candidates for the Vocational Instructional II Certificate must take the appropriate Praxis II: Vocational General Knowledge test.

- All candidates for instructional and specialist certificates must have 6 semester hours of mathematics, 3 semester hours of English composition, and 3 semester hours of English/American literature, all at the college level.

- All candidates must submit a health certificate signed by a U.S. licensed physician.

- Candidates for the Level I certificate must be U.S. citizens or file an intent to become a citizen within six years, except foreign language teachers who must have a permanent permit if they are not U.S. citizens. Only U.S. citizens and those converting a Level I foreign language certificate are eligible for the Level II certificate.

- Candidates who have not been Pennsylvania residents for the immediate past two years must submit fingerprints. All applicants must obtain a Child Abuse History Clearance.

## SPECIAL SITUATIONS AND NOTES

- Pennsylvania participates in the NASDTEC Interstate Agreement. Applicants from member states who have completed a teacher preparation program or have three years' experience under a valid certificate are eligible for a Pennsylvania certificate. Applicants must have a bachelor's degree with a 3.0 GPA, meet test requirements, have the requisite hours in math and English, and meet citizenship requirements. Applicants who meet all requirements except math and English may receive a Temporary Teaching Permit, valid for one year, to complete these requirements. Applicants who hold NBPTS certification receive the Level II Certificate and are exempt from test and course requirements. Applicants with three years' experience during the past seven years are exempt from taking the PPST, but must still take the Praxis II: Subject Assessment. Applicants who hold the ABCTE Passport to Teaching may also apply for the Temporary Teaching Permit to complete requirements for the Level I certificate.

- Foreign applicants must have their credentials evaluated by an evaluation service. They are also required to take the SPEAK test (a Pennsylvania-administered oral English proficiency test) if English is not their native language. See the Web site for more information.

- Paraprofessionals in Title I programs must have two years (48 semester hours) of study at an institution of higher education or an associate degree or pass a formal local assessment.

## USEFUL WEB SITES

- **Certification:** www.teaching.state.pa.us/teaching/cwp

- **Teaching in PA (job vacancies, approved programs forms, PA TTT, certification inquiry, application status):** www.teaching.state.pa.us/teaching/site/default.asp

- **School directory:** www.pde.state.pa.us/k12/cwp

- **Contacts:** www.teaching.state.pa.us/teaching/cwp

- **Testing:** www.tcs.ed.state.pa.us/PRAXIS/index.asp www.ets.org/praxis (select state requirements)

- **Alternate route:** www.teaching.state.pa.us/teaching/cwp/view.asp?a=6&q=32343

- **Foreign applicants:** www.teaching.state.pa.us/teaching/cwp/view.asp?a=3&Q=22571

- **NBPTS:** www.pde.state.pa.us/newsroom/cwp/view.asp?a=3&q=105493

- **ABCTE:** www.teaching.state.pa.us/teaching/cwp

# RHODE ISLAND

## OVERVIEW

*All teachers and specialists in Rhode Island must hold a certificate to teach at the elementary, middle, or secondary levels. There are two levels of certification.*

- **Certificate of Eligibility for Employment (CEE)** *is the initial certificate issued to beginning teachers. It allows the holder to accept employment, is valid for three years, and may be renewed every three years until the person is employed.*

- **Professional Certificate** *is issued to persons who hold the CEE and secure regular employment. Candidates must submit a five-year Professional Development Plan (I-Plan). The certificate is valid for five years and may be renewed upon completion of the I-Plan. Educators may receive an extension without completing the I-Plan if they were not employed for the entire five-year period.*

- *Candidates for School Nurse and Vocational Education have an additional level of certification. The* **One-Year Professional Certificate** *is issued to persons who hold the CEE and have additional coursework requirements to receive the Five-Year Professional Certificate. It may be renewed annually with 6 semester hours until all courses are completed.*

## TRADITIONAL ROUTE

Candidates for the Certificate of Eligibility for Employment must have a bachelor's degree and graduate from a teacher preparation program, including student teaching, in the certification area within the past five years. They must also satisfy testing requirements.

The **Transcript Analysis** method is available to persons who have not completed a preparation program. They may receive the CEE if they have completed 6 semester hours of student teaching and 24 semester hours (Early Childhood and Elementary) or 18 semester hours (Secondary) of required education coursework, including teaching reading in the content area and service to students with special needs. Candidates for certification in secondary subjects or special subjects must have 30 to 36 semester hours in the subject area. Teaching special education for those with severe/profound disabilities has additional requirements.

## ALTERNATE ROUTE

The **Non-Traditional Certification** program allows qualified individuals to begin teaching in documented teacher shortage areas while completing requirements for full certification. For admission to the program, prospective teachers must have a bachelor's degree with a 3.0 GPA and a major in the intended certification area as well as three years' work experience in the field. They must pass the basic skills assessment and have received an individualized plan based on a review of their education and experience. Upon admission to the program, candidates complete an intensive summer program. When they have an offer of employment, they receive a certificate allowing them to teach. They must complete one year of teaching with mentoring, their individualized plan, and an assessment.

## CERTIFICATES AND ENDORSEMENTS

Certificates are offered for Early Childhood (PreK–2), Elementary (1–6 and 7–8, if included in an elementary school), Secondary (Junior/High School), Special Subjects (PreK–12), Special Education (birth–K, K–8, 7–12, or severe/profound ages 3–21), School Nurse/Health Teacher (PreK–12), and English as a Second Language Specialist (PreK–12). Candidates for Special Education certification must be eligible for a certificate for the grade level in addition to completing a program for special education. Additional certificates may be added. Certified teachers with two years' experience may complete a one-year supervised internship at the new certification level in lieu of student teaching.

Endorsements expand the area of validity of a certificate. Endorsements are available for Bilingual/Bicultural (elementary or secondary), English as a Second Language (ESL), ESL for Content Teachers, Middle School (5–8), and Adapted Physical Education.

## SPECIALTY CERTIFICATES

- Support Professional Certificates include School Counselor, School Psychologist, School Social Worker, Speech-Language Pathologist, and Reading Specialist. The first four require a master's degree. School Social Worker also requires a professional license.

- The CEE for Vocational Education Teacher requires a high school diploma or equivalent, apprenticeship plus one year' work experience, written and practical exams, and 12 semester hours of education courses. Upon district employment, holders of the CEE receive the One-Year Professional Certificate until they receive a bachelor's degree. Those who already hold a bachelor's degree must complete 12 hours of professional education courses. Upon completion, they are eligible for the Five-Year Professional Certificate.

## TESTING AND SPECIAL REQUIREMENTS

- Candidates for Early Childhood, Elementary, and Elementary Special Education must take the Praxis II:

Elementary Education: Content Knowledge test and Elementary Education: Content Area Exercises test.

- Candidates for Secondary must take Praxis II: Principles of Learning and Teaching 7-12.

- Candidates for PreK–12 special subjects must take Praxis II: Principles of Learning and Teaching at either the K–6 level or the 7–12 level.

- Candidates for Bilingual Endorsement in Spanish must take Praxis II: Spanish Content Knowledge test and Spanish Productive Language Skills test.

- Candidates for admission to nontraditional certification programs must pass the Praxis I: Pre-Professional Skills Test (PPST).

- Candidates for vocational educator must pass the National Occupational Competency Testing Institute (NOCTI) exam.

- Candidates for CEE who do not have a master's degree must meet the recency requirement, which is 6 semester hours of college study during the past five years.

## SPECIAL SITUATIONS AND NOTES

- Rhode Island participates in the NASDTEC Interstate Agreement. Graduates of teacher education programs in participating states who have graduated within the past five years are eligible for the CEE. Applicants who hold a valid certificate from a participating state are eligible for a comparable Rhode Island certificate. Applicants who have been certified in any state, have a bachelor's degree, have completed a program leading to certification, and have met the test requirements, but do not currently meet all requirements may receive a Special Professional Certificate. It is valid for two years during which time applicants must complete all requirements. It is nonrenewable and may be issued only once.

- Rhode Island accepts the Northeast Regional Credential for employment up to two years.

- Instructional Teacher Assistants must have a high school diploma or equivalent and two years (48 college credits) of study at an institution of higher education or an associate degree or pass an assessment such as the ETS ParaPro Assessment. They must also complete a Teacher Assistant Training Program.

- Substitutes must hold the CEE or Professional Certificate for the grade level and subject they are assigned. If a substitute with the correct certification is not available, a substitute with any CEE or Professional Certificate may be used. If such person is not available, a person with a Substitute Permit may be used. This permit requires a bachelor's degree, is applicable for PreK–12, is valid for one year, and may be renewed.

## USEFUL WEB SITES

- **Certification:** www.ridoe.net/Certification_PD/Default.htm

- **Contacts:** www.ridoe.net/directions/Default.htm

- **School directory:** www.riedx.uri.edu/rimap.htm www.ridoe.net/School_Directory/details.htm

- **Jobs:** www.ridoe.net/teachers/ed_employment.htm

- **Certification inquiry:** www.ricert.ride.ri.gov/RIDE

- **Approved programs:** www.ridoe.net/Certification_PD/teacher_prep/Institutions.htm

- **Paraprofessionals:** ritap.org/ta

- **Testing:** www.ets.org/praxis (select state requirements)

- **Paraprofessionals:** www.ets.org/parapro

- **Alternate routes:** www.ridoe.net/Certification_PD/teacher_prep/Default.htm

- **NBPTS:** www.ridoe.net/Certification_PD/Natl_Board_Cert/Default.htm

- **Forms:** www.ridoe.net/Certification_PD/certification/Cert_Applications.htm

- **RI TTT:** www.nnettt.org

# SOUTH CAROLINA

## OVERVIEW

All teachers and support personnel in South Carolina are required to hold a teaching certificate to teach at the elementary, middle, or secondary level. There are two levels of certification. The first step is different for traditional and alternate routes.

■ **Initial Certificate (traditional route)** is issued to beginning teachers, is valid for three years, and may be renewed annually if the holder is employed. Those employed in nonpublic schools may renew their certificates annually as long as they meet renewal requirements every five years.

■ **Critical Need Certificate (alternate route)** allows a degreed person to begin teaching in a critical needs area while completing requirements. It is valid for one year and may be renewed twice if annual program requirements are met.

■ **Professional Certificate** is issued to educators who hold the Initial Certificate and to those who complete the Program of Alternative Certification for Educators. It is valid for five years. For renewal, educators must earn 120 renewal credits including at least 3 semester hours of graduate study for those who do not have a master's degree. This certificate is also issued to educators who achieve NBPTS certification, in which case it is valid for 10 years.

## TRADITIONAL ROUTE

Candidates for certification must hold a bachelor's degree through a teacher education program including student teaching. Three years of post-baccalaureate teaching experience in the certification area may be used in lieu of student teaching if all other requirements including testing are met. To move to the Professional Certificate, candidates must have three years' experience, and complete an induction program and formal evaluation.

## ALTERNATE ROUTE

**Program of Alternative Certification for Educators (PACE)** allows degreed individuals to teach in critical-needs subjects or geographical areas while completing requirements for certification. Critical-needs subject areas include art, business, student with emotional disabilities, English, family and consumer sciences, foreign languages, industrial technology, library science, math, music, science, speech, drama, and theater. Candidates must have a bachelor's degree with a major or 30 semester hours in the intended certification subject, two years' work experience, employment in a school district, and a passing score on the required subject assessment. Individuals who qualify for the program receive a **Critical Need Certificate.** During the program, candidates complete induction and mentoring, formal evaluation, graduate coursework, and a pedagogy exam. The PACE program and test requirements must be completed within three years. At that time, candidates are eligible for the Professional Certificate.

## CERTIFICATE AREAS

Certificates are offered in Early Childhood (PreK–3), Elementary (2–6), Middle level (5–8), and Secondary (9–12). The following areas are for PreK–12: art, music,

physical education, English for Speakers of Other Languages (ESOL), foreign languages, theater, and special education.

Beginning July 1, 2009, candidates who wish to add an area of certification must complete a program and pass the subject assessment. Until then, specific coursework and a passing score on the subject assessment are required for most areas.

## SPECIALTY CERTIFICATES

■ The Internship Certificate valid for one year is issued to candidates who have met all requirements except student teaching and who are enrolled in a teacher education program. This certificate is also issued to candidates for School Psychologist who are in a certification program and serving an internship. It may be renewed once. It is also issued to candidates for Speech-Language Pathologist who have a master's degree or a Certificate of Clinical Competence from the American Speech-Hearing Association (ASHA) and who have met test requirements. It is valid for one year and is converted to a Professional Certificate after one year of employment.

■ Guidance, School Psychologist, Speech-Language Therapist, and Media Specialist require a master's degree.

■ Special Subject Certificates are issued to qualifying teachers in noncore academic subjects. The certificate is valid for one year and may be renewed if the candidate meets test requirements.

■ Trade and industrial teachers must have an associate degree for most areas, complete a training institute, and pass the required exams. Candidates in work-based career and technology education are exempt from student teaching. Those who do not hold a nationally recognized license must pass a nationally recognized competency exam within two years. Candidates must pass the basic skills exam in the first year.

■ Audiologists, school nurses, and social workers are licensed by the state, not certified as education professionals.

## TESTING AND SPECIAL REQUIREMENTS

■ All candidates for initial certification must pass the appropriate level Praxis II: Principles of Learning and Teaching (PLT) and the appropriate Praxis II: Subject Assessments.

■ Candidates in the PACE program must take the appropriate PLT and Praxis II: Subject Assessments.

■ Candidates for work-based career and technology education must pass the Praxis I: Pre-Professional Skills Test (PPST) and the trade competency exam.

## SPECIAL SITUATIONS AND NOTES

■ South Carolina participates in the NASDTEC Interstate Agreement. Out-of-state applicants who hold valid certificates must submit test scores for the subject area exam and general professional knowledge exam required in the state where they are certified. If none were required, they must meet the South Carolina testing requirements. Applicants with less than three years' experience must take the PLT. Applicants receive comparable certification, and those with NBPTS certification receive full reciprocity.

■ Foreign applicants must have their credentials evaluated by an evaluation agency. An International Certificate is available to teachers from other countries whose credentials and visas have been verified by a recruiting agency. It may be renewed annually for a total of three years. Teachers must meet the Initial Certification test requirements.

■ Paraprofessionals in Title I programs must have two years of study at an institution of higher education or an associate degree or pass the ETS ParaPro Assessment or the ACT WorkKeys Proficiency Certificate for Teacher Assistants.

■ South Carolina does not certify substitute teachers. Individuals should contact the school district for information.

## USEFUL WEB SITES

■ **Certification:** www.scteachers.org

■ **CERRA SC** (job search, recruitment): www.cerra.org

■ **Contacts:** www.scteachers.org/cert/certcontact.cfm

■ **Forms:** www.scteachers.org/cert/index.cfm

■ **School directory:** www.myscschools.com/Public Information/schooldirectory.cfm

■ **Approved programs:** www.scteachers.org/educate/programstand.cfm

■ **Testing:** www.scteachers.org/cert/exam.cfm www.ets.org/praxis (select state requirements)

■ **Paraprofessionals:** www.ets.org/parapro www.act.org/workkeys/overview/profcert/index.html

■ **Alternate routes:** www.scteachers.org/cert/pace/overview.cfm

■ **Paraprofessionals:** www.scteachers.org/Titleii/newpara.cfm

■ **NBPTS:** www.scteachers.org/Cert/nbcert.cfm

■ **SC TTT:** www.scteachers.org/troops/index.cfm

# SOUTH DAKOTA

## OVERVIEW

*Teachers and school service specialists in South Dakota must hold a certificate to teach at the elementary, middle, or secondary levels. There is one standard certificate.*

- *The **Five-Year Certificate** is issued to individuals who have completed traditional teacher education programs or alternative route programs and meet all requirements. It is valid for five years. For renewal, 6 semester hours or Continuing Education Units (90 clock hours) are required including 3 semester hours of college credit.*

- *Candidates in alternative route programs first receive the **Alternative Teaching Certificate,** which is valid for three years and allows candidates to teach while completing requirements for full certification.*

## TRADITIONAL ROUTE

Candidates must hold a bachelor's degree, complete a teacher education program, and meet test requirements.

## ALTERNATE ROUTE

South Dakota has five alternative route programs. All require a bachelor's degree with a 2.5 GPA. Candidates must pass the subject assessments to be admitted and the pedagogy assessment by completion of the program. All candidates must meet the human relations and American Indian studies requirement. When the program has been completed and all requirements have been met, candidates are eligible for the five-year teaching certificate.

**State Program** is available only at the secondary level, but is not available for special education. Candidates must have a major in the subject area or five years' experience, and be employed by a school district. Candidates receive a two-year certificate, which may be renewed for an additional year. The program requires a maximum of three years and includes in-service induction, mentoring, and 6 semester hours of education courses that must be completed with a 2.5 GPA.

**Northern Plains Transition to Teaching (Montana State University)** is also available only at the secondary level, and takes from one to three years to complete. Candidates enter the program, complete 9 hours of preservice training, and then find employment. Portions of the program are conducted by distance learning. A one-year paid teaching experience is included. Candidates have the option to earn a master's degree in addition to certification.

**Teach for America** candidates are selected through a national search. They must secure employment and complete a summer preservice induction and training. Mentoring is included in the program, and the program takes two years to complete.

**Certification Only** program is conducted through universities and is only offered at the secondary level. Candidates do not have to be employed. The length of the program varies.

**Project Select (Black Hills State University)** is offered only at the secondary level. Candidates complete 6 hours of preservice training and then teach cooperatively with a mentor in a school district but are not under contract. The program takes one year to complete.

## CERTIFICATES AND AUTHORIZATIONS/ ENDORSEMENTS

Certificates are offered in Birth-Preschool, Early Childhood (birth–age 8), Elementary (K–8), Junior High/Middle School (5–8), Secondary (7–12), Special Education (K–12), and all level subjects (K–12).

Authorizations specify the grade or age level or the subject that the holder is authorized to teach. The terms "authorization" and "endorsement" are used interchangeably in the state. Authorizations may be added to an existing certificate. Some authorizations may be added by passing the subject assessment. In areas where no subject assessment has been approved, candidates must complete coursework. Some authorizations require both coursework and a subject assessment. Others require either coursework or a subject assessment.

## SPECIALTY CERTIFICATES

- Certificates for School Service Specialist are offered in the following areas: School Counselor, School Social Worker, School Psychologist, School Psychological Examiner (master's degree required), School Speech/ Language Pathologist, and School Library Media Specialist.

- For Vocational-Technical Education, endorsements with less than a bachelor's degree require a professional development plan. A two-year nonrenewable certificate is available for candidates who are offered employment and submit a professional development plan outlining criteria for the five-year certificate. Work experience is also necessary.

## TESTING AND SPECIAL REQUIREMENTS

- All candidates for certification must take the appropriate level Praxis II: Principles of Learning and Teaching (PLT) and the appropriate Praxis II: Subject Assessment.

- Candidates for admission to alternative route programs must take the appropriate Praxis II: Subject Assessments and they must take the appropriate PLT by the completion of the program.

- Candidates who are adding certain authorizations or certification areas must pass the appropriate Praxis II: Subject Assessment.

- All applicants must complete a course in Human Relations and a course in South Dakota Indian Studies. Each is 3 semester hours.

- Applicants who are U.S. citizens must sign an Oath of Allegiance. Those who are not citizens must have proof of legal alien status.

- Applicants are required to submit a Certification of Health.

## SPECIAL SITUATIONS AND NOTES

- Out-of-state applicants must pass the subject assessment for each area they plan to teach. Those with no previous experience must pass the appropriate PLT. Out-of-state licensure exams may be accepted. Applicants must meet the human relations and American Indian studies requirement to receive the Five-year certificate.

- Foreign applicants must have their credentials evaluated by an evaluation service. See the Web site for more information.

- Paraprofessionals in Title I programs must have two years (48 credits) of study at an institution of higher education or an associate degree or pass the ETS ParaPro Assessment.

## USEFUL WEB SITES

- **Certification:** doe.sd.gov/teachers/index.asp

- **Jobs:** doe.sd.gov/oatq/teachingjobs/index.asp

- **School directory:** doe.sd.gov/ofm/edudir

- **Contacts:** doe.sd.gov/contact/list.asp

- **Approved programs:** doe.sd.gov/oatq/postscndry/teachered.asp

- **Paraprofessionals:** doe.sd.gov/oatq/paraprocert/index.asp

- **NBPTS:** doe.sd.gov/secretary/NationalBoard/index.asp

- **Testing:** doe.sd.gov/oatq/praxis/index.asp www.ets.org/praxis (select state requirements)

- **Paraprofessionals:** www.ets.org/parapro

- **Forms:** doe.sd.gov/oatq/teachercert/index.asp

- **Alternate routes:** doe.sd.gov/oatq/teachercert/alternativecert.asp

- **Online application:** doe.sd.gov/oatq/teachercert/index.asp

- **SD TTT:** www.montana.edu/ttt

# TENNESSEE

## OVERVIEW

*Teachers and special service personnel in Tennessee must hold a license to teach at the elementary, middle, or secondary levels. Graduates of traditional programs have two levels of licensure, and candidates in alternate route programs have an additional initial level.*

- **Apprentice Teacher License** *is issued to beginning teachers who have completed a preparation program or alternative program. It is valid for three years of teaching. If the holder has not completed three years of teaching, the license can be extended to five years and requires 45 renewal points for renewal.*

- **Professional License** *is issued to persons who hold the Apprentice Teacher License and complete three years of teaching. It is valid for 10 years and requires 90 renewal points for renewal.*

## TRADITIONAL ROUTE

Candidates must graduate from a teacher education program in the area for which they intend to be licensed and meet test requirements.

## ALTERNATE ROUTE

**Alternative License** is issued to persons who hold a bachelor's degree and are completing requirements for full licensure. It is valid for one school year. Candidates may begin to teach under this license while completing requirements for the apprentice license. Upon completion of the program and test requirements, candidates are eligible for the Apprentice Teacher License.

- **Alternative License Type A:** Candidates must have a major in the intended endorsement area. However, candidates for early childhood, elementary, or middle grades education must also be admitted to a teacher preparation program and make adequate progress prior to receiving the license. All candidates must have an employment offer from a school district that will provide a mentor for the first two years. The license is valid for one year and may be renewed twice. For the first renewal, candidates must be admitted to a teacher preparation program, earn 6 semester hours each year, and continue to be employed. The license is available in all endorsement areas.

- **Alternative License Type C:** Candidates must have a degree in the teaching field, be admitted to an Alternative Type C program, and complete a summer program before being employed. Candidates are mentored during the first year. This license is available in all endorsement areas for which a university has an approved program. It is also offered online through six universities.

- **Alternative License Type E:** Candidates must have an academic major in the teaching field, receive verification from a certification officer that they have the necessary skills, or pass the appropriate subject assessment. This program is available for all areas except elementary and middle grades education. Candidates may be employed

up to three years while completing 24 semester hours of professional education courses. The license is valid for one year and may be renewed twice as long as the candidate continues to be employed and earns 6 semester hours of credit each year.

- **Teach Tennessee** allows candidates to teach at the secondary level in high-need districts and high-need subjects such as math, science, and foreign language while completing requirements for a license. The program requires a bachelor's degree with 24 semester hours in the content area and a 3.0 GPA. Candidates may also qualify by passing the appropriate subject assessment. They must have five years' work experience and complete an intensive training institute before entering the classroom. They then teach under a mentor.

- **Transition to Teaching** is open to candidates with a bachelor's degree in math, science, engineering, or nursing who commit to teach in a high-need middle or high school for three years. Candidates receive $5,000 toward their tuition for teacher training. This program is similar to the Type C licensing program.

## ENDORSEMENTS

Endorsements cover grade levels and subject areas, and may be added to an existing license. Candidates must complete a preparation program and meet test requirements.

## SPECIALTY CERTIFICATES

- The following educators receive the Apprentice Special Group License as their initial license: School Guidance Counselor, School Social Worker, and School Psychologist. All licenses are for PreK–12 and require a master's degree. After three years' experience, candidates advance to the Professional School Service Personnel License. The provisions of this professional license are the same as those for the Professional License for teachers.

- Occupational Educational Licenses are offered in Health Science and Trade and Industry. For Health Science, candidates must have an associate degree, three years' experience, and a current professional license. For Trade and Industry, candidates must have a high school diploma or equivalent and five years' experience. The Apprentice Occupational Education License is valid for three years. Coursework is required to advance to the Professional Occupational License.

## TESTING AND SPECIAL REQUIREMENTS

- All candidates for the Apprentice License including those in alternative programs are required to take the appropriate Praxis II: Subject Assessment and the appropriate level Praxis II: Principles of Learning and Teaching (PLT).

- Candidates adding an endorsement must take the appropriate Praxis II: Subject Assessment and those adding grade-level endorsements must take the appropriate level PLT.

- Candidates for School Counselor, School Psychologist, and Speech/Language Pathologist must take the appropriate Praxis II: Specialty Area assessment.

## SPECIAL SITUATIONS AND NOTES

- Tennessee participates in the NASDTEC Interstate Agreement. Out-of-state applicants who hold a valid license and have three years' experience during the past seven years may qualify for a license. Other applicants may have to meet test requirements. Candidates who meet all requirements receive an Out-of-State License, which may be converted to a Professional License with three years' experience. An Interim Type B License may be issued for up to two years to candidates who meet all requirements except the test requirements.

- Foreign applicants must have their credentials evaluated by an evaluation service. See the Web site for more information.

- Paraprofessionals in Title I programs must have two years study at an institution of higher education, or an associate degree, or pass the ETS ParaPro Assessment or an approved local assessment.

- A person without a license may serve as a substitute teacher for 20 consecutive days. Long-term substitutes must hold a license with proper endorsements for the assignment or be a retired teacher who held the proper license and endorsements.

## USEFUL WEB SITES

- **Licensing, contacts:** www.state.tn.us/education/lic

- **Teach in TN (job search):** www.k-12.state.tn.us/teachtn

- **School directory:** www.k-12.state.tn.us/SDE/default.asp

- **Certification inquiry:** www.k-12.state.tn.us/tcertinf Alternate routes: www.state.tn.us/education/lic/alt.shtml

- **Approved programs:** www.k-12.state.tn.us/ihelicense/ ProgramsList.asp

- **Paraprofessionals:** tennessee.gov/education/accthighly qualified.pdf

- **Forms:** www.state.tn.us/education/lic/forms.shtml

- **BASE TN (special ed):** www.k12.tn.us/base-tn

- **Testing:** www.state.tn.us/education/lic/nte.shtml www.ets.org/praxis (select state requirements) www.ets.org/parapro

- **Teach TN:** www.state.tn.us/education/teachtn

- **Transition to Teaching:** www.tnt2t.com

- **Foreign applicants:** www.state.tn.us/education/lic/foreign. shtml

- **NBPTS:** tennessee.gov/education/conbcert.htm

- **TN TTT:** www.state.tn.us/education/lic/troop.shtml

# TEXAS

## OVERVIEW

*Classroom teachers in Texas must hold a **Standard Educator Certificate** or Temporary Teaching Certificate for the grade level and subject areas they teach. Grade levels include early childhood–grade 4, grades 4–8, and grades 8–12. The Standard certificate is obtained directly through traditional route programs, is valid for five years, and requires 150 clock hours of continuing professional development for renewal. The Temporary certificate allows candidates in alternate route programs to teach while completing requirements for the Standard certificate. It is available only at the grades 8–12 level, and is valid for two years.*

### TRADITIONAL ROUTE

To qualify for the **Standard Educator Certificate,** candidates must have a bachelor's degree with an academic major (not education) and complete a teacher training program, which may be a baccalaureate or postbaccalaureate program. Candidates also must complete the test requirements. Certification for career and technology education is based on work experience rather than a degree.

### ALTERNATE ROUTE

To qualify for a **Temporary Teaching Certificate,** candidates must hold a bachelor's degree with a major related to one of the Texas certification areas with corresponding TExES exams at the grade 8–12 level. Candidates must request a review of credentials and pass the required TExES pedagogy and content exams. When these requirements have been met, the candidate receives a letter of eligibility to seek employment. Candidates must be employed in a school district with a Preparation, Support, and Mentoring Plan for the two-year period of the certificate. Upon completion of the program, candidates are eligible for the Standard Educator Certificate.

**Alternate route programs under No Child Left Behind** accept both elementary and secondary candidates. Requirements are similar to those of other alternate route programs. Elementary candidates must pass the TExES/ExCET exam, whereas secondary candidates may pass the exam or complete coursework equivalent to a major. Candidates receive a **Probationary Certificate** valid for one year while completing the program. The employing school must be a Title I school and the preparation program must be approved for NCLB.

### SUPPLEMENTAL CERTIFICATES AND ENDORSEMENTS

Texas offers the following supplemental certificates and endorsements for specific grade levels: Bilingual Education (Spanish and French), English as a Second Language, Gifted and Talented, and Visually Handicapped.

### TESTING AND SPECIAL REQUIREMENTS

- Candidates seeking initial Temporary or Standard certification for teaching in public schools through the traditional or alternate routes must pass the appropriate Texas Examinations of Educator Standards (TExES) exams. Where a TExES exam is not available, the Examination for the Certification of Educators in Texas (ExCET) exam maybe used. Charter school teachers must pass these exams in order to demonstrate content mastery. In some cases Authorization to Test may be required.

- Additional certification areas may be added to a Standard certificate by taking the required TExES/ExCET exams. This option is not available for career and technology education, special service areas, or any area where an exam has not been approved.

- TExES/ExCET include pedagogy and content exams. Candidates for initial certificates are required to take the appropriate grade-level pedagogy exam. Candidates for the Temporary Teaching Certificate must pass the 8–12 Pedagogy exam. Candidates for initial certificates, Temporary certification, or those adding an area of certification are required to take the appropriate content exams.

- The Texas Oral Proficiency Test (TOPT) is required for candidates who plan to teach Spanish or French or teach in a bilingual setting.

- The Texas Assessment of Sign Communication (TASC) and the Texas Assessment of Sign Communication—American Sign Language (TASC—ASL) are required for candidates who plan to teach ASL or hearing-impaired students. The exams are not required for those who will be teaching in a classroom in which an oral/aural or cued speech communication method is predominant.

### SPECIAL SITUATIONS AND NOTES

- Out-of-state applicants and foreign applicants who hold a certificate may qualify for a Texas teaching certificate if they have passed certification exams that have been determined to be "similar to and at least as rigorous as" the corresponding Texas exam. This also applies to applicants with NBPTS certification. Check the out-of-state Web site for a lists of tests that are considered comparable/not comparable to those in Texas. Applicants who have not passed comparable tests are required to take the TExES/ExCET tests. A One-Year Certificate (nonrenewable) is available to allow applicants to complete test requirements.

- Foreign applicants must have their credentials evaluated by an evaluation service. See the Web site for more information.

- Texas has teacher shortages in math, science, special education, foreign languages, bilingual education, and technology applications. The jobs Web site lists vacancies.

## USEFUL WEB SITES

- **Certification:** www.sbec.state.tx.us/SBECOnline/default.asp

- **Teach for TX (financial aid):** www.hhloans.com/borrowers/TFTLRAPFactSheet.cfm

- **School directory:** askted.tea.state.tx.us

- **NBPTS:** www.sbec.state.tx.us/SBECOnline/certinfo/nbptscand.asp

- **Jobs:** www.twc.state.tx.us/careers/teaching.html www.sbec.state.tx.us/SBECOnline/certinfo/schjobvac/sjobvaca.asp

- **Online application and status:** www.sbec.state.tx.us/SBECOnline/educator_why.asp

- **Approved programs:** www.sbec.state.tx.us/SBECOnline/approvedprograms.asp

- **TX TTT:** www.esc13.net/troops

- **Testing:** www.texes.nesinc.com www.sbec.state.tx.us/SBECOnline/standtest/testfram.asp

- **Contacts:** www.sbec.state.tx.us/SBECOnline/about/contact.asp

- **Alternate routes:** www.sbec.state.tx.us/SBECOnline/certinfo/tempcert/candinfo.asp

- **Certification inquiry:** www.sbec.state.tx.us/SBECONLINE/virtcert.asp

- **Out-of-state applicants:** www.sbec.state.tx.us/SBECOnline/standtest/compos.asp

- **Foreign applicants:** www.sbec.state.tx.us/SBECOnline/certinfo/tempcert/candinfo.asp

# UTAH

## OVERVIEW

All teachers and special service providers in Utah must hold a license to teach at the elementary, middle, or secondary levels. There are three levels of Professional Educator Licenses.

- **Level 1** is the entry-level license issued to candidates who have completed a traditional preparation or an alternative preparation program. It is valid for three years and may be renewed with 100 Professional Development Points.

- **Level 2** is issued to educators who hold the Level 1 license, have three years' experience under that license, and have completed the Entry Years Enhancement (EYE) program. This license is valid for five years and may be renewed if the holder has three years' work experience during the past five years and 100 Professional Development Points.

- **Level 3** is issued to persons who have three years' experience under a Level 1 or Level 2 license and complete a doctorate or achieve NBPTS certification. This license is valid for seven years and may be renewed if the holder has three years' work experience during the past five years and 100 Professional Development Points.

## TRADITIONAL ROUTE

Candidates must graduate from a teacher preparation program for their area of concentration. Candidates for Secondary Education must also complete a program in a subject area.

## ALTERNATE ROUTE

**Alternative Routes to Licensure (ARL)** allows persons who have a bachelor's degree to teach under a temporary license while completing requirements for full licensure. Special Education is not included in this program. Candidates for Secondary Education must have a major in a subject area, whereas candidates for Early Childhood or Elementary Education must have a broad liberal arts background (27 semester hours). Candidates may pursue **Licensing by Agreement,** which involves completing specific courses, or they may pursue **Licensing by Competency,** which involves passing content area and pedagogy tests, although not all content areas may be licensed through testing. Candidates who qualify receive a letter of eligibility allowing them to secure employment. To qualify for a Level 1 Professional Educator License, they must develop a Professional Growth Plan specifying requirements to be met, teach at least one year including mentoring, complete all program requirements and subject assessments, and be employed.

## AREAS OF CONCENTRATION AND ENDORSEMENTS

A Utah license includes an area of concentration, which specifies the grade level a person is authorized to teach. Candidates must apply for at least one area of concentration from among the following: Early Childhood (K–3), Elementary (1–8), Middle (5–9), Secondary (6–12), Special Education (birth–age 5 or K–12), and Communication Disorders.

Endorsements specify the subject area that a person is authorized to teach. Candidates with a Secondary school area of concentration must also apply for at least one endorsement. Endorsements may be added to a Level 1 or Level 2 license with an Elementary or Secondary school area of concentration. An endorsement may be added by completing an endorsement program or through demonstrated competency. Demonstrated competency requires that the applicant has taught the subject in Utah for two years during the previous five years, and has taken courses or in-service training, passed a standardized test, has the principal's recommendation, or can present successful student scores on achievement tests.

## SPECIALTY CERTIFICATES

- Level 2 Licenses for School Counselor, School Psychologist, and School Social Worker require a master's degree.

- There are three levels for Applied Technology Education (ATE) Licenses that correspond to the three professional educator license levels. Most ATE areas require either a Secondary license and endorsement in the specific field, or an ATE Alternative Preparation Program (ATE APP) license. A person may qualify for the ATE APP license with a bachelor's degree and two years' work experience, an associate degree and four years' experience, six years' experience, or by passing an approved competency exam. Nurses must also be Licensed Practical Nurses or Registered Nurses.

## TESTING AND SPECIAL REQUIREMENTS

- All candidates for an initial licensure are required to take the Praxis II: Subject Assessments appropriate to their area of concentration or endorsement. Only one exam is required.

- Teachers who hold a Level 1 license must take the appropriate grade level Praxis II: Principles of Learning and Teaching (PLT) as part of the EYE program required for advancing to a Level 2 license.

## SPECIAL SITUATIONS AND NOTES

- Utah participates in the NASDTEC Interstate Agreement. Candidates who hold a license in a member state receive a comparable Utah license if all requirements are met. Applicants must meet test requirements and if they have less than three years' experience, they must complete the EYE program. To fulfill the recency requirement, applicants must have three years' experience or 6 semester hours credit or 100 Professional Development Points within the past five years. Applicants who do not meet all requirements may receive a Conditional Level 1 Educator License and must complete requirements before it expires.

- Foreign applicants must have their credentials evaluated by an evaluation service and must also demonstrate proficiency in English through the TOEFL or the Michigan test. See the Web site for more information.

- Paraprofessionals in Title I programs must have a high school diploma and two years (48 semester hours) of study at an institution of higher education, or an associate degree, or pass the ETS ParaPro Assessment or the Western Governors University Test.

- School districts are responsible for hiring substitute teachers. First priority is given to those who hold a license for the area of concentration and endorsement, second priority is given to those who hold a license in any area, and last priority is given to those with a bachelor's degree but no license. A substitute may not serve more than eight weeks in the same assignment without appropriate licensing for that assignment.

- Signing bonuses are offered in math, science, information technology, learning technology, and preK–12 special education. See the Web site for details.

## USEFUL WEB SITES

- **Licensing:** www.schools.utah.gov/cert

- **Job search:** www.utaheducationjobs.com www.schools.utah.gov/cert/jobs.htm

- **School directory:** www.usoe.k12.ut.us/lea/districts.htm

- **Contacts:** www.schools.utah.gov/cert/other/STAFF.HTM

- **Approved programs:** www.schools.utah.gov/cert/PrepPrograms/prep.htm

- **Certification inquiry:** www.uen.org/educator/index.jsp

- **Fees:** www.usoe.k12.ut.us/cert/other/fees.htm

- **Paraprofessionals:** www.schools.utah.gov/cert/paraprofessional.htm

- **Substitutes:** www.rules.utah.gov/publicat/code/r277/r277-508.htm

- **Bonus program:** www.schools.utah.gov/cert/PEJEP/default.htm

- **UT TTT:** www.schools.utah.gov/cert/APT/Troops/default.htm

- **Testing:** www.schools.utah.gov/cert/OOS/OOSAPPL.HTM www.schools.utah.gov/cert/other/eye/required.htm www.ets.org/praxis (select state requirements)

- **Paraprofessionals:** www.ets.org/parapro www.wgu.edu (see admission requirements)

- **Alternate routes:** www.schools.utah.gov/cert/APT/default.htm

- **Application status (CACTUS):** www.schools.utah.gov/cert/require/renewal/unknown.htm

- **Foreign applicants:** www.schools.utah.gov/cert/OOS/FOREIGN%20CREDENTIA.htm www.ets.org/toefl www.internexus.to/contact.html

- **NBPTS:** www.schools.utah.gov/cert/NationalBoard/default.htm

# VERMONT

## OVERVIEW

*Educators and support professionals in Vermont must hold a license with appropriate endorsements to teach at the elementary, middle, or secondary levels. There are two levels of licensure.*

- **Level I: Beginning Educator License** *is the entry-level license, is valid for three years, and may be renewed once. If the educator has not taught in an endorsement area, 3 professional development credits in the endorsement area are necessary for renewal.*

- **Level II: Professional Educator License** *is issued to educators who have taught in an endorsement area for three years and have an approved Individual Professional Development Plan (IPDP) for the ensuing period. This license is valid for seven years and requires 9 relicensing credits per endorsement. Relicensing credits must be related to the IPDP and demonstrated via portfolio. Alternately, an NBPTS portfolio meets renewal requirements.*

## TRADITIONAL ROUTE

Candidates for an initial license must complete an educator preparation program through a bachelor's degree program and meet test requirements. Candidates for early childhood certification must complete a practicum at birth–age 5, ages 5–8, or both levels if they are seeking endorsement for birth–grade 3. Candidates for Elementary Education must complete a practicum at both grades K–3 and grades 4–6. Candidates for endorsements covering grades preK–12 must complete a practicum at both grades preK–6 and grades 7–12. Middle grade subjects require a minor or equivalent in coursework. Secondary subjects require a major or coursework equivalent.

## ALTERNATE ROUTE

**License by Evaluation or "Peer Review"** allows a person who holds a bachelor's degree but has not completed a traditional educator preparation program to be licensed. Any candidates may also use this route for adding an endorsement. This process involves applying for eligibility, preparing a portfolio demonstrating required competencies, evaluation of the portfolio with an interview, and applying for the license or endorsement if all competencies have been met. If they have not, the candidate must develop a plan of action to address any deficiencies. Candidates must meet the test requirements and have twelve consecutive weeks of student teaching or an equivalent supervised experience. Clinics are held monthly to assist and support candidates in the process.

## ENDORSEMENTS

Each license must have at least one endorsement. Endorsements specify the grade level and/or subject that the person is authorized to teach. Grade level endorsements include Early Childhood (birth–age 5, ages 5–8, or birth–grade 3), Elementary (PreK–6), Middle Grades subject areas (5–9), Secondary subject areas (7–12), all level subject areas (PreK–12). Additional endorsements require 18 credit hours. Endorsements may also be added

via Peer Review. An additional endorsement is added as a Level I license and may be converted to Level II after three years' experience in the area. Thus, an educator may hold a Level II license in one endorsement area and a Level I license in another.

## SPECIALTY LICENSES

- Support Professionals include School Nurse, School Counselor, Educational Speech Language Pathologist, School Social Worker, School Psychologist, and Consulting Teacher.

- School Counselor, School Social Worker, and Consulting Teacher require a master's degree.

- School Nurse requires a bachelor's degree in nursing, a Registered Nurse license, CPR/First Aid certification, four years of clinical experience, and completion of an educational orientation program. Candidates for Associate Nurse must meet the same requirements except only an associate degree is required.

- Candidates for Speech Language Pathologist (SLP) must have a clinical license and meet requirements for the SLP endorsement.

- Candidates for School Psychologist must meet requirements for the National Association of School Psychologists (NASP) Specialist Level or hold a doctorate.

- Educational Technology Specialists who provide direct instruction must hold an educator's license with the Educational Technology Specialist endorsement.

## TESTING AND SPECIAL REQUIREMENTS

- All candidates for an initial license, including support professionals and Peer Review candidates, must take Praxis I: Pre-Professional Skills Test (PPST) (written or computer-based) in reading, writing, and mathematics. Qualifying scores on the GRE, SAT, or ACT exams are accepted in place of PPST.

- All candidates for an initial license, including Peer Review candidates and candidates for additional endorsements in Mathematics (7–12), Social Studies (7–12), English (7–12), Science (7–12), Elementary Education (K–6), Art (K–12), Music (K–12), and Physical Education (K–12) must pass the appropriate Praxis II: Subject Assessments.

- Candidates for an initial license or endorsement in Modern and Classical Languages (French, German, and Spanish) must pass both the Praxis II: Content Knowledge and Productive Language Skills tests. For Latin, only the Content Knowledge test is required. For all other languages, the ACTFL or ASLTA (American Sign Language) proficiency test is required.

- Candidates for Speech-Language Pathologist must pass the appropriate Praxis II: Subject Assessment.

- Praxis II: Subject Assessments will be required in the future.

- Candidates who meet all other requirements and have achieved NBPTS certification are exempt from the test requirements.

- Candidates for a Level 1 Trades and Industry license must pass the PPST.

- U.S. citizens are required to sign an Oath of Allegiance.

## SPECIAL SITUATIONS AND NOTES

- Vermont participates in the NASDTEC Interstate Agreement. Credentials of applicants who hold a current license from another participating state and have three years' experience during the past seven years will be reviewed for a comparable license. They are exempt from test requirements but must meet all other Vermont requirements. Applicants who graduated from an educator preparation program in any state may qualify for licensing via transcript review. Vermont does not have reciprocity for support professionals. They must apply for licensing via transcript review.

- Foreign applicants must have their credentials evaluated by an evaluation service.

- Paraprofessionals in Title I programs must have two years (48 credit hours) study at an institution of higher education or an associate degree or pass the ETS ParaPro Assessment.

- Each school district determines qualifications for substitutes. Unlicensed substitutes must have a high school diploma and may serve up to 15 consecutive days in one assignment. Licensed substitutes may serve outside their endorsement for up to 30 days in one assignment.

## USEFUL WEB SITES

- **Licensing, contacts:** www.state.vt.us/educ/new/html/maincert.html

- **Job search:** www.state.vt.us/educ/new/html/mainemploy.html
www.schoolspring.com/searchResults.cfm?state=1
erecruit.per.state.vt.us/index.html

- **School directory:** www.state.vt.us/educ/new/html/directories/public_schools_A_C.html

- **Approved programs:** www.state.vt.us/educ/new/html/licensing/approved_teacher_prep.html

- **Paraprofessionals:** www.state.vt.us/educ/new/html/licensing/hqt.html

- **Testing:** www.state.vt.us/educ/new/html/licensing/testing.html
www.ets.org/praxis (select state requirements)

- **Paraprofessionals:** www.ets.org/parapro

- **Alternate routes:** www.state.vt.us/educ/new/html/licensing/alternate.html

- **Forms:** www.state.vt.us/educ/new/html/licensing/forms/initial_license.html

- **Substitutes:** www.state.vt.us/educ/new/html/licensing/regulations_endorsements.html

- **VT TTT:** www.nnettt.org

# VIRGINIA

## OVERVIEW

*Teachers in Virginia must hold a license to teach at the elementary, middle, or secondary levels. There are two levels of licensure for traditionally prepared teachers. Those coming through an alternate route have an additional initial level of licensure.*

### TRADITIONAL ROUTE

**Collegiate Professional License** is issued to persons who have earned a bachelor's degree through a teacher preparation program including student teaching and met the requirments of the Professional Teacher's Assessment. The license is valid for five years and may be renewed. See below.

**Postgraduate Professional License** is issued to persons who are qualified for the Collegiate Professional License and who have earned a graduate degree. It is valid for five years and may be renewed with

Renewal of both the Collegiate and Postgraduate Professional licenses requires 180 professional development points based on an individualized professional development plan. Those who do not have a master's degree must have 3 semester hours (90 points) in the endorsement area at the undergraduate or graduate level. The remaining 90 points may be accrued through various professional development activities.

### ALTERNATE ROUTE

**Provisional License** is issued to persons in alternate route programs leading to full licensure. It is valid for three years and is nonrenewable. A person who holds a bachelor's degree, satisfies the requirements for one or more endorsements, and is employed by a school may obtain a three-year, nonrenewable Provisional License. During the period of the license, candidates must complete the requirements of the Professional Teacher's Assessment and a program in a four-year institution or an alternative licensure program. They must also complete one year of full-time teaching with the support of a fully licensed experienced teacher. Upon completion of all requirements, candidates are eligible for the five-year renewable Collegiate Professional License.

**Career Switcher Alternative Route to Licensure Program** is designed for those who hold a bachelor's degree with required coursework in the intended teaching area, five years' experience, and passing scores on the Virginia Communication and Literacy Assessment. Priority is given to candidates to teach in critical shortage areas, which include foreign languages, mathematics, science, and technology education. Candidates complete an intensive 180-hour induction and then receive the Eligibility License allowing them to seek employment. During the first year of teaching, they attend five seminars and receive mentoring. Upon completion of all requirements, candidates are eligible for a Professional License.

### ENDORSEMENTS

Endorsements specify the grade level and/or subject that the holder is authorized to teach. Grade-level endorsements include Early/Primary (PreK–3), Elementary (PreK–6), Middle (6–8), Secondary subjects (6–12), and all grade-level subjects (PreK–12). Endorsements may be added to a license by completing an endorsement program or, for individuals who are employed, through an alternate route program.

### SPECIALTY LICENSES

■ Pupil Personnel Services License is issued to persons who hold the appropriate graduate degree and meet requirements for endorsement as Guidance Counselor, School Psychologist, School Social Worker, or Visiting Teacher. Teaching experience and the Professional Teacher's Assessment are not required.

■ Technical Professional License is issued to persons who have a high school diploma or GED, complete nine semester hours of professional studies, demonstrate competency, are employed in an educational setting, hold the appropriate Virginia license, complete a two-year apprenticeship, and have four years of training and experience at a supervisory level. This license is valid for five years and may be renewed with 3 semester hours (90 professional development points) at a two- or four-year college or university and 90 points in workshops or institutes.

### TESTING AND SPECIAL REQUIREMENTS

■ The Professional Teacher's Assessment consists of the Virginia Communication and Literacy Assessment (VCLA), Praxis II: Subject Assessments/Specialty Assessments, and the Virginia Reading Assessment (VRA).

■ Candidates for an initial teaching license must pass the VCLA. Candidates for initial licensure must pass only one Praxis II: Subject Assessment, but it must match one of the endorsements for initial licensure. Candidates for the Pupil Personnel Services License or the Technical Professional License are exempt.

■ Candidates for an initial license with the middle school education (6–8) endorsement with two areas of concentration must take the two corresponding Praxis II middle school assessments.

- Candidates for endorsement in the following areas must take the VRA for Elementary and Special Education Teachers: Early/Primary (PreK–3), Elementary Education (PreK–6), and Special Education (Emotional Disturbance, Specific Learning Disabilities, Mental Retardation, Hearing Impairments, and Visual Impairments). Candidates for the Reading Specialist endorsement must take the VRA for Reading Specialists.

- Candidates for foreign language endorsements must pass either the Modern Language Association (MLA) Proficiency Test for Teachers and Advanced Students or the ACTFL oral and written proficiency tests.

- All candidates for licensure must complete the Child Abuse Recognition and Intervention requirement. This course is available online and on CD-ROM.

- All candidates for licensure must meet the Technology Standards for Instructional Personnel requirement. This is included in Virginia teacher preparation programs.

## SPECIAL SITUATIONS AND NOTES

- Out-of-state applicants who have completed a teacher education program or hold a current teaching license may qualify for a comparable Virginia license. Those who hold full licenses and have two years of experience are exempt from the requirements of the Professional Teacher's Assessment.

- Foreign applicants must have their credentials evaluated by an evaluation service. See the Web site for more information.

- Paraprofessionals in Title I programs must have a high school diploma or equivalent and two years of study at an institution of higher education or an associate degree, or demonstrate competency on a formal state or local assessment.

- Substitute teachers must have a high school diploma or GED and attend an orientation on school procedures and policies.

- Virginia has a number of incentive and recruitment initiatives. See the main licensure Web site for more information.

## USEFUL WEB SITES

- **Licensure, forms, fees, foreign applicants, paraprofessionals, NBPTS, licensure inquiry:** www.pen.k12.va.us/VDOE/newvdoe/teached.html

- **Contacts:** www.pen.k12.va.us/VDOE/contact_us.html

- **Teach VA (job search, recruitment):** www.teachvirginia.org/index.cfm

- **Teach in VA (job search, recruitment):** www.teachinvirginia.org

- **School directory:** www.pen.k12.va.us/VDOE/dbpubs/doedir

- **VA TTT:** www.odu.edu/educ/education/ttt/index.htm

- **Testing:** www.pen.k12.va.us/VDOE/newvdoe/teached.html
  www.vra.nesinc.com
  www.ets.org/praxis (select state requirements)

- **Jobs:** www.pen.k12.va.us/VDOE/JOVE/home.shtml

- **Alternate routes:** www.pen.k12.va.us/VDOE/newvdoe/licroute.htm
  www.pen.k12.va.us/VDOE/newvdoe/CareerSwitcher

- **Approved programs:** www.pen.k12.va.us/VDOE/newvdoe/colleges.htm

# WASHINGTON

## OVERVIEW

Teachers and support personnel in Washington must have a certificate to teach at the elementary, middle, or secondary levels. There are two levels of teaching certificates.

- **Residency Certificate** is the entry-level certificate and is valid for a total of seven years. It is issued as provisional status for the first two years of employment and then reissued for five years. By the end of the seven years, teachers are expected to have met the requirements for the Professional Certificate. Teachers who do not meet all requirements have limited renewal options.

- **Professional Certificate** is the advanced certificate and is issued to persons who hold the Residency Certificate and complete a Professional Certification Program. It is valid for five years and may be renewed with 150 clock hours of coursework. This certificate is also issued to teachers who achieve NBPTS certification, in which case, it is valid for the duration of the NBPTS certificate.

## TRADITIONAL ROUTE

Candidates must have a bachelor's degree in an endorsement area, complete a teacher preparation program including internship or student teaching, and meet test requirements.

## ALTERNATE ROUTE

**Mid-Career Professionals: Route 3** is available to persons who hold a bachelor's degree with subject expertise in a high-needs area or who are willing to work in a high-needs geographic area. Subject shortage areas include special education, physics, Japanese, mathematics, biology, early childhood special education, and bilingual education. This list may change from year to year, and individual districts may have other high-needs areas. Alternative programs are offered at several colleges and universities as well as through Regional Consortia. However, the number of slots available is limited, and some programs are limited to secondary subjects. To qualify for the program, a person must have a bachelor's degree, five years' work experience, and meet the basic skills and subject area test requirements. Candidates attend an intensive summer academy and then complete a mentored internship for one year or less, if all requirements are met. A second summer academy may be necessary.

**Routes 1, 2, and 4** are for persons who are already working in school districts and have classified, conditional, or emergency status.

## ENDORSEMENTS

Endorsements specify the grade level and/or subject area that a person in authorized to teach. Grade-level endorsements include Early Childhood, Elementary, Middle Humanities, Middle Math/Science, Secondary, all grade-level subjects, and Special Education (Early Childhood, or PreK–12). Endorsements are added to an existing license by completing an endorsement program. If an endorsement is similar to one already held, the person may add it by taking the appropriate endorsement test or, in some cases,

the endorsement test plus a pedagogy assessment. Endorsements may also be added by achieving NBPTS certification in the area.

## SPECIALTY CERTIFICATES

- Educational Staff Associate (ESA): Candidates for School Counselor, School Psychologist, and School Social Worker must hold the appropriate degree and complete an approved program. Candidates for Occupational Therapist, Physical Therapist, School Nurse, and School Speech Language Pathologist or Audiologist must hold the appropriate degree and complete an Initial ESA Certification Course. Candidates for ESA certificates are exempt from test requirements.

- Career and Technology Education (CTE) Teaching Certificate: Candidates prepared through the College/University Route earn a bachelor's degree, complete a teacher preparation program, and are qualified to teach a broad range of courses. They must also have 2,000 hours of work experience. Candidate prepared through the Business and Industry Route must have extensive work experience (6,000 hours) and complete a business and industry route program. They are qualified to teach in one specific area. CTE Certificates are issued at the Initial and Continuing (advanced) levels.

## TESTING AND SPECIAL REQUIREMENTS

- Candidates for initial certification must pass the Washington Educator Skills Test—Basic (WEST–B) basic skills assessment. Passing scores on the California Basic Educational Skills Test (CBEST) or Praxis I: Pre-Professional Skills Test (PPST) are accepted in place of WEST—B.

- Candidates for initial certification and those adding an endorsement must pass the appropriate Praxis II: Subject Assessment for each endorsement. This is also sometimes called the Endorsement Test or Washington Educator Skills Test—Endorsements (WEST—E). Teachers with three years' experience may take up to twelve months to satisfy this requirement. All other candidates must satisfy it at the time they apply.

- Competency in bilingual education or foreign languages must be demonstrated through a teacher preparation program or through the ACTFL Oral Proficiency Interview.

- Candidates for the Professional Certificate must complete a course on issues of abuse and prevention.

## SPECIAL SITUATIONS AND NOTES

- Out-of-state applicants may apply for a Residency Certificate. They must pass the WEST—B within 12 months of receiving the first temporary permit and they must pass the appropriate Praxis II: Subject Assessment for each endorsement. Teachers with three years' experience may take up to twelve months to complete this requirement. All others must have completed it when applying. Applicants who hold advanced certificates from states whose advanced level certification program is comparable to that in Washington may be granted the Professional Certificate. Currently Oregon is the only state whose program qualifies as comparable to Washington's. Applicants who have alternate route certificates from other states must complete a teacher preparation program. Applicants who hold the equivalent of the Educational Staff Associate Certificate and have three years' experience qualify for the comparable Washington certificate.

- Foreign applicants must have their credentials evaluated by an evaluation service. See the Web site for more information.

- Paraeducators in Title I programs must have two years (48 semester hours) of study at an institution of higher education or an associate degree or complete a formal assessment. The formal assessment may be the ETS ParaPro Assessment, a portfolio, a district assessment, or an apprenticeship program.

- The Substitute Certificate may be issued to anyone who is qualified for a regular teaching certificate and is valid for life. A substitute may teach up to 30 consecutive days at any grade level in any subject. The Intern Substitute Certificate allows a student teacher to substitute for the supervising teacher. It is valid for one year and is nonrenewable. The Emergency Substitute Certificate may be issued to a person who is not fully qualified for a regular certificate, is valid for three years, and may be renewed.

## USEFUL WEB SITES

- **Certification, contacts:** www.k12.wa.us/certification/teacher/teacherinformation.aspx

- **Teach WA (recruitment):** www.teachwashington.org/pathways.php

- **Job search:** www.k12.wa.us/employment/k12opportunities.aspx

- **School directory:** www.k12.wa.us/maps/SDmainmap.aspx

- **Approved programs:** www.k12.wa.us/certification/profed/approvedprograms.aspx

- **CTE programs:** www.k12.wa.us/certification/CTE/CTEinformation.aspx

- **Substitutes:** www.k12.wa.us/certification/teacher/limited.aspx
www.k12.wa.us/certification/teacher/substitute.aspx

- **NBPTS:** www.k12.wa.us/certification/nbpts/default.aspx

- **Testing:** www.k12.wa.us/certification/teacher/teacherinformation.aspx
www.pesb.wa.gov/Assessment/WEST-E/WEST-E.htm
www.west.nesinc.com
www.ets.org/praxis (select state requirements)

- **Paraeducators:** www.ets.org/parapro

- **Online application and status:** eds.ospi.k12.wa.us/pda

- **Alternate routes:** www.pesb.wa.gov/AlternativeRoutes/AlternativeRoutes.htm

- **Forms:** www.k12.wa.us/certification/certapp/forms.aspx

- **Foreign applicants:** www.k12.wa.us/certification/colleges/reg_accred.html

- **Paraeducators:** www.k12.wa.us/Paraeducators/default.aspx

- **WA TTT:** www.k12.wa.us/certification/ProfEd/troops

# WEST VIRGINIA

## OVERVIEW

*Any credential issued by the West Virginia Board of Education is referred to as a "license." All persons employed in schools must hold a license appropriate to their position. Teaching and student support services licenses for elementary, middle, and secondary are divided into three levels. Alternate route credentialing is limited.*

## TRADITIONAL ROUTE

**Provisional Professional Certificate** is the entry-level certificate issued to candidates is valid for three years. Candidates must complete a bachelor's degree with a 2.5 GPA, complete an educational preparation program, and meet test requirements.

**Professional Certificate** is issued to a person who holds the three-year certificate, has two years experience, and has completed the beginning educator internship and 6 semester hours of credit. It is valid for five years and requires 6 semester hours with a 3.0 GPA for renewal.

**Permanent Certificate** is issued to a person who holds or is eligible for a Professional Certificate, has five years' experience, and earns a master's degree. It is also issued to persons who complete two five-year renewals of the Professional Certificate. This certificate is valid indefinitely unless suspended or revoked.

## ALTERNATE ROUTE

**Alternative Teaching Certificate** is issued in high-needs areas only and is not available in Elementary Education. To enroll in any alternative route program in general education and receive the Alternative Teaching Certificate, a candidate must have a bachelor's degree with a 2.5 GPA, meet test requirements, and be offered employment in a high-needs area. Candidates must complete 18 semester hours in the alternative certification program and complete three phases of training including supervision, mentoring, and evaluation. The certificate is valid for one year and may be renewed twice. The first renewal requires completing the beginning teacher internship program and 6 semester hours in the program. The second renewal requires an additional 6 semester hours. Upon completion of the program and all test requirements, candidates are eligible for the Provisional Professional Certificate.

**Special Education Alternative Program** is made up of two types of alternative programs. One is multicategorical and allows a person to teach students with learning disabilities, mental impairment, and behavior disorders. The other is for general education endorsements and is limited to the special education classroom in biology, English, general science, mathematics, or social studies. This program also allows certified special education teachers to become highly qualified by gaining content endorsements. To enroll, candidates must have a bachelor's degree with a 2.5 GPA. The program includes 15 semester hours in the content area, and candidates must also complete an internship or take 3 semester hours of content-specific methods and 3 semester hours of reading in the content area.

## ENDORSEMENTS

Certificates must have one or more endorsements that specify the grade (programmatic) level and subject area (specialization) that a person is authorized to teach. Programmatic level endorsements include Preschool Education (Birth–PreK), Early Education (PreK–K), Early Childhood Grades (K–4), Middle Childhood Grades (5–9), Adolescent Grades (9–12), and Adult. Specialization endorsements include Elementary Education (K–6), Secondary Subject (9–Adult), Student Support (PreK–Adult), Special Education (PreK–K, PreK–Adult, K–Adult, or 5–Adult), and all grade level subject (PreK–Adult or 5–Adult). New specializations may be added to a certificate by completing a program with a 2.5 GPA and meeting test requirements. Persons who complete a program to extend the programmatic level of a content area are exempt from the content area exam if they have three years' experience in the area.

## SPECIALTY CERTIFICATES

- Professional Student Support Certificates are offered for School Counselor, School Nurse, School Psychologist, Speech-Language Pathologist, and Attendance Director. The certificates are offered at three levels that correspond to the levels of teaching certificates. The initial certificate requires a master's degree for all areas except School Nurse, which requires a Registered Nurse License and completion of a School Nurse program, and Attendance Director, which requires completion of a Social Services and Attendance program.

- Career/Technical Education's initial certification requires completion of a program at an institution of higher education with a 3.0 GPA, two years of teaching experience in the endorsement area, and satisfaction of test requirements. Permits require at least a high school diploma or GED, credentials recognized in the industry, work experience, and satisfaction of test requirements.

- Authorizations are available for positions where no specialization exists for the Professional or Career/Technical Education Certificates (e.g., coaching, Junior ROTC, Psychologists for Test Administration). Generally, these authorizations require a bachelor's degree with minimum GPA and are valid for one year.

## TESTING AND SPECIAL REQUIREMENTS

- All candidates for the Provisional Professional Certificate must pass the Praxis I: Pre-Professional Skills Test (PPST). Waivers allow SAT or ACT scores to substitute for the PPST score.

- All candidates for the Provisional Professional Certificate must take the appropriate Praxis II: Subject Assessments/Specialty Area assessments and appropriate grade level Praxis II: Principles of Learning and Teaching (PLT).

- Candidates who passed the National Evaluation Systems (NES) test for special education are not required to take the Praxis II: Education of Exceptional Students: Core Content Knowledge Test.

- Candidates for admission to alternative route programs in general education must pass PPST and the appropriate Praxis II: Subject Assessment. Candidates for admission to alternate route programs in special education must pass the PPST. Alternate route candidates must pass the appropriate PLT to qualify for the Professional Certificate.

- Candidates who hold a Professional Certificate and wish to add a new specialization must pass the appropriate Praxis II: Subject Assessment.

- California Achievement Tests in reading, writing, and mathematics or the PPST are required for Career/Technical permits. Candidates for certificates must meet the same test requirements as professional teachers.

- All candidates for certification must complete 3 semester hours in special education and diversity.

- Candidates must be U.S. citizens. A Permit for Non-U.S. Citizen is available for qualified applicants.

## SPECIAL SITUATIONS AND NOTES

- West Virginia participates in the NASDTEC Interstate Agreement. Out-of-state applicants who have a bachelor's degree with a 2.5 GPA, have completed a teacher preparation program, and met the test requirements may qualify for the Initial (Provisional) Professional Certificate. Those who hold a valid license and have 3 years' experience during the past seven years qualify for a comparable Professional Certificate. Those who have a valid license and five years of experience may qualify for the Permanent Professional Certificate. At least one year of experience must be in West Virginia to obtain the five-year Professional Certificate or the Permanent

Certificate. Applicants who hold NBPTS certification or who have three years' experience are exempt from test requirements.

- Foreign applicants must have their credentials evaluated by an evaluation service.

- All Aides I, II, III, and IV and Paraprofessionals in Title I programs must meet NCLB requirements. They must have high school diploma or GED. In addition, they must have two years of study at an institution of higher education, hold an associate degree, pass a state competency exam, or complete requirements for the Paraprofessional Certificate. The Paraprofessional Certificate requires completing a 36-semester hour program and passing the state competency exam.

- Short-Term and Long-Term Substitute Permits require a bachelor's degree or Nursing Diploma/Associate Degree with a 2.0 GPA, and 18 clock hours of training provided by the local district. In addition, long-term substitutes must complete 12 semester hours of coursework in any specialization area. Long-term permits may also be issued to a person who holds an expired Professional Certificate or a valid or expired out-of-state professional certificate. A short-term substitute may replace the same teacher for 30 consecutive days. A long-term substitute may replace the same teacher for more than 30 consecutive days. Both permits are valid for three years and require 6 semester hours of coursework or 12 clock hours of in-service training for renewal. Substitute Career/Technical Education Permits are also available to persons with at least a high school diploma or GED, work experience, and 18 clock hours of training. Trade and industry specializations have additional requirements.

## USEFUL WEB SITES

- **Certification, contacts, forms, certification status:** wvde.state.wv.us/certification

- **Jobs:** wvde.state.wv.us/jobs

- **School directory:** wvde.state.wv.us/ed_directory

- **Approved programs:** wvde.state.wv.us/certification/educator/approved

- **VA TTT:** wvde.state.wv.us/certification/troops

- **Testing:** wvde.state.wv.us/certification/praxis_scores.html
www.ets.org/praxis (select state requirements)

- **Alternate routes:** wvde.state.wv.us/certification/educator/alternative/summary.html

- **NBPTS:** wvde.state.wv.us/certification/nbpts

# WISCONSIN

## OVERVIEW

Wisconsin has three stages of educator licenses for teaching at the elementary, middle, or secondary levels regardless of how candidates enter the system.

■ **Initial Educator License** is the entry-level license. It is valid for five years and is nonrenewable unless the educator has not been employed for at least two years, in which case a one-year nonrenewable license may be issued.

■ **Professional Educator License** is issued to persons who hold the Initial Educator License, have three years' experience, and complete a Professional Development Plan (PDP) through a portfolio. The license is valid for five years. Educators must design and complete a PDP for renewal. Renewal requirements are waived for persons who complete the NBPTS certification process.

■ **Master Educator License** is issued to persons who have five years' experience as a Professional Educator, hold a master's degree, and complete the Wisconsin Master Educator Assessment Process (WMEAP). It is also issued to persons who achieve NBPTS certification; however, the license is only for the same level and field as the NBPTS certification. The Master Educator license is valid for 10 years or until the NBPTS certification expires, and may be renewed with five years' experience and a formal assessment.

## TRADITIONAL ROUTE

Candidates must complete a bachelor's degree, a professional educator preparation program, and meet test requirements.

## ALTERNATE ROUTE

**Experimental/Innovative Educator Preparation Programs** are nontraditional accelerated programs often developed in partnership between a college/university or regional education agency and a school district to meet needs in shortage areas. A number of programs are offered. They generally require an individual to have a bachelor's degree and five years' experience in an identified subject shortage area. Through a combination of coursework, supervised teaching, mentoring, and assessment, candidates complete requirements for the Initial Educator License or for an additional license.

## TEACHING CATEGORIES

Licenses are offered for the following teaching categories: Early Childhood (Birth–Age 8), Early Childhood-Middle Childhood (Birth–Age 11), Middle Childhood-Early Adolescence (Age 6–12 or 13), Early Adolescence (Age 10–14), Early Adolescence-Adolescence (Age 10–21), and Early Childhood-Adolescence (Birth–Age 21).

Candidates for Middle Childhood Through Early Adolescence (MC-EA) must complete an approved minor. Candidates with minors in mathematics, computer science, language arts, social studies, and science are not required to take subject assessments in those areas because they are covered in the Middle School Content Knowledge exam. Candidates with other minors must take the appropriate subject assessments.

To extend the grade level of a license or to add a new category, an educator must complete a program and obtain endorsement from the institution.

## SPECIALTY CERTIFICATES

■ Pupil Services categories include School Counselor, School Nurse, School Psychologist, and School Social Worker. All require a master's degree except School Nurse, which requires a Registered Nurse License.

■ Supplementary categories include Adaptive Education, Adaptive Physical Education, Assistive Technology, Alternative Education, Bilingual-Bicultural Education, Coaching Athletics, Driver Education, Gifted and Talented, Instructional Library Media Specialist, Reading Teacher, Urban Educator, and Vocational Education.

■ To qualify for the Initial license as Library Media Specialist, candidates must hold or be eligible for a teaching license in another field and complete a library media specialist program. A master's degree is required for the Professional license.

■ Speech-Language Pathology License requires a master's degree and practicum.

■ To qualify for the Indian Language, History and Culture License, candidates must hold or be eligible for a teaching license and be recommended by the tribe.

■ School Audiologist License requires a master's degree.

■ Candidates for the School Occupational Therapy License and School Physical Therapy License, candidates must hold certification or licensure by the appropriate credentialing board.

## TESTING AND SPECIAL REQUIREMENTS

- Candidates for initial admission to professional education programs must pass the Praxis I: Pre-Professional Skills Test (PPST).

- All candidates in professional education programs and alternative programs must pass the appropriate Praxis II: Subject Assessments.

- Applicants who have worked, lived, or attended classes in a U.S. territory, Canada, Great Britain, or a state other than Wisconsin in the past 20 years (after age 17) must submit fingerprint cards. Others are not required to submit fingerprint cards.

## SPECIAL SITUATIONS AND NOTES

- Wisconsin does not have complete reciprocity with any other states. Therefore, most out-of-state applicants who graduated from a comparable teacher preparation program receive the Initial Educator License with Stipulations or the Professional Educator License with Stipulations. These licenses are nonrenewable and stipulations must be fulfilled within the term of the license. Wisconsin licenses are based on completion of teacher preparation programs in other states, not on licenses. However, Wisconsin does have an exchange agreement with Illinois, Iowa, Kansas, Michigan, Missouri, Nebraska, Oklahoma, and South Dakota. Persons who hold a valid license from one of these states have fewer stipulations. Out-of-state applicants must pass the PPST or an equivalent test required in the state where they were licensed. Applicants must also pass the Praxis II: Subject Assessments required in Wisconsin. A one-year nonrenewable license is available to applicants who need to meet this requirement. Applicants who hold NBPTS certification may apply for the Master Educator License when they meet all Wisconsin requirements.

- Foreign applicants must have their credentials evaluated by an evaluation service. See the Web site for more information.

- Specific requirements are set by local school districts by the Special Education Aide License. All paraprofessionals in Title I programs must have two years of study at an institution of higher education or an associate degree or demonstrate competency on a formal assessment. Each local school district has authority to develop its own assessment tool. Other districts are not required to accept the credentials of a paraprofessional who has completed an assessment in a different district.

- A person who has completed an educator training program in any state is eligible for the Five-Year Substitute Educator License, which allows the holder to substitute for more than 20 consecutive days in the same assignment in the area in which they are endorsed. Persons who hold the Three-Year Substitute Teaching Permit may not substitute more than 20 consecutive days in the same assignment. This permit requires a nonteaching bachelor's degree.

## USEFUL WEB SITES

- **Licensing:** dpi.wi.gov/tepdl/index.html

- **Contacts:** dpi.wi.gov/tepdl/feedback.html

- **Jobs:** dpi.wi.gov/tepdl/resource.html
  www.wisconsin.gov/state/core/education.html

- **School directory:** dpi.wi.gov/schldist.html

- **Approved programs:** dpi.wi.gov/tepdl/indexed.html

- **License inquiry:** dpi.wi.gov/tepdl/lisearch.html

- **Substitutes:** dpi.wi.gov/tepdl/sublic.html
  dpi.wi.gov/tepdl/bssub.html

- **Testing:** dpi.wi.gov/tepdl/index.html
  www.ets.org/praxis (select state requirements)

- **Alternate routes:** dpi.wi.gov/tepdl/altern.html

- **Forms:** dpi.wi.gov/tepdl/applications.html

- **Fees:** dpi.wi.gov/tepdl/appfee.html

- **Foreign applicants:** dpi.wi.gov/tepdl/foreign.html

- **NBPTS:** dpi.wi.gov/tepdl/nblicens.html

- **WI TTT:** dva.state.wi.us/Emp_troopsteachers.asp

- **Paraprofessionals:** dpi.wi.gov/cal/calpara.html

# WYOMING

## OVERVIEW

All teachers and pupil personnel in Wyoming must have a certificate to teach at the elementary, middle, or secondary level. Only one certificate is issued.

■ **Standard Certificate** is issued to persons who meet all requirements. It is valid for five years and may be renewed with five semester hours or 75 clock hours of continuing education. Certification by the NBPTS satisfies all renewal requirements.

### TRADITIONAL ROUTE

Candidates must complete a bachelor's degree from a teacher preparation program including student teaching, and meet the constitution requirement and all test requirements. Candidates who have completed a program may receive authorization to teach for one year while meeting test requirements.

### ALTERNATE ROUTE

Alternative certification allows a person who holds a bachelor's degree in a secondary subject area to begin teaching while completing requirements for a teaching certificate. Candidates must be employed in a school. A person may teach under a temporary permit for one year and the permit may be renewed twice. By the end of three years, candidates must complete a program or a portfolio that demonstrates how they meet the standards in order to qualify for certification. A person may also add an endorsement through an alternative certification program.

**Northern Plains Transition to Teaching (Montana State University)** is only available at the secondary level. Candidates enter the program, complete 9 hours of preservice training, and then find employment. It takes one to three years to complete the program. Portions of the program are conducted through distance learning. A one-year paid teaching experience is included. Candidates have the option to earn a master's degree in addition to certification.

### ENDORSEMENTS

Each certificate specifies a grade level and endorsements. Grade levels include Pre-School Years (Age 3–5), Elementary (K–6), Middle Level (5–8), Secondary areas (7–12), and all grade-level subjects (K–12). Endorsements specify subject areas that are valid for a particular grade level, or service areas for pupil personnel certificates.

### SPECIALTY CERTIFICATES

■ Teachers who hold the Standard Certificate may add the following areas: Coaching, Gifted and Talented, and Driver Education.

■ Candidates for School Nurse must have a bachelor's degree in nursing and a Registered Nurse License.

■ Graduate programs for Educational Diagnostician and School Counselor require completion of a teacher preparation program and appropriate experience.

■ Graduate programs for School Audiologist, School Psychologist, School Social Worker, and Speech-Language Pathologist do not require a teaching certificate.

■ An endorsement for assistant coach requires a high school diploma or GED, completion of Care and Prevention of Athletic Injuries course, CPR and First Aid training, and training in the philosophy of coaching and theory of the sport. In addition, an endorsement for head coach requires three years' experience and completion of courses in Child Growth and Development and Adolescent Psychology.

■ The Native Language Endorsement requires approval by the tribal council.

### TESTING AND SPECIAL REQUIREMENTS

■ All candidates for initial certification must take the appropriate Praxis II test. Candidates for Early Childhood, Elementary Education, and Elementary Special Education must take Elementary Education: Curriculum, Instruction, and Assessment. Candidates for Secondary Education must take Principles of Learning and Teaching (PLT): Grades 7–12. Candidates for Secondary Special Education, Social Worker, and K–12 subjects may choose PLT Grades 7–12 or Grades 5–9. Speech-Language Pathologists must take the Praxis II test required for American Speech-Language-Hearing Association (ASHA) certification.

■ All candidates must complete a course or exam on both the U.S. Constitution and the Wyoming Constitution.

### SPECIAL SITUATIONS AND NOTES

■ Wyoming participates in the NASDTEC Interstate Agreement. Out-of-state applicants who have completed a teacher preparation program or hold a current certificate may qualify for a comparable Wyoming certificate. Endorsement areas require a major or three years of experience during the past six years. Applicants who receive Standard Certificates have five years to complete all Wyoming requirements.

- Foreign applicants must have their credentials evaluated by an evaluation service. See the Web site for more information.

- Paraprofessionals must have a high school diploma or GED and have two years of study at an institution of higher education, or an associate degree, or demonstrate competency on a formal state or local assessment.

- The Substitute Permit allows the holder to substitute for 45 consecutive days in the same assignment. Candidates must have an associate degree or 65 semester hours of study at an institution of higher education, or they must have a high school diploma or GED, 24 clock hours of in-service training, and 10 clock hours of observation at each grade level (elementary, middle, or secondary) for which the permit will be authorized. The permit is valid for five years and requires five semester hours of development for renewal.

## USEFUL WEB SITES

- **Certification, contacts:** ptsb.state.wy.us

- **Jobs:** www.wsba-wy.org
www.teachers-teachers.com/wyoming.cfm
wyjobs.state.wy.us/appview/wjn_home.asp

- **School directory:** www.k12.wy.us/public_ed/schools.html

- **Testing:** ptsb.state.wy.us/testing.asp
www.ets.org/praxis (select state requirements)

- **Forms:** ptsb.state.wy.us/applicationsList.asp

- **Alternate routes:** ptsb.state.wy.us/altCert.asp

- **Foreign applicants:** ptsb.state.wy.us/faq.asp

- **WY TTT:** www.montana.edu/ttt

# Part III

# TEACHING OPPORTUNITIES

# Chapter 4

# FINDING JOBS IN TEACHING

The U.S. Bureau of Labor Statistics (BLS) predicts that student enrollment will rise slowly over the next ten years, and the number of students needing special education services is expected to increase more quickly. As a result, job prospects for teachers and other education personnel are expected to increase. In fact, the BLS projects that job opportunities in the education field should be good to excellent from 2004 to 2014. Opportunities are predicted to be particularly good in geographic and subject shortage areas. The projected increase in employment over the period is 16.7 percent for elementary and middle school teachers, 14.0 percent for secondary teachers, and 20.9 percent for special education teachers. The resulting overall projected increase is 18.3 percent, which is higher than the average across all industries. The increase in jobs for teacher assistants is expected to be about average, but demand will be greater for those in special education and those who can speak a language other than English. Vocational teachers will also be in demand.

In addition to the increase in young Americans, the graying of the teacher staff will add to the demand for teachers. In 2004, nearly 50 percent of elementary, middle, and secondary teachers, and over 50 percent of special education teachers were 45 or older according to the BLS. This greater-than-average number of older teachers is expected to contribute to a high retirement level over the next ten years. In the "Profile of Teachers in the U.S. 2005" the National Center for Education Information (NCEI) reports that in 2005, 42 percent of elementary and secondary teachers were over 50. Within five years, 40 percent of current teachers in public schools expect to have left teaching, because of retirement and other attrition, according to the profile.

The BLS reports that median earnings in 2004 were $43,160 for elementary teachers, $43,670 for middle school teachers, $45,650 for secondary teachers, and $45,700 for special education teachers. This places teaching among the high-paying occupations. From 2004 to 2014, the growth rate in teacher salaries is projected to be 17 percent, which is higher than the 14 percent projected for the average of all industries.

## TEACHER SHORTAGE AREAS

According to the National Teacher Recruitment Clearinghouse, teacher shortages occur in geographic areas, subject areas, and teacher diversity. The Clearinghouse Web site describes these shortages:

- **Geographic areas:** Teacher shortages are most acute in low-income urban and rural districts. According to the BLS, shortages will occur in states in the West where the population is growing rapidly, particularly Alaska, California, Hawaii, Idaho, New Mexico, and Utah. Shortages will occur to a lesser extent in states in the South where the population is rising but not as rapidly.

- **Subject areas:** The subjects most affected by teacher shortages are science, mathematics, special education, bilingual education, and English as a second language. Some states also report shortages of world language teachers.

- **Teacher diversity:** As the student population grows increasingly more multi-ethnic and multicultural, the demand grows for a more diverse teaching force. Urban districts in particular report a need for teachers of color. Male teachers are also in demand in urban districts, particularly at the elementary level.

## FINDING A JOB

The successful job search requires a variety of resources to identify opportunities and to secure employment. The following are some suggested resources:

- **College and University Placement Centers:** Placement centers have valuable information and also offer seminars and workshops on job vacancies, careers, resumes, and interviewing skills. In addition, the centers bring recruiters to campus to interview candidates.

- **School districts:** Applicants should forward their cover letter and resume to districts where they are interested in teaching.

- **Online job banks:**

  - Each state maintains a posting of education vacancies, usually accessible from the state department of education Web site or the certification Web site. Often, the postings are found on the state education recruiting Web site. Check the profiles in Chapter 3 for the URLs. Although not all districts post their vacancies, district Web sites are among the best places to search. These sites often contain additional resources, links to state certification requirements, summaries about state-approved preparation programs and alternate route programs, and information about living and working in the state. Most allow applicants to post their resumes online and apply for jobs at the same time.

  - Many states have a job bank on their state Web site. These are not specifically for education jobs, but they usually have a menu of occupations that includes education. Check the Web site information in the profiles in Chapter 3.

- A number of national education job banks post vacancies from school districts and other education organizations nationwide. Applicants may post their resumes online at no cost.

- **Classified ads:** Searching the classified ads in city newspapers is a good place to find local vacancies. Some states post classified ads from major newspapers on a section of the state Web site.

- **Job fairs:** Some states hold statewide job fairs for educators. Information about these may be found on state recruitment Web sites. See the National Teacher Recruitment Clearinghouse Web site for listings and links.

- **Networking:** As in all job searches, networking with other people often produces leads to job openings.

## INCENTIVES

The BLS projects that qualified teachers will be in demand and that states will offer bonuses and higher pay to attract and retain outstanding individuals. The Federal government, states, and large cities already offer some incentives and bonuses.

- **Loan forgiveness:** Federal student-aid loans may be canceled or deferred for teachers who serve in subject shortage areas or low-income areas.

- **The Teacher Next Door:** The U.S. Department of Housing and Urban Development (HUD) sponsors this program. It allows teachers to purchase homes for half of the list price in low- to moderate-income areas where they teach. The teacher must agree to live in the home for three years.

- New York City offers a housing subsidy to science, math, and special education teachers who work in high-needs schools. The subsidy will be as much as $14,600 over a several-year period.

- Some states offer signing bonuses for new teachers in high-needs districts or subject areas with a shortage of teachers. Scholarships and other forms of financial aid for students are also available. Where the programs are offered, state department of education or certification Web sites describe them.

- Most states offer stipends to pay for the cost of obtaining NBPTS certification. Teachers who obtain the certification also receive an annual bonus during the period of validity.

## VALUABLE RESOURCES

National Teacher Recruitment Clearinghouse is a comprehensive online resource for job seekers and employers. Recruiting New Teachers, Inc. (RNT) maintains the clearinghouse. The online job bank is actually a portal to more than 900 job banks. In addition, the Web site contains information on becoming a teacher, conducting a job

search, routes to teaching, licensure, and certification. Links are provided to state departments of education including their alternative route programs and sources of financial aid.

The American Association for Employment in Education (AAEE) is an organization of placement center directors at colleges and universities, recruiters from school systems, representatives from state education departments, teacher education faculty, administrators, and representatives of professional organizations. The Association publishes some guides for job hunters and hosts a job posting service.

Regional Education Applicant Placement (USREAP) is a nationwide online service for recruitment and application. School districts in REAP states post vacancies for teachers, support services personnel, and administrators, and applicants may apply for as many positions as they want. States that have REAP networks are Connecticut, Georgia, Iowa, Kentucky, Michigan, Missouri, New Mexico, New York, Ohio, Pennsylvania, Texas, and Wisconsin.

## TWO TARGETED PROGRAMS FOR ALTERNATE ROUTE CANDIDATES

Troops to Teachers (TTT) helps persons in the U.S. military transition to teaching. The program assists candidates in finding programs that lead to certification, obtaining information about certification requirements, and finding jobs. Stipends and bonuses are available to qualified persons who commit to teaching in high-needs schools for three years.

Spouses to Teachers (STT) is a complementary program to Troops to Teachers. It assists spouses of military personnel to become teachers. Financial aid is available to pay for certification exams. This is currently a pilot program and only available in the following states: California, Colorado, Florida, Georgia, Kansas, Louisiana, Nebraska, Nevada, New Mexico, North Carolina, South Carolina, Texas, Utah, and Virginia.

## ADDITIONAL RESOURCES

- **ABC Teaching Jobs:** www.abcteachingjobs.com
  Job postings for K–12 schools in all 50 States, the District of Columbia, and Puerto Rico. No fee for applicants. Teachers, support services, and administrators. Links to professional associations.

- **American Association for Employment in Education:** www.aaee.org

- **America's Career InfoNet:** www.acinet.org/acinet
  Resources for job searches, preparing a resume, and obtaining credentials. Links to job banks for primary, secondary, and special education teachers.

- **America's Job Bank:** www.ajb.org
  Posting of education positions mostly in private and corporate environments, few in public schools.

- **Bureau of Labor Statistics, U.S. Department of Labor:** *Occupational Outlook Handbook, 2006-07 Edition,* on the Internet at www.bls.gov/oco/home.htm (visited April 17, 2006).

Outlook and projections for occupations in education, including preschool, kindergarten, elementary, middle, secondary, and special education teachers, and counselors.

- **EducationAmerica.net:** www.educationamerica.net
Job postings nationwide. No fee for applicants. Teacher, support services, and administrators.

- **Federal Student Aid:** studentaid.ed.gov/PORTALSWeb App/students/english/teachercancel.jsp?tab=repaying
Teacher loan forgiveness and other financial assistance.

- **K–12 Jobs:** www.k12jobs.com
Job posting nationwide. No fee for applicants. Teachers and administrators. Links to state certification departments and school Web sites, listing of job fairs, salary information, and job outlook.

- **National Teacher Recruitment Clearinghouse:** www.recruitingteachers.org

- **Regional Education Applicant Placement (USREAP):** www.usreap.net

- **Teachers-Teachers:** www.teachers-teachers.com
Job postings for approximately 2,000 school districts nationwide. No fee for applicants. Teachers, support services, and administrators. E-mail service between prospective employers and candidates. Applicants prepare resumes online. Links to state departments of education; events directory; tips for cover letters, resumes, and interviews; salary information; guide to preparing resumes.

- **The Teacher Center:** www.theteachercenter.org
Information on the teaching profession, paths to teacher preparation, information on certification and testing requirements, links to job search sites in the Southern Regional Education Board (SREB) states (Alabama, Arkansas, Delaware, Florida, Georgia, Kentucky, Louisiana, Maryland, Mississippi, North Carolina, Oklahoma, South Carolina, Tennessee, Texas, Virginia, and West Virginia), links to teacher preparation programs and education resources in SREB states.

- **Troops to Teachers (TTT):** www.proudtoserveagain. com.
Program for military personnel transitioning to teaching. Provides assistance and funding. Maintains a job bank and links to other job banks.

- **Visiting International Faculty Program:** www. vifprogram.com
Teaching opportunities for international teachers in the United States.

- **Western States Certification Consortium:** www. pathway2teach.org
Works with Troops to Teachers and Spouses to Teachers to identify alternative pathways to certification that are distance-delivered.

# Part IV

# TEST PREPARATION AND PRACTICE

# Chapter 5

# TEST-TAKING TIPS

How well you handle test taking can make a difference in how well you do on tests. This chapter will help you improve your test-taking skills and master your test anxiety

## PREPARING FOR THE TEST

There are a number of things you can do to prepare for the test. One is to be enthusiastic about taking the test. Remember that this test is the means to the credential that will open a career as an educator to you.

Several days before the test, check out the test site. Take a test run to see how long it takes to get there. Find parking lots or garages in case there is no on-street parking. If you can, go inside the testing site and see the room in which you'll be taking the test. What does it look like? Find out where the restrooms are, too.

The night before the test, follow your regular routine. Don't do any special studying. Most of all, do get a good night's sleep. You need a clear head for the next day. Get ready what you need for the test. Be sure you have four number 2 pencils, an eraser, and a pen if you are taking a pencil-and-paper test. Regardless of how you take the test, you need your admission ticket, photo identification, a watch, and perhaps a sweater in case the room is cold. If the test takes several hours, bring a snack or lunch.

## ON TEST DAY

On the morning of the test, eat what you usually have for breakfast. If you don't eat breakfast, this is not the morning to have scrambled eggs and waffles, but you might want a light snack. Wear comfortable, layered clothes. Depending on the temperature in the testing room, you may need to take off or put on some layers. You don't have to dress like a model, but don't look sloppy. How we look affects how we feel and that can affect how we do.

Leave home so that you will arrive at least 30 minutes before the test. This will give you plenty of time to park, visit the restroom, get to the testing room, and check in without rushing.

If you have a choice of seats, sit where you think you can concentrate best. If you tend to look out the window a lot, sit across the room from the windows. Don't sit by the door if you can help it. If you're left-handed, ask for a left-handed desk. You may not get it, but it never hurts to ask.

### During the Test

Don't let others bother you. If someone near you sighs as though he is dying, or another person writes and erases furiously, block them out. Don't let their problems become

yours. Think only about doing your best. Use the relaxation techniques explained on page 127 to keep you focused.

Remember that you know a lot more than you think you do. You have studied this book and you know what to expect. Just keep working your way through the test. Think of the test as a game and your credential is the prize.

## SHARPENING YOUR TEST-TAKING SKILLS

Be sure that your name and all the supplementary information are correct. Even though you are familiar with the directions, read them carefully.

Mark machine-scored answer sheets carefully and completely. First, outline the answer oval or circle, and then fill it in. Any erasures should be complete. If you skip any questions, be sure to skip the same numbers on the answer sheet. Do not make any stray marks on the answer sheet.

If you are using a computer-assisted test, be sure that you understand how to use the particular computer model and how the test program works.

### Pacing Yourself

Be sure to pace yourself. When the proctor says you may start, note the time on your test booklet. Add a little less than half the time allotted for that section, and write that time at the middle question in the test booklet. Double the time and write it next to the last question. When you get to the half-way point as you work through the test, you can check and see whether your are ahead of or behind your schedule. This system allows for some time for review at the end of the test. Using this system, you will not need to look at your watch all the time either.

### Insurance

Before you start the test, mark the last ten answers in the section with the same letter (all Bs or Cs, for instance). Thus, if you haven't finished when the time is up, you have at least one chance in four or five of getting the last ten question correct. If you don't mark them, you have no chance of getting them right. As you work through the test and come to the last questions, you can readily change the answers. Remember, there is no penalty for guessing.

### Tackling a Question

Unless you are given scratch paper, write, mark, and solve problems on the test.

Read the questions carefully. Don't jump to conclusions. Does it say *must* or *may, and* or *or, always* or *sometimes*? Break complicated questions into parts. Check your answer against each part. Underline key words.

*Example:*

12. The fraction $\frac{12}{11}$ is between the numbers given in each of the following pairs except

    Underline *between* and *except.*

You may sometimes find it useful to cross out the answers that you can easily see are unlikely or impossible.

*Example:*

5. $\sqrt{32}$ is between

    **(A)** 100 and 1,000
    **(B)** 3 and 4
    **(C)** 5 and 6
    **(D)** 15 and 16
    **(E)** 60 and 64

The square root of 31 must be less than 31. So, eliminate choices (A) and (E). Choice (D) is half of 31, which is unlikely.

If you cannot decide between two answers, choose one, circle it, and put a mark by the number of the question. Indicate your choice on the answer sheet, and put a mark by that number as well. (Be sure to erase all extra marks on the answer sheet before you hand it in.) Don't leave an answer unmarked. You will lose your place more easily if you do, as well as missing a chance to get the right answer.

A question must earn your time and attention. If you haven't decided on an answer after 1 minute, mark it and go on. If you have no idea what the answer is, pick choice (B) or (C) or (D), but not the same letter as the answer just above or just below. Don't leave an answer blank. The mark by the number shows that you should go back to it after you have finished the section, if you have enough time. If the question is a super-puzzler, put two marks by it. There are only a few two-mark questions on each test. After you review each questionable answer, look only at the choices not crossed out. Make your decision and *erase* the mark by the number of the question on the answer sheet. Do the super-puzzlers (two marks) last. Since all the questions count equally, spend your time on those that are easiest for you. It's not a good idea to spend 5 minutes on a single question when in the same time you could be answering five questions.

When you guess, avoid such answers as "none of the above" and "it cannot be determined." They are usually put in when the test-maker cannot think of another choice. Of course, they must be correct once in a while, just to keep you guessing, but the averages are against it.

If you have a choice of combinations of numbered answers, and you're not sure of the answer, choose the one with the number that is used most often in the answers.

*Example:*

    **(A)** I
    **(B)** II
    **(C)** III
    **(D)** I and II
    **(E)** II and III

I is used two times, II is used three times, and III appears twice. The best guess is choice (B).

Work quickly, but not hastily. Mark your answers carefully. Go over the test after you have finished, making sure that all your answers are in the right space. Return to those questions you checked for further thought. Reread the directions, questions, and answers. Check your calculations. Don't be afraid to change an answer. *Erase all extra marks on the answer sheet.* Check identical answers on successive questions carefully, especially if there are three or more in a row.

## STRATEGIES FOR SPECIFIC QUESTIONS

### Reading

You will read a short passage, from one sentence to several paragraphs. There will be from one to five questions after each passage. First, quickly read the stems of the questions that pertain to the passage.

*Example:*

13. The most appropriate title is

    **(A)** Clarity
    **(B)** The Placement of Modifiers
    **(C)** The Purpose of Writing
    **(D)** The First Rule
    **(E)** Ideals

"The most appropriate title is" constitutes the stem of the question.

Decide whether the question involves interpretation or facts. Put I for interpretation and F for facts by the question. The, read the passage carefully, keeping the questions in mind. Underline key words ad you go, especially those that represent facts. Answer as many of the questions as you can. Then, reread the passage and answer the remaining questions. If absolutely necessary, read the paragraph a third time. Take your best shot at the remaining questions. Remember the marking technique.

Check the answer. Reread the sentence within the paragraph that supports the answer to be sure it is correct. Be certain the answer covers all parts of the question.

Don't add facts you happen to know. The questions test your ability to read and understand *only* the given passage. Forget your own conclusions.

Don't expect to find the answer to an inferential question stated word for word in a passage.

Don't pick a specific answer when a general one is asked for.

If you are still unsure about a question even after three reading of the passage, don't return to it unless you have extra time at the end. It takes too long to reread the passage.

### Sentence Completion

As you read the sentence, look for clues in its structure or rhythm that tell you what kinds of words will be best suited for filling in the blanks. Watch for key words in the sentence. Guess the answer even before consulting the choices. One choice will likely match or approximate your guess.

Look for clue words that indicate the blanks have contrasting meanings. For example, *not ... but, rather than,* and *whereas.* Be alert to clues of similarity, such as *not only ... but also* and *as well as.*

The part of the sentence without the blank will often define or suggest what the missing word should be. Start with that part of the sentence and work backward.

When there are two blanks, and you don't find an answer choice that fits the first one, try to find choices that fit the second blank. Then go back to the first blank.

### Mathematics

Some tests give formulas at the beginning of the test, others don't. Look for them, and if they are given, be sure to use them. However, don't depend on them being there.

Read each question carefully, so that you solve for what is asked. Estimate the answer first, and then work it out. Do all of your work on the test, unless scratch paper is provided. Cross out answers that are not possible. This narrows your choices and may leave you with only one answer.

Study graphs carefully. Are they to scale?

Round off amounts when you're asked for an approximate answer.

Draw a diagram or sketch and label it.

Check your calculations. Copy correctly. Make your work columns and figures neat to avoid errors. Work quickly, but don't get sloppy.

Watch for mixed units of measure in the questions and answers. Eliminate answers with wrong units, and, when in doubt, those with the highest and lowest figures.

When a question asks you to find an exception, look for some element common to all the choices except one. The choice without that element is your answer.

You can try out each answer to see whether it works in the question. Usually, there is a very simple or short-cut solution. Be alert for it.

Most of your mistakes will be due to carelessness in reading, not to your inability to do the math. Reread the question. Triple-check the problem, if there is time.

What to do if you don't have any idea what the answer is: If all the answer choices from a series, such as 4, 6, 8, 10, and 12, avoid the extremes—4 and 12. If you are to find the largest number that will work, pick the largest or next-to-largest number. Remember, there is no penalty for guessing.

### Writing

The topics are drawn from your personal observations and experiences. The topics are analytical or expressive. They are usually changed each time the tests are given. Everyone taking the test on the same day ordinarily writes on the same topic(s).

Spend 10 minutes on each topic, organizing your thoughts.

Do not stray from the topic title, or your essay will not count. If you don't like the topic and think you could write a better essay on another topic, resist the impulse.

Support your generalizations with specific examples. Be as specific and concrete as possible.

Write with care and precision. Scoring is based on organization, flow, cohesiveness, focus on the subject matter, level of vocabulary, strength of supporting arguments, mechanics, and style.

- **One essay:** You will have 45 minutes to write on one of two topics. Write on the topic with which you are most comfortable.

- **Two essay:** You will be asked to write about two topics in 60 minutes. Spend 30 minutes on each or twenty minutes on one and 40 minutes on the other. Write on the topic that you feel most comfortable about first.

### Grammar

Generally, choose the answer that "sounds" best to you. Remember that the grammar being tested is written, not spoken usage; therefore, the language will be somewhat formal. Beware, however, of sentences that sound too formal.

### Professional Knowledge

Some questions are factual, and you'll choose the answer you've learned or the one that seems most logical.

When questions deal with opinion, keep in mind current attitudes of educators and administrators. When in doubt, ask yourself: Which answer will benefit the child most? Which answer asks everyone's opinion? Which answer gets the most people involved?

## ABOUT THAT TEST ANXIETY

Now that you are armed with some specific information about how to prepare for Test Day and how to attack test questions, you should be feeling better. However, there are few people who don't experience some test anxiety. You may not be able to get rid of it completely, but you can tame it.

### Relaxation Techniques

Practice the following techniques to help you avoid tension and gain a degree of calmness. It's important to practice these techniques before the test, so that you can use them automatically during the test.

- First, close your eyes and take a mini vacation. Picture the calmest environment that you can think of—the beach, the mountains, a garden. Put yourself there. Enjoy the tranquility. After 15 to 30 seconds, open your eyes. You will feel relaxed and refreshed.

- Second, concentrate on your breathing. Breathe slowly, breathing out all the tension.

- Third, unclench your muscles. Stretch your legs and relax. Rotate your ankles. Stretch your arms forward and relax them. Clench your fists and relax them. Rotate your shoulders to release the tension in the muscles between your shoulder blades. Close your eyes and roll your head on your neck, four times to the right and four times to the left. These techniques are useful whenever you feel tense, not just during tests.

**Visualizing Test Day**

Preparing for the test psychologically can also help you keep your jitters in check. Begin by imagining the scene:

You arrive at the test site in plenty of time. You have all your supplies with you. You meet others who are also there to take the test. Some of them may be talking about how nervous they are about taking the test. You cannot control what others say, but you can control your reactions and responses. You can ignore them, walk away, try changing the subject, or say, "I'd rather not talk right now." Your job is to protect your inner calm and keep positive images in your mind.

You walk into the room, get checked off the master list, find a seat or go to your assigned seat, and sit down. Because you have plenty of time, you don't have to rush. You are now ready to take the test that will lead to your initial certification. Congratulations!

# Chapter 6

# PRACTICE TESTS

The reading, mathematics, and writing sections of the practice tests can be used to practice for the California Basic Educational Skills Test (CBEST) and the Pre-Professional Skills Test (PPST) or Praxis I. They are also useful in preparing for teacher certification tests administered by Arizona, Colorado, Florida, Illinois, Massachusetts, New York, and Oklahoma.

The pre-professional skills test is designed to test your knowledge of teaching concepts, theory, and educational law, with topics that range from classroom management to administration and organization.

# ANSWER SHEET PRACTICE TEST 1

## READING

1. Ⓐ Ⓑ Ⓒ Ⓓ Ⓔ   11. Ⓐ Ⓑ Ⓒ Ⓓ Ⓔ   21. Ⓐ Ⓑ Ⓒ Ⓓ Ⓔ   31. Ⓐ Ⓑ Ⓒ Ⓓ Ⓔ   41. Ⓐ Ⓑ Ⓒ Ⓓ Ⓔ
2. Ⓐ Ⓑ Ⓒ Ⓓ Ⓔ   12. Ⓐ Ⓑ Ⓒ Ⓓ Ⓔ   22. Ⓐ Ⓑ Ⓒ Ⓓ Ⓔ   32. Ⓐ Ⓑ Ⓒ Ⓓ Ⓔ   42. Ⓐ Ⓑ Ⓒ Ⓓ Ⓔ
3. Ⓐ Ⓑ Ⓒ Ⓓ Ⓔ   13. Ⓐ Ⓑ Ⓒ Ⓓ Ⓔ   23. Ⓐ Ⓑ Ⓒ Ⓓ Ⓔ   33. Ⓐ Ⓑ Ⓒ Ⓓ Ⓔ   43. Ⓐ Ⓑ Ⓒ Ⓓ Ⓔ
4. Ⓐ Ⓑ Ⓒ Ⓓ Ⓔ   14. Ⓐ Ⓑ Ⓒ Ⓓ Ⓔ   24. Ⓐ Ⓑ Ⓒ Ⓓ Ⓔ   34. Ⓐ Ⓑ Ⓒ Ⓓ Ⓔ   44. Ⓐ Ⓑ Ⓒ Ⓓ Ⓔ
5. Ⓐ Ⓑ Ⓒ Ⓓ Ⓔ   15. Ⓐ Ⓑ Ⓒ Ⓓ Ⓔ   25. Ⓐ Ⓑ Ⓒ Ⓓ Ⓔ   35. Ⓐ Ⓑ Ⓒ Ⓓ Ⓔ   45. Ⓐ Ⓑ Ⓒ Ⓓ Ⓔ
6. Ⓐ Ⓑ Ⓒ Ⓓ Ⓔ   16. Ⓐ Ⓑ Ⓒ Ⓓ Ⓔ   26. Ⓐ Ⓑ Ⓒ Ⓓ Ⓔ   36. Ⓐ Ⓑ Ⓒ Ⓓ Ⓔ   46. Ⓐ Ⓑ Ⓒ Ⓓ Ⓔ
7. Ⓐ Ⓑ Ⓒ Ⓓ Ⓔ   17. Ⓐ Ⓑ Ⓒ Ⓓ Ⓔ   27. Ⓐ Ⓑ Ⓒ Ⓓ Ⓔ   37. Ⓐ Ⓑ Ⓒ Ⓓ Ⓔ   47. Ⓐ Ⓑ Ⓒ Ⓓ Ⓔ
8. Ⓐ Ⓑ Ⓒ Ⓓ Ⓔ   18. Ⓐ Ⓑ Ⓒ Ⓓ Ⓔ   28. Ⓐ Ⓑ Ⓒ Ⓓ Ⓔ   38. Ⓐ Ⓑ Ⓒ Ⓓ Ⓔ   48. Ⓐ Ⓑ Ⓒ Ⓓ Ⓔ
9. Ⓐ Ⓑ Ⓒ Ⓓ Ⓔ   19. Ⓐ Ⓑ Ⓒ Ⓓ Ⓔ   29. Ⓐ Ⓑ Ⓒ Ⓓ Ⓔ   39. Ⓐ Ⓑ Ⓒ Ⓓ Ⓔ   49. Ⓐ Ⓑ Ⓒ Ⓓ Ⓔ
10. Ⓐ Ⓑ Ⓒ Ⓓ Ⓔ   20. Ⓐ Ⓑ Ⓒ Ⓓ Ⓔ   30. Ⓐ Ⓑ Ⓒ Ⓓ Ⓔ   40. Ⓐ Ⓑ Ⓒ Ⓓ Ⓔ   50. Ⓐ Ⓑ Ⓒ Ⓓ Ⓔ

## MATHEMATICS

1. Ⓐ Ⓑ Ⓒ Ⓓ Ⓔ   11. Ⓐ Ⓑ Ⓒ Ⓓ Ⓔ   21. Ⓐ Ⓑ Ⓒ Ⓓ Ⓔ   31. Ⓐ Ⓑ Ⓒ Ⓓ Ⓔ   41. Ⓐ Ⓑ Ⓒ Ⓓ Ⓔ
2. Ⓐ Ⓑ Ⓒ Ⓓ Ⓔ   12. Ⓐ Ⓑ Ⓒ Ⓓ Ⓔ   22. Ⓐ Ⓑ Ⓒ Ⓓ Ⓔ   32. Ⓐ Ⓑ Ⓒ Ⓓ Ⓔ   42. Ⓐ Ⓑ Ⓒ Ⓓ Ⓔ
3. Ⓐ Ⓑ Ⓒ Ⓓ Ⓔ   13. Ⓐ Ⓑ Ⓒ Ⓓ Ⓔ   23. Ⓐ Ⓑ Ⓒ Ⓓ Ⓔ   33. Ⓐ Ⓑ Ⓒ Ⓓ Ⓔ   43. Ⓐ Ⓑ Ⓒ Ⓓ Ⓔ
4. Ⓐ Ⓑ Ⓒ Ⓓ Ⓔ   14. Ⓐ Ⓑ Ⓒ Ⓓ Ⓔ   24. Ⓐ Ⓑ Ⓒ Ⓓ Ⓔ   34. Ⓐ Ⓑ Ⓒ Ⓓ Ⓔ   44. Ⓐ Ⓑ Ⓒ Ⓓ Ⓔ
5. Ⓐ Ⓑ Ⓒ Ⓓ Ⓔ   15. Ⓐ Ⓑ Ⓒ Ⓓ Ⓔ   25. Ⓐ Ⓑ Ⓒ Ⓓ Ⓔ   35. Ⓐ Ⓑ Ⓒ Ⓓ Ⓔ   45. Ⓐ Ⓑ Ⓒ Ⓓ Ⓔ
6. Ⓐ Ⓑ Ⓒ Ⓓ Ⓔ   16. Ⓐ Ⓑ Ⓒ Ⓓ Ⓔ   26. Ⓐ Ⓑ Ⓒ Ⓓ Ⓔ   36. Ⓐ Ⓑ Ⓒ Ⓓ Ⓔ   46. Ⓐ Ⓑ Ⓒ Ⓓ Ⓔ
7. Ⓐ Ⓑ Ⓒ Ⓓ Ⓔ   17. Ⓐ Ⓑ Ⓒ Ⓓ Ⓔ   27. Ⓐ Ⓑ Ⓒ Ⓓ Ⓔ   37. Ⓐ Ⓑ Ⓒ Ⓓ Ⓔ   47. Ⓐ Ⓑ Ⓒ Ⓓ Ⓔ
8. Ⓐ Ⓑ Ⓒ Ⓓ Ⓔ   18. Ⓐ Ⓑ Ⓒ Ⓓ Ⓔ   28. Ⓐ Ⓑ Ⓒ Ⓓ Ⓔ   38. Ⓐ Ⓑ Ⓒ Ⓓ Ⓔ   48. Ⓐ Ⓑ Ⓒ Ⓓ Ⓔ
9. Ⓐ Ⓑ Ⓒ Ⓓ Ⓔ   19. Ⓐ Ⓑ Ⓒ Ⓓ Ⓔ   29. Ⓐ Ⓑ Ⓒ Ⓓ Ⓔ   39. Ⓐ Ⓑ Ⓒ Ⓓ Ⓔ   49. Ⓐ Ⓑ Ⓒ Ⓓ Ⓔ
10. Ⓐ Ⓑ Ⓒ Ⓓ Ⓔ   20. Ⓐ Ⓑ Ⓒ Ⓓ Ⓔ   30. Ⓐ Ⓑ Ⓒ Ⓓ Ⓔ   40. Ⓐ Ⓑ Ⓒ Ⓓ Ⓔ   50. Ⓐ Ⓑ Ⓒ Ⓓ Ⓔ

**WRITING**

Topic A

_____

_____

_____

_____

_____

_____

_____

_____

_____

_____

_____

_____

_____

_____

_____

_____

_____

_____

_____

_____

_____

_____

_____

_____

_____

_____

_____

_____

_____

_____

_____

Topic B

# PRACTICE TEST 1 (CBEST)

## FORMAT OF THE CBEST

| Reading | 50 Questions | 65 minutes |
|---|---|---|
| Mathematics | 50 Questions | 70 minutes |

———————— *Break* ————————

| Writing | 2 Essays | 60 minutes |
|---|---|---|

## SCORING THE TEST

Raw scores for Reading and Mathematics sections are determined by totaling the number of questions answered correctly. There is no penalty for incorrect answers. Each of the two essays is scored on a scale of 1 (fail) to 4 (pass). Passing scores for both California and Oregon are set at a total scaled score of 123 for all three sections with no section below a scaled score of 37.

# READING

## 65 MINUTES—50 QUESTIONS

**Directions:** Choose the best answer for each question and blacken the corresponding space on the Answer Sheet for Sample Test 1. The correct answers and explanations follow the test.

### QUESTIONS 1–4 REFER TO THE FOLLOWING PASSAGE.

Halley's Comet has been known as the "evil star" since ancient times. It heralds death and disaster. In fact, the word "disaster" evolved from "evil star" or "bad star," which comets were often called. A chronological study shows that there is a correlation between the appearance of comets and waves of epidemics and suicides.

Halley's Comet appeared over Jerusalem in 66 AD, foreshadowing its destruction by the Romans. Mass suicides are recorded at this time, including 960 in Masada. When two comets appeared in 1347, the Black Death swept through Europe, killing 25 million, and a series of mass suicides occurred.

Recordings of associations between comets and mass suicides have been made every time Halley's Comet has neared Earth since the sixteenth century. There was clear evidence of a connection between the comet and suicides, particularly among children, in 1910. Waves of suicides were recorded at the time in Japan, Italy, and Spain. In 1985–1986, a wave of teenage suicides and airline crashes coincided with the return of Halley's Comet.

The appearance of the comet Kahoutek in 1973 coincided with the Watergate scandal, President Nixon's fall, the assassination of Spanish Premier Luis Carrero Blanco, earthquakes in Mexico and Pakistan, which killed 5,500, and droughts in Africa and India, which left 200,000 dead.

Comet Halley frames these events, but does not cause them. Other spectacular comets seem to have influenced some people, resulting in their suicide. Further research of these phenomena continues.

1.  The earliest date linking Halley's Comet with disaster is

    (A) 66 AD
    (B) 960 AD
    (C) 1347 AD
    (D) 1910 AD
    (E) 25,000,000 years ago

2.  The comet Kahoutek caused

    (A) the Watergate scandal and President Nixon's fall
    (B) the assassination of Spanish Premier Luis Carrera Blanco
    (C) earthquakes in Mexico and Pakistan
    (D) droughts in Africa and India
    (E) None of the above

3.  The central idea of the passage is that

    (A) Halley's Comet causes suicides
    (B) comet Kahoutek causes political and natural disasters
    (C) comets cause disasters
    (D) some comets influence some people
    (E) when two comets appear, they cause series of mass suicides

4.  From reading the passage, it can be deduced that a meaning of "distemper" is

    (A) not tempered
    (B) absence of temper
    (C) expelling temper
    (D) deprived of temper
    (E) bad temper

### QUESTIONS 5–7 REFER TO THE FOLLOWING PASSAGE.

Most of us hold jobs most of our lives, yet how many of us really enjoy that work and gain feelings of accomplishment, confidence, fulfillment, and serenity from it? No job is perfect. Regardless of how successful we are, at some time or another we all experience feelings of doubt, inferiority, disgust, or boredom with what we are doing. To gain perspective and add variety to our lives, we need to get away from our work at times.

Usually, people in steady, secure jobs tend to pursue exciting hobbies or competitive sports, while those in dangerous or insecure jobs are content to choose quiet hobbies such as reading, art, or music. Some presidents are known to have read westerns or mysteries for relaxation, while Nathaniel Hawthorne wrote *The Scarlet Letter* during his career as a customs house inspector.

We may wonder that some people's hobbies seem more important to them than their work. Perhaps this is because the hobby makes use of an aptitude the person possesses that is not used in work. If a woman has an aptitude for music, but does not make music her career, joining a band may satisfy her need to express herself musically. Despite a considerable investment of money and many hours of practice, she considers the activity worthwhile because she enjoys it and it makes use of her musical talent. If she does not use her musical aptitude in some way, she might become frustrated. In addition to providing a salary, her job makes use of some of her aptitudes; her hobby makes use of other aptitudes.

In this way, a person can lead a fulfilled and balanced life.

5. From the passage, it can be assumed that Nathaniel Hawthorne

   (A) poured great mental energy into his hobby
   (B) was a boring writer
   (C) wrote westerns and mystery stories
   (D) had an insecure and dangerous job
   (E) revealed his inner feelings only in his writing

6. According to the passage, which of the following is true about a hobby?

   (A) It requires considerable investment of time and money.
   (B) It has value because of the enjoyment we derive from it.
   (C) It is monetarily rewarding.
   (D) It should be related to work in order to be of benefit.
   (E) It uses aptitudes we do not possess.

7. From the passage, we can conclude that

   (A) a person who is deeply interested in her hobby is not leading a balanced life
   (B) we should get away from our jobs as often as possible, or we will lose perspective
   (C) most of us don't have careers that use all of our abilities
   (D) it is essential that everyone have a hobby in order to live a balanced life
   (E) if you have a dangerous job, you should not go white-water rafting

8. This past winter, pilots reported changes in the mighty jet stream, the "rivers" of wind in the upper atmosphere. The weather has deviated considerably from normal: severe snow storms, thunderstorms, tornadoes in unlikely places, exceptionally cold weather, greater amounts of snow and rainfall than usual.

   From this information, one can conclude that

   (A) the weather affects the jet stream
   (B) the jet stream affects the weather
   (C) there will be no more unusual weather
   (D) the weather will return to normal shortly
   (E) it will be an unusually hot summer

9. After members of the Japanese Alpine Club reached the top of Mount Everest, Y. Muira, one of Japan's foremost skiers, skied nearly two miles down a seventy-degree slope. High winds buffeted him, and during the run he fell, losing his right ski. He skied the rest of the distance on one ski, terminating his run just short of a crevasse.

   Muira did not continue his run because

   (A) he was at the bottom of the mountain
   (B) it was too windy
   (C) he couldn't continue skiing on one ski
   (D) it was too difficult to breathe at that altitude
   (E) there was a deep crack in the ice

### QUESTIONS 10–11 REFER TO THE FOLLOWING PASSAGE.

We think of musicals as pure entertainment, but some have explored social issues that were not generally discussed at the time they were produced. The messages were slipped in between the singing and dancing. For example, *Showboat* and *South Pacific* both addressed racial prejudice. In *South Pacific,* there were parallel stories, each emphasizing a certain aspect of racial prejudice.

10. The opinions expressed in the passage

    (A) are racially prejudiced
    (B) are informative without bias
    (C) advocate portraying social issues in musical theatre
    (D) oppose musicals portraying social issues
    (E) have nothing to do with social injustics

11. The people who wrote the words and music for the musicals mentioned in the passage

    (A) did not intend to explore racial prejudice
    (B) deliberately explored racial prejudice
    (C) had strong feelings against racial prejudice
    (D) were unconcerned about racial prejudice
    (E) There is not enough information to make a judgment

12. Two-year colleges received a larger share of their total financial support from state funds and a smaller share from local governments in 2003–04 than they did in the previous year.

    From this we can conclude that

    (A) state governments will increase their influence over two-year colleges
    (B) state governments will decrease their influence over two-year colleges
    (C) local governments will increase their influence over two-year colleges
    (D) two-year colleges will have increased funding
    (E) two-year colleges will have decreased funding

13. Scotland is a kingdom united with England and Wales in Great Britain.

    We can conclude that

    (A) England is the same as Great Britain
    (B) Wales and England make up Great Britain
    (C) Scotland is part of England
    (D) Scotland is part of Great Britain
    (E) Scotland is not part of Great Britain

## QUESTIONS 14–15 REFER TO THE FOLLOWING INFORMATION.

Quicksand pits are found in virtually every part of the world, but falling into one is seldom as horrible as it is depicted in stories.

14. Quicksand is found

    (A) practically everywhere
    (B) here and there
    (C) seldom
    (D) only in stories
    (E) in horrible parts of the world

15. The stories mentioned

    (A) have pictures of quicksand
    (B) have illustrations of quicksand
    (C) describe quicksand experiences
    (D) explain what quicksand is
    (E) give a realistic account of experiences with quicksand

## QUESTIONS 16–21 REFER TO THE FOLLOWING INFORMATION.

### COMPARISON OF AUTO INSURANCE COSTS

|  | With Usual Deductible | With Higher Deductible |
|---|---|---|
| Deductible | $ 150.00 | $ 500.00 |
| Monthly premium | $ 125.00 | $ 100.00 |
| Total coverage | $5,000.00 | $5,000.00 |

One way to hold down the cost of auto insurance is to raise the amount of deductible costs you are willing to pay before the insurance company assumes financial responsibility. This can lower monthly premiums without risking the basic purpose of auto insurance—to cover losses you can't afford to absorb.

16. Besides lower premium payments, what effect does a higher deductible have?

    (A) You pay less if there is damage.
    (B) You must pay more if there is damage.
    (C) You will have more total insurance.
    (D) Your insured amount will be more.
    (E) Your insured amount will be less.

17. How much will be saved in premiums over one year by taking a higher deductible?

    (A) $1,200.00
    (B) $300.00
    (C) $150.00
    (D) $125.00
    (E) $500.00

18. Sam chooses the higher deductible and has an accident with total damages of $1,000.00 after one year. You conclude that

    (A) he saves money with the higher deductible
    (B) he should have kept the usual deductible
    (C) the results would be the same with both policies
    (D) the policies cannot be compared
    (E) Sam should change insurance companies

19. What is Sam's total cost for insurance and repair of the accident in question 18 compared with what he would have paid on the usual deductible?

    (A) $350 more
    (B) $50 less
    (C) $350 less
    (D) $400 more
    (E) $50 more

20. If Sam (who has the higher deductible policy) has an accident that causes $7,000 damage to his car, he will have to pay

    (A) $7,000
    (B) $5,000
    (C) $2,500
    (D) $2,000
    (E) $500

21. Who will benefit the most from the policy he or she has chosen as opposed to the other policy?

| | Person | Deductible | Repair costs per accident | Accidents per year |
|---|---|---|---|---|
| (A) | John | usual | $ 400 | 4 |
| (B) | Harry | usual | $ 500 | 1 |
| (C) | Sam | higher | $ 400 | 2 |
| (D) | Betsy | higher | $4,000 | 1 |
| (E) | Barbara | higher | $ 650 | 4 |

22. "Counting their toes and counting candles on birthday cakes are some of the ways that children can learn math." How can you use this information in the classroom?

    (A) Tell children that math can be used in everyday situations.
    (B) Teach more math in class.
    (C) Start teaching math at a higher level because children already know math.
    (D) Show how math can be used in everyday situations.
    (E) None of the above

**QUESTIONS 23–24 REFERS TO THE FOLLOWING STATEMENT.**

"Growth in state funds for colleges is expected to slow further in 2005."

23. This statement means that state funds for colleges

 (A) will increase in 2005
 (B) will decrease in 2005
 (C) will increase in 2005, but at a lower rate
 (D) will decrease in 2005, but at a lower rate
 (E) decreased during 2005

24. What action would you expect a college to consider because of the statement above?

 I. decreasing enrollment
 II. seeking other sources of funding
 III. decreasing services to students

 (A) I only
 (B) II only
 (C) III only
 (D) I and III only
 (E) I, II, and III

25. "There have been significant increases in four other types of health insurance provided by insurance companies." A logical conclusion is that

 (A) some types of health insurance have decreased
 (B) the previous sentence discussed a type or types of health insurance
 (C) all types of health insurance have increased
 (D) only four types of health insurance have increased
 (E) only insurance companies provide health insurance

26. Complete the following sentence:

 "Students cannot learn to write and compute well unless they first learn how to think; therefore,

 (A) we need to teach students to think."
 (B) writing and computing should be delayed."
 (C) students need to stay home until they can think."
 (D) students need to stay in school longer."
 (E) students who don't learn to think cannot learn to write and compute."

27. Driven by a high wind, dunes creep across deserts, forming a relentless tide of sand.

 Sand in the desert

 (A) can be controlled by planting shrubbery
 (B) stays in the same place
 (C) looks like waves
 (D) goes back and forth like a tide
 (E) cannot be controlled

28. "The Star-Spangled Banner" was written by F.S. Key in 1814. President Wilson ordered it played at military services in 1916. It was designated the national anthem by Act of Congress in 1931.

 (A) "The Star-Spangled Banner" was played at President Wilson's inauguration.
 (B) "The Star-Spangled Banner" became the national anthem under President Wilson.
 (C) President Wilson thought "The Star-Spangled Banner" should be our national anthem.
 (D) "The Star-Spangled Banner" was written more than 100 years before being designated the national anthem.
 (E) F.S. Key and President Wilson were acquaintances.

29. The coming of the railroads proved a boon to California agriculture.

 We can conclude that

 (A) the railroads were a problem for California farmers
 (B) the railroads brought more people to California
 (C) without the railroads, California agriculture would not have increased as rapidly as it did
 (D) the railroads made products cheaper
 (E) the railroads made products more expensive

30. "Not a ship escaped heavy damage" means

 (A) no ship had damage
 (B) every ship had heavy damage
 (C) all ships had some damage, but not all had heavy damage
 (D) some ships had heavy damage
 (E) some ships had damage

31. "Students learn more when they are praised." If you applied this statement in the classroom, you would

 (A) praise each student for everything he or she does
 (B) praise each student when he or she has done a good job
 (C) praise at least one student every day
 (D) praise each student at least once a week
 (E) make the praise valuable by praising only in exceptional circumstances

**QUESTIONS 32–33 REFER TO THE FOLLOWING INFORMATION.**

When a cold air layer lies below a warm layer, mirage images appear above the real object. When the layers are reversed, the image is inverted below the real object.

**32.** Which drawing illustrates the above information?

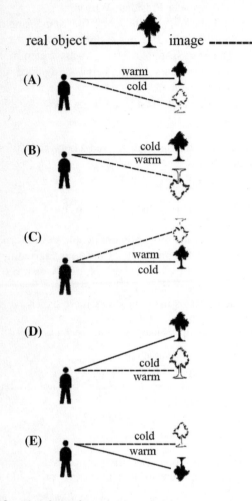

**33.** A mirage is

(A) an inversion
(B) an air layer
(C) a reversion
(D) an image
(E) an object

**34.** "People can have clean air if they demand it. The remedies for most forms of air pollution are known; they need only be applied."

This statement would be most strengthened by which of the following statements?

(A) The death rate has decreased in some cities.
(B) Pollution-control regulations have been passed.
(C) Smog-control devices are required in some states.
(D) Environmental lessons have been added to the curriculum in many schools.
(E) In several cities air-pollution-control programs are in effect with striking improvement of the air quality.

**QUESTIONS 35–38 REFER TO THE FOLLOWING PASSAGE.**

Knowledge of words has become our most valuable tool today. With a good vocabulary, we can better understand others and communicate our thoughts to them. There is a high correlation between a large precise vocabulary and achievement in worldly success, earnings, and management status.

Frustration over the inability to express thoughts in words often results in physical aggressiveness. For some years, the nation's vocabulary level has been decreasing every year, while crime has been steadily increasing. A limited vocabulary is a serious handicap. Hard working people can advance only so far, before they reach a plateau beyond which they are hampered by their lack of vocabulary. As a result of being stymied in their employment, these people change jobs frequently. By middle-age, many low-vocabulary people are stuck in routine jobs. When companies reduce personnel due to mergers or economic constraints, it's often the low-vocabulary people who are left without jobs.

**35.** We can conclude that people with a low level of vocabulary

(A) all have routine jobs
(B) have difficulty expressing themselves in words
(C) are unemployed most of the time
(D) are physically aggressive
(E) are laid off when companies merge

**36.** There is a high correlation between

(A) a large vocabulary and job success
(B) size of vocabulary and the crime rate
(C) low vocabulary and retention rate upon the merger of two companies
(D) size of vocabulary and lack of communication
(E) lack of advancement and extent of vocabulary

37. All of the following are mentioned as disadvantages of a limited vocabulary except

    (A) lack of opportunity to be promoted to higher paid positions
    (B) difficulty in understanding others
    (C) more apt to be let go from job
    (D) less apt to have interesting work
    (E) lack of opportunity to use manual dexterity

38. Developing a large vocabulary enables one to

    I. be promoted
    II. change jobs easily
    III. understand others easily

    (A) III only
    (B) II and III only
    (C) I and II only
    (D) I and III only
    (E) I, II, and III

39. What probable effect will a decreasing birthrate have on education?

    I. Fewer teachers will be needed.
    II. Fewer schools will be needed.
    III. Fewer students will enroll.

    (A) I only
    (B) II only
    (C) III only
    (D) II and III only
    (E) I, II, and III

40. "Moderation in all things, including moderation" leads one to think that

    (A) one should always be moderate
    (B) one should sometimes be immoderate
    (C) it is mediocre to be moderate
    (D) moderation is dull
    (E) moderation is modern

41. Earthquakes cause damage and loss of life, but scientists point out that they are vital to the continued development of our earth. Mountains are constantly eroding, and if they were not raised again, the world would become a place of stagnant seas and swamps.

    The likely effect of the above information on a reader is

    (A) no change in attitude
    (B) that he will understand the benefits of earthquakes
    (C) that he will be better prepared for earthquakes
    (D) that he will understand that earthquakes are beneficial as well as harmful
    (E) that he will know what to do in case of an earthquake

## QUESTIONS 42–46 REFER TO THE FOLLOWING CHART.

**Years of Life Expected at Birth**

| Year | Total | Male | Female |
| --- | --- | --- | --- |
| 1970 | 70.5 | 67.0 | 74.3 |
| 1960 | 69.7 | 66.6 | 73.1 |
| 1950 | 68.2 | 65.6 | 71.1 |
| 1940 | 62.9 | 60.8 | 65.2 |
| 1930 | 59.7 | 58.1 | 61.6 |
| 1920 | 54.1 | 53.6 | 54.6 |
| 1910 | 50.0 | 48.4 | 51.8 |
| 1900 | 47.3 | 46.3 | 48.3 |

42. The largest increase in total life expectancy is between

    (A) 1900 and 1910
    (B) 1910 and 1920
    (C) 1920 and 1930
    (D) 1930 and 1940
    (E) 1940 and 1950

43. What is the last census year in which a person who is still living in 1985 could have been born and outlived his or her expected life span?

    (A) 1900
    (B) 1910
    (C) 1920
    (D) 1930
    (E) 1940

44. A man born in 1950 can expect to live to the year

    (A) 2015
    (B) 2000
    (C) 2018
    (D) 2021
    (E) 2026

45. Which of the following are true, according to the chart?

    I. Women live longer than men.
    II. Life expectancy has increased every reporting period.
    III. Women have increased their life expectancy more than men.

    (A) I only
    (B) II only
    (C) I and II only
    (D) I and III only
    (E) I, II, and III

46. Projecting the information into the future, the following conclusion can be made:

    I. Life expectancy will increase, but at a slower rate.

    II. There will be an increasing number of older people.

    III. The life expectancy of men will decrease.

    (A) I only
    (B) II only
    (C) III only
    (D) I and II only
    (E) I, II, and III

## QUESTIONS 47–49 REFER TO THE FOLLOWING PASSAGE.

Vocabulary is acquired, not innate. Vocabulary grows faster in the first year of life than at any other time. At age ten, vocabulary is learned twice as fast as a few years later and three times as fast as at college age. Contrary to public belief, vocabulary test scores rarely improve because of formal learning. Children of high-vocabulary parents have a head start. Parents are urged to start a child's vocabulary building at an early age. A limited vocabulary leads to school problems, leaving the young person with feelings of failure.

Many people view vocabulary building as a formidable task, but they already know many words. Only about 3,500 words separate the high- and low-vocabulary person, and spell the difference between success and failure. English is based on Anglo-Saxon word order, but the words of subtlety and precision are Latin. The number of years a person studies Latin correlates with a large and exact English vocabulary, which in turn correlates with earnings. Vocabulary building requires both patience and effort, but the rewards are worthwhile.

47. Learning vocabulary

    (A) is done most readily before a child's first birthday
    (B) is an inherited ability
    (C) is fastest at age ten
    (D) is easiest during the college years
    (E) depends on how many years of Latin you study

48. The passage states that parents should begin vocabulary building for their child

    (A) during the first year
    (B) at age ten
    (C) at age thirteen
    (D) during the college years
    (E) not specified

49. Only about 3,500 words is

    (A) the number of words known by a person of low-vocabulary level
    (B) the number of words known by a person of high-vocabulary level
    (C) the difference between the number of words known by a high-vocabulary and a low-vocabulary person.
    (D) the number of words known before age ten
    (E) the average number of words learned during college

50. Nuclear plants use large amounts of water for cooling. One likely effect of this is

    (A) a shortage of water
    (B) contamination of water
    (C) higher water temperatures down-stream
    (D) fewer nuclear plants near water
    (E) higher humidity

# MATHEMATICS

## 70 MINUTES—50 QUESTIONS

**Directions:** Choose the best answer for each question and blacken the corresponding space on the Answer Sheet for Sample Test 1. The correct answers and explanations follow the test.

1. The 7 in 1234.5678 represents

   **(A)** ones
   **(B)** tens
   **(C)** tenths
   **(D)** hundredths
   **(E)** thousandths

2. Round off 76,569 to the nearest thousand.

   **(A)** 76
   **(B)** 77
   **(C)** 76,000
   **(D)** 76,500
   **(E)** 77,000

3. $\frac{7}{9}$ lies between each of the following pairs of numbers EXCEPT

   **(A)** $\frac{2}{3}$ and $\frac{3}{2}$

   **(B)** $\frac{7}{11}$ and $\frac{9}{7}$

   **(C)** $\frac{1}{2}$ and 1

   **(D)** 0.7 and 0.9

   **(E)** $\frac{7}{8}$ and $\frac{9}{8}$

4. To check whether $\frac{x^2 - 4}{x + 2} = x - 2$, you could

   **(A)** multiply $x - 2$ by $x^2 - 4$
   **(B)** multiply $x - 2$ by $x + 2$
   **(C)** multiply $x - 2$ by $x$
   **(D)** multiply $x + 2$ by $x$
   **(E)** multiply $x - 2$ by 2

5. $\boxed{16{,}752 \div 3 =}$

   When James tried to solve this problem, he found that it

   **(A)** has a remainder of 1
   **(B)** has a remainder of 2
   **(C)** has no remainder
   **(D)** cannot be divided
   **(E)** is smaller than 5,500

6. $\boxed{\text{Jessica has 7 bills totaling \$135.00 in \$50.00, \$20.00, \$10.00, and \$5.00 denominations. How many \$20.00 bills does she have?}}$

   When Jeremy began to solve this problem, he started with five $20.00 bills. After he tried that, he knew that

   **(A)** he was right
   **(B)** there were more than five $20.00 bills
   **(C)** there were four $5.00 bills
   **(D)** there was one $50.00 bill
   **(E)** there were four $20.00 bills

7. Harlan paid $45.05, including sales tax, for a pair of tennis shoes. If the rate of sales tax was 6%, how much tax did he pay?

   **(A)** $2.55
   **(B)** $2.70
   **(C)** $42.50
   **(D)** $45.59
   **(E)** $47.75

8. Which fraction is smallest?

   **(A)** $\frac{2}{3}$

   **(B)** $\frac{4}{9}$

   **(C)** $\frac{1}{2}$

   **(D)** $\frac{5}{11}$

   **(E)** $\frac{3}{7}$

9. For which problem would you use $\frac{1}{2} \times \frac{1}{3}$ to get the answer?

   (A) | Jerry wants a third less than half of a pie. |

   (B) | Jeffrey wants to divide a third by a half. |

   (C) | Jeremy wants to find a half less than a third. |

   (D) | Jurgen wants to divide a half by a third. |

   (E) | Jerome wants half of a third of a pie. |

10. Muriel works part time at a drug store. She works 5 hours Monday, 4 hours on Tuesday, 3 hours Wednesday, 2 hours Thursday, and 6 hours on Friday. What were her average dollar earnings per day?

    (A) 3
    (B) 4
    (C) 5
    (D) 20
    (E) There is not enough information

11. Which pair of numbers has a ratio of 4 to 11?

    (A) 49, 110
    (B) 16, 33
    (C) 77, 28
    (D) 28, 77
    (E) 110, 49

12. On an assignment, Sidney did 18 problems correctly and 6 incorrectly. The ratio of problems attempted to problems solved incorrectly is

    (A) 1:4
    (B) 4:3
    (C) 4:1
    (D) 3:4
    (E) 18:6

13. The scale on a house plan is 1:36. This means that

    (A) 1 in = 36 yds
    (B) 1 ft = 6 yds
    (C) 1 ft = 3 yds
    (D) 1 in = 1 yd
    (E) 1 in = 3 yds

14. To get a B (80%) on a test, Susan had to answer at least 104 questions correctly. The number of questions on the test was

    (A) 140
    (B) 130
    (C) 107
    (D) 100
    (E) 64

15. In a dominoes tournament, each player plays every other player once. The winner is the person who wins the greatest number of games. What is the total number of games played if 8 people participate?

    (A) 8
    (B) 15
    (C) 28
    (D) 32
    (E) 64

16.

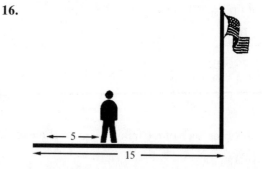

A man 6 feet tall casts a shadow 5 feet long. The flagpole nearby casts a 15-foot shadow. How tall is the flagpole?

    (A) 11 ft
    (B) 15 ft
    (C) 18 ft
    (D) 21 ft
    (E) 26 ft

17. Brenda earns six times as much as Marvin. Marvin earns

    (A) $6.00
    (B) one sixth of their combined income
    (C) six divided by Brenda's earnings
    (D) six times Brenda's earnings
    (E) Brenda's earnings divided by six

18. The prime factors of 60 are

    (A) 1, 2, 3, 5
    (B) 2, 3, 5
    (C) 1, 3, 4, 5
    (D) 12, 5
    (E) 6, 10

19. $\sqrt{4725}$ is closest to

    (A) 65
    (B) 68
    (C) 69
    (D) 75
    (E) 225

20. The temperature in Kevin's room has been fluctuating between 65° and 80°. The average temperature for the past five days has been 72°. What is the lowest average temperature the room can have for the week?

    (A) 65°
    (B) 70°
    (C) 72°
    (D) 75°
    (E) 80°

21. A person would be weighed in

    (A) milligrams
    (B) grams
    (C) kilograms
    (D) liters
    (E) meters

22. Convert 35° Celsius to Fahrenheit.

    (A) 7°F
    (B) 20°F
    (C) 52°F
    (D) 67°F
    (E) 95°F

23. The basic rate for a telephone is $6.00 per month. Each call is charged at 30¢. How much will Nancy pay for March if she made 25 calls?

    (A) $6.55
    (B) $13.50
    (C) $15.30
    (D) $15.75
    (E) $18.25

24. Sidney is baking 50 muffins. How many muffin tins will he need if there are 8 muffin cups in each tin?

    (A) 6
    (B) 6.25
    (C) 7
    (D) 8
    (E) 9

25. Tammy is the owner of a lamp store. A $50.00 lamp has been marked down 10% but hasn't sold. She decides to mark it down another 20%. What price will she put on it?

    (A) $20.00
    (B) $30.00
    (C) $35.00
    (D) $36.00
    (E) $40.00

26. Gudelia is five years older than Francis. Five years ago, she was twice as old as Francis. How old is Francis?

    (A) 5
    (B) 10
    (C) 15
    (D) 20
    (E) None of the above

27. The difference between a two-digit number and the number reversed is 36. The sum of the digits is 10. What is the number?

    (A) 56
    (B) 64
    (C) 73
    (D) 82
    (E) 91

28. Margaret borrowed $2,700 from the credit union to be paid back at the end of three years at 12% annual simple interest. How much will she pay back?

    (A) $972.00
    (B) $2,700.00
    (C) $3,105.00
    (D) $3,672.00
    (E) $3,780.00

29. David filled a container that was 12 inches long by 8 inches wide, to a depth of 6 inches. How should he determine the number of cubic inches of water in the container?

    (A) $2(12 + 8 + 6)$
    (B) $8(6 + 12)$
    (C) $6(8 + 12)$
    (D) $12(6 + 8)$
    (E) $6 \times 8 \times 12$

**30.** Diane is going to put fringe around a tablecloth that is 3 feet by 5 feet. How many yards of fringe will she need to buy?

(A)  16 yds

(B)  $2\frac{2}{3}$ yds

(C)  5 yds

(D)  $5\frac{1}{3}$ yds

(E)  10 yds

**31.** $(b - 4)(b + 3) =$

(A)  $b^2 - 12$
(B)  $2b - 1$
(C)  $b^2 - 1$
(D)  $b^2 - b - 12$
(E)  $b^2 - b + 12$

**32.**

> You can buy eight CDs for $60.00 at Tape World upon presentation of a $4.00 discount certificate. Under these terms, how much does one CD cost?

Which formula would you use to solve this problem?

(A)  $8x = 60$
(B)  $8x + 4 = 60$
(C)  $8x - 4 = 60$
(D)  $8x + 60 = -4$
(E)  $4 - 8x = 60$

**33.** $3k^2 - 4k + 7 - 2k^2 =$

(A)  $k^2 - 4k + 7$
(B)  $-4k + 7$
(C)  $6k^2 - 4k + 7$
(D)  $-6k^4 - 4k + 7$
(E)  $-3k^5 + 7$

**34.** What is the area of a rectangular chart that is $3a^2$ wide and $4a^3$ long?

(A)  $7a^5$
(B)  $12a^5$
(C)  $7a^6$
(D)  $144a^6$
(E)  $72a$

**35.** $678 + K - M - 401 = 385;$ $K = 5M.$ Find the value of M.

(A)  27
(B)  108
(C)  277
(D)  18
(E)  411

**36.** $x° + y° =$

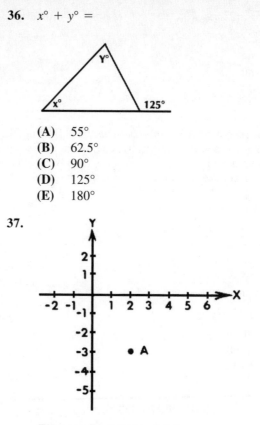

(A)  55°
(B)  62.5°
(C)  90°
(D)  125°
(E)  180°

**37.**

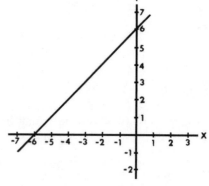

The coordinates of point A are

(A)  $x = 3, y = 2$
(B)  $x = -3, y = 2$
(C)  $x = 2, y = -3$
(D)  $x = -2, y = -3$
(E)  None of the above

**38.**

The equation for the above line is

(A)  $x - y = 6$
(B)  $x + y = 6$
(C)  $x = 6$
(D)  $y = 6$
(E)  $y - x = 6$

**QUESTIONS 39–40 REFER TO THE FOLLOWING GRAPHIC.**

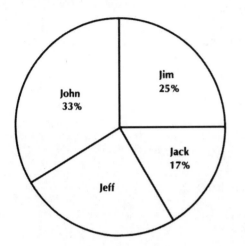

39. Jeff, Jill, Jack, and John formed the Jay-Four company. Their investments in the company are shown in the pie graph above. What fraction of the total investment was Jeff's?

(A) $\frac{1}{3}$

(B) $\frac{1}{4}$

(C) $\frac{1}{5}$

(D) $\frac{1}{6}$

(E) $\frac{2}{7}$

40. How many degrees does Jim's investment represent?

(A) 25°
(B) 50°
(C) 75°
(D) 90°
(E) 100°

41.

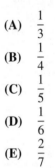

What is the area of the shaded portion of the circle above?

(A) 3π
(B) 9π
(C) 12π
(D) 27π
(E) 36π

42. The formula for the area of a circle is $A = \pi r^2$. Find the area of a circle with a radius of 4.

(A) 8
(B) 4π
(C) 16π
(D) 8π
(E) 16

43. Jason paid $11.60 for a shirt that was marked down by 20%. How much money did he save by buying at the sale price rather than the original price?

(A) $2.00
(B) $2.90
(C) $2.32
(D) $14.50
(E) $11.60

44. Ken has a drawer full of marker pens. Four are black, three are red, two are green, and six are blue. If he pulls out one pen at random, what are his chances of pulling out a red one?

(A) 1 in 15
(B) 1 in 2
(C) 1 in 5
(D) 2 in 15
(E) 4 in 6

45. If the area of a square is more than the area of a triangle with a base of 12 and a height of 8, what is length of one side of the square?

(A) 8
(B) 15
(C) 48
(D) 64
(E) 96

46. James is arranging a display of coffee tins on a table 40 inches wide and 42 inches long. How many tins, each 6 inches in diameter, can be placed on the surface of the table without stacking the tins?

(A) 42
(B) 46
(C) 47
(D) 182
(E) 186

47. There were 180 parents and students at graduation. At least a third of the audience consisted of students. How many students attended?

(A) 60–179
(B) 60–180
(C) 61–180
(D) 120–179
(E) 121–180

## QUESTIONS 48–50 REFER TO THE FOLLOWING INFORMATION.

The community swimming pool is being filled at a steady rate. The depth of the water is measured every 15 minutes and recorded in inches and centimeters.

| Time | Inches | Centimeters |
| --- | --- | --- |
| 9:00 a.m. | 7 | 17.92 |
| 9:15 a.m. | 14 | 35.84 |
| 9:30 a.m. | 21 | 53.76 |
| 9:45 a.m. | 28 | 71.86 |
| 10:00 a.m. | 35 | 89.60 |
| 10:15 a.m. | 42 | 107.52 |

**48.** At which time was an incorrect measurement logged?

- **(A)** 9:15 a.m.
- **(B)** 9:30 a.m.
- **(C)** 9:45 a.m.
- **(D)** 10:00 a.m.
- **(E)** At no time

**49.** At the same rate, when will the water in the pool be 7 feet deep?

- **(A)** 10:30 a.m.
- **(B)** 11:00 a.m.
- **(C)** 11:15 a.m.
- **(D)** 11:45 a.m.
- **(E)** 12:00 a.m.

**50.** How deep will the water be at noon?

- **(A)** 6 ft
- **(B)** 7 ft
- **(C)** 7 ft 7 in
- **(D)** 8 ft
- **(E)** More than 8 ft

# WRITING

## 60 MINUTES—TWO ESSAYS

> **Directions:** You have 60 minutes in which to write two essays. The essay topics are intended to measure how well you write, given limitations on time and subject. Quality is more important than quantity. Spend some of your time organizing your thoughts. Use specific examples to support your opinions. Write only on the assigned topic. Write legibly and within the lines provided. Space for notes is provided below.

### Topic A

John Molloy found that students reacted differently when he dressed casually from the way they reacted when he dressed more formally. From your observations and experiences, relate how what you wear affects you and others and how you would use this information.

### Topic B

Do you agree or disagree with the statement, "Good teachers are born, not made"? Support your position with examples from your experience with teachers you have met.

# ANSWER KEY AND EXPLANATIONS

## READING

| | | | | | | | | | |
|---|---|---|---|---|---|---|---|---|---|
| 1. A | 8. B | 15. C | 21. A | 27. E | 33. D | 39. E | 45. D |
| 2. E | 9. E | 16. B | 22. D | 28. D | 34. E | 40. B | 46. D |
| 3. D | 10. B | 17. B | 23. C | 29. C | 35. B | 41. D | 47. A |
| 4. E | 11. B | 18. B | 24. E | 30. B | 36. A | 42. C | 48. E |
| 5. A | 12. A | 19. E | 25. B | 31. B | 37. E | 43. C | 49. C |
| 6. B | 13. D | 20. C | 26. A | 32. B | 38. D | 44. A | 50. C |
| 7. C | 14. A | | | | | | |

1. **The correct answer is (A).** The second paragraph states the earliest date mentioned.

2. **The correct answer is (E).** The comet did not cause these events.

3. **The correct answer is (D).** The last paragraph states this.

4. **The correct answer is (E).** *Disaster* means *evil* or *bad* star; similarly, *distemper* means *bad temper.*

5. **The correct answer is (A).** In paragraph 2, Hawthorne is contrasted to presidents who have very demanding jobs. He probably had a job which did not tax his mental ability and, therefore, had a hobby which did.

6. **The correct answer is (B).** As stated in paragraph 3, a hobby is for enjoyment.

7. **The correct answer is (C).** The other statements are too extreme.

8. **The correct answer is (B).** Rivers of wind have widespread effects on weather.

9. **The correct answer is (E).** A crevasse is a deep cut in ice or rock.

10. **The correct answer is (B).** No advocacy or bias is shown.

11. **The correct answer is (B).** "The messages were slipped in," but we don't know what opinions they expressed.

12. **The correct answer is (A).** According to the information in the passage, no other statement is logical.

13. **The correct answer is (D).** England, Scotland, and Wales make up Great Britain.

14. **The correct answer is (A).** *Virtually* means *practically.*

15. **The correct answer is (C).** *Depict* means *describe.*

16. **The correct answer is (B).** A higher deductible means that you pay more for repairs before the insurance company starts paying.

17. **The correct answer is (B).** $25.00 per month, or $25 × 12 = $300.00 per year.

18. **The correct answer is (B).** He saves $300.00 in premiums, but pays $500.00 − $150.00 = $350.00 more deductible, for a loss of $50.00.

19. **The correct answer is (E).** See answer to question 18.

20. **The correct answer is (C).** He pays the first $500.00. He is insured for $5,000.00, so he will have to pay any amount over that: $7,000.00 − $5,000.00 = $2,000.00. Altogether he will have to pay $2,500.00

21. **The correct answer is (A).** The best deals are the usual policy and several accidents, or higher deductible and few accidents. Eliminate choices (B), (C), and (E). This is a time-consuming problem, so if you're short of time, choose (A) or (D) and move on.

Check (A):

| | Usual | |
|---|---|---|
| Premiums | $125 × 12 = | $1,400 |
| Deductible | $150 × 4 = | 600 |
| Total Cost | | $2,100 |

| | Higher | |
|---|---|---|
| Premiums | $100 × 12 = | $1,200 |
| Deductible | $400 × 4 = | 1,600 |
| Total Cost | | $2,800 |

$700 savings.

Check (D):

| | Usual | |
|---|---|---|
| Premiums | $125 × 12 = | $1,400 |
| Deductible | $150 × 1 = | 150 |
| Total Cost | | $1,650 |

| | Higher | |
|---|---|---|
| Premiums | $100 × 12 = | $1,200 |
| Deductible | $500 × 1 = | 500 |
| Total Cost | | $1,700 |

$50 savings.

22. **The correct answer is (D).** *Show* beats *tell.*

23. **The correct answer is (C).** Growth has decreased, but it's still growth.

24. **The correct answer is (E).** They will *consider* all three, but perhaps act only on II.

25. **The correct answer is (B).** *Other* is the key word.

26. **The correct answer is (A).** Choice (E) is the only other logical choice to consider. Notice, however, that the passage says, "write and compute WELL."

27. **The correct answer is (E).** *Relentless* means *steady* and *persistent.* The implication is that the movement of the sand cannot be stopped.

28. **The correct answer is (D).** 1931 − 1814 = 117 years

29. **The correct answer is (C).** A *boon* is a benefit.

30. **The correct answer is (B).** If no ships escaped heavy damage, then every ship had heavy damage.

31. **The correct answer is (B).** Students sense when praise is not deserved.

32. **The correct answer is (B).** Both drawings below are correct.

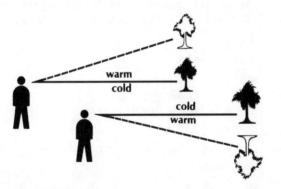

33. **The correct answer is (D).** The passage refers to *mirage images.*

34. **The correct answer is (E).** Only choice (E) illustrates the argument.

35. **The correct answer is (B).** The second sentence states, "With a good vocabulary, we can better . . . communicate our thoughts. . . ." Conversely, people without a good vocabulary would have difficulty expressing themselves.

36. **The correct answer is (A).** Sentence 3 states this.

37. **The correct answer is (E).** All the others are listed as disadvantages.

38. **The correct answer is (D).** I and III are mentioned. II is possible but not mentioned.

39. **The correct answer is (E).** If there are fewer children, there will be fewer students, and fewer teachers and schools will be needed.

40. **The correct answer is (B).** Even moderation has to be tempered, which means that sometimes one should not be moderate.

41. **The correct answer is (D).** Choice (A) is possible, but choice (D) is more likely.

42. **The correct answer is (C).** Look for a large difference.

    Choice (A): About 3
    Choice (B): About 4
    Choice (C): About 5
    Choice (D): About 3
    Choice (E): About 5

    Work out choices (C) and (E) to find that choice (C) is the correct answer.

43. **The correct answer is (C).** Underline *last.* Add the year and life expectancy. It has to be less than 1985.

44. **The correct answer is (A).** 1950 + 65.6 = 2015.6

45. **The correct answer is (D).** All are true.

46. **The correct answer is (D).** I and II are valid. III is doubtful.

47. **The correct answer is (A).** The second sentence gives this information.

48. **The correct answer is (E).** Beginning vocabulary development is suggested "at an early age" but no age is specified.

49. **The correct answer is (C).** The second sentence of the second paragraph contains the answer.

50. **The correct answer is (C).** Choice (C) is the most logical. Using the water for cooling means the water will be heated.

## MATHEMATICS

| | | | | | | |
|---|---|---|---|---|---|---|
| 1. E | 8. E | 15. C | 21. C | 27. C | 33. A | 39. B | 45. A |
| 2. E | 9. E | 16. C | 22. E | 28. D | 34. B | 40. D | 46. A |
| 3. E | 10. E | 17. E | 23. B | 29. E | 35. A | 41. D | 47. A |
| 4. B | 11. D | 18. B | 24. C | 30. D | 36. D | 42. C | 48. C |
| 5. C | 12. C | 19. C | 25. D | 31. D | 37. C | 43. B | 49. D |
| 6. D | 13. D | 20. B | 26. B | 32. C | 38. E | 44. C | 50. C |
| 7. A | 14. B | | | | | | |

1. **The correct answer is (E).** The numeral 7 is in the thousandths place.

2. **The correct answer is (E).**

$$76,569$$
↑    5 or more, round up.
$$\underline{1,000}$$
$$77,000$$

3. **The correct answer is (E).** Compare by cross-multiplication.

Choice (A):    18       21/14      27
$$\frac{2}{3} \times \frac{7}{9} \times \frac{3}{2}$$

Choice (B):    63       77/49      81
$$\frac{7}{11} \times \frac{7}{9} \times \frac{9}{7}$$

Choice (C):    9        14/7       9
$$\frac{1}{2} \times \frac{7}{9} \times \frac{1}{1}$$

Choice (D):    63       70/70      81
$$\frac{7}{10} \times \frac{7}{9} \times \frac{9}{10}$$

Choice (E):    63       56/63      72
$$\frac{7}{8} \times \frac{7}{9} \times \frac{8}{9}$$

$\frac{7}{9}$ is smaller than both $\frac{7}{8}$ and $\frac{8}{9}$.

4. **The correct answer is (B).** To check $\frac{12}{3} = 4$, you would multiply 3 by 4. Similarly, you would multiply $(x + 2)$ by $(x - 2)$ to check $\frac{x^2 - 4}{x + 2} = x - 2$.

5. **The correct answer is (C).** $1 + 6 + 7 + 5 + 2 = 21$, which is divisible by 3; therefore, 16,752 is divisible by 3 and has no remainder.

6. **The correct answer is (D).** Try the various answer choices. Choice (A): $5 \times 20 = 100$. You have $35.00 to make up with two bills; this isn't possible.

Choice (B): $6 \times 20 = 120$; you need one $15.00 bill; this is not possible.

Choice (C): You need an odd number of $5.00 bills. So, this answer is incorrect.

Choice (D): $3 \times 20 = 60$. This leaves $75.00 to be made up with four bills; $50 + 10 + 10 + 5 = 75$.

Choice (E): $4 \times 20 = 80$. This leaves $55.00 to be made up with three bills; this is not possible.

7. **The correct answer is (A).** Your sales tax will be less than $3.00; eliminate choices (C), (D), and (E).

$$\begin{array}{cc} \$ & \% \\ \dfrac{x}{\$45.05} & = \dfrac{6}{106} \end{array}$$
$$106x = (45.06)(6)$$
$$x = 270.3 \div 106$$
$$x = \$2.55$$

8. **The correct answer is (E).** Compare by cross-multiplication.

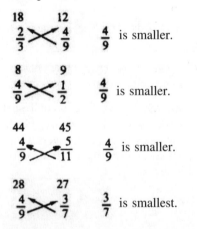

    18       12
$$\frac{2}{3} \times \frac{4}{9} \qquad \frac{4}{9} \text{ is smaller.}$$

    8        9
$$\frac{4}{9} \times \frac{1}{2} \qquad \frac{4}{9} \text{ is smaller.}$$

    44       45
$$\frac{4}{9} \times \frac{5}{11} \qquad \frac{4}{9} \text{ is smaller.}$$

    28       27
$$\frac{4}{9} \times \frac{3}{7} \qquad \frac{3}{7} \text{ is smallest.}$$

With this type of question, first check to determine whether there are any answers you can eliminate, e.g., $\frac{2}{3}$ is 0.67, $\frac{1}{2}$ is 0.50.

9. **The correct answer is (E).** You need to try out the choices.

Choice (A): $\dfrac{1}{2} - \dfrac{1}{3}$

Choice (B): $\dfrac{1}{3} \div \dfrac{1}{2}$

Choice (C): $\dfrac{1}{3} - \dfrac{1}{2}$

Choice (D): $\dfrac{1}{2} \div \dfrac{1}{3}$

Choice (E): $\dfrac{1}{2} \times \dfrac{1}{3}$

10. **The correct answer is (E).** You need to know how much she earned per hour. There's not enough information.

11. **The correct answer is (D).** Look for the smaller number to be placed first. Eliminate choice (C) and (E). Next, test whether the first number is divisible by 4. Eliminate choice (A). Is the second number divisible by 11? "When the first number is divided by 4 and the second number is divided by 11, are the quotients (answers) the same?"

Try choice (B): $\dfrac{16}{4} = 4$; $\dfrac{33}{11} = 3$; eliminate this answer.

Try choice (D): $\dfrac{28}{4} = 7$; $\dfrac{77}{11} = 7$; this is correct.

12. **The correct answer is (C).**

$$18 + 6 : 6$$
$$24 : 6$$
$$4 : 1$$

13. **The correct answer is (D).** Convert to same measure.

Choice (A): 1 in = 36 × 36 in
Choice (B): 1 ft = 6 × 3 ft
Choice (C): 1 ft = 3 × 3 ft
Choice (D): 1 in = 36 in
Choice (E): 1 in = 3 × 36 in

14. **The correct answer is (B).**

$$\frac{80\%}{100\%} = \frac{104}{n}$$

$$80n = 104(100)$$

$$n = \frac{104(100)}{80} = 130$$

15. **The correct answer is (C).**

Player 1 plays players 2, 3, 4, 5, 6, 7, 8 = 7 games
Player 2 plays players 3, 4, 5, 6, 7, 8 = 6 games
Player 3 plays players 4, 5, 6, 7, 8 = 5 games
Player 4 plays players 5, 6, 7, 8 = 4 games
Player 5 plays players 6, 7, 8 = 3 games
Player 6 plays players 7, 8 = 2 games
Player 7 plays players 8 = 1 games

Total number of games played = 28 games

Each player plays the others only once. Player 1 plays player 2, therefore that game is not counted in player 2's number of games. Player 8 has already played each of the others.

16. **The correct answer is (C).**

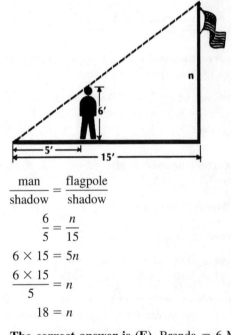

$$\frac{\text{man}}{\text{shadow}} = \frac{\text{flagpole}}{\text{shadow}}$$

$$\frac{6}{5} = \frac{n}{15}$$

$$6 \times 15 = 5n$$

$$\frac{6 \times 15}{5} = n$$

$$18 = n$$

17. **The correct answer is (E).** Brenda = 6 Marvin

$$\text{Marvin} = \frac{\text{Brenda}}{6} \text{ or } \frac{1}{6} \text{ Brenda.}$$

If Brenda earns 6 times what Marvin earns, then Marvin earns $\dfrac{1}{6}$ of what Brenda earns.

18. **The correct answer is (B).**

$$\begin{array}{c|c} 2 & 60 \\ 2 & 30 \\ 3 & 15 \\ 5 & 5 \end{array}$$

Choice (A): 1 is not prime.
Choice (C): 1 and 4 are not prime.
Choice (D): 12 is not prime.
Choice (E): 6 and 10 are not prime.

**19. The correct answer is (C).**

$$\sqrt{47\,25}$$

1. 2 places in answer; eliminate choice (E).
2. square root closest to 47 is 6 ($6^2 = 36$); eliminate choice (D).
3. 47 is close to 49, so try 68 or 69.
   $68^2 = 4,624$
   $69^2 = 4,721$ (closest)

**20. The correct answer is (B).** The lowest temperature will be less than 72°; eliminate choices (C), (D), and (E).

$5 \times 72 = 360$

$2 \times 65 + \dfrac{130}{490}$    $\dfrac{490}{7} = 70$

**21. The correct answer is (C).** Pounds is the equivalent measure to kilograms.

**22. The correct answer is (E).** C → F larger; eliminate choices (A) and (B).

Approximation       Formula
$2C + 30° = F$       $9/5C + 32° = F$
$2 \times 35° + 30° = 100°$    $9/5(35)° + 32° = 95°$

**23. The correct answer is (B).** $6.00 + 25 \times 0.30 = 6.00 + 7.50 = \$13.50$

**24. The correct answer is (C).** $50 \div 8 = 6\dfrac{1}{4}$. He'll need 7.

**25. The correct answer is (D).**

10% off = 90%    $\$50 \times 0.9 = \$45$
20% off = 80%    $\$45 \times 0.8 = \$36$

**26. The correct answer is (B).** Five years ago, Francis was less than a year old; eliminate. Substitute 10 for Francis. Now, G = 15, F = 10. Five years ago: $15 - 5 = 2(10 - 5)$; $10 = 2 \times 5$

**27. The correct answer is (C).** Is the sum of the digits 10? Eliminate choice (A). Subtract the digits reversed. Look for 36.

Choice (B):    65
          −46
          18

Choice (C):    73
          −37
          36

**28. The correct answer is (D).** Total to be repaid is more than amount borrowed; so, eliminate choices (A) and (B).

Total = Principal + Interest
Interest = Principal × Rate × Time
$$= \$2,700 \times \dfrac{12}{100} \times 3 = \$972$$

Total = $\$2,700 + \$972 = \$3,672$

**29. The correct answer is (E).**

Volume $= l \times w \times h$
         $= 12 \times 8 \times 6$

**30. The correct answer is (D).**

Perimeter $= 2(l + w)$
          $= 2(3 + 5)$
          $= 2(8) = 16$ ft

16 ft $\div$ 3 $= 5\dfrac{1}{3}$ yds

**31. The correct answer is (D).**

**32. The correct answer is (C).** The $60 is paid for the 8 CDs after the $4 discount. The cost of 1 CD is $x$. $8x - 4 = 60$.

**33. The correct answer is (A).**

$3k^2 - 4k + 7 - 2k^2 =$
$3k^2 - 2k^2 - 4k + 7 =$
     $k^2 - 4k + 7$

**34. The correct answer is (B).**

Area = length × width
      $= 4a^3 \times 3a^2$
      $= 12a^5$

**35.    The correct answer is (A).**

Estimate:
$$700 + 4M - 400 = 400$$
$$300 + 4M = 400$$
$$4M = 100$$
$$M = 25$$

Eliminate choices (B), (C), and (E).

Now solve the problem:

$$678 + K - M - 401 = 385; \quad K = 5M$$

Substitute    $678 + 5M - M - 401 = 385$
Combine      $678 - 401 + 4M = 385$
$$277 + 4M = 385$$
Subtract 277 $\quad\quad\quad -277 \quad\quad -277$
$$4M = 108$$
Divide by 4 $\quad\quad\quad\quad M = 27$

**36.    The correct answer is (D).** The exterior angle equals the sum of the two opposite interior (inside) angles. The three inside angles of a triangle add up to 180°.

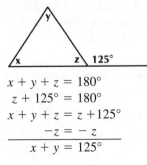

$$x + y + z = 180°$$
$$z + 125° = 180°$$
$$x + y + z = z + 125°$$
$$\underline{-z = -z}$$
$$x + y = 125°$$

**37.    The correct answer is (C).**

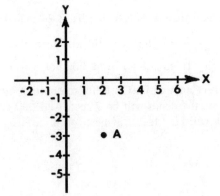

The $x$-direction is listed first, then the $y$-direction. A is 2 units to the right $(+)$ along $x$, hence $x = 2$. A is 3 units down $(-)$ along $y$, hence $y = -3$.

**38.    The correct answer is (E).**

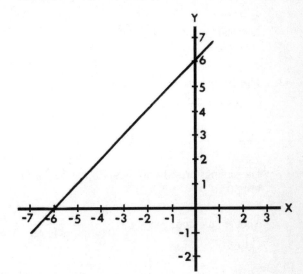

When $x$ is 0, $y$ is 6. When $y$ is 0, $x$ is $-6$. Try out the answer choices.

Choice (A):  Cover $x$ with your finger (0): $-y = 6$ or $y = -6$. Cover $y$ with your finger (0): $x = 6$. Eliminate this answer choice.

Choice (B):  When $x = 0$, $y = 6$. When $y = 0$ $x = 6$. Eliminate this answer choice.

Choice (C):  vertical

Choice (D):  horizontal

Choice (E):  When $y = 0$, $-x = 6$ or $x = -6$. When $x = 0$, $y = 6$. This is correct.

**39.    The correct answer is (B).**

$$\begin{array}{ll} 33\% & \\ 17\% & 100\% \\ \underline{+25\%} & \underline{-75\%} \\ 75\% \text{ others} & 25\% \text{ Jeff} = \dfrac{1}{4} \end{array}$$

**40.    The correct answer is (D).** $\dfrac{25\%}{100\%} = \dfrac{d°}{360°}$

$$\frac{25 \times 360}{100} = d° = 90°$$

*or* 25% is $\dfrac{1}{4}$

$$\frac{1}{4} \times 360° = 90°$$

**41.    The correct answer is (D).** Area of a circle $A = \pi r^2$. You want $\dfrac{3}{4}$ of the area:

$$\frac{3}{4}\pi r^2 = \frac{3}{4}\pi 6^2 = 27\pi$$

**42.** **The correct answer is (C).**

$$A = \pi r^2$$
$$= \pi 4^2$$
$$= 16\pi$$

**43.** **The correct answer is (B).** $\dfrac{\text{part}}{\text{whole}} = \dfrac{\$11.60}{p} = \dfrac{80\%}{100\%}$ (marked down 20%)

$$\frac{\$11.60 \times 100}{80} = p = \$14.50$$

The savings are $\$14.50 - \$11.60 = \$2.90$, or $\$14.50 \times 20\% = \$2.90$

Another method: Saving is $\dfrac{20\%}{80\%} = \dfrac{p}{\$11.60}$ or $\dfrac{1}{4}$ of $\$11.60$

$$\frac{\$20 \times 11.60}{80} = p = \$2.90$$

**44.** **The correct answer is (C).** There are fifteen pens altogether. Three are red. 3 out of $15 = \dfrac{3}{15} = \dfrac{1}{15}$. The chances of getting a red pen are 1 in 5.

**45.** **The correct answer is (A).** Start with the area of the triangle:

$$A = \frac{1}{2} \times b \times h = \frac{1}{2} \times 12 \times 8 = 48$$

The area if the square is $\dfrac{1}{3}$ more than 48:

$$\frac{1}{3} \times 48 = 16.$$

The area of the square is $48 + 16 = 64$.

$$A = s^2 = 64$$

$s = \sqrt{64} = 8$; One side of the square $= 8$.

**46.** **The correct answer is (A).**

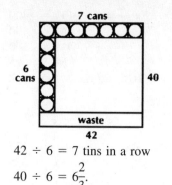

$42 \div 6 = 7$ tins in a row

$40 \div 6 = 6\dfrac{2}{3}$.

Number of cans $= 6 \times 7 = 42$

(You can't put $\dfrac{2}{3}$ of a tin on the table.)

**47.** **The correct answer is (A).** $180 \div 3 = 60$. There were at least 60 students. There was at least one parent. The number of students was 60 to 179.

**48.** **The correct answer is (C).** Look for a discrepancy. There is none in time or inches, but there is one in centimeters. The error occurred at 9:45.

| Time | Change | Inches | Change | Centi-meters | Change |
|------|--------|--------|--------|--------------|--------|
| 9:00 | 0 | 7 | 0 | 17.92 | 0 |
| 9:15 | 15 | 14 | 7 | 35.84 | 17.92 |
| 9:30 | 15 | 21 | 7 | 53.76 | 17.92 |
| 9:45 | 15 | 28 | 7 | 71.86 | 18.10 |
| 10:00 | 15 | 35 | 7 | 89.60 | 17.74 |
| 10:15 | 15 | 42 | 7 | 107.52 | 17.92 |

**49.** **The correct answer is (D).** It fills at 28 inches per hour. $\dfrac{7 \text{ ft} \times 12}{28} = 3$ hours to fill to 7 feet. The pool started being filled at 8:45. Add 3:00 hours $= 11:45$.

**50.** **The correct answer is (C).** Refer to question 49. At 11:45 a.m., the depth will be 7 feet. At 12:00 noon, the depth will be 7 feet 7 inches.

# SCORING FOR PRACTICE TEST 1

Each institution or the state decides on the passing score. In general, 35 correct answers on the Reading section and 33 correct answers on the Mathematics sections should give you a passing score.

### How to Score the Writing Section

The writing section is scored holistically, which makes it difficult to grade. You may want to have someone else score it and make suggestions on how to improve your writing, or you may want or need to score it yourself.

Here is a suggestion for scoring the essay yourself. Start with a total of 50 points for each essay. Then subtract as follows for errors.

### Subtract

- $1\frac{1}{2}$ points for every line that you wrote over the limit

- 1 point for every punctuation, spelling or minor grammatical error

- 3 points for each major grammatical error, incorrectly used word or failure to paragraph correctly

- 5 points for low vocabulary level or jargon

- 10 points if your arguments don't support your statement

- 10 points if you didn't fill more than the first page

- 10 points if you did not have a conclusion

- 25 points if you didn't stay on the topic

This will give you a raw score for each essay. Add the two raw scores together to get your total.

# ANSWER SHEET PRACTICE TEST 2

## READING

1. Ⓐ Ⓑ Ⓒ Ⓓ Ⓔ  11. Ⓐ Ⓑ Ⓒ Ⓓ Ⓔ  21. Ⓐ Ⓑ Ⓒ Ⓓ Ⓔ  31. Ⓐ Ⓑ Ⓒ Ⓓ Ⓔ  41. Ⓐ Ⓑ Ⓒ Ⓓ Ⓔ
2. Ⓐ Ⓑ Ⓒ Ⓓ Ⓔ  12. Ⓐ Ⓑ Ⓒ Ⓓ Ⓔ  22. Ⓐ Ⓑ Ⓒ Ⓓ Ⓔ  32. Ⓐ Ⓑ Ⓒ Ⓓ Ⓔ  42. Ⓐ Ⓑ Ⓒ Ⓓ Ⓔ
3. Ⓐ Ⓑ Ⓒ Ⓓ Ⓔ  13. Ⓐ Ⓑ Ⓒ Ⓓ Ⓔ  23. Ⓐ Ⓑ Ⓒ Ⓓ Ⓔ  33. Ⓐ Ⓑ Ⓒ Ⓓ Ⓔ  43. Ⓐ Ⓑ Ⓒ Ⓓ Ⓔ
4. Ⓐ Ⓑ Ⓒ Ⓓ Ⓔ  14. Ⓐ Ⓑ Ⓒ Ⓓ Ⓔ  24. Ⓐ Ⓑ Ⓒ Ⓓ Ⓔ  34. Ⓐ Ⓑ Ⓒ Ⓓ Ⓔ  44. Ⓐ Ⓑ Ⓒ Ⓓ Ⓔ
5. Ⓐ Ⓑ Ⓒ Ⓓ Ⓔ  15. Ⓐ Ⓑ Ⓒ Ⓓ Ⓔ  25. Ⓐ Ⓑ Ⓒ Ⓓ Ⓔ  35. Ⓐ Ⓑ Ⓒ Ⓓ Ⓔ  45. Ⓐ Ⓑ Ⓒ Ⓓ Ⓔ
6. Ⓐ Ⓑ Ⓒ Ⓓ Ⓔ  16. Ⓐ Ⓑ Ⓒ Ⓓ Ⓔ  26. Ⓐ Ⓑ Ⓒ Ⓓ Ⓔ  36. Ⓐ Ⓑ Ⓒ Ⓓ Ⓔ  46. Ⓐ Ⓑ Ⓒ Ⓓ Ⓔ
7. Ⓐ Ⓑ Ⓒ Ⓓ Ⓔ  17. Ⓐ Ⓑ Ⓒ Ⓓ Ⓔ  27. Ⓐ Ⓑ Ⓒ Ⓓ Ⓔ  37. Ⓐ Ⓑ Ⓒ Ⓓ Ⓔ  47. Ⓐ Ⓑ Ⓒ Ⓓ Ⓔ
8. Ⓐ Ⓑ Ⓒ Ⓓ Ⓔ  18. Ⓐ Ⓑ Ⓒ Ⓓ Ⓔ  28. Ⓐ Ⓑ Ⓒ Ⓓ Ⓔ  38. Ⓐ Ⓑ Ⓒ Ⓓ Ⓔ  48. Ⓐ Ⓑ Ⓒ Ⓓ Ⓔ
9. Ⓐ Ⓑ Ⓒ Ⓓ Ⓔ  19. Ⓐ Ⓑ Ⓒ Ⓓ Ⓔ  29. Ⓐ Ⓑ Ⓒ Ⓓ Ⓔ  39. Ⓐ Ⓑ Ⓒ Ⓓ Ⓔ  49. Ⓐ Ⓑ Ⓒ Ⓓ Ⓔ
10. Ⓐ Ⓑ Ⓒ Ⓓ Ⓔ  20. Ⓐ Ⓑ Ⓒ Ⓓ Ⓔ  30. Ⓐ Ⓑ Ⓒ Ⓓ Ⓔ  40. Ⓐ Ⓑ Ⓒ Ⓓ Ⓔ  50. Ⓐ Ⓑ Ⓒ Ⓓ Ⓔ

## MATHEMATICS

1. Ⓐ Ⓑ Ⓒ Ⓓ Ⓔ  11. Ⓐ Ⓑ Ⓒ Ⓓ Ⓔ  21. Ⓐ Ⓑ Ⓒ Ⓓ Ⓔ  31. Ⓐ Ⓑ Ⓒ Ⓓ Ⓔ  41. Ⓐ Ⓑ Ⓒ Ⓓ Ⓔ
2. Ⓐ Ⓑ Ⓒ Ⓓ Ⓔ  12. Ⓐ Ⓑ Ⓒ Ⓓ Ⓔ  22. Ⓐ Ⓑ Ⓒ Ⓓ Ⓔ  32. Ⓐ Ⓑ Ⓒ Ⓓ Ⓔ  42. Ⓐ Ⓑ Ⓒ Ⓓ Ⓔ
3. Ⓐ Ⓑ Ⓒ Ⓓ Ⓔ  13. Ⓐ Ⓑ Ⓒ Ⓓ Ⓔ  23. Ⓐ Ⓑ Ⓒ Ⓓ Ⓔ  33. Ⓐ Ⓑ Ⓒ Ⓓ Ⓔ  43. Ⓐ Ⓑ Ⓒ Ⓓ Ⓔ
4. Ⓐ Ⓑ Ⓒ Ⓓ Ⓔ  14. Ⓐ Ⓑ Ⓒ Ⓓ Ⓔ  24. Ⓐ Ⓑ Ⓒ Ⓓ Ⓔ  34. Ⓐ Ⓑ Ⓒ Ⓓ Ⓔ  44. Ⓐ Ⓑ Ⓒ Ⓓ Ⓔ
5. Ⓐ Ⓑ Ⓒ Ⓓ Ⓔ  15. Ⓐ Ⓑ Ⓒ Ⓓ Ⓔ  25. Ⓐ Ⓑ Ⓒ Ⓓ Ⓔ  35. Ⓐ Ⓑ Ⓒ Ⓓ Ⓔ  45. Ⓐ Ⓑ Ⓒ Ⓓ Ⓔ
6. Ⓐ Ⓑ Ⓒ Ⓓ Ⓔ  16. Ⓐ Ⓑ Ⓒ Ⓓ Ⓔ  26. Ⓐ Ⓑ Ⓒ Ⓓ Ⓔ  36. Ⓐ Ⓑ Ⓒ Ⓓ Ⓔ  46. Ⓐ Ⓑ Ⓒ Ⓓ Ⓔ
7. Ⓐ Ⓑ Ⓒ Ⓓ Ⓔ  17. Ⓐ Ⓑ Ⓒ Ⓓ Ⓔ  27. Ⓐ Ⓑ Ⓒ Ⓓ Ⓔ  37. Ⓐ Ⓑ Ⓒ Ⓓ Ⓔ  47. Ⓐ Ⓑ Ⓒ Ⓓ Ⓔ
8. Ⓐ Ⓑ Ⓒ Ⓓ Ⓔ  18. Ⓐ Ⓑ Ⓒ Ⓓ Ⓔ  28. Ⓐ Ⓑ Ⓒ Ⓓ Ⓔ  38. Ⓐ Ⓑ Ⓒ Ⓓ Ⓔ  48. Ⓐ Ⓑ Ⓒ Ⓓ Ⓔ
9. Ⓐ Ⓑ Ⓒ Ⓓ Ⓔ  19. Ⓐ Ⓑ Ⓒ Ⓓ Ⓔ  29. Ⓐ Ⓑ Ⓒ Ⓓ Ⓔ  39. Ⓐ Ⓑ Ⓒ Ⓓ Ⓔ  49. Ⓐ Ⓑ Ⓒ Ⓓ Ⓔ
10. Ⓐ Ⓑ Ⓒ Ⓓ Ⓔ  20. Ⓐ Ⓑ Ⓒ Ⓓ Ⓔ  30. Ⓐ Ⓑ Ⓒ Ⓓ Ⓔ  40. Ⓐ Ⓑ Ⓒ Ⓓ Ⓔ  50. Ⓐ Ⓑ Ⓒ Ⓓ Ⓔ

**WRITING**

Topic A

_____

_____

_____

_____

_____

_____

_____

_____

_____

_____

_____

_____

_____

_____

_____

_____

_____

_____

_____

_____

_____

_____

_____

_____

_____

_____

_____

_____

_____

_____

_____

_____

_____

Topic B

# PRACTICE TEST 2 (CBEST)

## FORMAT OF THE CBEST

| | | |
|---|---|---|
| Reading | 50 Questions | 65 minutes |
| Mathematics | 50 Questions | 70 minutes |
| ——————— Break ——————— | | |
| Writing | 2 Essays | 60 minutes |

## SCORING THE TEST

Raw scores for Reading and Mathematics sections are determined by totaling the number of questions answered correctly. There is no penalty for incorrect answers. Each of the two essays is scored on a scale of 1 (fail) to 4 (pass). Passing scores are set at a total scaled score for all three sections.

# READING

**65 MINUTES—50 QUESTIONS**

**Directions:** Choose the best answer for each question and blacken the corresponding space on the Answer Sheet for Sample Test 1. The correct answers and explanations follow the test.

## QUESTIONS 1–3 REFER TO THE FOLLOWING PASSAGE.

The number of first-aid information classes for children ages four to fourteen is increasing. Because of the rising maternal employment rate, growing numbers of children are spending part of the day alone or with foreign-speaking housekeepers. This increases the likelihood that children will have to deal with emergencies partially or entirely on their own. The first-aid programs are designed to help prevent household and other accidents, home fires, child abuse, and kidnapping. Children can choose among courses such as first aid, fingerprinting and photo identification, fire safety, emergency telephone calling, personal safety, and babysitting safety. Children ten or older can also attend an hour-long cardiopulmonary resuscitation class.

Children practice emergency calling know-how and the use of the 911 number, but only after they have learned that this number should be called only when a police officer, firefighters, or an ambulance is needed quickly. Children learn about such things as wearing seat belts and the do's and don'ts for treating burns and broken bones. They learn not to put butter on burns, because it insulates the burn and retains heat. They also learn that they should not try to straighten broken bones but to leave that for the doctor to do.

1. A child who is nine can participate in which of the following programs?

   **(A)** Fingerprinting and photo identification
   **(B)** How to deal with broken bones
   **(C)** Cardiopulmonary resuscitation
   **(D)** All of the above
   **(E)** Choices (A) and (B) only

2. The underlying cause of the increasing number of children's first-aid programs is

   **(A)** increased crime rate
   **(B)** better health awareness
   **(C)** more mothers working
   **(D)** federal funding for the programs
   **(E)** increase in the number of emergency situations

3. According to the passage, children can learn all of the following EXCEPT

   **(A)** how to call the emergency number
   **(B)** what to put on a burn
   **(C)** how to straighten a broken bone
   **(D)** how to prevent household accidents
   **(E)** how to prevent kidnapping

## QUESTIONS 4–7 REFER TO THE FOLLOWING PASSAGE.

A nationwide study may shatter the widely held notion that a mother's employment is detrimental to her children. It states that school-age children of working mothers outscore children of mothers who do not work outside the home in math and reading. They have a lower absentee rate from school and have significantly higher IQ scores. The new study also found that children of employed mothers are more self-reliant than children of nonworking mothers. This supports earlier studies that showed a higher sense of self-esteem and greater skill in handling personal relationships among children of working mothers. Employed mothers participate in significantly more recreational activities with their children than do their nonworking counterparts. All significant social and academic criteria favor children of employed mothers. However, working mothers were shown to rely more heavily on babysitters and relatives for evening childcare than mothers who are not employed. Families of nonworking mothers were more likely to have more members of the family present at the evening meal. Nonworking mothers expressed higher satisfaction with their own parenting, and their children also reported better mother-child relations.

4. According to the study, mothers working outside the home

   **(A)** had more family members at the evening meal
   **(B)** were more satisfied with their parenting than nonworking mothers
   **(C)** felt more guilty about their work
   **(D)** did more recreational things with their children
   **(E)** stayed home more in the evenings

5. Who reported higher satisfaction with parenting and mother-child relationships?

   **(A)** Employed mothers
   **(B)** Children of employed mothers
   **(C)** Mothers staying home
   **(D)** Children of mothers who stay at home
   **(E** Choices (C) and (D)

6. We can infer from the passage that it was previously believed that

   (A)   a mother's work had detrimental effects on her children

   (B)   children of working mothers had a high sense of self-esteem

   (C)   children of nonworking mothers had a high absentee rate from school

   (D)   working mothers had a high sense of satisfaction with their parenting

   (E)   children of working mothers were left alone a great deal

## QUESTIONS 7–8 REFER TO THE FOLLOWING PASSAGE.

Why and how did Europeans, alone among the peoples of the world, disperse around the globe? For most of human history, oceans were unbreachable barriers to the movement of people from one continent to another. As a result, Asians are principally in Asia, Africans are primarily in Africa, Arabs are mainly in the Middle East, Polynesians in the islands of the Pacific, Indians in India, and so forth. But Europeans are everywhere—Greenland, Iceland, Australia, North and South America, and parts of Africa. Why is this?

One reason that has been put forth is technology. The Renaissance gave European seamen ships that could cross oceans, and sufficient seamanship and navigational skills to make such voyages possible. It also gave them tools and weapons to conquer stone-age civilizations with dispatch. Why only Europeans had this technology is yet another question.

Another approach to the spread of European influence is that rather than technology, it was the plants and microbes that the Europeans brought with them that enabled them to conquer many of the lands they surveyed. Among the living things they brought with them, which included plants and animals, were the diseases that gave them the upper hand. In Europe, periodic smallpox epidemics wiped out large numbers of people, but conferred immunity on those who survived. In the New World, the native people had no such diseases and no such immunity. As a result, the natives of America and Australia were almost defenseless against the onslaught of microbes brought in by the Europeans. Measles could wipe out an entire native population.

7. "The Europeans dispersed all over the world and readily conquered native civilizations primarily because of the diseases they brought with them and their immunity to most of them."

Which of the following describes this statement?

   (A)   Factual

   (B)   A supposition

   (C)   A conclusion based on interpretation of facts

   (D)   Unrelated to the passage

   (E)   Based on technical knowledge

8. Why were the Europeans able to spread to all areas of the world?

   (A)   Because there were too many of them

   (B)   Because they had navigational knowledge

   (C)   Because they had superior armies

   (D)   Because they had superior medical knowledge

   (E)   Though several theories have been presented, we still don't know.

9. There has long been a tradition of firefighters in my family. Although we fight fires all over the United States, most of us come from the Southwest. We follow in our fathers' footsteps. We have all been trained to protect our neighborhoods but are eager to help elsewhere. We have a natural dedication to preserving the land because of our strong ties to the earth. Natural resources mean more to my family than to most other people.

According to the passage, the author's family

   (A)   feels strongly about preserving nature

   (B)   is able to withstand the rigors of fire-fighting

   (C)   fights fires wherever they occur

   (D)   views firefighting as a good livelihood

   (E)   All of the above

10. The most prominent piece of sculpture in a city-center mall has disappeared. Various persons have tried to figure what happened to it. Outstanding in the investigation is that most people didn't even notice the sculpture was missing. There is speculation as to what happened to it. It may have been bulldozed accidentally or on purpose.

What is the central idea of the passage?

   (A)   The sculpture was too small to be noticed.

   (B)   The sculpture wasn't important to begin with.

   (C)   The sculpture wasn't noticed to begin with.

   (D)   Everyone hated it.

   (E)   People wanted to get rid of it.

## QUESTIONS 11–15 REFER TO THE FOLLOWING PASSAGE.

It is too late to start thinking about your retirement on the day you pick up your gold watch, if you are lucky enough to get a gold watch. Regardless of your age, now is the time to figure out how much you will need in order to make your retirement secure, and where that money will come from. When you are in your thirties, start setting priorities for your spending, so that your major expenses will be paid off when you retire. For example, buy a house or apartment so that your mortgage will be paid off by the time you leave your job. Try to save at least 5 percent of your pay, and build an emergency fund equal to three to six months of your living expenses. When you reach 45, try to invest 10 percent of your income and, if possible, try not to switch jobs until you are fully vested in your pension plan. If you anticipate large college expenses for your children, start savings and investment accounts in their names. In your fifties, try to save 10 to 15 percent of your income. When you reach 60, you may already be collecting your pension. Many companies are encouraging employees to take early retirement. Do your research carefully before deciding to take advantage of this option. Early retirees' pension checks are considerably less than the checks for those who retire at 65. The difference in payments can be substantial. In some cases, retiring at 55 may entitle you to only 25 percent of the pension you would have received had you worked until age 65. If you decide to retire early, figure out what you want to do, and whether you can afford to do it. Most retirees need at least 60 to 70 percent of their preretirement salary to maintain their standard of living. Your needs may fall at the lower end of that range if your major outlays such as housing, children's education expenses, and medical bills are under control or taken care of. If not, you will need more. If the combination of your pension and social security falls short of your requirements, you will have to make up the difference through savings and investments or a second career.

11. The amount of money you will need for retirement

    (A) is the same for everyone
    (B) is covered by social security
    (C) depends on what your expenses are
    (D) can be projected in your thirties
    (E) is inflation-proof because it's tax free

12. The amount of money recommended to be set aside for retirement

    (A) varies with your age
    (B) depends on how much you earn
    (C) doesn't take into consideration people's varying retirement expenses
    (D) is too conservative
    (E) does not allow for inflation

13. The factors which affect your retirement income are

    (A) whether your house is paid for or not
    (B) whether your children are self-sufficient
    (C) whether you have paid medical insurance or not
    (D) whether you are vested in your pension plan or not
    (E) All of the above

14. The passage could be classified as

    (A) informative
    (B) persuasive
    (C) factual
    (D) biased
    (E) cause and effect

15. According to the passage, early retirement

    (A) should be taken advantage of because it extends your enjoyable life span
    (B) affords you the opportunity of a second career
    (C) makes the best use of your earning power
    (D) should be carefully checked out
    (E) gives you the option of investing your retirement income at your discretion

## QUESTIONS 16–19 REFER TO THE FOLLOWING PASSAGE.

A subject that generally is not discussed before marriage is money and how it should be handled. Many divorced couples will agree that the way money is handled can break up a marriage. Do happily married couples and those later divorced differ in how they decide to spend money? Researchers say, "Yes." A ten-year study in which couples were regularly interviewed to determine their marital satisfaction and financial decision-making and consumer behavior agrees. At the end of the ten-year period, one sixth of the couples had divorced, while another one sixth were happily married. The rest of the group was dropped from the study because they did not agree on the status of their relationship. Allocation of financial responsibility at the beginning of marriage was strongly related to subsequent marital satisfaction. Happily married couples tend to develop areas of specialization and greater joint influence or joint decision-making than couples who were later divorced. Divorced couples showed more dominance by the husband and less influence by the wife. Couples who later divorced spent more money on items such as stereos and color television sets, while happily married couples spent more money for homes, furniture, appliances, and recreational vehicles—purchases that reflect family commitment.

16. The factor that did not seem to make a difference between happily married couples and those who divorced was

   (A) the allocation of fiscal duties
   (B) extent of joint influence on spending
   (C) the extent of dominance in spending decisions
   (D) the total amount of income
   (E) the proportion of spending on electronic entertainment

17. A factor which is not mentioned as one leading to marital satisfaction is

   (A) early decision about which partner will be responsible for which expenses
   (B) the extent to which decisions are made jointly
   (C) the proportion of money spent on a home
   (D) the extent of spending on home entertainment
   (E) equal dominance of the partners in fiscal decisions

18. What part of the original study group was used to draw the conclusions from?

   (A) One sixth
   (B) One third
   (C) Two thirds
   (D) Five sixths
   (E) All

19. Mabel and Eric have been married for fifteen years. They own a house, a stereo, a color television, and just put new carpeting in their home. Mabel pays for all the groceries, her children's clothes, gifts, and outings. Eric takes care of the rest. Last year, Eric bought a car without discussing it with Mabel, as all major decisions are made by him. From this we can conclude that

   (A) Eric and Mabel are divorced and in the study
   (B) Eric and Mabel are happily married and in the study
   (C) Eric and Mabel are not in the study because they can't agree on their status
   (D) Eric and Mabel will not be married much longer
   (E) The information is inconclusive.

## QUESTIONS 20–22 REFER TO THE FOLLOWING PASSAGE.

Thousands of Americans who return from vacation suffer from a disease known as post-vacation depression. It usually lasts for only one to three weeks. Symptoms include feeling blue, not being able to sleep at night, short-temperedness, and not being able to get going in the morning. What should be done about it? Nothing. There are many theories about the cause of the depression. One psychologist speculates that people feel let down because they had such a good time on vacation and now they find themselves back at work doing something they don't like. Another psychologist says post-vacation depression stems from not being able to complete things before leaving on vacation. Yet another psychologist thinks that many people assume incorrectly that a vacation will resolve problems. Upon returning home, they are disappointed to find the problems are still there.

A vacation can refresh you and improve your outlook, but it can seldom resolve problems which were there before vacation time. Not only are the problems still there, but it will be an extended time before you can get away again. To prevent this, people should try to resolve their problems and get their lives in order before leaving on vacation, and use their vacations as a reward and celebration.

20. The number of theories advanced on the causes of post-vacation depression is

   (A) none
   (B) one
   (C) two
   (D) three
   (E) four

21. Post-vacation depression is caused by

   (A) the contrast between vacation and work
   (B) not tying up loose ends before leaving on vacation
   (C) disappointment that unresolved problems remain
   (D) All of these things
   (E) None of these things

22. A vacation can accomplish all of the following EXCEPT

   (A) be a reward for hard work
   (B) give you rest and relaxation
   (C) refresh your outlook on life
   (D) be a change of pace and scenery
   (E) eliminate problems in your life

## QUESTIONS 23–24 REFER TO THE FOLLOWING PASSAGE.

Ancient Greece had a democratic form of government, with all citizens voting on many issues. One issue decided by popular vote was whether or not a person should be banished. Citizens cast their ballots by writing the names of those they thought should be banished on pieces of tile, pottery, or oyster shell fragments, called ostrakons. The term of exile was determined by the number of votes cast. Because the names of the people to be banished were written on ostrakons, the people were said to be ostracized. The modern-day Amish in Pennsylvania have a similar form of punishment, called "shunning." A person who is shunned is not to be acknowledged or spoken to by any member of the community, including immediate family, for the period of time decided upon by the group. Shunning can last from one week to more than a year.

23. Currently, a person who is ostracized is considered to be

    (A) voted out of office
    (B) socially excluded
    (C) unpopular
    (D) exiled from the country
    (E) a collector of tile, pottery, or oyster shell fragments

24. The Amish custom of shunning is

    (A) a strong form of peer pressure
    (B) considered illegal in the United States
    (C) a custom copied from the Greeks
    (D) cruel and unusual punishment
    (E) a form of brainwashing

## QUESTION 25 REFERS TO THE FOLLOWING PASSAGE.

When you switch your television set to watch a classic movie like "Casablanca" or "Citizen Kane" you may be surprised to find that the film is in color, courtesy of a computerized process called colorization. The use of this process may be growing, to the chagrin of a large number of people who denounce the vulgarization of some of the best films ever made. The day may come when you will be able to see them only in color. What future generations, growing up only dimly aware that anything but color movies ever existed, will miss is an art form that, as employed by its most skillful directors, conveyed a sense of time, place, and mood in a way that color rarely achieves.

25. According to the passage, what is an advantage of black-and-white movies being shown in black and white as opposed to colorized?

    (A) They convey a sense of time appropriately.
    (B) They set the stage in a special manner.
    (C) They interpret the emotions involved sensitively.
    (D) All of the above
    (E) None of the above

## QUESTIONS 26–28 REFER TO THE FOLLOWING GRAPH.

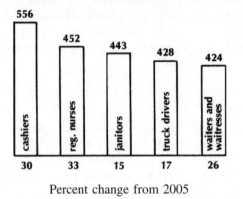

Where the New Jobs Will Be
(Shown in thousands)

Percent change from 2005

26. What conclusion can be drawn from the graph?

    (A) Many more people will need college education.
    (B) There will be fewer restaurants and food outlets.
    (C) Many jobs will become obsolete due to robotization.
    (D) The level of education needed for the majority of new jobs is low.
    (E) More people will be sick.

27. Which of the occupations listed already has the largest group of people employed?

    (A) Cashiers
    (B) Registered nurses
    (C) Janitors
    (D) Truck drivers
    (E) Waitresses and waiters

28. From the graph what projections can you make about business in 2015?

    (A) There will be an increase in the number of retail stores.
    (B) The trucking industry will diminish.
    (C) The increase in restaurants will be primarily in cafeteria and fast-food types.
    (D) Many of the jobs currently done by registered nurses will be taken over by licensed vocational nurses.
    (E) Scanners will affect the number of grocery store cashiers.

## QUESTIONS 29–31 REFER TO THE FOLLOWING PASSAGE.

Students headed toward many of the state universities this fall were picked from a record number of applicants despite higher tuition and tougher entrance requirements. Many students are driven to state colleges by spiraling private college costs. A student mirrored the current thinking when he said, "I figure I can get as good an education here, and the cost is far less." Out-of-state students also have been hit hard by rising tuition. One state university tripled its out-of-state tuition. Quality is also a lure at many state colleges.

In recent years, thirty-six states have raised their entrance requirements, requiring more English, science, math, and language courses. "Since we are a state-supported college with limited enrollment, we have no choice but to increase standards," stated an admissions officer. The average SAT scores for entering freshmen has gone up considerably as a result.

29. To what does the passage attribute the increase in average SAT scores of entering freshmen at state colleges?

(A) High schools are doing a better job of preparing students for college.

(B) There are more students trying to get into state colleges, and since the enrollment can't be raised, the competition for the number of places available is more intense.

(C) The increased cost of attending private schools has made many students change their focus.

(D) The education at public colleges was poor for many years, but now it is improving.

(E) Out-of-state tuition has been increased, thereby lessening competition.

30. Students are attending state-supported colleges in increasing numbers because of

   I. higher tuition at private colleges
   II. higher out-of-state tuition
   III. quality of the education available at state colleges
   IV. higher SAT scores needed for entrance to state colleges
   V. increase in subject requirements needed for entrance to state colleges

(A) I, II, and III only

(B) I, II, and IV only

(C) I, IV, and V only

(D) II, IV, and V only

(E) III and V only

31. Based upon the information provided, we can assume that fourteen states

(A) have lowered their entrance requirements

(B) have not increased their entrance requirements

(C) have not changed their entrance requirements

(D) require lower SAT scores

(E) require higher SAT scores

## QUESTIONS 32–35 REFER TO THE FOLLOWING PASSAGE.

Here are some tips on creating a favorable environment for schoolwork your child must do at home. Be a good role model for your child. Do chores that require thinking in front of your child, such as balancing your checkbook, reading, writing letters, or working on a home computer.

A child needs a quiet setting for studying, preferably away from television or other distractions; therefore, you should create a special place for studying. Children should be discouraged from studying in bed.

Keep good research sources handy for your child. It is easier for a child to do homework and check facts if the parents keep a good dictionary, atlas, encyclopedia, and almanac in the house.

Check your child's homework. Though a child may not bring homework home every night, you should be suspicious if he or she never brings any home.

Show interest in your child's learning by staying in contact with his or her teacher. Ask questions about what he or she is learning at school. The dinner table is an excellent setting for these chats.

Let your child know you're proud of his or her accomplishments, but that mistakes are human. Acknowledge your child's efforts to learn in order to teach that the act of learning is worthwhile. Try not to let your child get too uptight or too relaxed about schoolwork. If a child is overwhelmed or overly anxious, he or she may give up. If he or she is overconfident, the child may not exert the effort necessary to master the subject. Teach self-discipline. Your child needs to learn that work comes before play.

Start reading to your child when he or she is young. When your child is able to read alone, have fun reading material on hand. Get him or her a library card, and go often, so he or she will feel comfortable at the library.

Monitor school schedules. Parents with older children should keep track of how much time is spent on outside jobs. An after-school job is fine, but parents should be sure it is not interfering with schoolwork.

**32.** The central idea of the passage is that parents

**(A)** should follow prescribed outlines to ensure their child's progress

**(B)** play an important role in their child's educational progress

**(C)** should be involved in every aspect of their child's life

**(D)** should read to their child as often as possible

**(E)** need to invest a lot of money in their children's education

**33.** In order to create a good atmosphere for a child's learning environment, parents

**(A)** should follow those suggestions that are appropriate for their family

**(B)** must follow all the suggestions in the passage

**(C)** should plan the child's day so there is no free time to get into trouble.

**(D)** should not let their child have an outside job, as that interferes with studies

**(E)** should join a parents' support group

**34.** The format of this passage is

**(A)** premise and a number of reasons to support it

**(B)** cause and effect

**(C)** premise and a listing of examples

**(D)** chronological sequences

**(E)** thesis and disproof of antithesis

**35.** In which area does the passage suggest that parents should try to keep a balance?

**(A)** Self-discipline

**(B)** Study settings

**(C)** Learning efforts

**(D)** Reading

**(E)** Inquiry about schoolwork

**36.** "The symphony will give a performance tonight at 8 p.m. through Sunday."

This sentence

**(A)** is a concise and accurate statement

**(B)** is misleading because it gives the impression that the performance will last from 8 p.m. tonight until Sunday.

**(C)** is misleading because it gives the impression that the symphony will perform at 8 p.m. every evening through Sunday

**(D)** clarifies that the performance starts at 8 p.m. tonight and goes on until Sunday

**(E)** makes it clear that the performance is at 8 p.m. each night through Sunday

## QUESTIONS 37–42 REFER TO THE FOLLOWING PASSAGE.

Plague in the United States? It's unthinkable! The plague killed millions of people in the Orient, Western Europe, and the Americas during the three great pandemics of history. During the second pandemic in the fourteenth century, it was called the Black Plague because the disease darkened the victims' skin just before they died.

There has hardly been a time when the world has been without plague, but there are some areas of the world that have been plague-free so far. It may be that the rodents that carry the plague fleas do not live there. Plague tends to thrive in cool, high altitudes. In the United States, it's found in the West and the Southwest. Plague flourishes in host rodents such as rats, squirrels, and chipmunks until the animal die of it. Then, the fleas move to other living hosts, like cats. Humans usually contract plague by means of a flea bite. Much of the danger comes from the increasing intimacy between creatures and humans. For example, ground squirrels populate parks and accept treats from people, and in the mountains, marmots sneak into summer cabins to nest. Most deaths from plague occur because victims wait too long to seek medical help and doctors diagnose the disease too late. Plague's symptoms are fever, chills, headache, muscle aches, feeling of weakness, and swollen and tender lymph nodes. It is essential to contact a doctor if any of these symptoms develop within seven days of possible exposure to plague.

To avoid plague, the Department of Public Health suggests that you avoid dead or sick animals, especially cats. Deny rodents food and shelter. Put a bell on your cat's collar to minimize its contact with rodents. When camping with pets, confine or leash them to reduce their exposure to rodents. Don't feed rodents in campgrounds and picnic areas. Spray insect repellent on socks and pants' cuffs, and tuck trousers into boot tops to reduce exposure to fleas.

**37.** According to the passage, people can contract plague from

**(A)** contact with rodents

**(B)** flea bites

**(C)** other people who have plague

**(D)** All of the above

**(E)** None of the above

**38.** The first pandemic occurred

**(A)** during 1400 BC

**(B)** before 1300 AD

**(C)** before 1400 AD

**(D)** during 1400 AD

**(E)** before 1400 BC

39. The third pandemic

   (A) spread over a wide geographic area and affected a high proportion of people
   (B) spread over a small geographic area and affected a high proportion of people
   (C) spread over a small geographic area and affected a small proportion of people
   (D) spread over a wide geographic area and affected a small proportion of people
   (E) caused pandemonium over a wide geographical area

40. To avoid contracting plague, it is suggested that one adhere to all of the following suggestions EXCEPT

   (A) keep your cat on a leash when you take her along camping
   (B) put out feed for the squirrels in your back yard
   (C) don't bury the cat that was killed on the mountain road
   (D) don't feed the chipmunks that come to your picnic table in the park
   (E) use insecticide liberally

41. Rodents mentioned include all of the following EXCEPT

   (A) rats
   (B) squirrels
   (C) lemmings
   (D) chipmunks
   (E) marmots

42. Plague could be found in all of these areas EXCEPT

   (A) China
   (B) Cuba
   C) Chile
   (D) France
   (E) Colorado

43. Too little fluoride can deprive children of protection against cavities, but too much can cause discoloration of tooth enamel.

   Based on the above information, what action should be taken?

   (A) Children should not be given fluoride at all.
   (B) Children should be given only a moderate amount of fluoride.
   (C) Children should be given a generous amount of fluoride.
   (D) Children should be given as much fluoride as they can handle.
   (E) None of these actions should be taken.

## QUESTIONS 44–45 REFER TO THE FOLLOWING PASSAGE.

Thirteen percent of American adults are illiterate. As a result, about nineteen million Americans have difficulty reading want ads, filling out employment applications, and reading job instructions.

44. From the above information we can conclude that these people

   (A) don't want to work
   (B) don't want to learn to read
   (C) have a high unemployment rate
   (D) are immigrants
   (E) are illegal aliens

45. People who are illiterate

   (A) learn to compensate for their lack of reading ability
   (B) have below-average intelligence
   (C) are not willing workers
   (D) have not had an opportunity to learn to read
   (E) are opposed to education

## QUESTIONS 46–48 REFER TO THE FOLLOWING PASSAGE.

One psychologist equates SAT scores with the size of families. As families become larger, the children tend to be less mature intellectually. For the twenty years leading up to 1980, test scores dropped. Since then they have increased, a reflection of the size of the test-takers' families. This trend is expected to continue until the year 2010.

46. Based on the passage, family size

   (A) will remain stable over a fifty-year period
   (B) will start to decrease in 2010
   (C) started to decrease in 1960
   (D) will decrease until the year 2010
   (E) started to decrease in 1975

47. Based upon the information in the passage, SAT test-takers of the year 2010 will

   (A) come from a large family and be intellectually mature
   (B) come from a small family and be intellectually mature
   (C) come from a small family and be intellectually immature
   (D) come from a large family and be intellectually immature
   (E) have a lower SAT score regardless of family size

**48.** If the information in the passage were charted, it would look like this.

(A)  SAT Scores

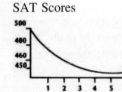

Year  1960      1980      2000

(B)  SAT Scores

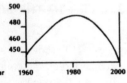

Number of Children

(C)  SAT Scores

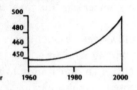

Year   1960      1980      2000

(D)  SAT Scores

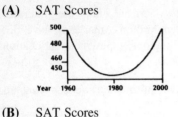

Year  1960      1980      2000

(E)  SAT Scores

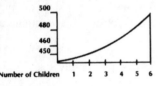

Number of Children  1   2   3   4   5   6

**49.** Only about one tenth of an iceberg is visible above the water. Eight to nine times as much ice is hidden below the water line. In the Antarctic Ocean, near the South Pole, there are icebergs that rise as high as 300 feet above the water.

The paragraph best supports the statement that icebergs in the Antarctic Ocean

(A)  are usually 300 fee high.
(B)  can be as much as 3,000 feet in total height.
(C)  are difficult to spot.
(D)  are a hazard to navigation.
(E)  are near the South Pole.

**50.** It is a common assumption that city directories are prepared and published by the cities concerned. However, the directory business is as much a private business as is the publishing of dictionaries and encyclopedias. The companies financing the publication make their profits through the sales of the directories themselves and through the advertising in them.

The paragraph best supports the statement that

(A)  the publication of a city directory is a commercial enterprise.
(B)  the size of a city directory limits the space devoted to advertising.
(C)  many city directories are published by dictionary and encyclopedia concerns.
(D)  city directories are sold at cost to local residents and businessmen.
(E)  city directories are published by nonprofit organizations.

# MATHEMATICS

**70 MINUTES—50 QUESTIONS**

**Directions:** Choose the best answer for each question and blacken the corresponding space on the Answer Sheet for Sample Test 1. The correct answers and explanations follow the test.

1. What is $x$ if $4x + 7 < -9$?

   (A) $x < 4$
   (B) $x > 4$
   (C) $x < -4$
   (D) $x > -4$
   (E) $x < -\dfrac{1}{2}$

2. The prime factors of 2,310 are

   (A) $10 \times 5 \times 7 \times 11$
   (B) $2 \times 3 \times 5 \times 77$
   (C) $2 \times 15 \times 7 \times 11$
   (D) $2 \times 3 \times 5 \times 7 \times 11$
   (E) $1 \times 2 \times 3 \times 5 \times 7 \times 11$

3. If $K$ represents an odd number and $M$ represents an even number, which of the following statements are odd?

   I. $2K^3 + 3K^2 + K$
   II. $2M^3 + 3M^2 + M$
   III. $M^2 K^2 + MK + K$

   (A) I only
   (B) II only
   (C) III only
   (D) I and III only
   (E) I and II only

4. $7 - 4(3 - 6) =$

   (A) $-11$
   (B) $-9$
   (C) $1$
   (D) $5$
   (E) $19$

5. When Richard wanted to find out what percent 32 is of 45, he tried it five different ways. Which one is correct?

   (A) $\dfrac{32}{45}$

   (B) $\dfrac{45}{32} \times 100$

   (C) $\dfrac{45 \times 32}{100}$

   (D) $\dfrac{45}{32 \times 100}$

   (E) $\dfrac{32 \times 100}{45}$

6. When public service channel EDUC held its auction, one company offered to match funds with donors. For every \$15.00 a donor pledged, the company would donate \$13.00. How much did the company give when Paul donated \$105.00?

   (A) \$13.00
   (B) \$28.00
   (C) \$90.00
   (D) \$91.00
   (E) \$120.00

7. If $x^2 = \sqrt{y}$ then $y =$

   (A) $x^4$
   (B) $x$
   (C) $x^2$
   (D) $\sqrt{2^x}$
   (E) $y$

8. If $P = 7$, find the value of $2P^3 + 3P^2 - 4P + 5$.

   (A) $61$
   (B) $180$
   (C) $810$
   (D) $866$
   (E) $3,162$

9. $7 \times 10^6 + 6 \times 10^5 + 8 \times 10^4 + 5 \times 10^3 =$

   (A) $7,685$
   (B) $76,850$
   (C) $768,500$
   (D) $76 \times 10^3$
   (E) $7.685 \times 10^6$

10. $\dfrac{4}{10,000}$ would be written

   (A)  40,000
   (B)  2,500
   (C)  0.004
   (D)  0.0004
   (E)  0.00004

11. $0.0146 \div 0.125 =$

   (A)  0.0117
   (B)  0.117
   (C)  0.8506
   (D)  1.170
   (E)  8.506

12. $8\dfrac{5}{8} \div 6\dfrac{4}{7} =$

   (A)  $\dfrac{28}{1587}$

   (B)  $\dfrac{16}{21}$

   (C)  $1\dfrac{5}{16}$

   (D)  $1\dfrac{5}{56}$

   (E)  $9\dfrac{1}{3}$

13. $5a^2 (2a^3 + 6a^2 - a) =$

   (A)  $35a^6$
   (B)  $10a^6 + 30a^4 + 5a^3$
   (C)  $10a^6 + 30a^4 - 5a^2$
   (D)  $10a^5 + 30a^4 + 5a^3$
   (E)  $10a^5 + 30a^4 - 5a^3$

14. If $2x + y = 9$ and $3x - y = 1$, what is the value of $x$?

   (A)  $\dfrac{8}{5}$

   (B)  10
   (C)  2
   (D)  $-4$
   (E)  5

**QUESTIONS 15–16 REFER TO THE FOLLOWING INFORMATION.**

Before the sluice gates of the dam were opened, the level of the reservoir was 8 feet below the normal water level. After the gates had been open for 5 hours, the level was 7 feet above the normal level.

15. How much did the level of the reservoir rise?

   (A)  1 ft
   (B)  5 ft
   (C)  7 ft
   (D)  8 ft
   (E)  15 ft

16. How many feet per hour did the water in the reservoir rise?

   (A)  $1\dfrac{3}{5}$ ft per hour

   (B)  $\dfrac{5}{7}$ ft per hou

   (C)  $1\dfrac{2}{5}$ ft per hou

   (D)  $1\dfrac{1}{7}$ ft per hou

   (E)  3 ft per hour

**QUESTIONS 17–18 REFER TO THE FOLLOWING FIGURE.**

EF = 2 CD
AG = FG

17. What is the perimeter of the enclosed area?

   (A)  40
   (B)  36
   (C)  37
   (D)  32
   (E)  29

**18.** What is the area of the enclosed figure?

    **(A)** 58
    **(B)** 37
    **(C)** 64
    **(D)** 40
    **(E)** Not enough information

**19.**

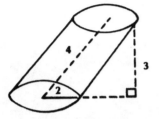

The volume of a cylinder is $\pi r^2 \times$ altitude. What is the volume of the cylinder shown above?

    **(A)** $12\pi$
    **(B)** $16\pi$
    **(C)** $18\pi$
    **(D)** $24\pi$
    **(E)** $32\pi$

**20.**

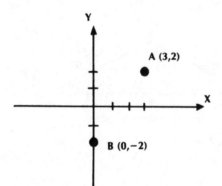

What is the distance between points A and B?

    **(A)** 5
    **(B)** 4
    **(C)** 0
    **(D)** 3
    **(E)** $-5$

**21.** ABC is an isosceles triangle with AB = AC.

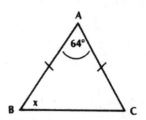

What is the measurement of angle $x$?

    **(A)** $64°$
    **(B)** $60°$
    **(C)** $58°$
    **(D)** $116°$
    **(E)** $32°$

**22.**

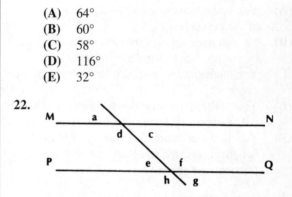

Lines MN and PQ are parallel. Which angles are equal?

    **(A)** a, b, and c
    **(B)** a, c, e, and g
    **(C)** a, d, e, and h
    **(D)** a, c, f, and g
    **(E)** b, d, e, and f

**23.**

| S | M | T | W | Th | F | S |
|---|---|---|---|----|---|---|
| 9 | 10 | 11 | 12 | 13 | 14 | 15 |
| 16 | 17 | 18 | 19 | 20 | 21 | 22 |

Susan can see only part of her calendar. On which day of the week was the first of the month shown?

    **(A)** Wednesday
    **(B)** Thursday
    **(C)** Friday
    **(D)** Saturday
    **(E)** Sunday

**QUESTIONS 24–25 REFER TO THE FOLLOWING PROBLEM.**

$$\frac{1}{3} \times \frac{4}{9} \times \frac{7}{6} \times \frac{18}{21} \times \frac{15}{24} =$$

24. When Sharon tried to do this problem, she found the multiplication difficult. She thought there might be an easier way. Is there?

  (A) Yes, add the numerators and divide by the sum of the denominators.
  (B) No, you must multiply the numerators and divide by the product of the denominators.
  (C) Yes, numerators and denominators can be canceled.
  (D) Yes, multiply the first two fractions, then multiply that product by the next fraction, and so on.
  (E) Yes, find a common denominator, add the first two fractions, reduce, then add it to the next fraction, and so on.

25. The answer to the problem above is

  (A) $\frac{44}{63}$

  (B) $\frac{5}{81}$

  (C) $\frac{28}{39}$

  (D) $\frac{1}{9}$

  (E) $\frac{5}{54}$

26. To determine what part 18 is of 81, you would use which of the following expressions?

  (A) $18 \div 81$
  (B) $81 \div 18$
  (C) $(18 \div 81) \times 100$
  (D) $(81 \div 18) \times 100$
  (E) None of these

27. $\dfrac{\sqrt{1600}}{\sqrt{64}}$

  (A) 5
  (B) 7
  (C) 25
  (D) 50
  (E) Cannot be solved

28. A right triangle may have

  (A) three right angles
  (B) two right angles
  (C) all sides of equal length
  (D) two angles of equal measure
  (E) one angle greater than a right angle

29. $\dfrac{3}{5}$ changed to a decimal is

  (A) 3.5
  (B) 0.60
  (C) 0.06
  (D) 5.3
  (E) 0.35

30. Jill and two friends bought a lottery ticket together. Jill's share was 28%. When the ticket won, she got $70.00. What was the full amount of the winnings?

  (A) $19.60
  (B) $196.00
  (C) $142.00
  (D) $98.00
  (E) $250.00

31.

Note: Graphic not drawn to scale.

The smallest angle is

  (A) $\angle ABC$
  (B) $\angle CBA$
  (C) $\angle BCA$
  (D) $\angle BAC$
  (E) $\angle CAB$

32. $\dfrac{1}{8} + \dfrac{1}{6}$

The least common denominator for the above problem is

  (A) 24
  (B) 48
  (C) 8
  (D) 6
  (E) $\dfrac{7}{24}$

**33.** Grandfather gave the children a riddle. "I am 60 years old. I am 4 years younger than 8 times Sally's age. How old is Sally?" What is the answer to the riddle?

(A) 7
(B) 7.5
(C) 8
(D) 15
(E) 30

**34.** $10 - 6 [3 \times 4 - (7 - 3)^2 + 12 \div 6] =$

The first step in this problem would be

(A) $10 - 6 [12 - (7 - 3)^2 + 12 \div 6] =$
(B) $10 - 6 \times 3 \times 4 - (7 - 3)^2 + 2 =$
(C) $4 [3 \times 4 - (7 - 3)^2 + 12 \div 6] =$
(D) $10 - 6 [12 - 4^2 + 2] =$
(E) $10 - 6 [3 \times 4 - 4^2 + 12 \div 6] =$

**35.** $(4a + 6)(2a + 3) =$

(A) $6a + 18$
(B) $6a^2 + 18$
(C) $8a^2 + 12a + 18$
(D) $8a^2 + 18$
(E) $8a^2 + 24a + 18$

### QUESTIONS 36–37 REFER TO THE FOLLOWING INFORMATION.

Jonathan bought items at the grocery store, some of which were taxed at 5% and some of which were not taxed. He bought a candy bar for 35 cents (taxable), two pencils at 20 cents each (taxable), three apples at 17 cents each (nontaxable) and a note pad (taxable) for $1.69.

**36.** How much tax did Jonathan pay?

(A) 11 cents
(B) 12 cents
(C) 13 cents
(D) 14 cents
(E) 15 cents

**37.** How much did Jonathan pay altogether?

(A) $2.53
(B) $2.56
(C) $2.86
(D) $3.07
(E) $3.10

**38.** $3K^2 - 4K + 7 - 2K^2 =$

(A) $K^2 - 4K + 7$
(B) $-4 + 7$
(C) $6K^2 - 4K + 7$
(D) $-6K^4 - 4K + 7$
(E) $-3K^5 + 7$

**39.**

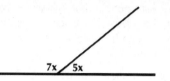

How big is the larger angle?

(A) 10°
(B) 52°
(C) 56°
(D) 105°
(E) 120°

**40.** The temperature on Sunday rose from 51°F to 86°F. What was the high temperature in Centigrade?

(A) 16°C
(B) 30°C
(C) 35°C
(D) 51°C
(E) 86°C

**41.** 84, 81, 85, 87, 86, 89, 79, 93, 89

Of the above list of numbers, 86 is the

(A) mode
(B) range
(C) median
(D) mean
(E) deviation

**42.** Eggs are packed in crates which hold 7 rows of 6 eggs in each layer, with a total of 5 layers. If the average breakage rate is 1.9%, on the average how many eggs are broken per crate?

(A) 2
(B) 4
(C) 5
(D) 6
(E) 7

**43.** Paul bought $2\frac{1}{2}$ lbs. of candy at 69 cents per pound and $1\frac{1}{2}$ pounds at 89 cents per pound. How much did he pay for all of the candy?

(A) $1.73
(B) $2.23
(C) $3.55
(D) $3.95
(E) $4.45

**44.** Brian had lost one test, but has scores of 76, 78, 81, and 96 on the others. His teacher says his average on the five tests is 83. When he tried to figure out the score on the missing test,

(A) he got an answer of 81
(B) he got an answer of 82
(C) he got an answer of 83
(D) he got an answer of 84
(E) he found it couldn't be done

**45.** It was discount day at Great Day Market. Mrs. Swanson bought $69.50 of groceries, on which she got a 12% discount. How much did she pay for her groceries?

(A) $8.34
(B) $61.16
(C) $69.50
(D) $68.67
(E) $77.84

**46.** Twelve posters can be purchased for $13.80. How many posters can Shannon buy if she has $5.00?

(A) One
(B) Two
(C) Three
(D) Four
(E) Five

**47.** An elementary school's enrollment of 300 consisted of 45% girls. Then, 150 additional girls were enrolled. Which of the following cannot be calculated from this information?

(A) The total percentage of boys after the addition of 150 girls
(B) The original number of boys
(C) The total number of girls
(D) How many students were first-graders
(E) The percentage of girls after the 150 girls enrolled

**48.** Rob holds a compass pointing NW. If he rotates it 225° clockwise, in which direction will it point?

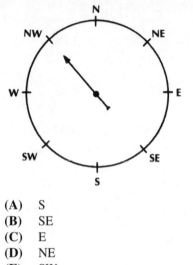

(A) S
(B) SE
(C) E
(D) NE
(E) SW

**49.** Sean took out a $10,000.00 loan at the credit union to buy a new car. The loan was for six years at 11.5% interest. What is the total interest paid by Sean?

(A) $1,150.00
(B) $6,900.00
(C) $10,000.00
(D) $11,000.00
(E) $16,900.00

**50.** Sean had a chance to get the same $10,000 loan for the car at 10.5% interest for eight years. Which of the two loans would result in the least total interest paid?

(A) There is no difference between the amount of total interest paid.
(B) 11.5% for six years
(C) 10.5% for eight years
(D) There is not enough information.
(E) 11.5% for eight years

# WRITING

## 60 MINUTES—TWO ESSAYS

**Directions:** You have 60 minutes in which to write two essays. The essay topics are intended to measure how well you write, given limitations on time and subject. Quality is more important than quantity. Spend some of your time organizing your thoughts. Use specific examples to support your opinions. Write only on the assigned topic. Write legibly and within the lines provided. Space for notes is provided below.

### Topic A

A good teacher needs more than a teaching credential and knowledge of the subject. Good teachers have special qualities that make them stand out. What special quality or qualities do you have that make you a good teacher? Tell about these qualities and how your having them makes you a better teacher.

### Topic B

An increasing number of states are requiring that candidates pass teacher competency tests to get a teaching credential. It has been suggested that the same test should be used in each state. State why you agree or disagree with this suggestion.

# ANSWER KEY AND EXPLANATIONS

## READING

| | | | | | | | |
|---|---|---|---|---|---|---|---|
| 1. E | 8. E | 15. D | 21. D | 27. C | 33. A | 39. A | 45. A |
| 2. C | 9. E | 16. D | 22. E | 28. A | 34. C | 40. B | 46. D |
| 3. C | 10. C | 17. D | 23. B | 29. B | 35. C | 41. C | 47. B |
| 4. D | 11. C | 18. B | 24. A | 30. A | 36. B | 42. B | 48. A |
| 5. E | 12. A | 19. E | 25. D | 31. B | 37. D | 43. B | 49. B |
| 6. A | 13. E | 20. D | 26. D | 32. B | 38. B | 44. C | 50. A |
| 7. C | 14. B | | | | | | |

1. **The correct answer is (E).** Cardiopulmonary resuscitation is for children ten or older.

2. **The correct answer is (C).** The underlying cause of the increasing number of children's first-aid programs is higher maternal employment rate.

3. **The correct answer is (C).** The answer can be found in the last sentence.

4. **The correct answer is (D).** According to the passage, employed mothers participate in significantly more recreational activities with their children than do nonworking mothers.

5. **The correct answer is (E).** The answer can be found in the last sentence.

6. **The correct answer is (A).** The answer can be found in the first sentence.

7. **The correct answer is (C).** That Europeans brought communicable disease with them is factual, but the conclusion is an interpretation of that fact.

8. **The correct answer is (E).** The passage mentions several possible reasons but does not settle upon one answer.

9. **The correct answer is (E).** All are mentioned in the passage.

10. **The correct answer is (C).** If people didn't notice the loss of the sculpture, they probably didn't notice it before it was gone.

11. **The correct answer is (C).** If your house and other major expenses are taken care of, you will need less money for retirement.

12. **The correct answer is (A).** The passage suggests setting aside 5 percent of your income at age 30, 10 percent at age 45, and 10 to 15 percent at age 55.

13. **The correct answer is (E).** All are mentioned in the passage.

14. **The correct answer is (B).** The article is trying to persuade you to save money for retirement.

15. **The correct answer is (D).** Early retirement may give you considerably less income.

16. **The correct answer is (D).** The amount of income is not mentioned.

17. **The correct answer is (D).** Divorced couples spend a larger amount on television and stereos.

18. **The correct answer is (B).** One sixth of the group was divorced and one sixth was happily married, which makes up a total of one third of the original group.

19. **The correct answer is (E).** The information doesn't point strongly one way or another.

20. **The correct answer is (D).** Three theories are given.

21. **The correct answer is (D).** All three causes are mentioned in the passage.

22. **The correct answer is (E).** Problems you left behind will still be there. The others are all listed as benefits.

23. **The correct answer is (B).** Currently, the banishment is social.

24. **The correct answer is (A).** The punishment is decided on and carried out by one's peers.

25. **The correct answer is (D).** All reasons are listed in the passage.

26. **The correct answer is (D).** Of the jobs shown, only nursing requires college education.

27. **The correct answer is (C).** The number of janitors will increase almost as much as the number of cashiers, but that only represents a 15 percent increase in the number of janitors, compared to a 30 percent increase in the number of cashiers.

28. **The correct answer is (A).** Since the greatest increase in jobs will be in cashiers, that must mean that there will be more stores.

29. **The correct answer is (B).** This information can be found in the last paragraph.

30. **The correct answer is (A).** IV and V are not reasons for attending state-supported colleges.

31. **The correct answer is (B).** Thirty-six states have increased their requirements.

32. **The correct answer is (B).** All of the suggestions discuss the parents' involvement. Choice (A) is too rigid, and choice (C) is overdoing it.

33. **The correct answer is (A).** Common sense leads to choice (A).

34. **The correct answer is (C).** The passage presents a list of suggestions on how parents can improve their child's learning environment.

35. **The correct answer is (C).** "Try not to let your child get too uptight or too relaxed about schoolwork."

36. **The correct answer is (B).** The sentence is unclear. It seems that the symphony will put on a marathon performance, which isn't likely.

37. **The correct answer is (D).** All are possible sources of contagion.

38. **The correct answer is (B).** If the second pandemic was in the fourteenth century, the first occurred before that.

39. **The correct answer is (A).** A pandemic is spread over a wide geographic area and affects a high proportion of its people.

40. **The correct answer is (B).** The passage strongly suggests not to feed rodents.

41. **The correct answer is (C).** Lemmings live in the Arctic and are not mentioned in the passage.

42. **The correct answer is (B).** Cuba is not cool and does not have high altitudes.

43. **The correct answer is (B).** Some fluoride is fine, but not too much.

44. **The correct answer is (C).** If people have difficulty reading want ads and application forms, they have difficulty getting into the job market. Eliminate the other answers.

45. **The correct answer is (A).** They compensate so well that most people are unaware that they know illiterates. Eliminate the other answers.

46. **The correct answer is (D).** Scores will continue to go up; therefore, families will decrease in size according to the reasoning expressed in the passage.

47. **The correct answer is (B).** Families will have fewer but more intellectually mature children.

48. **The correct answer is (A).** Graph (A) mirrors the information in the passage.

59. **The correct answer is (B).** If an iceberg towers 300 feet above the water line and only one tenth of its height is visible, its total height may well be 3,000 feet.

50. **The correct answer is (A).** The business of publishing city directories is a private business operated for profit. As such, it is a commercial enterprise.

## MATHEMATICS

| | | | | | | | | | | |
|---|---|---|---|---|---|---|---|---|---|---|
| 1. **C** | 8. **C** | 15. **E** | 21. **C** | 27. **A** | 33. **C** | 39. **D** | 45. **B** |
| 2. **D** | 9. **E** | 16. **E** | 22. **B** | 28. **D** | 34. **E** | 40. **B** | 46. **D** |
| 3. **C** | 10. **D** | 17. **A** | 23. **D** | 29. **B** | 35. **E** | 41. **C** | 47. **D** |
| 4. **E** | 11. **B** | 18. **E** | 24. **C** | 30. **E** | 36. **B** | 42. **B** | 48. **A** |
| 5. **E** | 12. **C** | 19. **A** | 25. **E** | 31. **C** | 37. **D** | 43. **D** | 49. **B** |
| 6. **D** | 13. **E** | 20. **A** | 26. **A** | 32. **A** | 38. **A** | 44. **D** | 50. **B** |
| 7. **A** | 14. **C** | | | | | | |

1. **The correct answer is (C).**

$$
\begin{aligned}
4x + 7 &< -9 \\
-7 &\quad -7 \\
\hline
4x &< -16 \\
\frac{4x}{4} &< -\frac{-16}{4} \\
x &< -4
\end{aligned}
$$

2. **The correct answer is (D).** Eliminate before factoring.

Choice (A): 10 is not a prime number.
Choice (B): 77 is not a prime number.
Choice (C): 15 is not a prime number.
Choice (D): All are primes.
Choice (E): 1 is not a prime.

The answer must be choice (D).

3. **The correct answer is (C).** Remember:

Even $\times$ Odd = Even
Odd $\times$ Odd = Odd
Even $\times$ Even = Even
Even + Odd = Odd
Even + Even = Even
Odd + Odd = Even

  I. E $\times$ O $\times$ O $\times$ O + O $\times$ O $\times$ O + O
    Even + Odd + Odd = Even

  II. 2 $\times$ E $\times$ E $\times$ E + O $\times$ E $\times$ E + E
    Even + Even + Even = Even

  III. O $\times$ O $\times$ E $\times$ E + O $\times$ E + O
    Even + Even + Odd = Odd

4. **The correct answer is (E).** $7 - 4(3 - 6) = 7 - 4(-3) = 7 - (-12) = 7 + 12 = 19$

5. **The correct answer is (E).** $\frac{is}{of} \times 100 = \frac{32}{45} \times 100$

6. **The correct answer is (D).** It will be close to, but less than what Paul donated. This eliminates choices (A) and (B) (too small) and choice (E) (too big).

$$
\frac{13}{15} = \frac{x}{105}
$$
$$
13 \times 105 = 15x
$$
$$
\frac{13 \times 105}{15} = x
$$
$$
\$91.00 = x
$$

7. **The correct answer is (A).** $x^2 = \sqrt{y}$

To find $y$, square $\sqrt{y}$
$(\sqrt{y})^2 = (x^2)^2$
$y = x^4$

8. **The correct answer is (C).**

$$
\begin{aligned}
2(7)^3 + 3(7)^2 - 4(7) + &= \\
2(343) + 3(40) - 28 + 5 &= \\
686 + 147 - 28 + 5 &= 810
\end{aligned}
$$

9. **The correct answer is (E).**

$$
\begin{aligned}
7 \times 10^6 &= 7,000,000 \\
6 \times 10^5 &= \phantom{7,}600,000 \\
8 \times 10^4 &= \phantom{7,60}80,000 \\
5 \times 10^3 &= \phantom{7,600}5,000 \\
\hline
&\phantom{7,}7,685,000
\end{aligned}
$$

Choices (A), (B), and (C) are too small. Check choice (E): $7.685 \times 10^6 = 7,685,000$

10. **The correct answer is (D).**

$$
\frac{4}{10} = .4
$$
$$
\frac{4}{100} = .04
$$
$$
\frac{4}{1,000} = .004
$$
$$
\frac{4}{10,000} = .0004
$$

11. **The correct answer is (B).** $0.125\overline{)0.0146}$

Move decimals three places to the right.

$$
\begin{array}{r}
.177 \\
125\overline{)14.600} \\
125 \\
\overline{\phantom{0}210} \\
125 \\
\overline{\phantom{0}850} \\
875
\end{array}
$$

12. **The correct answer is (C).** Estimate $9 \div 7 = 1+$. Eliminate choices (A), (B), and (E).

$$8\frac{5}{8} \div 6\frac{4}{7} =$$

$$\frac{69}{8} \div \frac{46}{7} =$$

$$\frac{69}{8} \times \frac{7}{46} =$$

$$\frac{3}{8} \times \frac{7}{2} = \frac{21}{16} = 1\frac{5}{16}$$

13. **The correct answer is (E).**

$5a^2(2a^3 + 6a^2 - a) = 5a^2(2a^3) + 5a^2(6a^2) + 5a^2(-a)$
$= 10a^5 + 30a^4 - 5a^3$

14. **The correct answer is (C).**

$$
\begin{array}{r}
2x + y = 9 \\
\text{Add } 3x - y = 1 \\
\overline{\phantom{xx}5x \phantom{+y} = 10} \\
x = 2
\end{array}
$$

15. **The correct answer is (E).** It was 8 feet to the normal level plus 7 feet above the normal level for a total of 15 feet.

16. **The correct answer is (E).** $\dfrac{15 \text{ ft.}}{5 \text{ hrs.}} = 3$ ft. per hour.

17. **The correct answer is (A).**

$$
\begin{array}{ll}
AB = & 5 \\
BC = & 8 \\
CD = & 4 \\
DE = & 9 \\
EF = & 8 \; (2 \times 4) \\
FG = & 3 \\
GA = & 3 \\
& \overline{40}
\end{array}
$$

18. **The correct answer is (E).** There is not enough information.

19. **The correct answer is (A).** 3 is the altitude.

$V = \pi r^2 h$
$V = \pi 2^2 \cdot 3$
$V = \pi 4^2 \cdot 3$
$V = 12\pi$

20. **The correct answer is (A).** Distance is always positive, so eliminate choices (C) and (E). This is simply a right triangle problem. Construct a right triangle. The distance between A and B is the hypotenuse of the triangle. Use the Pythagorean theorem to find its length.

$a^2 + b^2 = c^2$
$4^2 + 3^2 = c^2$
$16 + 9 = c^2$
$25 = c^2$
$5 = c$

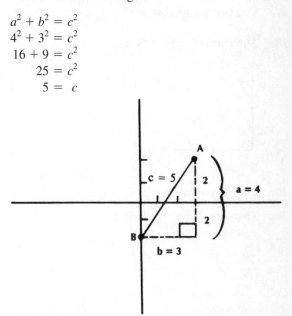

21. **The correct answer is (C).** $\angle B = \angle C$, because in an isosceles triangle, angles opposite equal sides are equal.

$\angle B + \angle C = 2x$
$2x + 64° = 180°$

(The sum of the angles in a triangle $= 180°$)

$2x = 180° - 64°$
$2x = 116°$
$x = 58°$

22. **The correct answer is (B).** $a = c = e = g$ and $b = d = f = h$

23. **The correct answer is (D).**

| S | M | T | W | Th | F | S |
|---|---|---|---|----|---|---|
| | | | | | | 1 |
| 2 | 3 | 4 | 5 | 6 | 7 | 8 |
| 9 | 10 | 11 | 12 | 13 | 14 | 15 |
| 16 | 17 | 18 | 19 | 20 | 21 | 22 |

**24.** **The correct answer is (C).**

$$\frac{1}{\cancel{2}} \times \frac{\cancel{4}}{\cancel{9}} \times \frac{\cancel{7}}{\cancel{8}} \times \frac{\overset{3}{\cancel{18}}}{\underset{3}{\cancel{21}}} \times \frac{\overset{5}{\cancel{15}}}{\underset{6}{\cancel{24}}} =$$

**25.** **The correct answer is (E).** $\dfrac{5}{54}$

**26.** **The correct answer is (A).** $\dfrac{is}{of} = \dfrac{18}{81}$ or $18 \div 81$.

**27.** **The correct answer is (A).** $\dfrac{\sqrt{1600}}{\sqrt{64}} = \dfrac{40}{8} = 5$

**28.** **The correct answer is (D).**

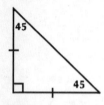

Eliminate.

**29.** **The correct answer is (B).** $5\overline{)3.00}$ with $.60$

**30.** **The correct answer is (E).**

$$\begin{array}{cc} \% & \$ \\ \dfrac{28}{100} & = \dfrac{70}{x} \end{array}$$
$$28x = 7,000$$
$$x = \$250.00$$

**31.** **The correct answer is (C).** The sizes of the angles of a triangle correspond to their opposite sides. The largest angle is opposite the largest side, and the smallest angle is opposite the smallest side. Since side AB is smallest, the angle at C ($\angle$BCA) is smallest.

**32.** **The correct answer is (A).** The LCD is the least number both denominators, 8 and 6, will divide into evenly. Eliminate choice (E).

$$8 = 2 \times 2 \times 2$$
$$6 = 2 \times 3$$
$$LCD = 2 \times 2 \times 2 \times 3 = 24$$

Or you can try each of the answers.

**33.** **The correct answer is (C).**

$$\begin{array}{rl} 8S - 4 = & 60 \\ +4 \quad +4 & \\ 8S = & 64 \\ s = & 8 \end{array}$$

**34.** **The correct answer is (E).** The first step in multiple operations is to do the operation in the innermost bracket.

$$(7 - 3)^2 = 4^2$$
$$10 - 6[3 \times 4 - (7 - 3)2 + 12 \div 6] =$$
$$10 - 6[3 \times 4 - 42 + 12 \div 6]$$

**35.** **The correct answer is (E).**

$$\begin{array}{r} 4a + 6 \\ 2a + 3 \\ \hline 12a + 18 \\ 8a^2 + 12a \\ \hline 8a^2 + 24a + 18 \end{array}$$

**36.** **The correct answer is (B).**

| Candy bar | $ .35 |
|---|---|
| Pencils | .20 |
| | .20 |
| Note pad | 1.69 |
| | $ 2.44 |
| Tax | × .05 |
| | $ .1220 = 12 cents |

**37.** **The correct answer is (D).** See the solution for question 36.

| Candy, Pencils, Note pad | $2.44 |
|---|---|
| Tax | .12 |
| 3 Apples × 17 cents | .51 |
| | $3.07 |

**38.** **The correct answer is (A).**

$$3K^2 - 4K + 7 - 2K^2 =$$
$$3K^2 - 2K^2 - 4K + 7 =$$
$$K^2 - 4K + 7$$

**39.** **The correct answer is (D).**

$$\begin{array}{rl} 7x + 5x = & 12x \\ 12x = & 180° \\ x = & 15° \\ 7x = & 105° \end{array}$$

**40.** **The correct answer is (B).** °F → °C is smaller

$$\frac{5}{9}(°F - °32) = C$$

$$\frac{5}{9}(86 - 32) =$$

$$\frac{5}{9}(54) = 5 \times 6 = 30°C$$

or approximately $\dfrac{°F - 30}{2} = \dfrac{86 - 30}{2} = \dfrac{56}{2} = 29°C$

41. **The correct answer is (C).** When the numbers are arranged according to size, the median is the middle number.

42. **The correct answer is (B).** $6 \times 7 \times 5 = 210$ Total Eggs Per Crate

    $210 \times 0.019 = 3.99 = 4$ Eggs Broken.

43. **The correct answer is (D).** He bought the same of each, so it's the same as if he had bought 5 pounds at the average price.

    $$\frac{(69 + 89)}{2} = 79 \text{ cents per pound}$$

    $$5 \times 79 = \$3.95$$

    $or \quad 2\frac{1}{2} \times 69 = \$1.725$

    $$2\frac{1}{2} \times 89 = \underline{2.225}$$
    $$\$3.950 = \$3.95$$

    approximate $5 \times 80 = \$4.00$

44. **The correct answer is (D).**

    $$5 \times 83 = 415 \text{ total points}$$
    $76 + 78 + 81 + 96 = 331$
    Subtract $415 - 331 = \overline{84}$ the missing store

45. **The correct answer is (B).** $\$69.50 \times .12 = \$8.34$ discount. $\$69.50 - \$8.34 = \$61.16$

46. **The correct answer is (D).** $\$13.80 \div 12 = \$1.15$

    Each $\$5.00 \div 1.15 = 4\frac{40}{115}$.

    Estimate—It costs more than $\$1.00$ per poster, so she can't buy 5.

47. **The correct answer is (D).** Grade enrollment is not mentioned. All the others can be worked out.

48. **The correct answer is (A).** There are $360°$ in a circle, and it is divided into 8 parts.

    $360 \div 8 = 45°$ in each section
    $225 \div 45 = 5$

    5 sections clockwise to the South.

49. **The correct answer is (B).** Estimate: $11\% \times 6 = 66\%$ of $\$10,000.00$ equals more than half of $\$10,000.00$, which is more than $\$5,000.00$.

    Interest = Principal $\times$ Rate $\times$ Time
    I = $\$10,000 \times .115 \times 6 = \$6,900.00$

50. **The correct answer is (B).**

    $I = P \times R \times T$
    $= \$10,000 \times 10.5\% \times 8$
    $= \$10,000 \times .105 \times 8$
    $= \$8,400.00$

    Sean will pay $\$1,500$ less in total interest at $11.5\%$ for 6 years.

# SCORING FOR PRACTICE TEST 2

Each institution or the state decides on the passing score. In general, 35 correct answers on the Reading section and 33 correct answers on the Mathematics sections should give you a passing score.

## How to Score the Writing Section

The writing section is scored holistically, which makes it difficult to grade. You may want to have someone else score it and make suggestions on how to improve your writing, or you may want or need to score it yourself.

Here is a suggestion for scoring the essay yourself. Start with a total of 50 points for each essay. Then subtract as follows for errors.

## Subtract

- $1\frac{1}{2}$ points for every line that you wrote over the limit

- 1 point for every punctuation, spelling or minor grammatical error
- 3 points for each major grammatical error, incorrectly used word or failure to paragraph correctly
- 5 points for low vocabulary level or jargon
- 10 points if your arguments don't support your statement
- 10 points if you didn't fill more than the first page
- 10 points if you did not have a conclusion
- 25 points if you didn't stay on the topic

This will give you a raw score for each essay. Add the two raw scores together to get your total.

# ANSWER SHEET PRACTICE TEST 3

### SECTION I: READING

1. Ⓐ Ⓑ Ⓒ Ⓓ Ⓔ  11. Ⓐ Ⓑ Ⓒ Ⓓ Ⓔ  21. Ⓐ Ⓑ Ⓒ Ⓓ Ⓔ  31. Ⓐ Ⓑ Ⓒ Ⓓ Ⓔ
2. Ⓐ Ⓑ Ⓒ Ⓓ Ⓔ  12. Ⓐ Ⓑ Ⓒ Ⓓ Ⓔ  22. Ⓐ Ⓑ Ⓒ Ⓓ Ⓔ  32. Ⓐ Ⓑ Ⓒ Ⓓ Ⓔ
3. Ⓐ Ⓑ Ⓒ Ⓓ Ⓔ  13. Ⓐ Ⓑ Ⓒ Ⓓ Ⓔ  23. Ⓐ Ⓑ Ⓒ Ⓓ Ⓔ  33. Ⓐ Ⓑ Ⓒ Ⓓ Ⓔ
4. Ⓐ Ⓑ Ⓒ Ⓓ Ⓔ  14. Ⓐ Ⓑ Ⓒ Ⓓ Ⓔ  24. Ⓐ Ⓑ Ⓒ Ⓓ Ⓔ  34. Ⓐ Ⓑ Ⓒ Ⓓ Ⓔ
5. Ⓐ Ⓑ Ⓒ Ⓓ Ⓔ  15. Ⓐ Ⓑ Ⓒ Ⓓ Ⓔ  25. Ⓐ Ⓑ Ⓒ Ⓓ Ⓔ  35. Ⓐ Ⓑ Ⓒ Ⓓ Ⓔ
6. Ⓐ Ⓑ Ⓒ Ⓓ Ⓔ  16. Ⓐ Ⓑ Ⓒ Ⓓ Ⓔ  26. Ⓐ Ⓑ Ⓒ Ⓓ Ⓔ  36. Ⓐ Ⓑ Ⓒ Ⓓ Ⓔ
7. Ⓐ Ⓑ Ⓒ Ⓓ Ⓔ  17. Ⓐ Ⓑ Ⓒ Ⓓ Ⓔ  27. Ⓐ Ⓑ Ⓒ Ⓓ Ⓔ  37. Ⓐ Ⓑ Ⓒ Ⓓ Ⓔ
8. Ⓐ Ⓑ Ⓒ Ⓓ Ⓔ  18. Ⓐ Ⓑ Ⓒ Ⓓ Ⓔ  28. Ⓐ Ⓑ Ⓒ Ⓓ Ⓔ  38. Ⓐ Ⓑ Ⓒ Ⓓ Ⓔ
9. Ⓐ Ⓑ Ⓒ Ⓓ Ⓔ  19. Ⓐ Ⓑ Ⓒ Ⓓ Ⓔ  29. Ⓐ Ⓑ Ⓒ Ⓓ Ⓔ  39. Ⓐ Ⓑ Ⓒ Ⓓ Ⓔ
10. Ⓐ Ⓑ Ⓒ Ⓓ Ⓔ  20. Ⓐ Ⓑ Ⓒ Ⓓ Ⓔ  30. Ⓐ Ⓑ Ⓒ Ⓓ Ⓔ  40. Ⓐ Ⓑ Ⓒ Ⓓ Ⓔ

### SECTION II: MATHEMATICS

1. Ⓐ Ⓑ Ⓒ Ⓓ Ⓔ  11. Ⓐ Ⓑ Ⓒ Ⓓ Ⓔ  21. Ⓐ Ⓑ Ⓒ Ⓓ Ⓔ  31. Ⓐ Ⓑ Ⓒ Ⓓ Ⓔ
2. Ⓐ Ⓑ Ⓒ Ⓓ Ⓔ  12. Ⓐ Ⓑ Ⓒ Ⓓ Ⓔ  22. Ⓐ Ⓑ Ⓒ Ⓓ Ⓔ  32. Ⓐ Ⓑ Ⓒ Ⓓ Ⓔ
3. Ⓐ Ⓑ Ⓒ Ⓓ Ⓔ  13. Ⓐ Ⓑ Ⓒ Ⓓ Ⓔ  23. Ⓐ Ⓑ Ⓒ Ⓓ Ⓔ  33. Ⓐ Ⓑ Ⓒ Ⓓ Ⓔ
4. Ⓐ Ⓑ Ⓒ Ⓓ Ⓔ  14. Ⓐ Ⓑ Ⓒ Ⓓ Ⓔ  24. Ⓐ Ⓑ Ⓒ Ⓓ Ⓔ  34. Ⓐ Ⓑ Ⓒ Ⓓ Ⓔ
5. Ⓐ Ⓑ Ⓒ Ⓓ Ⓔ  15. Ⓐ Ⓑ Ⓒ Ⓓ Ⓔ  25. Ⓐ Ⓑ Ⓒ Ⓓ Ⓔ  35. Ⓐ Ⓑ Ⓒ Ⓓ Ⓔ
6. Ⓐ Ⓑ Ⓒ Ⓓ Ⓔ  16. Ⓐ Ⓑ Ⓒ Ⓓ Ⓔ  26. Ⓐ Ⓑ Ⓒ Ⓓ Ⓔ  36. Ⓐ Ⓑ Ⓒ Ⓓ Ⓔ
7. Ⓐ Ⓑ Ⓒ Ⓓ Ⓔ  17. Ⓐ Ⓑ Ⓒ Ⓓ Ⓔ  27. Ⓐ Ⓑ Ⓒ Ⓓ Ⓔ  37. Ⓐ Ⓑ Ⓒ Ⓓ Ⓔ
8. Ⓐ Ⓑ Ⓒ Ⓓ Ⓔ  18. Ⓐ Ⓑ Ⓒ Ⓓ Ⓔ  28. Ⓐ Ⓑ Ⓒ Ⓓ Ⓔ  38. Ⓐ Ⓑ Ⓒ Ⓓ Ⓔ
9. Ⓐ Ⓑ Ⓒ Ⓓ Ⓔ  19. Ⓐ Ⓑ Ⓒ Ⓓ Ⓔ  29. Ⓐ Ⓑ Ⓒ Ⓓ Ⓔ  39. Ⓐ Ⓑ Ⓒ Ⓓ Ⓔ
10. Ⓐ Ⓑ Ⓒ Ⓓ Ⓔ  20. Ⓐ Ⓑ Ⓒ Ⓓ Ⓔ  30. Ⓐ Ⓑ Ⓒ Ⓓ Ⓔ  40. Ⓐ Ⓑ Ⓒ Ⓓ Ⓔ

### SECTION III: WRITING

1. Ⓐ Ⓑ Ⓒ Ⓓ Ⓔ  13. Ⓐ Ⓑ Ⓒ Ⓓ Ⓔ  24. Ⓐ Ⓑ Ⓒ Ⓓ Ⓔ  35. Ⓐ Ⓑ Ⓒ Ⓓ Ⓔ
2. Ⓐ Ⓑ Ⓒ Ⓓ Ⓔ  14. Ⓐ Ⓑ Ⓒ Ⓓ Ⓔ  25. Ⓐ Ⓑ Ⓒ Ⓓ Ⓔ  36. Ⓐ Ⓑ Ⓒ Ⓓ Ⓔ
3. Ⓐ Ⓑ Ⓒ Ⓓ Ⓔ  15. Ⓐ Ⓑ Ⓒ Ⓓ Ⓔ  26. Ⓐ Ⓑ Ⓒ Ⓓ Ⓔ  37. Ⓐ Ⓑ Ⓒ Ⓓ Ⓔ
4. Ⓐ Ⓑ Ⓒ Ⓓ Ⓔ  16. Ⓐ Ⓑ Ⓒ Ⓓ Ⓔ  27. Ⓐ Ⓑ Ⓒ Ⓓ Ⓔ  38. Ⓐ Ⓑ Ⓒ Ⓓ Ⓔ
5. Ⓐ Ⓑ Ⓒ Ⓓ Ⓔ  17. Ⓐ Ⓑ Ⓒ Ⓓ Ⓔ  28. Ⓐ Ⓑ Ⓒ Ⓓ Ⓔ  39. Ⓐ Ⓑ Ⓒ Ⓓ Ⓔ
6. Ⓐ Ⓑ Ⓒ Ⓓ Ⓔ  18. Ⓐ Ⓑ Ⓒ Ⓓ Ⓔ  29. Ⓐ Ⓑ Ⓒ Ⓓ Ⓔ  40. Ⓐ Ⓑ Ⓒ Ⓓ Ⓔ
7. Ⓐ Ⓑ Ⓒ Ⓓ Ⓔ  19. Ⓐ Ⓑ Ⓒ Ⓓ Ⓔ  30. Ⓐ Ⓑ Ⓒ Ⓓ Ⓔ  41. Ⓐ Ⓑ Ⓒ Ⓓ Ⓔ
8. Ⓐ Ⓑ Ⓒ Ⓓ Ⓔ  20. Ⓐ Ⓑ Ⓒ Ⓓ Ⓔ  31. Ⓐ Ⓑ Ⓒ Ⓓ Ⓔ  42. Ⓐ Ⓑ Ⓒ Ⓓ Ⓔ
9. Ⓐ Ⓑ Ⓒ Ⓓ Ⓔ  21. Ⓐ Ⓑ Ⓒ Ⓓ Ⓔ  32. Ⓐ Ⓑ Ⓒ Ⓓ Ⓔ  43. Ⓐ Ⓑ Ⓒ Ⓓ Ⓔ
10. Ⓐ Ⓑ Ⓒ Ⓓ Ⓔ  22. Ⓐ Ⓑ Ⓒ Ⓓ Ⓔ  33. Ⓐ Ⓑ Ⓒ Ⓓ Ⓔ  44. Ⓐ Ⓑ Ⓒ Ⓓ Ⓔ
11. Ⓐ Ⓑ Ⓒ Ⓓ Ⓔ  23. Ⓐ Ⓑ Ⓒ Ⓓ Ⓔ  34. Ⓐ Ⓑ Ⓒ Ⓓ Ⓔ  45. Ⓐ Ⓑ Ⓒ Ⓓ Ⓔ
12. Ⓐ Ⓑ Ⓒ Ⓓ Ⓔ

**ESSAY**

# PRACTICE TEST 3 (PRAXIS/PPST)

## FORMAT OF THE PPST

Section I: Reading      40 Questions      60 minutes

Section II: Mathematics      40 Questions      60 minutes

———————————— *Break* ————————————

Section III: Writing      45 questions      30 minutes

                     1 essay      30 minutes

## SCORING THE TEST

Separate scores are reported for each of the three sections. Reading and Mathematics scores are based on the number of questions answered correctly. No deductions are made for incorrect answers, so it pays to answer every question even if you have to take a wild guess. The Writing score is a composite score that is scaled to give equal weight to the multiple-choice and essay sections.

# SECTION I: READING

**40 MINUTES—40 QUESTIONS**

**Directions:** Each statement or passage is followed by one or more questions based on its content. After reading the statement or passage, choose the best answer for each question and blacken the corresponding space on the Answer Sheet for Sample Test 3. The correct answers and explanations follow the test.

## QUESTIONS 1–3 REFER TO THE FOLLOWING PASSAGE.

Who has the better memory, men or women? The answer depends on what is being recalled. Women excel in verbal memory—the recall of words, information, writing, and faces. Men excel in spatial memory—in recalling landmarks, maps, and positions of objects. As observers, men are more accurate in remembering men or cars, while women are more accurate at recalling what people wore, for example.

1. Based on the passage, a woman at the scene of an accident would probably be more accurate in recalling

   (A) the make of the car
   (B) the direction of the street
   (C) the license-plate number of the car
   (D) where the impact occurred
   (E) the weather conditions

2. The passage might explain why a

   (A) man misplaces things in a house
   (B) woman has difficulty with travel directions
   (C) woman forgets a person's name but not his face
   (D) man remembers names
   (E) man can quote passages from a book

3. From the information given, it may be inferred that a woman might have trouble remembering each of the following items EXCEPT

   (A) where she left her car keys
   (B) when to turn while driving to an acquaintance's house
   (C) what was on her shopping list
   (D) which fender of her car was dented
   (E) what Nick, the garage mechanic, looks like

## QUESTIONS 4–6 REFER TO THE FOLLOWING INFORMATION.

A group of boys went to the doughnut shop and bought doughnuts, which they then consumed. Alex ate fewer doughnuts than Charlie. Bob ate fewer doughnuts than Fred. Dan ate more doughnuts than Alex. Elmer ate more doughnuts than Dan. Fred ate fewer doughnuts than Alex, and Charlie ate fewer doughnuts than Dan.

4. Who ate the most doughnuts?

   (A) Alex
   (B) Bob
   (C) Charlie
   (D) Dan
   (E) Elmer

5. Who ate the fewest doughnuts?

   (A) Bob
   (B) Charlie
   (C) Dan
   (D) Elmer
   (E) Fred

6. Charlie ate more doughnuts than

   (A) Elmer, Fred, and Bob
   (B) Elmer, Dan, and Alex
   (C) Dan, Fred, and Bob
   (D) Alex, Fred, and Bob
   (E) Dan, Alex, and Bob

## QUESTIONS 7–13 REFER TO THE FOLLOWING PASSAGE.

Most people have never heard of the mathematical achievements that affect their everyday lives. Nor are they aware that mathematics has progressed in quantum leaps over the last thirty-five years. It is generally believed that mathematicians work in an abstract world no lay person can understand and that mathematics has no practical purposes.

It is true that most of us don't understand a great deal of mathematics, and that mathematics is an abstract field in which things must be discovered, invented, or created. It is also difficult to comprehend. As with other technical fields, even understanding the language of mathematics is difficult. When mathematicians discuss their science, it sounds so abstract and esoteric that the lay person feels hopelessly lost. Mathematicians are the first to admit that their work is almost impossible to discuss with non-mathematicians. However, they do acknowledge that they have been reluctant to discuss their work with people outside their field.

Mathematicians, unlike other experimental scientists, do most of their work alone, without teams of assistants and experimental apparatus. Most mathematicians do their work without direct regard to the application of the results; mathematical research is seldom concerned with solving a specific practical problem. Surprisingly enough, the abstract mathematical concepts thus developed are often the very tools needed and used to solve specific problems—in mathematics or other fields. Godfrey Hardy developed a number theory and proclaimed that it would not have any effect on the world. His work is now the basis for constructing secret codes, which is central to national security issues. Many mathematical developments that were once thought to be too abstract to have practical application have astonished physicists as being the exact tool needed to explain ideas about nature. Mathematics has become so important in physics, astronomy, and economics that it is hard to tell where mathematics leaves off and the other sciences begin. Mathematics has made fundamental improvements in the design of computer software. Many recent technological developments such as supersonic aircraft wings and medical scanners would not have been possible without the recently evolved mathematical tools.

7. Based on the passage which of the following statements is (are) correct?

I. Mathematics is an abstract science with no practical applications.
II. Mathematics has many practical applications
III. Mathematics has been instrumental in opening a world of new technological advances.

(A) I only
(B) II only
(C) III only
(D) I and III only
(E) II and III only

8. The author's purpose in the passage is to

(A) inform people about the role of math in their lives
(B) criticize mathematicians for not communicating with lay people
(C) let people know about the importance of mathematics
(D) encourage more people to pursue mathematics
(E) enhance people's concept of mathematics

9. The author's tone in the passage is

(A) informative, without bias
(B) anti-mathematicians
(C) supercilious
(D) critical of people who don't understand mathematics
(E) not written for lay people

10. According to the passage, most people

(A) are unaware of current mathematical thinking
(B) think mathematics is worthless
(C) know that mathematics is important, but not why
(D) think mathematical research is a waste of funding and resources
(E) think of mathematics as an experimental science

11. A high school teacher could use this information to

(A) interest students in mathematics
(B) let students know that mathematics has useful applications
(C) encourage students to enter the fields of mathematics
(D) show students that math is in the forefront of technological advances
(E) All of the above

12. The main idea of the passage is that

(A) mathematicians don't communicate well with lay people
(B) mathematics is an abstract field with practical application
(C) mathematics is not developed to solve specific problems
(D) the abstract concepts of mathematics are not easy to comprehend
(E) mathematicians developed supersonic aircraft wings

13. The author would probably be in favor of

(A) less mathematical research
(B) better communication by mathematicians regarding the benefits of mathematics
(C) more research by mathematicians
(D) separation of mathematics and other experimental fields
(E) mathematicians keeping to themselves

**QUESTIONS 14–17 REFER TO THE FOLLOWING PASSAGE.**

A recent study showed that leading scholars in the humanities and social sciences have strongly criticized the scholarly journals in their fields. Many of those surveyed think the peer-review system of deciding what gets published in the journals is biased in favor of established researchers, scholars from prestigious institutions, and those who use currently fashionable approaches to a subject. About one third say they rarely find articles of interest in their discipline's primary journal. One scholar claimed that the leading journal in his field was controlled by a small group that shut out any challenges to the theories on which they have made their reputations, resulting in stagnation. Nearly one fourth of the respondents regard prepublication material by their colleagues to be at least as important as articles published in the journals. About one third of those surveyed expressed dissatisfaction with the length of time it takes for articles to appear in print after they have been accepted for publication.

14. Of those surveyed regarding scholarly publications, how many were critical?

   (A) All
   (B) Many
   (C) One third
   (D) One fourth
   (E) Nearly one fourth

15. The survey showed dissatisfaction with all of the following EXCEPT

   (A) the peer-review system of deciding what gets published
   (B) the lack of articles of interest
   (C) too much variety in journals
   (D) the control of journals by a coterie
   (E) not enough new information relevant to their field

16. The greatest dissatisfaction with journals was expressed by

   (A) history professors
   (B) new Ph.D.s
   (C) administrators
   (D) editors of journals
   (E) None of the above

17. The passage

   (A) draws conclusions from a survey
   (B) recommends change in how articles should be reviewed
   (C) furnishes data from a survey
   (D) is biased in favor of the journalist
   (E) is biased in favor of the scholars

**QUESTIONS 18–21 REFER TO THE FOLLOWING PASSAGE.**

This is the sixth consecutive year in which college costs have risen at a rate higher than inflation. At public colleges and universities, the rate of increase has slowed. At two-year public colleges, tuition is up 4 percent, while at four-year public colleges and universities, it is up 6 percent. At private institutions, tuition has risen 8 percent. The most common reasons for the higher charges are increases in faculty pay, increased student aid, higher insurance costs, and the need for more computers and new facilities.

Students who live on campus at four-year public colleges will pay slightly more than half the amount paid by students at private colleges. Students who live at home and commute to college save almost $1,200 per year.

18. According to the passage, tuition at public institutions has

   (A) decreased
   (B) increased more than the inflation rate
   (C) increased the same as the inflation rate
   (D) increased less than the inflation rate
   (E) increased

19. The least expensive education would be

   (A) living on campus at a private college
   (B) commuting to a private college
   (C) living on campus at a public university
   (D) commuting to a public university
   (E) Not enough information to decide

20. From the passage, we can conclude that the current rate of inflation is less than

   (A) 4 percent
   (B) 5 percent
   (C) 6 percent
   (D) 7 percent
   (E) 8 percent

21. Reasons for higher college costs include all of the following EXCEPT the

   (A) need for more computers
   (B) need to raise salaries
   (C) rise in financial aid costs
   (D) rise in insurance costs
   (E) rise in housing costs

**QUESTIONS 22–24 REFER TO THE FOLLOWING PASSAGE.**

Some state leaders are critical of a national report that calls for the elimination of undergraduate education programs. The report advocates that prospective teachers complete an undergraduate degree in liberal arts, and then continue to a master's degree in education. It states that too many graduates of education programs lack adequate knowledge of the subjects they teach. State officials critical of the report say that the proposed changes would cost too much, and that the report focuses attention on the wrong issues. Some states are already shifting toward the recommended program, but others call it an easy out and impractical. Many more teachers will be needed in the next five to ten years. Taking an extra year to complete a credential program would delay the entry of many into the ranks of much-needed teachers.

22. "All states will be required to offer education programs at the graduate, rather than the undergraduate level."

    Based on the information in the passage, how should you respond to this statement?

    (A) Agree
    (B) Disagree
    (C) Not in passage
    (D) Not enough information
    (E) Agree partially

23. The report _____ that teachers have an undergraduate degree in liberal arts before pursuing a master's degree in education.

    (A) mandates
    (B) recommends
    (C) rules
    (D) requires
    (E) cautiously suggests

24. We can assume that the purpose of the report was to

    (A) improve education
    (B) improve the caliber of new teachers
    (C) increase departments of education
    (D) save money on educational programs
    (E) provide more teachers in the next five to ten years

**QUESTIONS 25–27 REFER TO THE FOLLOWING GUIDELINES.**

In order to be admitted to North State Community College, a resident needs to have a high school diploma, a General Education Diploma, have passed the state high school equivalency test, or be 18 years of age. An out-of-state student needs to have a high school diploma and have finished in the upper half of his or her graduating class. Service personnel are considered the same as in-state students.

25. According to the guidelines above, which of the following applicants is (are) admissible to North State Community College?

    I. Carrie, who is 17, lives in North State, and dropped out of school after she passed the high school equivalency test
    II. Sean, who ran away from his home in Lincoln State at 15, joined the service, and has finished his 3-year tour of duty
    III. Hillary, who lives in South State and was valedictorian of her class

    (A) I only
    (B) II only
    (C) III only
    (D) I and II only
    (E) I, II, and III

26. Ruth, who lives in North State and is 16, dropped out of high school. What will enable her to enroll in North State Community College?

    (A) Waiting two years
    (B) Joining the service
    (C) Getting the General Education Diploma
    (D) Both (A) and (C)
    (E) Either (A) or (C)

27. Despite persistent claims that admissions tests are unfair and unnecessary, the widely used tests seem to be as entrenched as ever at selective colleges and universities.

    From the above statement we can conclude that admissions tests

    (A) are used more frequently than ever across the nation
    (B) are used less frequently across the nation
    (C) will be eliminated
    (D) are used as much as ever at certain colleges
    (E) are unfair and unnecessary

**QUESTIONS 28–29 REFER TO THE FOLLOWING PASSAGE.**

Computers and software are increasingly being used in higher education. Some colleges have software development programs in which professors are given time off from teaching in order to write software programs for their classes. One professor developed a program that allows his students to experiment with ways of staging various Shakespearean scenes. With the advent of the software development programs, some administrators worried that faculty members would not be willing to use materials developed on other campuses; however, professors look for good software just as they look for good textbooks. Another area of concern was whether the developer of a program would have to spend all his time answering questions about the software. This fear, too, has proven false. Actually, faculty members are increasingly computer-literate and less likely to need help. The problem that has yet to be solved is incompatibility of hardware. New questions that must be addressed are how students can use the materials and whether they can get access to the necessary computers.

28. A fear which proved unfounded was

   (A) professors wasting time answering questions about the program
   (B) incompatibility of hardware
   (C) getting the program to the ultimate user
   (D) not enough computers
   (E) the students not knowing how to use the programs

29. A continuing problem is

   (A) professors spending time answering questions about programs
   (B) incompatibility of hardware
   (C) getting the programs to the ultimate user
   (D) professors not using other programs
   (E) professors not looking for other programs

30. In one state, student aid work-study funds have been appropriated to pay college students to teach illiterate adults to read.

   The concept in the statement could be

   (A) young learning from old
   (B) illiterates teaching college students
   (C) college students teach illiteracy
   (D) multiple benefits from one program
   (E) waste not, want not

31. In Midway County, all high school graduates have been offered full-tuition scholarships to attend the local community college. The foundation granting the scholarships is trying to stimulate the economy by encouraging people to stay in the area. "The ripple effect is tremendous," said the president of the foundation. Every student who takes advantage of this offer stays in the community. This is $10,000 per year that doesn't leave Midway.

   As used in this passage, "ripple effect" refers to a(an)

   (A) wavy effect
   (B) irregular effect
   (C) up-and-down effect
   (D) increasingly greater effect
   (E) undulating effect

**QUESTIONS 32–35 REFER TO THE FOLLOWING GRAPH.**

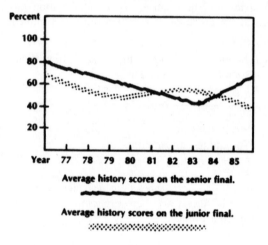

Average history scores on the senior final.

Average history scores on the junior final.

32. Senior history scores are shown to be

   (A) declining steadily
   (B) increasing steadily
   (C) increasing after a small decline
   (D) increasing after years of steady decline
   (E) variable without a trend

33. The lowest senior scores were in

   (A) 1982 and 44%
   (B) 1983 and 44%
   (C) 1984 and 44%
   (D) 1982 and 55%
   (E) 1983 and 55%

34. The juniors and seniors had the same scores in

   (A) 1981
   (B) 1984
   (C) 1981 and 1984
   (D) 1977 and 1986
   (E) 1982 and 1983

**35.** The juniors had better scores than the seniors

(A) one year
(B) two years
(C) three years
(D) four years
(E) five years

**QUESTIONS 36–40 REFER TO THE FOLLOWING GRAPH.**

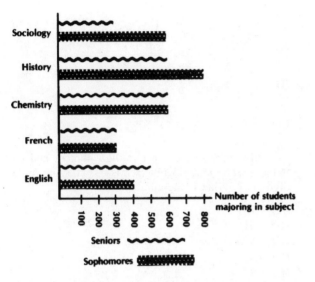

**36.** From the data in the graph, one can project that

(A) the overall trend is toward more students major-ing in the subjects listed as a whole
(B) English is gaining popularity
(C) more students are majoring in each subject
(D) these subjects are all less popular as majors
(E) total enrollment is declining

**37.** Which subject is gaining most in being chosen as a major?

(A) Sociology
(B) History
(C) Chemistry
(D) French
(E) English

**38.** Which subject is decreasing as a major choice?

(A) Sociology
(B) History
(C) Chemistry
(D) French
(E) English

**39.** Which subject shows no appreciable change?

(A) Sociology
(B) History
(C) Chemistry
(D) French
(E) English

**40.** According to the graph, which subject has the largest total number of students majoring in it?

(A) Sociology
(B) History
(C) Chemistry
(D) French
(E) English

# SECTION II: MATHEMATICS

**50 MINUTES—40 QUESTIONS**

**Directions:** Choose the best answer for each question and blacken the corresponding space on the Answer Sheet for Sample Test 3. Correct answers and solutions follow the test.

1. What is the remainder when 5,619 is divided by 39?

    (A) $\frac{3}{13}$

    (B) 3

    (C) $144\frac{1}{1}$

    (D) $\frac{1}{39}$

    (E) 144

2. $\frac{2x - y}{2} =$

    (A) $x - y$

    (B) $2x - y$

    (C) $x - \frac{y}{2}$

    (D) $2x - \frac{y}{2}$

    (E) $2(2x - y)$

3. Packages are delivered every fourth working day. If packages were delivered on Thursday, what is the next delivery date?

    (A) Saturday
    (B) Monday
    (C) Wednesday
    (D) Thursday
    (E) Friday

4. Which fraction is largest?

    (A) $\frac{2}{3}$

    (B) $\frac{3}{4}$

    (C) $\frac{7}{11}$

    (D) $\frac{3}{5}$

    (E) $\frac{5}{9}$

5. The difference between a two-digit number and the number with the digits reversed is 63. The sum of the digits is 7. What is the number?

    (A) 70
    (B) 61
    (C) 52
    (D) 43
    (E) 81

6. 3,487.9652

    The 2 in the above number represents

    (A) units
    (B) hundredths
    (C) thousandths
    (D) thousands
    (E) ten-thousandths

7. Paul's age is one year less than double Carmen's age. Seven years ago he was three times as old as Carmen. How old is Paul?

    (A) 25
    (B) 22
    (C) 18
    (D) 13
    (E) 6

8. 20 is what percent of 16?

    (A) 80%

    (B) $\frac{16}{20}$

    (C) 75%
    (D) 32%
    (E) 125%

9. Round off 14,494 to the nearest 100.

    (A) 14,000
    (B) 15,000
    (C) 14,400
    (D) 14,500
    (E) 14,490

10. To check $\dfrac{x^2 - 9}{x - 3}$, you could

    I. multiply $x - 3$ by $x + 3$
    II. substitute a number for $x$
    III. work the problem over again

    (A) I only
    (B) II only
    (C) III only
    (D) I and II only
    (E) II and III only

11. $\dfrac{9}{20}$ converted into a decimal is

    (A) 0.18
    (B) 1.80
    (C) 0.9
    (D) 0.20
    (E) 0.45

12. $\dfrac{7}{9}$ equals

    (A) $\dfrac{9}{63}$

    (B) $\dfrac{42}{54}$

    (C) $\dfrac{7}{21}$

    (D) $\dfrac{87}{114}$

    (E) $\dfrac{9}{7}$

13. Henry was building a 1:24 scale model of a boat. If the boat's width is 2 yards, how wide should the model be?

    (A) $\dfrac{1}{2}$ inch

    (B) 1 inch
    (C) 2 inches
    (D) 3 inches
    (E) 4 inches

14. Acme Rental Car Company charges $40.00 per day for a car, while Zenith Cars charges $37.50 per day. Which of the following can be answered with this information?

    (A) The weekly rental charge for Acme
    (B) The rental cost for half a day of use from Zenith
    (C) The cost for renting a car for two days from Acme
    (D) The surcharge for gasoline by both companies
    (E) The difference between what Acme and Zenith charge per day

15.

Mrs. Purden set up a wheel for her children to spin to decide when each one would be responsible for washing the dishes. If Charlene spins the wheel, what are her chances of not having any chores?

    (A) $\dfrac{1}{6}$

    (B) $\dfrac{1}{7}$

    (C) $\dfrac{1}{8}$

    (D) $\dfrac{6}{7}$

    (E) $\dfrac{7}{8}$

16. 20° Centigrade converted to Fahrenheit is

    (A) −7°F
    (B) 7°F
    (C) 36°F
    (D) 68°F
    (E) 93.6°F

17. 1.025 + 30.76 + 2.087 + 0.1567 + 417.6 =

    (A) 1.1931
    (B) 11.931
    (C) 75.7887
    (D) 1,119.31
    (E) 451.6287

18. David can complete a paper route in 3 hours, while Scott can do it in 2 hours. How long will it take if they work together?

    (A)  1 hr
    (B)  $1\frac{1}{5}$
    (C)  2 hrs
    (D)  3 hrs
    (E)  5 hrs

19. An elevator can carry 6 people. How many trips will it have to make to transport 26 people?

    When Chris worked this problem he got an answer of 4.2. What should he do now?

    (A)  Redo the problem
    (B)  Choose 4 as the answer
    (C)  Choose 5 as the answer
    (D)  Choose 4.2 as the answer
    (E)  Assume there is an error in the answer choices

20. A triangle's altitude is $\frac{1}{2}$ of its base of $3\frac{1}{4}$ inches. What is the measurement of the altitude?

    (A)  $\frac{1}{2}$ in
    (B)  $1\frac{1}{4}$ in
    (C)  $1\frac{5}{8}$ in
    (D)  $3\frac{1}{3}$ in
    (E)  $6\frac{1}{2}$ in

21. How many hours will it take a train going 78 kilometers per hour to travel 37 kilometers?

    (A)  0.47 hr
    (B)  0.5 hr
    (C)  1.2 hrs
    (D)  2.0 hrs
    (E)  2.1 hrs

22. Melissa checked the acidity level of her experiment every 10 minutes. After 10 hours, how many times had she checked it?

    (A)  1
    (B)  10
    (C)  6
    (D)  60
    (E)  100

23.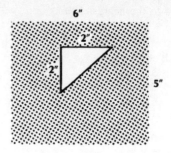

    Sue cut a triangle out of a sheet of paper. How much paper did she waste?

    (A)  2 sq. in
    (B)  4 sq. in
    (C)  26 sq. in
    (D)  28 sq. in
    (E)  30 sq. in

24. Rick and Russell collect stamps and have 450 stamps between them. Rick has 50% more than Russell. How many stamps does Rick have?

    (A)  180 stamps
    (B)  225 stamps
    (C)  270 stamps
    (D)  405 stamps
    (E)  675 stamps

25.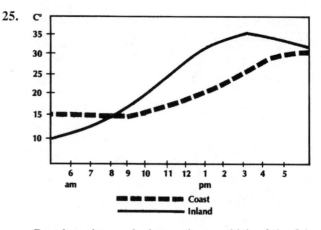

    Based on the graph shown above, which of the following is true?

    I.   The temperature varies more inland than at the coast.
    II.  Temperatures inland and at the coast were the same at 6 p.m.
    III. At noon the temperature at the coast was 30°.

    (A)  I only
    (B)  II only
    (C)  III only
    (D)  I and II only
    (E)  II and III only

**26.**

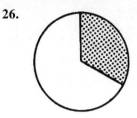

One third of the circle is shaded. Find the shaded area if the radius is 7.

(A) $\dfrac{49}{3}\pi$

(B) $\dfrac{49}{3}$

(C) 497

(D) 49

(E) $\dfrac{7}{3}\pi$

**27.**

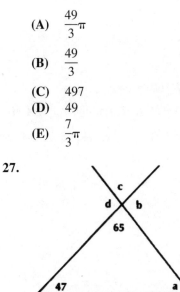

Which angle equals 115°?

(A) a
(B) b
(C) c
(D) d
(E) b and d

**28.** Which fraction is the smallest?

(A) $\dfrac{7}{11}$

(B) $\dfrac{8}{12}$

(C) $\dfrac{9}{13}$

(D) $\dfrac{10}{14}$

(E) $\dfrac{10}{15}$

**29.** $727{,}654 \div 9 =$

The solution to this problem has

(A) no remainder
(B) a remainder of 1
(C) a remainder of 2
(D) a remainder of 3
(E) a remainder of 4

**30.** $3\dfrac{7}{8} + 5\dfrac{5}{6} - 4\dfrac{3}{4}$

(A) $4\dfrac{5}{6}$

(B) $4\dfrac{23}{24}$

(C) $8\dfrac{41}{24}$

(D) $9\dfrac{17}{24}$

(E) $14\dfrac{2}{3}$

**31.** Change $\dfrac{39}{24}$ to a decimal.

(A) 0.625
(B) 1.15
(C) 1.58
(D) 1.625
(E) 2.04

**32.** $\dfrac{1}{3}\%$ of the kernels in popcorn do not pop. At this rate, how many kernels will not pop out of 600 kernels?

(A) 2 kernels
(B) 6 kernels
(C) 18 kernels
(D) 100 kernels
(E) 200 kernels

**33.** $\sqrt{236}$ is closest to

(A) 14
(B) 15
(C) 16
(D) 46
(E) 118

**34.** In a class of 35 students, 15 took a test. The ratio of students who did not take the test to students who did is

(A) $\dfrac{4}{3}$

(B) $\dfrac{3}{7}$

(C) $\dfrac{4}{7}$

(D) $\dfrac{3}{4}$

(E) $\dfrac{7}{4}$

**35.** What percent is 21 of 15?

(A) 21%
(B) 60%
(C) 70%
(D) 129%
(E) 140%

**36.** Which of the following groups contain only prime factors?

I. (1, 2, 3, 5)
II. (2, 3, 4, 5)
III. (0, 7, 11, 13)

(A) I only
(B) II only
(C) III only
(D) I and III only
(E) None of the above

**37.** Ron wants to arrange the following weights in order from largest to smallest. Which order is correct?

I. Milligram
II. Gram
III. Kilogram

(A) I, II, III
(B) II, III, I
(C) I, III, II
(D) III, II, I
(E) II, I, III

**38.** $3x(x - 2y) =$

(A) $3x - 6y$
(B) $3x^2 + xy$
(C) $3x^2 - 6xy$
(D) $3x^2 - 2y$
(E) $3x - 2xy$

**39.** $(b - 3)(b + 4) =$

(A) $b^2 - 12$
(B) $b^2 + 12$
(C) $b^2 + b - 12$
(D) $b^2 - b - 12$
(E) $b^2 - b + 12$

**40.** $360 - 4M + 6K + 160 = 640$

In the equation above, $K = 2$, find the value of $M$.

(A) 12
(B) 15
(C) 20
(D) 30
(E) 120

# SECTION III: WRITING

**30 MINUTES—45 QUESTIONS**

## PART A

> **Directions:** Some of the sentences below contain errors in grammar, word use or punctuation; others are correct. For each question, blacken the answer space that corresponds to the letter of the underlined portion that contains an error. If the sentence is correct as it stands, blacken space E on your answer sheet. No sentence contains more than one error.

1. Every algebra teacher must make up their own tests.
   (A)        (B)                        (C)        (D)
   No error
   (E)

2. Both the student and the teacher wants good results.
   (A)          (B)                  (C)        (D)
   No error
   (E)

3. Neither the parents nor the teacher understand the
   (A)              (B)    (C)              (D)
   problem. No error
              (E)

4. None of the teachers were prepared to return to school
   (A)                    (B)          (C)
   a week before the semester started. No error
                                   (D)        (E)

5. Either you or I am to blame for not rewinding the
   (A)            (B)(C)              (D)
   cassette tape. No error
                  (E)

6. Every teacher would be at school on time if I was the
   (A)                  (B)                    (C) (D)
   principal. No error
              (E)

7. He feels bad about having run over the dog, even
   (A) (B)        (C)    (D)
   though it was unavoidable. No error
                              (E)

8. Because he has practiced all summer, he runs faster
              (A)                              (B)
   than any boy in school. No error
   (C)              (D)        (E)

9. Both Cindy and Mark are tall, a characteristic inherited
                        (A)          (B)              (C)
   from their father, but Mark is the tallest. No error
                                    (D)          (E)

10. After having corrected test papers all evening, Susan
    (A)    (B)
    decided to relax with a cup of tea. No error
    (C)        (D)                            (E)

11. Neither Jonathan nor his friends, who are baseball
                        (A)            (B)    (C)
    enthusiasts also, wants to stop the game to eat supper.
                      (D)
    No error
    (E)

12. The four brothers have only one bicycle between
                                              (A)
    them. This forces them to walk a great deal and keeps
    (B)  (C)                    (D)
    them fit. No error
              (E)

13. After snowing all night, the roads were impassable
          (A)                                (B)
    the next morning, as a result the school buses were
                      (C)                        (D)
    delayed. No error
              (E)

14. Our teachers are very well prepared. In particular, our
                            (A)          (B)              (C)
    master teachers who have had special training. No error
                    (D)                          (E)

15. Student teachers benefit by participating in extracur-
                    (A)
    ricular school activities, they help provide an overall
                              (B)                      (C)
    view of the teacher's day. No error
              (D)              (E)

16. On his vacation Benjamin wanted to climb rocks, to
    (A)                                          (B)
    swim in the ocean and scuba diving in the Caribbean.
                        (C)                (D)
    No error
    (E)

17. Either the counselors or Vince Johnson, the vice principal,
    $\underline{\hspace{2em}}$
    (A)
    makes the decision whether to suspend students or not.
    $\underline{\hspace{1em}}$  $\underline{\hspace{2em}}$  $\underline{\hspace{2em}}$
    (B)          (C)                    (D)
    No error
    $\overline{\hspace{2em}}$
    (E)

18. She works very hard at her studies, and as a result,
    $\underline{\hspace{1em}}$ $\underline{\hspace{1em}}$
    (A)  (B)
    she has better grades than anyone in class. No error
    $\underline{\hspace{2em}}$  $\underline{\hspace{2em}}$  $\overline{\hspace{2em}}$
    (C)    (D)              (E)

19. Even though she lives a solitary existence in the
    $\underline{\hspace{2em}}$  $\underline{\hspace{1em}}$
    (A)          (B)
    jungle she has a wonderful kind of a life. No error
    $\underline{\hspace{2em}}$          $\underline{\hspace{2em}}$  $\overline{\hspace{2em}}$
    (C)                    (D)              (E)

20. After having coped with commuter traffic on the way
    $\underline{\hspace{2em}}$
    (A)
    to work, I did not need a broken copier to further
    $\underline{\hspace{1em}}$                            $\underline{\hspace{2em}}$
    (B)                                          (C)
    aggravate me. No error
    $\underline{\hspace{2em}}$  $\overline{\hspace{2em}}$
    (D)          (E)

21. The Parent Support Group will have a pot-luck sup-
    $\underline{\hspace{3em}}$
    (A)
    per for all new and returning teachers at the beginning
    $\underline{\hspace{3em}}$
    (B)
    of school. We should all try and attend it. No error
    $\underline{\hspace{2em}}$ $\underline{\hspace{1em}}$ $\overline{\hspace{2em}}$
    (C)      (D)      (E)

22. Be sure to turn in your year-end attendance reports on
    $\underline{\hspace{1em}}$ $\underline{\hspace{1em}}$ $\underline{\hspace{1em}}$ $\underline{\hspace{1em}}$
    (A)      (B)    (C)      (D)
    time. No error
    $\overline{\hspace{2em}}$
    (E)

23. The reason I could not attend the last session of the
    $\underline{\hspace{3em}}$
    (A)
    seminar is because a faculty meeting was scheduled
    $\underline{\hspace{2em}}$                  $\underline{\hspace{2em}}$
    (B)                          (C)
    for the same time. No error
    $\underline{\hspace{1em}}$          $\overline{\hspace{2em}}$
    (D)              (E)

24. Because it is a difficult procedure, it is something that
    $\underline{\hspace{2em}}$                      $\underline{\hspace{2em}}$
    (A)                              (B)
    should be done by myself. No error
    $\underline{\hspace{1em}}$      $\underline{\hspace{2em}}$ $\overline{\hspace{2em}}$
    (C)          (D)      (E)

25. This is the most perfect camp location of all the ones
    $\underline{\hspace{2em}}$                  $\underline{\hspace{1em}}$ $\underline{\hspace{1em}}$
    (A)                          (B)    (C)
    we have looked at. No error
    $\underline{\hspace{2em}}$  $\overline{\hspace{2em}}$
    (D)      (E)

**PART B**

**Directions:** Some of the sentences below contain errors in grammar, word choice, sentence construction and punctuation. Part or all of each sentence is underlined. Beneath each sentence are five ways of writing the underlined part. Choice A repeats the original sentence, but the other four choices are different. If you think the original sentence is the best one, select A. Otherwise, select one of the other answer choices that produces the most effective version of the original sentence. On your answer sheet, blacken the space that corresponds to your choice.

26. Since the baby boomers have graduated from college, there are less application this year than in the past.

    (A) there are less application this year than in the past
    (B) there are less applications this year than in the past
    (C) there are fewer application this year than in the past
    (D) there are fewer applications this year than in the past
    (E) there are less applications this year than last

27. The secretary reported that you are to call home right away.

    (A) reported that you are to call home right away
    (B) reported that, "You are to call home right away"
    (C) reported, "You are to call home right away"
    (D) reported, you are to call home right away
    (E) reported that, you are to call home right away

28. He will go farther in school administration than his peers, because he has already earned his doctoral degree.

    (A) He will go farther in school
    (B) He will succeed farther in school
    (C) He will go farther in school
    (D) He will go further as to school
    (E) He will go further in school

29. What is the latest development on the controversial education bill now before the legislature?

    (A) latest development on the controversial
    (B) late development on the controversial
    (C) recent development with the controversial
    (D) late development with the controversial
    (E) recent development on the controversial

30. The future of video tape use in the classroom is hard to predict because of the uncertainty of it's uses.

    (A) because of the uncertainty of it's uses
    (B) because of the uncertainty of its uses
    (C) due the uncertainty of its uses
    (D) due the uncertainty of it's uses
    (E) because of the uncertainty of their uses

31. The resource teacher at our school not only does his work well, but goes out of his way to be helpful also.

    (A) but goes out of his way to be helpful also
    (B) but goes out of his way also to be helpful
    (C) but also goes out of his way to be helpful
    (D) but goes out of his way to be helpful
    (E) but goes out of his way to be helpful too

32. As a senior, his course load was very heavy. He was taking English, Calculus, American History and Psychology I.

    (A) English, Calculus, American History and Psychology I
    (B) English, calculus, American History and Psychology I
    (C) English, calculus, American History and psychology I
    (D) English, Calculus, American history and psychology I
    (E) English, Calculus, American history and Psychology I

33. "As a result of the energy crisis," she stated, "we have worked diligently to make our home energy-efficient."

    (A) crisis," she stated, "we have
    (B) crisis, she stated, we have
    (C) crisis. She stated, "We have
    (D) crisis," she stated, "We have
    (E) crisis, she stated. "We have

34. It is very difficult to determine the detrimental affects that will result from flooding this valley.

    (A) affects that will result from
    (B) affects that shall result as
    (C) effects that will result as
    (D) effects that shall result from
    (E) effects that will result from

35. I have always thought these kind of mountains were particularly beautiful.

    (A) these kind of mountains
    (B) these kinds of mountains
    (C) this kinds of mountains
    (D) this kind of mountains
    (E) this kind of mountain

36. After I observed the class for six weeks, I student taught the following nine weeks.

    (A) observed the class for six weeks,
    (B) observed for six weeks in the classroom,
    (C) had observation for six weeks in the classroom.
    (D) observing the class for six weeks,
    (E) had observed the class for six weeks,

37. Not one of the teachers has their lesson plans in on time.

    (A) Not one of the teachers has their
    (B) None of the teachers has their
    (C) All of the teachers has their
    (D) Not one of the teachers has his
    (E) Not one of the teachers have their

38. He is one of the staff members who teaches on a provisional credential.

    (A) He is one of the staff members who teaches
    (B) He is one of the staff members who teach
    (C) He is the only one of the staff members who teach
    (D) He is one of those staff members who teaches
    (E) He is the staff members who teaches

39. Harriet is the only one of the teachers in that building who have a classroom equipped with a sink.

    (A) the only one of the teachers in that building who have
    (B) the only teacher in that building who have
    (C) the only one of the teachers in that building who has
    (D) the only teacher in that building whose
    (E) the only one in that building who has

40. Each of the students in the class needs a separate study plan.

    (A) Each of the students in the class needs
    (B) Each of the students in the class need
    (C) Each of the student in the class needs
    (D) Every one of the student in the class need
    (E) Every student in the class need

41. Waiting for the mountains to finally come into view, their magnificence overwhelmed us.

    (A) Waiting for the mountains to finally come into view
    (B) While waiting for the mountains to finally come into view
    (C) After waiting for the mountains to finally come into view
    (D) Waiting for the mountains finally coming into view
    (E) When the mountains finally came into view

42. The shock of the <u>barely averted accident</u> had her in tears. We <u>couldn't hardly</u> blame her.

    (A) barely averted accident . . . couldn't hardly
    (B) averted accident . . . couldn't hardly
    (C) barely averted accident . . . could hardly
    (D) bare averted accident . . . could hardly
    (E) averted accident . . . could hardly

43. Of all the books he had read, his favorite was <u>The rise and fall of athens</u>.

    (A) *The rise and fall of athens*
    (B) *The Rise and Fall of Athens*
    (C) The Rise and Fall of Athens
    (D) <u>The rise and fall of Athens</u>
    (E) "The Rise and Fall of Athens"

44. Last Thursday Jeffrey and I saw the <u>blue jays flying south for the winter</u>.

    (A) blue jays flying south for the winter
    (B) blue jays flying South for the winter
    (C) blue jays flying South for the Winter
    (D) blue jays flying south for the Winter
    (E) blue jays flying south during the winter

45. Since our exhibits paralleled each other, the award was given to <u>both you and I</u>.

    (A) both you and I
    (B) both of us
    (C) both I and you
    (D) both you and me
    (E) both me and you

# ESSAY

## 30 MINUTES—ESSAY TOPIC

**Directions:** You have 30 minutes in which to write an essay on the topic specified. The essay section is intended to measure how well you write, given limitations on time and subject. Quality is more important than quantity. Spend some of your time organizing your thoughts. Use specific examples to support your statements. Write only on the assigned topic. Write legibly and within the lines provided. You may use the space below the topic for notes.

## TOPIC

Describe one experience that you had in college which made you a different person from the one you were when you entered college.

# ANSWER KEY AND EXPLANATIONS

## SECTION I: READING

| | | | | | | | |
|---|---|---|---|---|---|---|---|
| 1. **C** | 6. **D** | 11. **E** | 16. **E** | 21. **E** | 26. **E** | 31. **D** | 36. **A** |
| 2. **B** | 7. **E** | 12. **B** | 17. **C** | 22. **B** | 27. **D** | 32. **D** | 37. **A** |
| 3. **C** | 8. **C** | 13. **B** | 18. **E** | 23. **B** | 28. **A** | 33. **B** | 38. **E** |
| 4. **E** | 9. **A** | 14. **B** | 19. **D** | 24. **B** | 29. **B** | 34. **C** | 39. **C** |
| 5. **A** | 10. **A** | 15. **C** | 20. **E** | 25. **E** | 30. **D** | 35. **B** | 40. **B** |

1. **The correct answer is (C).** Women recall written material well; therefore, they are likely to recall license-plate numbers.

2. **The correct answer is (B).** Travel directions include landmarks and maps.

3. **The correct answer is (C).** A shopping list is written material.

4. **The correct answer is (E).** Arrange the boys in order from the one who ate most to the one who ate least:

   Elmer — Dan — Charlie — Alex — Fred — Bob
   most ————————————————————— least

5. **The correct answer is (A).** See the explanation to question 4.

6. **The correct answer is (D).** See the explanation to question 4.

7. **The correct answer is (E).** Rule out statement I, because mathematics is abstract, but it has practical applications.

8. **The correct answer is (C).** The author does not criticize or encourage. He discusses more than mathematics' role in our lives; therefore, choice (C) is the best answer.

9. **The correct answer is (A).** Eliminate all other choices.

10. **The correct answer is (A).** Choice (C) is a possible answer, but choice (A) is more exact.

11. **The correct answer is (E).** The teacher could use all four points.

12. **The correct answer is (B).** Choices (A), (C), and (D) are too specific. Choice (E) is incorrect, leaving choice (B) as the correct answer.

13. **The correct answer is (B).** He discusses problems of communication between mathematicians and lay people.

14. **The correct answer is (B).** No specific numbers were given. Choice (A) is too broad; therefore, choice (B) is the best choice.

15. **The correct answer is (C).** All answer choices except choice (C) are mentioned in the passage.

16. **The correct answer is (E).** The article doesn't state which category was most dissatisfied.

17. **The correct answer is (C).** The article is based on data from a survey, and neither gives opinions nor draws conclusions.

18. **The correct answer is (E).** "At public institutions the rate of increase has slowed"—but it still increased. No specific figure is given for the inflation rate.

19. **The correct answer is (D).** Attending a public university and living at home is the cheapest.

20. **The correct answer is (E).** There are two possible rankings of rising costs:

    4% — two-year college costs
    6% — public four-year college costs; inflation; average four-year college costs
    8% — private four-year college costs

    *or*

    4% — two-year colleges; inflation; average four-year college costs
    6% — public four-year college costs
    8% — private four-year college costs

    In each case inflation is definitely less than 8 percent.

21. **The correct answer is (E).** All the other answer choices are mentioned as reasons for increased costs.

22. **The correct answer is (B).** The passage states that some states have already adopted such a program; however, the program is not mandatory.

23. **The correct answer is (B).** The report recommends, or advocates.

24. **The correct answer is (B).** It is specifically geared to improving teacher education. Improved education is a hoped-for by-product.

25. **The correct answer is (E).** Carrie has passed the high school equivalency test. Sean has been in the service and is 18. Hillary was first in her class.

26. **The correct answer is (E).** Joining the service will not help her enter NSCC. She will be eligible at age 18 (in two years) or after earning a General Education Diploma.

27. **The correct answer is (D).** The word "entrenched" is the key. The others are not stated as fact in the passage.

28. **The correct answer is (A).** The words "unfounded fear" help us find the answer. "The fear has proven false."

29. **The correct answer is (B).** "The problem that has yet to be solved is incompatibility of hardware."

30. **The correct answer is (D).** Both the students and the adults who learn to read benefit.

31. **The correct answer is (D).** All the others describe wave motion.

32. **The correct answer is (D).** The seniors' scores went down for seven years before increasing.

33. **The correct answer is (B).** The low point was in 1983 and was between 40% and 50%.

34. **The correct answer is (C).** The lines cross in 1981 and 1984.

35. **The correct answer is (B).** The juniors' scores were better in 1982 and 1983.

36. **The correct answer is (A).** Eliminate the others.

37. **The correct answer is (A).** The largest increase is in sociology; 300 more sophomores than seniors.

38. **The correct answer is (E).** English is the only subject showing a decline.

39. **The correct answer is (C).** Chemistry has no change.

40. **The correct answer is (B).** Combine the numbers of sophomores and seniors.

## SECTION II: MATHEMATICS

| 1. B | 6. E | 11. E | 16. D | 21. A | 26. A | 31. D | 36. E |
| 2. C | 7. A | 12. B | 17. E | 22. D | 27. E | 32. A | 37. D |
| 3. B | 8. E | 13. D | 18. B | 23. D | 28. A | 33. B | 38. C |
| 4. B | 9. D | 14. E | 19. C | 24. C | 29. E | 34. A | 39. C |
| 5. A | 10. D | 15. C | 20. C | 25. A | 30. B | 35. E | 40. B |

1. **The correct answer is (B).**

$$\begin{array}{r} 144 \text{ R3} \\ 39\overline{\smash{\big)}\,5619} \\ \underline{39} \\ 171 \\ \underline{156} \\ 159 \\ \underline{156} \\ 3 \end{array}$$

The key word is "remainder."

2. **The correct answer is (C).** $\dfrac{2x - y}{2} = \dfrac{2x}{2} = x - \dfrac{y}{2}$

3. **The correct answer is (B).**

| Thursday | Friday | ~~Saturday~~ | ~~Sunday~~ |
| Delivery | 1 Delivery | | |
| Monday | Tuesday | Wednesday | |
| 2 delivery | 3 Delivery | 4 Delivery | |

4. **The correct answer is (B).** Underline *largest*. Are there any numbers you can eliminate immediately? Compare the answer choices:

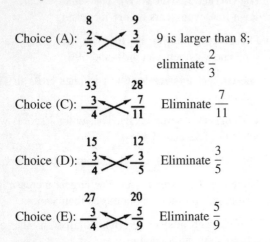

Choice (A): $\dfrac{2}{3}$ ✕ $\dfrac{3}{4}$  9 is larger than 8; eliminate $\dfrac{2}{3}$

Choice (C): $\dfrac{3}{4}$ ✕ $\dfrac{7}{11}$  Eliminate $\dfrac{7}{11}$

Choice (D): $\dfrac{3}{4}$ ✕ $\dfrac{3}{5}$  Eliminate $\dfrac{3}{5}$

Choice (E): $\dfrac{3}{4}$ ✕ $\dfrac{5}{9}$  Eliminate $\dfrac{5}{9}$

5. **The correct answer is (A).** Check: sum of digits is 7. Eliminate choice (E). Reverse number and subtract.

Choice (A):  $\begin{array}{r} 70 \\ -70 \\ \hline 63 \end{array}$

No further calculations are needed.

6. **The correct answer is (E).**

$\begin{array}{r} 3\,4\,8\,7\,.\,9\,6\,5\,2 \\ 2 \\ \hline 1\,0\,0\,0\,0 \end{array}$

7. **The correct answer is (A).** The answer must fit in both equations.

$$P = 2C$$
$$P - 7 = 3(C - 7)$$

Paul can't be 6, because the problem talks about "7 years ago." So, eliminate choice (E). The answer has to be choice (A). Check:

$\begin{array}{r} 25 = 2C - 1 \\ +\ 1 \qquad +1 \\ \hline 26 = 2C \\ 13 = C \end{array}$

$$25 - 7 = 3\,(13 - 7)$$
$$18 = 3\,(16)$$
$$18 = 18$$

Paul is 25.

8. **The correct answer is (E).** The question asks for percentage. Eliminate choice (B). Estimate: 20 is more than 16, therefore it is more than 100%. Only choice (E) qualifies.

$$\frac{\text{is}}{\text{of}} \quad \frac{20}{16} \times 100 = 125\%$$

9. **The correct answer is (D).**

14,494
↑ number above first 0 is 5 or bigger, so add 1.

$\begin{array}{r} 100 \\ \hline 14,500 \end{array}$

10. **The correct answer is (D).** To check division, e.g., $\dfrac{12}{3} = 4$, multiply $3 \times 4$, therefore I fits; eliminate choices (B), (C), and (E). You can also substitute a number for $x$; therefore II fits. The correct answer is choice (D).

11. **The correct answer is (E).** Estimate: $\dfrac{9}{20}$ is a little less than $\dfrac{1}{2}$.

$\begin{array}{r} .45 \\ 20\overline{)9.00} \\ -8\,0 \\ \hline 1\,00 \\ -1\,00 \\ \hline 0 \end{array}$

12. **The correct answer is (B).** The numerator is smaller than the denominator, so eliminate choice (E). The numerator must be divisible by 7. Eliminate choices (A) and (D). The denominator must be divisible by 9, so eliminate choice (C).

$$\frac{42 \div 6}{54 \div 6} = \frac{7}{9}$$

13. **The correct answer is (D).**

Model $\dfrac{1}{\text{Boat}\ 24} = \dfrac{W}{2\ \text{yds.}}$  Change 2 yards to inches ($2 \times 36$)

$$\frac{1}{24} = \frac{W}{72}$$

Cross-multiply:

$$24W = 72$$
$$W = 3\ \text{inches}$$

14. **The correct answer is (E).** $\$40.00 - \$37.50 = \$2.50$. There is not enough information to answer the rest.

15. **The correct answer is (C).** This wheel is divided into eighths. "No chores" is 1 of those 8. Her chances are 1 in 8, or $\frac{1}{8}$.

16. **The correct answer is (D).** C → F = bigger. Eliminate choices (A) and (B):

$$\frac{9}{5}°C + 32 = °F$$

$$\frac{9}{5}(20) + 32 =$$

$$36 + 32 = 68°F$$

*Or estimate:*

$$2C + 30 =$$
$$2(20) + 30 =$$
$$40 + 30 = 70 \text{ D is closest.}$$

17. **The correct answer is (E).** Round off all numbers and estimate: $1 + 31 + 2 + 418 = 452$. Choice (E) is the only possibility

18. **The correct answer is (B).** It will take less time than 2 hours. Eliminate choices (C), (D), and (E). David completes route in 3 hours. In 1 hour, he does $\frac{1}{3}$. Scott completes route in 2 hours. In 1 hour, he does $\frac{1}{2}$. David and Scott complete $\frac{1}{3} + \frac{1}{2} = \frac{5}{6}$ in 1 hour. They complete all of it in $\frac{6}{5} = 1\frac{1}{5}$. In estimating how long it takes for two people working together to do a job, keep in mind that it will take less time than it will take either one to do it alone. In general, it will take less time than the faster worker, but more than $\frac{1}{2}$ that time.

19. **The correct answer is (C).** The elevator will need to make five trips. The excess verbiage is only window dressing.

20. **The correct answer is (C).**

$$3\frac{1}{4} \div 2 =$$

$$\frac{13}{4} \times \frac{1}{2} = \frac{13}{8} = 1\frac{5}{8}''$$

21. **The correct answer is (A).** It will take a little less than half an hour. There is no need to work it out: $37 \div 78 = 0.47$.

22. **The correct answer is (D).** She checked it 6 times per hour: $60 \div 10 = 6$. In 10 hours, she checked it $6 \times 10 = 60$ times.

23. **The correct answer is (D).**

= shaded area

The area of the rectangle ($5 \times 6$) − area of triangle ($\frac{1}{2} \times 2 \times 2$) = amount of wasted paper. Thus, $30 - 2 = 28$ square inches of wasted paper.

24. **The correct answer is (C).** Eliminate choice (E). Rick has 50 percent more than Russell. For every 100 stamps Russell has, Rick has 150; or Rick has three stamps for every two Russell has.

$$\frac{1000}{150} = \frac{2}{3}$$

$$x = \text{Russell's stamps}$$
$$1.5x = \text{Rick's stamps}$$
$$x + 1.5x = 450$$
$$2.5x = 450$$
$$x = 180$$

$$1.5x = 270$$

There are $2 + 3 = 5$ parts
$450 \div 5 = 90$ stamps

Check: Rick has $\frac{3}{5} = \frac{x}{450}$

$$(3)(450) = 5x$$
$$270 = x$$

*Or estimate:* Rick has more than half (225); eliminate choices (A), (B), and (E).

25. **The correct answer is (A).** Statement I is correct; inland temperatures ranged from 10° to 35°. You can't verify statement II. Statement III is incorrect; it was 30° inland at noon. It was 20° at the coast at noon.

26. **The correct answer is (A).**

$$A = \pi r^2$$
$$A = \pi \cdot 7^2$$
$$A = 49\pi$$

$$\frac{1}{3}A = \frac{1}{3} \times 49\pi = \frac{49}{3}\pi$$

**27.** **The correct answer is (E).**

$a = 180 - (65 + 47) = 68$

$b = 180 - 65 = 115$

$c = 65$ (opposite angle)

$d = 180 - 65 = 115$ or $b$

**28.** **The correct answer is (A).** Compare by cross-multiplication.

Choice (B): Reduce $\dfrac{8}{12} = \dfrac{2}{3}$

Choice (D): Reduce $\dfrac{10}{14} = \dfrac{5}{7}$

Choice (E): Reduce $\dfrac{10}{15} = \dfrac{2}{3}$

Note that choice (E) is the same as choice (B). Eliminate both of these answer choices.

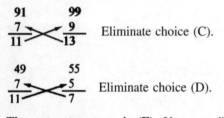

Eliminate choice (C).

Eliminate choice (D).

**29.** **The correct answer is (E).** You can divide it out, which is the long way, or add the digits and divide the total by 9. The remainder is your answer. $7 + 2 + 7 + 6 + 5 + 4 = 31$. $31 \div 9 = 3$ with a remainder of 4.

**30.** **The correct answer is (B).** Estimate $4 + 6 - 5 = 5$. This means the correct answer is either choice (A) or choice (B). The common denominator is 24.

$$+3\dfrac{7}{8} = \quad 3\dfrac{21}{24}$$

$$+5\dfrac{5}{6} = +\dfrac{5\dfrac{20}{24}}{8\dfrac{41}{24}}$$

$$4\dfrac{3}{4} = -\dfrac{4\dfrac{18}{24}}{4\dfrac{23}{24}}$$

**31.** **The correct answer is (D).**

$$\dfrac{39}{24} = \dfrac{13}{8} = 1\dfrac{5}{8}$$

$13 \div 8 = 1.625$

**32.** **The correct answer is (A).**

1% of $600 = 6$

$\dfrac{1}{3}$% of $600 = 2$

**33.** **The correct answer is (B).** You can try squaring the answers. Start with the middle number.

$16^2 = 256$—too big

$15^2 = 225$—too small

236 is closer to 225 than 256.

**34.** **The correct answer is (A).**

$$\dfrac{\text{Didn't Take Test}}{\text{Did Take Test}} = \dfrac{35 - 15}{15} = \dfrac{20}{15} = \dfrac{4}{3}$$

**35.** **The correct answer is (E).,** or

$$\dfrac{\text{is}}{\text{of}} \times 100 = \dfrac{21}{15} \times 100 = 140\%,$$

or $\dfrac{21}{15} = \dfrac{x}{100}$; $x = 140\%$

**36.** **The correct answer is (E).** Statement I is incorrect, because 1 is not a prime number. Statement II is incorrect, because 4 is not a prime number. Statement III is incorrect, because 0 is not a prime number.

**37.** **The correct answer is (D).**

**38.** **The correct answer is (C).**

$$3x(x - 2y) = 3x \bullet x - 3x \bullet 2y = 3x^2 - 6xy$$

**39.** **The correct answer is (C).**

$$\begin{array}{r} b - 3 \\ b + 4 \\ \hline b^2 - 3b \\ + 4b - 12 \\ \hline b^2 + b - 12 \end{array}$$

**40.** **The correct answer is (B).**

$$360 - 4M + 6K + 160 = 640$$
$$360 - 4m + 12M + 160 = 640$$
$$360 + 8M + 160 = 640$$
$$520 + 8M = 640$$
$$8M = 120$$
$$M = 15$$

## SECTION III: WRITING

| 1. C | 6. D | 11. D | 16. C | 21. C | 26. D | 31. C | 36. E | 41. E |
| 2. C | 7. E | 12. A | 17. E | 22. E | 27. C | 32. B | 37. D | 42. C |
| 3. D | 8. C | 13. A | 18. D | 23. B | 28. E | 33. A | 38. B | 43. B |
| 4. B | 9. D | 14. B | 19. D | 24. D | 29. A | 34. E | 39. C | 44. A |
| 5. E | 10. E | 15. B | 20. D | 25. A | 30. B | 35. B | 40. A | 45. D |

1. **The correct answer is (C).** "Every" is singular, so the correct pronoun is *his*.

2. **The correct answer is (C).** "Both . . . and" takes a plural verb.

3. **The correct answer is (D).** With "neither . . . nor," the verb agrees with the noun closest to it.

4. **The correct answer is (B).** "None" is singular, so the correct verb is *was*.

5. **The correct answer is (E).** The sentence is correct.

6. **The correct answer is (D).** The subjunctive of "was" is "were".

7. **The correct answer is (E).** The sentence is correct.

8. **The correct answer is (C).** The correct expression is "any other"; he cannot be faster than himself.

9. **The correct answer is (D).** When comparing two items, use "-er" ending.

10. **The correct answer is (E).** The sentence is correct.

11. **The correct answer is (D).** "Want" agrees with "friends," which is plural.

12. **The correct answer is (A).** You use *among* if you talk about more than two people.

13. **The correct answer is (A).** The original is a dangling participle.

14. **The correct answer is (B).** The original is a sentence fragment.

15. **The correct answer is (B).** The original is a run-on sentence.

16. **The correct answer is (C).** The original is not parallel.

17. **The correct answer is (E).** The sentence is correct.

18. **The correct answer is (D).** She cannot have better grades than herself.

19. **The correct answer is (D).** "A" should be omitted.

20. **The correct answer is (D).** *Aggravate* means "to make worse."

21. **The correct answer is (C).** The infinitive is needed.

22. **The correct answer is (E).** The sentence is correct.

23. **The correct answer is (B).** "Reason" and "because" are redundant.

24. **The correct answer is (D).** "Myself" has to be preceded by I or me.

25. **The correct answer is (A).** "Perfect" does not need a qualifier.

26. **The correct answer is (D).** Applications can be counted; therefore, the correct word to use is "fewer."

27. **The correct answer is (C).** This is a direct quote, so delete "that."

28. **The correct answer is (E).** This is used figuratively.

29. **The correct answer is (A).** The sentence is correct.

30. **The correct answer is (B).** "It's" is the contraction for "it is;" "its" is the possessive of "it."

31. **The correct answer is (C).** The words "Not only" and "but also" should be kept together.

32. **The correct answer is (B).** Calculus is not capitalized. The other subjects are capitalized because they are the name of a language, country, or a specific course.

33. **The correct answer is (A).** The sentence is correct.

34. **The correct answer is (E).** "Effect" is a noun; "affect" is a verb.

35. **The correct answer is (B).** "These" is plural, therefore, it needs the plural "kinds."

36. **The correct answer is (E).** I had observed first, then I taught. "Observed" needs to be in the past-perfect tense in order to show that the observation occurred before the teaching.

37. **The correct answer is (D).** "his"—"not one" is singular, therefore it should be "his lesson plans."

38. **The correct answer is (B).** He is one of several who teach on a provisional credential, he is not the only one; therefore use the plural form "teach."

**39.** **The correct answer is (C).** Harriet is the only one (singular), and she has a classroom equipped with a sink.

**40.** **The correct answer is (A).** The sentence is correct.

**41.** **The correct answer is (E).** A gerundial phrase, which begins with a word ending in *-ing,* must refer to the subject of the main clause. The subject is "magnificence," referring to mountains; therefore the subordinate clause must refer to it also.

**42.** **The correct answer is (C).** "Hardly" and "scarcely" are negative and should not be used with other negatives.

**43.** **The correct answer is (B).** The first and last words of a book title are capitalized, as well as nouns and verbs. Book titles are either underlined or printed in italics.

**44.** **The correct answer is (A).** The sentence is correct.

**45.** **The correct answer is (D).** The indirect object uses "me," not "I."

# ANSWER SHEET PRACTICE TEST 4

## MATHEMATICS

1. Ⓐ Ⓑ Ⓒ Ⓓ
2. Ⓐ Ⓑ Ⓒ Ⓓ
3. Ⓐ Ⓑ Ⓒ Ⓓ
4. Ⓐ Ⓑ Ⓒ Ⓓ
5. Ⓐ Ⓑ Ⓒ Ⓓ
6. Ⓐ Ⓑ Ⓒ Ⓓ
7. Ⓐ Ⓑ Ⓒ Ⓓ
8. Ⓐ Ⓑ Ⓒ Ⓓ
9. Ⓐ Ⓑ Ⓒ Ⓓ
10. Ⓐ Ⓑ Ⓒ Ⓓ
11. Ⓐ Ⓑ Ⓒ Ⓓ
12. Ⓐ Ⓑ Ⓒ Ⓓ

13. Ⓐ Ⓑ Ⓒ Ⓓ
14. Ⓐ Ⓑ Ⓒ Ⓓ
15. Ⓐ Ⓑ Ⓒ Ⓓ
16. Ⓐ Ⓑ Ⓒ Ⓓ
17. Ⓐ Ⓑ Ⓒ Ⓓ
18. Ⓐ Ⓑ Ⓒ Ⓓ
19. Ⓐ Ⓑ Ⓒ Ⓓ
20. Ⓐ Ⓑ Ⓒ Ⓓ
21. Ⓐ Ⓑ Ⓒ Ⓓ
22. Ⓐ Ⓑ Ⓒ Ⓓ
23. Ⓐ Ⓑ Ⓒ Ⓓ

24. Ⓐ Ⓑ Ⓒ Ⓓ
25. Ⓐ Ⓑ Ⓒ Ⓓ
26. Ⓐ Ⓑ Ⓒ Ⓓ
27. Ⓐ Ⓑ Ⓒ Ⓓ
28. Ⓐ Ⓑ Ⓒ Ⓓ
29. Ⓐ Ⓑ Ⓒ Ⓓ
30. Ⓐ Ⓑ Ⓒ Ⓓ
31. Ⓐ Ⓑ Ⓒ Ⓓ
32. Ⓐ Ⓑ Ⓒ Ⓓ
33. Ⓐ Ⓑ Ⓒ Ⓓ
34. Ⓐ Ⓑ Ⓒ Ⓓ

35. Ⓐ Ⓑ Ⓒ Ⓓ
36. Ⓐ Ⓑ Ⓒ Ⓓ
37. Ⓐ Ⓑ Ⓒ Ⓓ
38. Ⓐ Ⓑ Ⓒ Ⓓ
39. Ⓐ Ⓑ Ⓒ Ⓓ
40. Ⓐ Ⓑ Ⓒ Ⓓ
41. Ⓐ Ⓑ Ⓒ Ⓓ
42. Ⓐ Ⓑ Ⓒ Ⓓ
43. Ⓐ Ⓑ Ⓒ Ⓓ
44. Ⓐ Ⓑ Ⓒ Ⓓ
45. Ⓐ Ⓑ Ⓒ Ⓓ

## READING

1. Ⓐ Ⓑ Ⓒ Ⓓ
2. Ⓐ Ⓑ Ⓒ Ⓓ
3. Ⓐ Ⓑ Ⓒ Ⓓ
4. Ⓐ Ⓑ Ⓒ Ⓓ
5. Ⓐ Ⓑ Ⓒ Ⓓ
6. Ⓐ Ⓑ Ⓒ Ⓓ
7. Ⓐ Ⓑ Ⓒ Ⓓ
8. Ⓐ Ⓑ Ⓒ Ⓓ

9. Ⓐ Ⓑ Ⓒ Ⓓ
10. Ⓐ Ⓑ Ⓒ Ⓓ
11. Ⓐ Ⓑ Ⓒ Ⓓ
12. Ⓐ Ⓑ Ⓒ Ⓓ
13. Ⓐ Ⓑ Ⓒ Ⓓ
14. Ⓐ Ⓑ Ⓒ Ⓓ
15. Ⓐ Ⓑ Ⓒ Ⓓ
16. Ⓐ Ⓑ Ⓒ Ⓓ

17. Ⓐ Ⓑ Ⓒ Ⓓ
18. Ⓐ Ⓑ Ⓒ Ⓓ
19. Ⓐ Ⓑ Ⓒ Ⓓ
20. Ⓐ Ⓑ Ⓒ Ⓓ
21. Ⓐ Ⓑ Ⓒ Ⓓ
22. Ⓐ Ⓑ Ⓒ Ⓓ
23. Ⓐ Ⓑ Ⓒ Ⓓ

24. Ⓐ Ⓑ Ⓒ Ⓓ
25. Ⓐ Ⓑ Ⓒ Ⓓ
26. Ⓐ Ⓑ Ⓒ Ⓓ
27. Ⓐ Ⓑ Ⓒ Ⓓ
28. Ⓐ Ⓑ Ⓒ Ⓓ
29. Ⓐ Ⓑ Ⓒ Ⓓ
30. Ⓐ Ⓑ Ⓒ Ⓓ

## WRITING–EDITING

1. Ⓐ Ⓑ Ⓒ Ⓓ
2. Ⓐ Ⓑ Ⓒ Ⓓ
3. Ⓐ Ⓑ Ⓒ Ⓓ
4. Ⓐ Ⓑ Ⓒ Ⓓ
5. Ⓐ Ⓑ Ⓒ Ⓓ

6. Ⓐ Ⓑ Ⓒ Ⓓ
7. Ⓐ Ⓑ Ⓒ Ⓓ
8. Ⓐ Ⓑ Ⓒ Ⓓ
9. Ⓐ Ⓑ Ⓒ Ⓓ
10. Ⓐ Ⓑ Ⓒ Ⓓ

11. Ⓐ Ⓑ Ⓒ Ⓓ
12. Ⓐ Ⓑ Ⓒ Ⓓ
13. Ⓐ Ⓑ Ⓒ Ⓓ
14. Ⓐ Ⓑ Ⓒ Ⓓ
15. Ⓐ Ⓑ Ⓒ Ⓓ

16. Ⓐ Ⓑ Ⓒ Ⓓ
17. Ⓐ Ⓑ Ⓒ Ⓓ
18. Ⓐ Ⓑ Ⓒ Ⓓ
19. Ⓐ Ⓑ Ⓒ Ⓓ
20. Ⓐ Ⓑ Ⓒ Ⓓ

## PROFESSIONAL KNOWLEDGE

1. Ⓐ Ⓑ Ⓒ Ⓓ
2. Ⓐ Ⓑ Ⓒ Ⓓ
3. Ⓐ Ⓑ Ⓒ Ⓓ
4. Ⓐ Ⓑ Ⓒ Ⓓ
5. Ⓐ Ⓑ Ⓒ Ⓓ

6. Ⓐ Ⓑ Ⓒ Ⓓ
7. Ⓐ Ⓑ Ⓒ Ⓓ
8. Ⓐ Ⓑ Ⓒ Ⓓ
9. Ⓐ Ⓑ Ⓒ Ⓓ
10. Ⓐ Ⓑ Ⓒ Ⓓ

11. Ⓐ Ⓑ Ⓒ Ⓓ
12. Ⓐ Ⓑ Ⓒ Ⓓ
13. Ⓐ Ⓑ Ⓒ Ⓓ
14. Ⓐ Ⓑ Ⓒ Ⓓ
15. Ⓐ Ⓑ Ⓒ Ⓓ

16. Ⓐ Ⓑ Ⓒ Ⓓ
17. Ⓐ Ⓑ Ⓒ Ⓓ
18. Ⓐ Ⓑ Ⓒ Ⓓ
19. Ⓐ Ⓑ Ⓒ Ⓓ
20. Ⓐ Ⓑ Ⓒ Ⓓ

# PRACTICE TEST 4

This is not a true practice test, but rather a sample of question types used in teacher certification tests in Colorado, Massachusetts, Michigan, New York, and Oklahoma (OGET and OPTE). The number of questions will vary from state to state, and not every section is used in each state, so study the sections that are appropriate for your state.

**Colorado** (PLACE): Study the reading, writing, mathematics, and professional knowledge sections. The PLACE Test also includes scientific process, historical and scientific awareness, artistic expression, and humanities not included here.

**Massachusetts:** Study the reading comprehension and editing sections.

**Michigan:** Study the reading comprehension and writing, both essay and editing sections.

**New York** (NYSTCE): The LAST (Liberal Arts and Science Test) includes questions similar to the reading, mathematics, and writing (both editing and essay) sections. The ATS-W-assessment of teaching skills-written, includes questions similar to the professional knowledge section. The LAST also includes areas other than those in this book such as science, history, sociology, art and humanities.

**Oklahoma:** To study for the OGET (Oklahoma General Education Test), go over the reading, mathematics, and writing (both editing and essay) sections. The OGET also includes questions about science, art, literature and social sciences which are not addressed here. For the OPTE (Oklahoma Professional Teacher's Examination), study the professional knowledge portion.

Each state's tests vary in format, time, number of questions, and scoring. Read your state's bulletin carefully. Some states may sell or provide study guides for their specific test.

# MATHEMATICS

**45 QUESTIONS**

**Directions:** Choose the best answer for each question and blacken the corresponding space on the answer sheet.

1. A recipe for biscuits calls for $\frac{1}{2}$ cup lard to $2\frac{1}{2}$ cups flour. What is the ratio of lard to flour?

   **(A)** $1:2\frac{1}{2}$
   **(B)** 5:1
   **(C)** 1:5
   **(D)** 1:6

2. 7,500 times what number is 75?

   **(A)** 0.01
   **(B)** 10
   **(C)** 0.1
   **(D)** 100

3. Kim is sent to the store with $10.00. She can spend what is left on comic books, after she has bought five packages of gelatin at $1.65 each. How much can she spend on comic books?

   **(A)** $8.25
   **(B)** $2.25
   **(C)** $1.75
   **(D)** $1.25

4. If comic books cost 57 cents each, how many can Kim buy if she has $2.25?

   **(A)** 2
   **(B)** 3
   **(C)** $3\frac{54}{57}$
   **(D)** 4

5. If Pete and Mike can rake all the leaves on the property in 6 hours, how long will it take to rake the property if Barbara and Karen pitch in to help, assuming that all four work at the same speed.

   **(A)** 3 hours
   **(B)** 4 hours
   **(C)** 6 hours
   **(D)** 8 hours

6. Find the Celsius (°C) reading if its equivalent Fahrenheit (°F) reading is 104 degrees.

   $$°C = \frac{5}{9}(°F - 32)$$

   **(A)** 26 degrees
   **(B)** 40 degrees
   **(C)** 58 degrees
   **(D)** 72 degrees

7. How much ground can a worm cover in one day if it travels at a speed of 4 mm/second?

   **(A)** 345,600 cm
   **(B)** 34,560 cm
   **(C)** 345.6 km
   **(D)** 0.3456 km

8. Milk is measured in

   **(A)** kilograms
   **(B)** milligrams
   **(C)** liters
   **(D)** meters

9. $\frac{3}{8}$ changed to a percent is equivalent to

   **(A)** 36%
   **(B)** 37.5%
   **(C)** 38%
   **(D)** 83%

10. The directions for making concrete call for two parts cement, four parts sand, three parts rock, and one part water. If you use 3 gallons of cement in the mixture, how much water should you use?

    **(A)** 1 gallon
    **(B)** $\frac{1}{2}$
    **(C)** $1\frac{1}{2}$
    **(D)** 2 gallons

11. How many degrees above freezing is it on the outdoor Fahrenheit thermometer shown below?

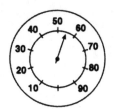

(A) 5 degrees
(B) 23 degrees
(C) 25 degrees
(D) 55 degrees

12. If every item in a store is taxable at 7%, what is the total cost of an item priced at $t$ dollars?

(A) $7t$
(B) $t + 7$
(C) $t + .07$
(D) $1.07t$

13. If $\dfrac{24}{a} = \dfrac{15}{b}$, find $a$ when $b = 10$.

(A) 16
(B) 62.5
(C) 15
(D) 6.25

14. When a number $N$ is divided by a number $M$ that is less than 1, the result is always larger than $N$. Which example disproves this statement?

(A) $50 + \left(-\dfrac{1}{2}\right) = -100$
(B) $50 \div 0.2 = 250$
(C) $50 \div .8 = 62.5$
(D) $50 + \left(-\dfrac{1}{2}\right) = +100$

15. Given the formula $V = lwh$, all the following are true EXCEPT

(A) $\dfrac{V}{l} = wh$
(B) $\dfrac{V}{lw} = h$
(C) $\dfrac{V}{lwh} = 1$
(D) $\dfrac{1}{lw} = Vh$

16. Ken is going to paint a room using paint that covers 125 sq. ft. per gallon. What information must he have before he goes to the store to purchase the paint?

(A) the number of square feet in the room
(B) the price per gallon of the paint
(C) whether the paint covers well or not
(D) nothing, he has all the information he needs

17. 76% of $48.00 is approximately

(A) $12.00
(B) $36.00
(C) $37.00
(D) $38.00

18. A $7.50 belt is on sale for $5.50. How should the percent discount be determined?

(A) $(200 \div 7.50)\,100$
(B) $(5.50 \div 7.50)\,100$
(C) $2.00 \div 100$
(D) $(2.00)(100)$

19. Which of the following decimal fractions is between 0.05 and 0.4?

(A) 0.42
(B) 0.049
(C) 0.062
(D) 0.45

20. If 40 pounds of gravel cost $2.50, how much do 3 tons of gravel cost?

(A) $100
(B) $125
(C) $375
(D) $500

21.

| Word Processors | Pages Complete | Hours |
| --- | --- | --- |
| Janelle | 7 | 2 |
| David | 16 | 5 |
| Ronald | 10 | 3 |
| Kathryn | 13 | 4 |

According to the table above, which word processor works most slowly?

(A) Janelle
(B) David
(C) Ronald
(D) Kathryn

22. Miss Felling's class is going to make placemats. Each placemat will be 9 inches by 12 inches. How many yards of 36-inch material will she need for 34 placemats?

(A) 2 yds
(B) 4 yds
(C) 3 yds
(D) 5 yds

**23.** Mr. Evarard's house payment uses up $240.50 of his monthly salary of $1,850.00. What percent of his salary is his house payment?

 (A) 13%
 (B) 1.3%
 (C) 1.6%
 (D) 16%

**24.** In order to enroll in kindergarten, a child must be at least $5\frac{1}{2}$ years old before the first day of school. Which child will be eligible to start school on September 2, 2006?

 (A) Clarissa—born April 2, 2001
 (B) Jamie—born February 28, 2002
 (C) Margaret—born March 4, 2001
 (D) Donald—born February 28, 2001

**25.** What is $\frac{7}{9}$ of $\frac{3}{14}$?

 (A) $\frac{10}{23}$

 (B) $\frac{1}{6}$

 (C) $\frac{98}{27}$

 (D) $\frac{27}{98}$

**26.** Mark spends $\frac{3}{8}$ of his day at work, $\frac{1}{4}$ of it sleeping, $\frac{1}{12}$ exercising or playing sports, and $\frac{1}{6}$ on incidentals such as eating or driving to work. How much time does that leave him for his hobby of fly-tying?

 (A) None
 (B) 1 hour
 (C) 2 hours
 (D) 3 hours

**27.** Coriane wanted an A on her physics test. She needed 24 more points to get an A, which is 90%. What score did she get?

 (A) 66%
 (B) 76%
 (C) 90%
 (D) 114%

**28.** Which area is bigger?

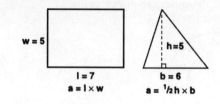

 (A) The rectangle, by 50
 (B) The triangle, by 15
 (C) The triangle, by 35
 (D) The rectangle, by 20

**29.** $6.7 [3.2 - (0.8 \times 9 - 3.8)] =$

 (A) $-13.4$
 (B) $-1.34$
 (C) $1.34$
 (D) $13.4$

**30.** There was a large amount of poster paper in the supply room. First, June took $\frac{3}{8}$ of it. Then, Karla took $\frac{3}{5}$ of what was left. What fraction of the original supply was left when the next student came to the storeroom?

 (A) $\frac{5}{8}$

 (B) $\frac{2}{5}$

 (C) $\frac{3}{8}$

 (D) $\frac{1}{4}$

**31.** Barbara scored 69 on each of her first three tests and 76, 79, and 82 on the next three tests. What is her average for these tests?

 (A) 69
 (B) 74
 (C) 76
 (D) 79

**32.** Geneva gets paid $4.00 per hour. She worked $2\frac{1}{3}$ hours Monday, $1\frac{1}{2}$ hours Tuesday, $2\frac{3}{4}$ hours each on Wednesday and Thursday, and $3\frac{2}{3}$ hours on Friday. How much was she paid for the week?

 (A) $44.00
 (B) $52.00
 (C) $50.00
 (D) $48.00

33. To call from Great Falls to Lexington costs 50 cents for the first minute and 33 cents per minute thereafter. A flat fee for 10 minutes costs $3.45. Which way of calling is cheaper?

   (A) No difference
   (B) Flat fee
   (C) 50 cents and 33 cents
   (D) There is not enough information

34. The temperature on Monday was 87 degrees, it fell 5 degrees on Tuesday; rose 3 degrees on Wednesday, warmed another 4 degrees on Thursday, and dropped 6 degrees on Friday. What was the difference in the temperature between Monday and Friday?

   (A) −4 degrees
   (B) +7 degrees
   (C) +5 degrees
   (D) +4 degrees

35. If a car travels 532 miles on 18 gallons of gasoline, how many miles per gallon does it get?

   (A) 26
   (B) 27
   (C) 28
   (D) 29

36. Walter paid $75.00 down on a stereo system, and he will make 32 payments of $17.50 each. How much will he pay in all?

   (A) $75.00
   (B) $635.00
   (C) $560.00
   (D) $114.50

37. In the previous problem, how much interest will Walter pay if the stereo system's cash price is $427.95?

   (A) $207.05
   (B) $132.05
   (C) $297.95
   (D) $132.95

38. 85 is 34% of what number?

   (A) 29
   (B) 25
   (C) 250
   (D) 290

39. The fall enrollment at Columbia Junior College is 14,780, up from 12,890 the previous year. What is the increase in enrollment?

   (A) 1,890
   (B) 1,910
   (C) 1,980
   (D) 2,110

**QUESTIONS 40–41 REFER TO THE FOLLOWING INFORMATION.**

New linoleum is being put in Mr. Ketcham's classroom, which measures 42 feet by 51 feet. It sells for $7.00 per square yard.

40. How many square yards of linoleum will be needed?

   (A) 79 square yards
   (B) 238 square yards
   (C) 714 square yards
   (D) 2142 square yards

41. How much is being spent on the linoleum in Mr. Ketcham's classroom?

   (A) $555.00
   (B) $1,666.00
   (C) $4,998.00
   (D) $14,994.00

42. Madge's baby weighs 21 lbs 5 oz, while her sister Joan's baby weighs 17 lbs 7 oz. What is the difference in their weights?

   (A) 3 lbs 14 oz
   (B) 4 lbs 2 oz
   (C) 3 lbs 8 oz
   (D) 18 lbs 12 oz

43. The total of 2,839 + 62,987 + 247 + 1,755 + 487 is

   (A) 68,135
   (B) 68,315
   (C) 68,531
   (D) 6,835

44. $-9 - (-4) =$

   (A) −13
   (B) −5
   (C) +5
   (D) +13

45. $\dfrac{5}{7} - \dfrac{1}{8} =$

   (A) $\dfrac{3}{5}$
   (B) $\dfrac{1}{4}$
   (C) $\dfrac{47}{56}$
   (D) $\dfrac{33}{56}$

# READING

**30 QUESTIONS**

**Directions:** Choose the best answer for each question and blacken the corresponding space on the answer sheet.

1. "This diet will enable you to lose up to 85% of your excess weight."

   Which of the following can you assume from this statement?

   (A) Everyone will lose 85% of his or her excess weight.
   (B) 85% of the people trying the diet will lose 85% of their excess weight.
   (C) Some people could lose 85% of their excess weight.
   (D) 85% of the people trying to diet will lose their weight.

2. "There is a 10% chance that the seeds will not sprout."

   What is the best interpretation of this statement?

   (A) 10% of the seeds will not sprout.
   (B) There is a 90% chance that the seeds will sprout.
   (C) 1 out of 10 seeds will not sprout.
   (D) 900 out of 1,000 seeds will sprout.

3. Which of the following charts represents the graph shown here?

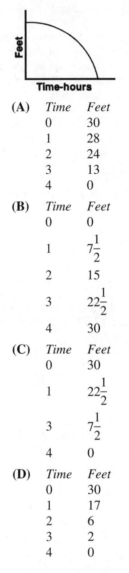

   (A)
   | Time | Feet |
   | --- | --- |
   | 0 | 30 |
   | 1 | 28 |
   | 2 | 24 |
   | 3 | 13 |
   | 4 | 0 |

   (B)
   | Time | Feet |
   | --- | --- |
   | 0 | 0 |
   | 1 | $7\frac{1}{2}$ |
   | 2 | 15 |
   | 3 | $22\frac{1}{2}$ |
   | 4 | 30 |

   (C)
   | Time | Feet |
   | --- | --- |
   | 0 | 30 |
   | 1 | $22\frac{1}{2}$ |
   | 3 | $7\frac{1}{2}$ |
   | 4 | 0 |

   (D)
   | Time | Feet |
   | --- | --- |
   | 0 | 30 |
   | 1 | 17 |
   | 2 | 6 |
   | 3 | 2 |
   | 4 | 0 |

4. In a recent administration of the CST, one fifth of the students scored above average on the verbal part, and two fifths scored above average on the math portion. Based upon this information, which of the following is a valid conclusion?

   (A) Two fifths of the students scored below average in both math and verbal.
   (B) Three fifths of the students scored above average in both math and verbal.
   (C) One fifth of the students scored above average on both math and verbal.
   (D) Three fifths of all the students are above average in math, verbal, or both.

## QUESTIONS 5–8 REFER TO THE FOLLOWING GRAPH.

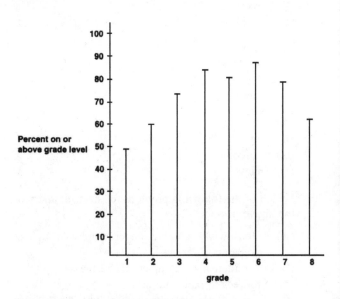

5. Which grades have the same percent of students scoring on grade level?

   (A) Third and seventh grade
   (B) Second and eighth grade
   (C) Fifth and seventh grade
   (D) There is not enough information

6. If each student performs the same next year as this year, which class will have the highest percentage on grade level?

   (A) Fourth grade
   (B) Fifth grade
   (C) Sixth grade
   (D) Seventh grade

7. Which class has the least number of students on grade level?

   (A) First grade
   (B) Second grade
   (C) Eighth grade
   (D) There is not enough information

8. Which class has the smallest percentage of students below grade level?

   (A) First grade
   (B) Fourth grade
   (C) Sixth grade
   (D) Eighth grade

## QUESTIONS 9–15 REFER TO THE FOLLOWING PASSAGE.

For questions 9–13, choose the word that makes the best sense for each numbered blank.

Is vision _____ surgery the fad of our times? There is
        9
a tremendous amount of television advertising about radial keratotomy. It's as if you could go to the _____
                                                          10
drugstore to get it. The surgery requires cutting several slits in the cornea of the eye to temporarily ease nearsightedness. No one knows what the _____ effects are, and
                                        11
some experts still say it may impair vision. A small fraction of all _____ who have had the surgery have problems
        12
with glare, visual functions and night driving. The effects of the surgery in years to come are _____, yet it is
                                              13
being sold like breakfast cereal.

9. (A) enhancement
   (B) lifting
   (C) reduction
   (D) refraction

10. (A) medical
    (B) neighborhood
    (C) super
    (D) specialty

11. (A) present
    (B) current
    (C) immediate
    (D) long-term

12. (A elderly
    (B) men
    (C) women
    (D) patients

13. (A) unknown
    (B) many
    (C) negative
    (D) visible

14. Which of the following best describes the writer's tone in the passage above?

    (A) Enthusiastic
    (B) Argumentative
    (C) Cautious
    (D) Neutral

15. According to the passage, what percent of patients who have had the surgery have had none of the problems listed?

    (A) $\frac{1}{4}$%

    (B) 25%

    (C) $\frac{3}{4}$%

    (D) 75%

## QUESTIONS 16– 23 REFER TO THE FOLLOWING PASSAGE.

For questions 16–19, choose the word that makes the best sense for each numbered blank.

Tax preparation services rely on a large, _____, and

                              16

well-trained work force. For many years it consisted

primarily of housewives, who enjoyed the temporary work

and additional income. With the _____ number of

                                      17

older people, tax preparation companies now woo retired

people to _____ their incomes. In doing this, tax

          18

preparation services have joined the _____ of other

                                      19

businesses who have realized the value of retired

people—and their ready availability. Look around at the

fast-food services, restaurants and doughnut shops you

frequent. You'll quickly see that many of the employees are

no longer the pimply teenagers, but the gray-haired

grandfathers.

16. (A) permanent
    (B) ubiquitous
    (C) highly paid
    (D) temporary

17. (A) failing
    (B) increasing
    (C) reduced
    (D) stable

18. (A) use
    (B) supplant
    (C) keep
    (D) supplement

19. (A) ranks
    (B) merger
    (C) forces
    (D) class

20. Which of the following provides the best summary of the above passage?

    (A) Housewives are no longer employed by tax preparation services.
    (B) An increasing number of businesses employ retirees in part-time jobs.
    (C) Retired persons are taking jobs away from housewives and teenagers.
    (D) Businesses employ retirees part-time because the retirees cannot work full-time and retain their pensions.

21. As used in the passage above, the word *frequent* means most nearly

    (A) often
    (B) habitual
    (C) go to repeatedly
    (D) like best

22. Which word means "to take the place of"?

    (A) Supportive
    (B) Supplement
    (C) Supplant
    (D) Supposition

23. The writer uses "pimply teenagers" and "gray-haired grandfathers"

    (A) to disparage teens
    (B) as a generalization
    (C) to emphasize contrasts
    (D) Both (B) and (C)

**QUESTIONS 24–27 REFER TO THE FOLLOWING PASSAGE.**

There are two theories of what constitutes a college education. One theory holds that this education should lead directly to a well-paid position or profession. The primary aim is to prepare the student to take his place in society as one who supports himself and his family and thereby benefits society. The theory is reflected in the instructional mode, which consists primarily of lecture, specific reading assignments, multiple-choice tests, papers written but not discussed, and, in fact, little or no discussion at all. Indeed, this is a thoroughly practical approach.

The other theory espouses that a college education should train the person to think, to be able to see through to the heart of the matter and support his viewpoint of it. This graduate is groomed to make his contribution to society in intangible ways, by forwarding the knowledge of the past through his application of it to the future. The instruction for this method of learning is imprecise, calling for the student to present and defend his interpretation of what he has heard or listened to. There are no cut-and-dried answers, which may be disconcerting, but which reflects life.

Is one method superior to another, and are they mutually exclusive?

24. Which theory of what constitutes a college education is easier to define?

(A) Education should lead directly to a profession.
(B) Education should train the person to think.
(C) Both (A) and (B)
(D) None of the above

25. Does the writer of this passage come to a conclusion?

(A) Yes
(B) No

26. The writer of this passage is biased

(A) in favor of professional education
(B) in favor of education designed to train people to think
(C) toward neither theory
(D) but can't make up his mind

27. What is the writer's purpose in ending the passage with a question?

(A) He doesn't know how to finish it.
(B) He is uncertain of his conclusions.
(C) He wants the reader to ponder the question and draw his own conclusions.

**QUESTIONS 28–30 REFER TO THE FOLLOWING PASSAGE.**

With would-be teachers all looking for jobs, it may seem paradoxical that school districts in the Southwest United States are recruiting across the nation. By 2010, more than one million new teachers will be needed nationally. Then why are there unemployed teachers?

The answer is that school districts are looking for teachers in particular fields—specifically, bilingual teachers, teachers of math, science, or special education. Large school districts have recruiters who travel to Canada and the Northeast because there is a surplus of teachers there. They extol the virtues of their area and their school district. They may even help arrange relocation loans and find employment for spouses.

Smaller districts with limited resources are encouraging teachers to become credentialed in the areas needing more teachers, and promote future-teacher clubs to encourage high school students to become teachers.

Small communities find it particularly difficult to get and keep teachers. Many of the teachers commute from urban areas, and as soon as possible, secure positions close to home. Some small-town districts have programs that encourage local residents to become teachers.

While some school districts deal with the problem of closing schools, others try to cope with overcrowding. The methods are as diverse as the districts. Harrison Unified has put three elementary schools on an all-year schedule. All the elementary schools in Whiteman District are on double sessions. Portable classrooms are used by the Evans School District, while Hawkins and Wynona Schools are building new schools. None of the choices are palatable, whether they involve inconvenience or spending more money, but children must be educated.

28. According to the passage, why are some teachers unemployed?

(A) They are not credentialed.
(B) They don't have credentials in the fields that are needed.
(C) They live in an area of growing school enrollment.

29. From this passage we can conclude that

(A) all school districts are growing
(B) only small school districts are growing
(C) only large school districts are growing
(D) some districts are growing while others deal with dwindling student enrollments

30. To cope with increasing enrollments, school districts

(A) use an all-year schedule
(B) use double sessions
(C) add portable classrooms
(D) employ a variety of measures

# WRITING—EDITING

## 20 QUESTIONS

**Directions:** Choose the best answer for each question and blacken the corresponding space on the answer sheet.

1. Each student will turn in _____ examination paper before leaving class.

    The correct word to fill in the blank is

    **(A)** his
    **(B)** their

## QUESTIONS 2–3 REFER TO THE FOLLOWING:

_____2_____ the two of us, who has _____3_____ students?

2. The correct word to fill in blank 2 is

    **(A)** Between
    **(B)** Among

3. The correct word to fill in blank 3 is

    **(A)** the most
    **(B)** more

4. From what you say, I _____ that you are familiar with our neighborhood.

    The correct word to fill in the blank is

    **(A)** imply
    **(B)** infer

## QUESTIONS 5–6 REFER TO THE FOLLOWING:

Please _____5_____ so I can see whether _____6_____ you are sitting on the newspaper _____.

5. The correct word to fill in blank 5 is

    **(A)** rise
    **(B)** raise

6. Blank number 6

    **(A)** is correct as it stands
    **(B)** should be filled in with the words "or not."

7. Young Henderson' behavior is beginning to _____ me.

    The correct word to fill in the blank is

    **(A)** aggravate
    **(B)** irritate

8. Amanda studies American History, French composition,
    $\overline{(A)}$    $\overline{(B)}$    $\overline{(C)}$
    and Astral Physics.
    $\overline{(D)}$    $\overline{(E)}$

    Which of the underlined letters above is in the correct (capitalized or lower) case?

9. Mr. Harris teaches several classes, but his favorite is

    **(A)** English history II
    **(B)** English History II
    **(C)** english history II
    **(D)** english History II

## QUESTIONS 10–11 REFER TO THE FOLLOWING:

The students were _____10_____ to go to the picnic. _____11_____ of the weather, they were eager to go.

10. The correct word to fill in blank 10 is

    **(A)** all ready
    **(B)** already

11. The correct word to fill in blank 11 is

    **(A)** Regardless
    **(B)** Irregardless

## QUESTIONS 12–13 REFER TO THE FOLLOWING:

I will _____12_____ come to class promptly next time. The reason I was late to class this time _____13_____ the bus was late.

12. The correct words to fill in blank 12 are

    **(A)** try and
    **(B)** try to

13. The correct words to fill in blank 13 are

    **(A)** is that
    **(B)** is because

**14.** I would rather be safe _____ sorry.

The correct word to fill in the blank is

(A) then
(B) than

**15.** The antonym of <u>praise</u> is

(A) laud
(B) detest
(C) chide
(D) emulate

**Directions:** For questions 16–20, choose the correct punctuation for each underlined and numbered part of the passage.

The idea of people meeting people is used in a previously racially torn city to build <u>understanding through</u> the
16
generosity of an anonymous donor, people come together for dinner once a month. The only stipulation is that each person must bring a guest of a different race. There is no agenda, or formal discussion—just people <u>eating discussing</u>
17
every day <u>events and</u> getting to know each other on a
18
one-to-one basis as people. This creates a friendly atmosphere in which problems can be solved. The group seeks to get at a basic need of all communities—the need for people to get to know one another, across all lines and differences. As one member put <u>it, when</u> people get to
19
know each other and are friends, they're more likely to work things <u>out.</u>
20

**16.** (A) Correct as is
(B) understanding. Through

**17.** (A) Correct as is
(B) eating, discussing

**18.** (A) Correct as is
(B) events; and

**19.** (A) Correct as is
(B) it, "When

**20.** (A) Correct as is
(B) out."

# WRITING—ESSAY

**Directions:** Write an essay on the assigned topic. The essay topic is intended to measure how well you write, given limitations on time and subject. Quality is more important than quantity. Before you begin to write, take some time to organize your thoughts. Use specific examples to support your statements. Write only on the assigned topic. Write legibly and within the lines provided on the answer sheet.

## TOPIC

The school district that is considering hiring you is particularly concerned that its teachers sponsor at least one extracurricular activity. Write a letter to the principal telling him about your interest, qualifications, and background in such extracurricular activity.

# PROFESSIONAL KNOWLEDGE

**20 QUESTIONS**

> **Directions:** Choose the best answer for each question and blacken the corresponding space on the answer sheet.

## ANSWER QUESTIONS 1–3 ABOUT THE PASSAGE BELOW AS IF YOU WERE A PRESCHOOL TEACHER.

Children's temper tantrums occur at the most undesirable times and locations. A child usually outgrows the tendency toward tantrums before kindergarten, but not always. Such behavior is not unheard of at preschool. The problem is how to handle it, preferably without making a scene. Often, taking the child away from the audience works wonders. But a teacher who has charge of a roomful of children can seldom do that. Some children hold their breath during tantrums. This is disconcerting at first, but there's nothing to worry about. To stop the tantrum, try blowing gently in the child's face or apply a cold, wet washcloth. Say something unusual or silly. Whispering might make a child quiet down to try to hear you. Most of all, try to not let it upset you, which is easier said than done.

1. As you are teaching a song to a class of twelve preschool children, one child has a temper tantrum. Your responsibility is to

   **(A)** the child who is having the tantrum
   **(B)** the rest of the class
   **(C)** keep the classroom quiet so as not to disturb other classes
   **(D)** Both (A) and (B)

2. According to the passage, which of the following is your best reaction to the incident described in question 1?

   **(A)** Tell the child having the tantrum to go to the time-out corner.
   **(B)** Carry the child having the tantrum to the time-out corner.
   **(C)** Ignore the child having the tantrum and continue teaching the song.
   **(D)** Wipe a disposable towelette over the face of the child having the tantrum.

3. Immediately after the incident of the temper tantrum you should

   **(A)** inform the parents about their child's temper tantrum
   **(B)** inform the vice-principal of the incident
   **(C)** inform the vice-principal of the incident and ask for follow-up such as telephoning the parents
   **(D)** talk to the child who had the tantrum in a gentle manner

4. Peer instruction is most often used

   **(A)** for reinforcement
   **(B)** in multilevel classes
   **(C)** in large classes
   **(D)** All of the above

5. Most people who volunteer in a classroom anticipate

   **(A)** working directly with students
   **(B)** doing clerical work
   **(C)** being rewarded
   **(D)** All of the above

6. Most teachers who use volunteers in the classroom anticipate

   **(A)** help with individual tutoring of students
   **(B)** help with clerical work, to free them to teach
   **(C)** help with record-keeping
   **(D)** someone who can take over the class for a short time so they can take a break

7. The information volunteers must have before going into the classroom includes

   **(A)** the school's policies about accidents and insurance
   **(B)** expectations of the time and service involved
   **(C)** what training and supervision they can expect
   **(D)** All of the above

8. A teacher of English as a Second Language uses vocabulary cards, fill-in-the-blank sentences, dialogues, dictation, and writing exercises in teaching a lesson about grocery shopping. Based on this information, which of the following is a valid conclusion?

   (A) The teacher is reinforcing learning by giving the same information in a variety of methods.
   (B) The teacher is teaching in a variety of ways because not all students learn in the same manner.
   (C) The teacher is displaying the Broze Hierarchy of Cognitive Learning.
   (D) Both (A) and (B)

9. A teacher has some excellent outside material she wishes to use to enhance a topic. Before deciding how to use this material, the readability level must be determined by a formula. Most of these formulas measure difficulty by

   (A) sentence length
   (B) number of syllables
   (C) syntax, grammar and concept load
   (D) Both (A) and (B)

10. For a readability scale to be used effectively and frequently by a teacher, it must be

    (A) absolutely accurate
    (B) officially adopted by the school district
    (C) quick and easy to use
    (D) recognized by the Reading Council of the USA

11. A student is repressed and quiet at home. Her behavior is a reflection of

    (A) her behavior in her home environment
    (B) her behavior with her peers
    (C) her behavior at school
    (D) All of the above

12. In competency-based instruction, time is

    (A) inflexible and results are norm-referenced
    (B) flexible and results are criterion-referenced
    (C) inflexible and results are criterion-referenced
    (D) flexible and results are norm-referenced

13. A pretest to a topic can be used as

    I. an effective opener
    II. a screen so that students are kept from relearning things they already know
    III. a measure of which sub-objectives of the topic need special emphasis

    (A) I and II only
    (B) I and III only
    (C) II and III only
    (D) I, II, and III

14. One kindergarten teacher who used to teach her students the alphabet and numbers found that an increasing number of her students already knew the alphabet and their numbers before coming to school, but did not know any nursery rhymes, which her earlier students had known. The primary reason for this is

    (A) parents think it is more important that their children know the alphabet than that they know nursery rhymes
    (B) an increasing number of mothers are working and sending their children to day care or preschool
    (C) an increasing number of preschoolers are learning the alphabet
    (D) Both (B) and (C)

15. In light of the information in the previous question, what changes would you as the teacher make in your curriculum?

    (A) Make no change
    (B) Reduce the time spent on the alphabet and numbers
    (C) Add the learning of nursery rhymes
    (D) Both (B) and (C)

## QUESTIONS 16–18 REFER TO THE FOLLOWING INFORMATION.

Mr. Herbert teaches a government class at Union High School. During the semester he has administered only true-false or multiple-choice question tests. The students have done well on the previous tests. He decides to make the final consist of five essay questions.

16. Which of the following is the most likely effect of this decision to use an all essay final on student scores?

    (A) The students will not do as well as on the previous tests.
    (B) The students will do as well as on the previous tests.
    (C) The students will do better than they have on the previous tests.
    (D) There will be no correlation between the final and the previous tests.

17. What is the basis for your answer to the previous question?

    (A) The preparation is different for different types of tests. Students prepared for multiple-choice questions are not likely to do as well on essay tests.

    (B) If the students know the material, the type of test is immaterial.

    (C) It is easier to explain one's thinking in essay form, as it is less confining.

    (D) There is no basis for thinking the type of test will make a difference.

18. If you taught Mr. Herbert's class, what would you do to ensure that your students' test scores accurately reflect their knowledge of the subject?

    (A) Let each student select the type of test he or she is most comfortable with.

    (B) Use different types of tests during the semester, so that students are familiar with the various types of tests.

    (C) Give the same type of test all year, so that there are no surprises.

    (D) If the students know the material, it doesn't matter what type of test is used.

19. You have presented a lesson on the habits and habitats of kit foxes. At the end, you ask if there are any questions. There are none. You can take this to mean that

    (A) the students understand everything you presented

    (B) the students are not interested in kit foxes

    (C) you need to ask specific questions to elicit responses

    (D) the students didn't understand what you were talking about

20. As a second grade teacher preparing for the year, you arrange the class schedule. Which of the following schedules is best?

    (A) Morning: physical education, music and art, mathematics

    Afternoon: spelling, reading, writing

    (B) Morning: mathematics, spelling, reading

    Afternoon: writing, physical education, music and art

    (C) Morning: spelling, reading, writing

    Afternoon: physical education, music and art, mathematics

    (D) Morning: music and art, mathematics, spelling

    Afternoon: reading, writing, physical education

# ANSWER KEY AND EXPLANATIONS

## MATHEMATICS

| | | | | | | | | |
|---|---|---|---|---|---|---|---|---|
| 1. C | 6. B | 11. B | 16. A | 21. B | 26. D | 31. B | 36. B | 41. B |
| 2. A | 7. D | 12. D | 17. B | 22. C | 27. A | 32. B | 37. A | 42. A |
| 3. C | 8. C | 13. D | 18. A | 23. A | 28. D | 33. D | 38. C | 43. B |
| 4. B | 9. B | 14. A | 19. C | 24. D | 29. B | 34. A | 39. A | 44. B |
| 5. A | 10. C | 15. D | 20. C | 25. B | 30. D | 35. D | 40. B | 45. D |

1. **The correct answer is (C).** Lard : Flour $= \frac{1}{2} : 2\frac{1}{2} =$ 1:5

2. **The correct answer is (A).** $7{,}500x = 75$; $x = \frac{75}{7500} = \frac{1}{100} = 0.01$

3. **The correct answer is (C).** $\$1.65 \times 5 = \$8.25$; $\$10.00 - \$8.25 = \$1.75$

4. **The correct answer is (B).** $2.25 \div 57 = 3\frac{54}{57}$. She only buys whole comic books, therefore, she can afford to buy 3 comic books.

5. **The correct answer is (A).** If twice as many people work, it will take half as long to do the job.

6. **The correct answer is (B).**
$$^\circ C = \frac{5}{9}(^\circ F - 32)$$
$$^\circ C = \frac{5}{9}(104 - 32)$$
$$^\circ C = \frac{5}{9}(72)$$
$$^\circ C = 40^\circ$$

7. **The correct answer is (D).** $4 \text{ mm} \times 60 \text{ sec} \times 60 \text{ min} \times 24 \text{ hrs} = 345{,}600 \text{ mm} = 34{,}560 \text{ cm} = 345.6 \text{ m} = 0.3456 \text{ km}$

8. **The correct answer is (C).** Liquid is measured in liters.

9. **The correct answer is (B).** $\frac{3}{8} \times 100 = 37.5\%$

10. **The correct answer is (C).**

| Cement | | Water |
|---|---|---|
| $\frac{2}{3}$ | $=$ | $\frac{1}{x}$ |

$2x = 3$

$x = \frac{3}{2} = 1\frac{1}{2}$ gallons

11. **The correct answer is (B).** The reading shows 55 degrees. Freezing is 32 degrees. Therefore, it is $55 - 32 = 23$ degrees above freezing.

12. **The correct answer is (D).** $t + .07t = 1.07t$

13. **The correct answer is (D).**
$$\frac{24}{a} = \frac{15}{10}$$
$$24 \times 10 = 15a$$
$$240 = 15a$$
$$16 = a$$

14. **The correct answer is (A).** 50 divided by $\left(-\frac{1}{2}\right) = 50 \times (-2) = -100$, which is less than 50.

15. **The correct answer is (D).** If $\frac{1}{lw}$, then $\frac{1}{lwh} = V$. But $V = lwh$, so this statement must be false.

16. **The correct answer is (A).** Answer choices (B) and (C) may be desirable, but choice (A) is essential.

17. **The correct answer is (B).** 76% is close to 75%, which is $\frac{3}{4}$. $\frac{3}{4} \times \$48 = 3 \times 12 = \$36$.

18. **The correct answer is (A).** The sale price represents a discount of $2.00. The discount is compared to the original price and multiplied by 100 to find the percentage. ($2.00 divided by $7.50 $\times$ 100)

19. **The correct answer is (C).** Write the decimals 0.05 and 0.40 or move each decimal two places to the right: 5 and 40. Then, choice (A) becomes 41—too big. Choice (B) becomes 4.9—too small. Choice (C) becomes 6.2—just right. Choice (D) becomes 45—too big.

**20.** The correct answer is **(C)**. Make sure you do not mix up pounds and tons.

$$\frac{40}{3 \times 2,000} = \frac{\$2.50}{x}$$

$$\frac{1}{350} = \frac{\$2.50}{x}$$

$$x = \$2.50(150)$$

$$x = \$375.00$$

**21.** The correct answer is **(B)**. The key phrase is "most slowly." We are looking for the person who completes the fewest pages per hour.

Janelle — $\frac{7}{2} = 3\frac{1}{2}$

David — $\frac{16}{5} = 3\frac{1}{5}$ (least number of pages)

Ronald — $\frac{10}{3} = 3\frac{1}{3}$

Kathryn — $\frac{13}{4} = 3\frac{1}{4}$

**22.** The correct answer is **(C)**. She can get 3 across (36 divided by 12 = 3) and 4 per yard (36 divided by 9 = 4) for a total of 12 placemats per yard. Or she can get 4 across (36 divided by 9 = 4) and 3 per yard (36 divided by 12 = 3) for the same total of 12 placemats per yard. She'll need 34 divided by 12 = 2.83, or 3 yards.

**23.** The correct answer is **(A)**. The payment is more than 10%. Eliminate choices (B) and (C). Next, try choice (A): 240.50 ÷ 1,850.00 × 100 = 13%. Or: 1,850 × 0.13 = 240.50

**24.** The correct answer is **(D)**.

| | Sept. 2, 2006 | 9 | 2 | 06 |
|---|---|---|---|---|
| − | 6 months, 5 years | − 6 | | 5 |
| | March 2, 2001 | 3 | 2 | 2001 |

In order to be eligible to start school on September 2, 2006, the child must be born before March 2, 2001.

**25.** The correct answer is **(B)**.

$$\frac{\overset{1}{\cancel{7}}}{\underset{3}{\cancel{9}}} \cdot \frac{\overset{1}{\cancel{3}}}{\underset{2}{\cancel{14}}} = \frac{1}{6}$$

**26.** The correct answer is **(D)**. Change everything to hours:

$$\frac{3}{8} = \frac{9}{24} = 9 \text{ hours}$$

$$\frac{1}{4} = \frac{6}{24} = 6 \text{ hours}$$

$$\frac{1}{12} = \frac{2}{24} = 2 \text{ hours}$$

$$\frac{1}{6} = \frac{4}{24} = 4 \text{ hours}$$

Total 21 hours

He has 24 − 21 = 3 hours for this hobby.

**27.** The correct answer is **(A)**. 90 − 24 = 66

**28.** The correct answer is **(D)**.

$$5 \times 7 = 35$$

$$\frac{1}{2} \times 5 \times 6 = 15$$

$$20$$

**29.** The correct answer is **(B)**. Remove the brackets from the inside to the outside.

6.7 [3.2 − (0.8 × 9 − 3.8)] =
6.7 [3.2 − (7.2 − 3.8)] =
6.7 (3.2 − 3.4) =
6.7 (− 0.2) = −1.34

**30.** The correct answer is **(D)**. Jane took $\frac{3}{8} \cdot 1 - \frac{3}{8} =$ $\frac{5}{8} = \frac{5}{8}$ left. Karla took $\frac{3}{5}$ of $\frac{5}{8} \cdot \frac{3}{5} \times \frac{5}{8} = \frac{3}{8}$. That left $\frac{5}{8} - \frac{3}{8} = \frac{2}{8}$ or $\frac{1}{4}$.

**31.** The correct answer is **(B)**.

```
  69
  69
  69
  76
  79
+ 82
―――
444 ÷ 6 = 74
```

**32.** The correct answer is **(B)**. $2\frac{1}{3} + 1\frac{1}{2} + 2\frac{3}{4} + 3\frac{2}{3} =$ 13. 13 × $4.00 = $52.00

**33.** The correct answer is **(D)**. If the call is less than 10 minutes, the 50 cents + 33 cents rate is cheaper. If the call is 10 minutes or longer, the flat fee is cheaper. Since we don't know how long the call is for which the rate should be calculated, we do not have enough information to answer this question.

**34.** **The correct answer is (A).** $(-5 + 3 + 4 - 6) = -4$

**35.** **The correct answer is (D).** 532 divided by 18 = 29.

**36.** **The correct answer is (B).** $\$75.00 + 32 \times 17.50 = \$75.00 + 560.00 = \$635.00$.

**37.** **The correct answer is (A).**

$$
\begin{array}{r}
635.00 \\
- 427.95 \\
\hline
\$207.05
\end{array}
$$

**38.** **The correct answer is (C).** $\dfrac{85}{34} \times 100 = \dfrac{8,500}{34} = 250$. Check: $250 \times .34 = 85$

**39.** **The correct answer is (A).**

$$
\begin{array}{r}
14,780 \\
- 12,890 \\
\hline
1,890
\end{array}
$$

**40.** **The correct answer is (B).** The key is "square yards." $\dfrac{42 \times 51}{9} = 238$, or $\dfrac{42}{3} \times \dfrac{51}{3} = 238$.

**41.** **The correct answer is (B).** $238 \times \$7.00 = \$1,666.00$

**42.** **The correct answer is (A).**

$$
16 \text{ oz.} = 1 \text{ lb.}
$$

$$
\begin{array}{r}
21 \text{ lbs. } 5 \text{ oz.} = 20 \text{ lbs. } 21 \text{ oz} \\
- 17 \text{ lbs. } 7 \text{ oz} \\
\hline
3 \text{ lbs. } 14 \text{ oz}
\end{array}
$$

**43.** **The correct answer is (B).** Estimate: the answer is about 68,000. Now add the last three digits of each number:

$$
\begin{array}{r}
839 \\
987 \\
247 \\
755 \\
487 \\
\hline
315
\end{array}
$$

**44.** **The correct answer is (B).**

$$
-9 - (-4) = -9 + 4 = -5
$$

**45.** **The correct answer is (D).** $\dfrac{5}{7} - \dfrac{1}{8} = \dfrac{5 \times 8}{7 \times 8} - \dfrac{1 \times 7}{8 \times 7}$

$$
= \dfrac{40 - 7}{56} = \dfrac{33}{56}
$$

## READING

| | | | | | |
|---|---|---|---|---|---|
| 1. C | 6. D | 11. D | 16. D | 21. C | 26. C |
| 2. B | 7. D | 12. D | 17. B | 22. C | 27. C |
| 3. A | 8. C | 13. A | 18. D | 23. D | 28. B |
| 4. C | 9. A | 14. C | 19. A | 24. A | 29. D |
| 5. B | 10. B | 15. D | 20. B | 25. B | 30. D |

**1.** **The correct answer is (C).** The key words are "lose up to 85%." Not everyone will lose 85% of excess weight. So, eliminate choice (A). Also, eliminate choices (B) and (D); one can't assume what percent of people on this diet will lose weight.

**2.** **The correct answer is (B).** "There is a chance" that the seeds will sprout, but it is not for sure. Eliminate choices (A), (C), and (D). Answer choice (B) correctly restates the statement.

**3.** **The correct answer is (A).** The chart starts with feet at its highest point. Eliminate choice (B). The feet fall very little at first and then faster.

**4.** **The correct answer is (C).** By using "below average," no account is being taken of those whose scores are "average."

**5.** **The correct answer is (B).** Second and eighth grades have the same percent of students score on grade level.

**6.** **The correct answer is (D).** The highest scores are the sixth grade. The ones in the sixth grade this year will be in the seventh grade next year.

**7.** **The correct answer is (D).** The question asks for *number* of students, but the information is given in percentages.

**8.** **The correct answer is (C).** "Smallest" and "below" are important. This statement means the same as "which class has the largest percentage of students on or above grade level."

**9.** **The correct answer is (A).** The surgery "eases nearsightedness," which enhances vision.

**10.** **The correct answer is (B).** The television ads make it seem so easy that you could get it at the *neighborhood* drugstore.

**11.** **The correct answer is (D).** In the short-term, vision is enhanced, but no one knows the *long-term* effects.

12. **The correct answer is (D).** There is no indication given of the gender or age of the people having the surgery, but all are *patients*.

13. **The correct answer is (A).** No one knows the long-term effects, so they are *unknown*.

14. **The correct answer is (C).** The writer is cautious, warning that there could be problems in the future.

15. **The correct answer is (D).** $\frac{1}{4}$ of patients have had problems. This is 25%. The percent with no problems is 75%.

16. **The correct answer is (D).** The work is described as *temporary* in the second sentence.

17. **The correct answer is (B).** Retired people are readily available, which indicates that their numbers are increasing.

18. **The correct answer is (D).** The only word that makes sense in this sentence is *supplement*, meaning "to add to."

19. **The correct answer is (A).** The expression is "to join the *ranks*."

20. **The correct answer is (B).** The essence of the passage is that more and more businesses are hiring retirees to fill part-time jobs. This is best expressed by choice (B).

21. **The correct answer is (C).** As used in this passage, the word *frequent* means "to go to repeatedly."

22. **The correct answer is (C).** *Supplement* means "to add to," "to make up for a lack of," or "to take the place of."

23. **The correct answer is (D).** He generalizes about teenagers and grandfathers, and he draws contrasts between the two groups.

24. **The correct answer is (A).** About education that trains a person to think the author says, "The instruction for this method of learning is imprecise . . ." and "There are no cut-and-dried answers."

25. **The correct answer is (B).** The author offers no conclusion.

26. **The correct answer is (C).** The writer presents both methods equally.

27. **The correct answer is (C).** The author wants to make the readers think.

28. **The correct answer is (B).** You can find the answer in the first sentence of the second paragraph.

29. **The correct answer is (D).** You can find the answer in the first sentence in the fourth paragraph.

30. **The correct answer is (D).** The passage states that "the methods are as diverse as the districts."

## WRITING—EDITING

| | | | | |
|---|---|---|---|---|
| 1. A | 5. A | 9. B | 13. A | 17. B |
| 2. A | 6. B | 10. A | 14. B | 18. A |
| 3. B | 7. B | 11. A | 15. C | 19. B |
| 4. C | 8. B | 12. B | 16. B | 20. B |

1. **The correct answer is (A).** "Each" is singular, so "his" is correct.

2. **The correct answer is (A).** When talking about two people, you would use the word "between." If there are three or more people, you would use "among."

3. **The correct answer is (B).** "More" compares two things, while "most" compares three or more things.

4. **The correct answer is (C).** A speaker "implies," while a listener "infers."

5. **The correct answer is (A).** A person can "rise." One "raises" something else.

6. **The correct answer is (B).** "Whether" has "or not" as a partner.

7. **The correct answer is (B).** "Irritate" means to make someone angry, but "aggravate" means to make something worse.

8. **The correct answer is (B).** "French" like "American" is capitalized because the word comes from the name of a country.

9. **The correct answer is (B).** This is the title of a specific class, so both words are capitalized.

10. **The correct answer is (A).** "All ready" means "prepared," while "already" means "in the past."

11. **The correct answer is (A).** "Regardless" is correct; "irregardless" is not Standard English.

12. **The correct answer is (B).** The correct form is "to try to."

13. **The correct answer is (A).** After "reason," the word "that" is used. One can use either "reason" or "because," but not both.

14. **The correct answer is (B).** "Then" refers to time, while "than" is used in a comparison.

15. **The correct answer is (C).** "Chide" means to criticize.

16. **The correct answer is (B).** The two complete sentences need to be separated with a period.

17. **The correct answer is (B).** A comma is needed to separate the elements in a series.

18. **The correct answer is (A).** The semicolon is incorrect in this series.

19. **The correct answer is (B).** A direct quote starts with quotation marks and a capital letter.

20. **The correct answer is (B).** Quotation marks are needed to indicate the end of the direct quote.

## PROFESSIONAL KNOWLEDGE

| | | | | |
|---|---|---|---|---|
| 1. **D** | 5. **A** | 9. **D** | 13. **D** | 17. **A** |
| 2. **D** | 6. **B** | 10. **C** | 14. **D** | 18. **B** |
| 3. **D** | 7. **D** | 11. **A** | 15. **D** | 19. **C** |
| 4. **D** | 8. **D** | 12. **B** | 16. **A** | 20. **B** |

1. **The correct answer is (D).** As a teacher, you are responsible for all the children.

2. **The correct answer is (D).** As indicated in sentence 8, the trick is to do something unexpected that gets the child's attention.

3. **The correct answer is (D).** Unless this is a daily occurrence, talking gently to the child is enough.

4. **The correct answer is (D).** All of these are good reasons for peer instruction.

5. **The correct answer is (A).** They volunteer because they want to work with students.

6. **The correct answer is (B).** If a teacher can assign the necessary clerical work to a volunteer, he or she is left with more time to "just teach," which is the part that is most important to most teachers.

7. **The correct answer is (D).** All of the information is important.

8. **The correct answer is (D).** The method mentioned in choice (C) does not exist.

9. **The correct answer is (D).** Choice (C) is desirable but complex to determine. Most reading scales employ sentence length and number of syllables to determine readability.

10. **The correct answer is (C).** For a teacher to use a scale "frequently," it must be quick and easy to use.

11. **The correct answer is (A).** The student may be outgoing, aggressive, or social in other situations.

12. **The correct answer is (B).** Competency-based instruction asks, "Can you do it?" It does not ask how fast or how well compared to others are task can be completed.

13. **The correct answer is (D).** A pretest has many uses.

14. **The correct answer is (D).** Nursery rhymes were taught by mothers who are now often working outside the home.

15. **The correct answer is (D).** This is most logical.

16. **The correct answer is (A).** Preparation varies for different types of tests.

17. **The correct answer is (A).** Students who have prepared for a multiple-choice test are not likely to do as well if they are given an essay exam.

18. **The correct answer is (B).** If students are accustomed to different types of tests, they will study accordingly and be prepared.

19. **The correct answer is (C).** Just because students don't have questions at first doesn't mean questions won't surface later.

20. **The correct answer is (B).** Students are usually alert in the morning, so teach core subjects that need concentration then. After lunch, students are often quiet, which is a good time for writing. Physical education gives the students an opportunity to move around, and music and art give the students an opportunity to express themselves but do not require precision.

# APPENDIXES

# DIRECTORY OF PROFESSIONAL ASSOCIATIONS AND RESOURCES

Joining a professional association has several benefits. First, professional associations are in the forefront of developments in their areas of concentration. Each association publishes newsletters and other materials about research and instructional methods in its subject. By reading an organization's publications and going to its meetings, you will learn about new developments in your field. Second, you will meet people with similar interests with whom you can share ideas and resources. Third, membership in professional associations often includes a number of benefits. These may range from discounts on insurance to access to professional development opportunities abroad.

The following directory lists contact information for the national headquarters of professional associations for educators. Many of these organizations also have state affiliates. Contact the association directly to find out about your state or even county chapter.

American Association of Physics Teachers (AAPT)
1 Physics Ellipse
College Park, MD 20740-3845
(301)209-3300
www.aapt.org

American Association of School Administrators (AASA)
801 N. Quincy Street, Suite 700
Arlington, VA 22203-1730
(703)528-0700
www.aasa.org

American Association of School Librarians (AASL)
50 East Huron Street
Chicago, Illinois 60611
(800)545-2433
www.ala.org

American Council on the Teaching of Foreign Languages (ACTFL)
700 S. Washington Street, Suite 210
Alexandria, VA 22314
(703)894-2900
www.actfl.org

American School Counselor Association (ASCA)
1101 King Street, Suite 625
Alexandria, VA 22314
(800)306-4722
www.schoolcounselor.org

Association for Educational Communications and Technology (AECT)
1800 N. Stonelake Drive, Suite 2
Bloomington, IN 47404
(812)335-7675
www.aect.org

Association for Supervision and Curriculum Development (ASCD)
1703 N. Beauregard Street
Alexandria, VA 22311-1714
(800)933-2723
www.ascd.org

Association for the Advancement of Computing in Education (AACE)
PO Box 1545
Chesapeake, VA 23327-1545
(757)366-5606
www.aace.org

Consortium for School Networking (CoSN)
1710 Rhode Island Avenue, NW
Suite 900
Washington, DC 20036-3007
(866)267-8747
www.cosn.org

International Technology Education Association (ITEA)
1914 Association Drive, Suite 201
Reston, VA 20191
(703)860-2100
www.itea.org

Music Teachers National Association (MTNA)
441 Vine Street, Suite 505
Cincinnati, OH 45202
(888)512-5278
www.mtna.org

National Alliance of Black School Educators (NABSE)
310 Pennsylvania Avenue SE
Washington, DC 20003
(800)221-2654
www.nabse.org

National Association of Biology Teachers (NABT)
12030 Sunrise Valley Drive, Suite 110
Reston, VA 20191
(800)406-0775
www.nabt.org

National Association of Elementary School Principals
(NAESP)
1615 Duke Street
Alexandria, VA 22314
(800)386-2377
www.naesp.org

National Association of Secondary School Principals
(NASSP)
1904 Association Drive
Reston, VA 20191-1537
(703)860-0200
www.nassp.org

National Council for the Social Studies (NCSS)
8555 Sixteenth Street, Suite 500
Silver Spring, MD 20910
(301)588-1800
www.ncss.org

National Council of Teachers of English (NCTE)
1111 W. Kenyon Road
Urbana, Illinois 61801-1096
(217)328-3870
www.ncte.org

National Council of Teachers of Mathematics (NCTM)
1906 Association Drive
Reston, VA 20191-1502
(703)476-2970
www.nctm.org

National Middle School Association (NMSA)
4151 Executive Parkway, Suite 300
Westerville, OH 43081
(800)528-6672
www.nmsa.org

National Science Teachers Association (NSTA)
1840 Wilson Boulevard
Arlington, VA 22201-3000
(703)243-7100
www.nsta.org

Teachers of English to Speakers of Other Languages
(TESOL)
700 South Washington Street, Suite 200
Alexandria, VA 22314
(888)547-3369
www.tesol.org

The Council for Exceptional Children (CEC)
1110 North Glebe Road
Suite 300
Arlington, VA 22201
(703)620-3660
www.cec.sped.org

The International Reading Association (IRA)
800 Barksdale Road
PO Box 8139
Newark, DE 19714-8139
(800)336-7323
www.reading.org

The National Association for the Education of Young
Children (NAEYC)
1509 16th Street, NW
Washington, DC 20036
(800)424-2460
www.naeyc.org

## Appendix B

# NATIONAL TESTING CONTACT INFORMATION

For information on state testing, check your State Profile, pages 14–115.

For information on taking Praxis I and II and ParaPRO, contact

ETS
PO Box 6051
Princeton, NJ 08541-6051
(800)772-9476
www.ets.org

For information on ACT, Inc., contact

ACT
500 ACT Drive
PO Box 168
Iowa City, IA 52243-0168

For information on other types of board certification, contact

Certification Board for Music Therapists (CBMT)—Music Therapists
506 E. Lancaster Avenue, Suite 102
Downingtown, PA 19335
(800)765-2268
www.cbmt.org

National Association of School Psychologists
4340 East West Highway, Suite 402
Bethesda, MD 20814
(301)657-0270
www.nasponline.org

National Board for Professional Teacher Standards
Certification Renewal
National Office
1525 Wilson Blvd.
Suite 500
Arlington, VA 22209
(703)465-2700
www.nbpts.org/standards/renewal.cfm

National Board for Certification of School Nurses
c/o National Association of School Nurses
1416 Park Street, Suite A
Castle Rock, CO 80109
(303)663-2329
www.nbcsn.com

**NOTES**

# NOTES

# NOTES

**NOTES**

# NOTES

# Thomson Peterson's
## Book Satisfaction Survey

## Give Us Your Feedback

Thank you for choosing Thomson Peterson's as your source for personalized solutions for your education and career achievement. Please take a few minutes to answer the following questions. Your answers will go a long way in helping us to produce the most user-friendly and comprehensive resources to meet your individual needs.

When completed, please tear out this page and mail it to us at:

Publishing Department
Thomson Peterson's
2000 Lenox Drive
Lawrenceville, NJ 08648

You can also complete this survey online at **www.petersons.com/booksurvey.**

1. **What is the ISBN of the book you have purchased? (The ISBN can be found on the book's back cover in the lower right-hand corner. )** _____

2. **Where did you purchase this book?**
   ❑ Retailer, such as Barnes & Noble
   ❑ Online reseller, such as Amazon.com
   ❑ Petersons.com or Thomson Learning Bookstore
   ❑ Other (please specify) _____

3. **If you purchased this book on Petersons.com or through the Thomson Learning Bookstore, please rate the following aspects of your online purchasing experience on a scale of 4 to 1 (4 = Excellent and 1 = Poor).**

|  | 4 | 3 | 2 | 1 |
|---|---|---|---|---|
| Comprehensiveness of Peterson's Online Bookstore page | ❑ | ❑ | ❑ | ❑ |
| Overall online customer experience | ❑ | ❑ | ❑ | ❑ |

4. **Which category best describes you?**
   ❑ High school student
   ❑ Parent of high school student
   ❑ College student
   ❑ Graduate/professional student
   ❑ Returning adult student

   ❑ Teacher
   ❑ Counselor
   ❑ Working professional/military
   ❑ Other (please specify) _____

5. **Rate your overall satisfaction with this book.**

| Extremely Satisfied | Satisfied | Not Satisfied |
|---|---|---|
| ❑ | ❑ | ❑ |

**6. Rate each of the following aspects of this book on a scale of 4 to 1 (4 = Excellent and 1 = Poor).**

| | 4 | 3 | 2 | 1 |
|---|---|---|---|---|
| Comprehensiveness of the information | ❑ | ❑ | ❑ | ❑ |
| Accuracy of the information | ❑ | ❑ | ❑ | ❑ |
| Usability | ❑ | ❑ | ❑ | ❑ |
| Cover design | ❑ | ❑ | ❑ | ❑ |
| Book layout | ❑ | ❑ | ❑ | ❑ |
| Special features (e.g., CD, flashcards, charts, etc.) | ❑ | ❑ | ❑ | ❑ |
| Value for the money | ❑ | ❑ | ❑ | ❑ |

**7. This book was recommended by:**
❑ Guidance counselor
❑ Parent/guardian
❑ Family member/relative
❑ Friend
❑ Teacher
❑ Not recommended by anyone—I found the book on my own
❑ Other (please specify) _____

**8. Would you recommend this book to others?**

| Yes | Not Sure | No |
|---|---|---|
| ❑ | ❑ | ❑ |

**9. Please provide any additional comments.**

_____

_____

_____

_____

_____

Remember, you can tear out this page and mail it to us at:

Publishing Department
Thomson Peterson's
2000 Lenox Drive
Lawrenceville, NJ 08648

or you can complete the survey online at **www.petersons.com/booksurvey.**

Your feedback is important to us at Thomson Peterson's, and we thank you for your time!

If you would like us to keep in touch with you about new products and services, please include your e-mail here: _____